In Search of European Liberalisms

European Conceptual History

Editorial Board:
Michael Freeden, University of Oxford
Diana Mishkova, Centre for Advanced Study Sofia
Javier Fernández-Sebastián, Universidad del País Vasco, Bilbao
Willibald Steinmetz, University of Bielefeld
Henrik Stenius, University of Helsinki

The transformation of social and political concepts is central to understanding the histories of societies. This series focuses on the notable values and terminology that have developed throughout European history, exploring key concepts such as parliamentarianism, democracy, civilization and liberalism to illuminate a vocabulary that has helped to shape the modern world.

In Search of European Liberalisms

Concepts, Languages, Ideologies

Edited by

Michael Freeden, Javier Fernández-Sebastián
and Jörn Leonhard

berghahn
NEW YORK · OXFORD
www.berghahnbooks.com

First published in 2019 by
Berghahn Books
www.berghahnbooks.com

Library of Congress Cataloging-in-Publication Data
Names: Freeden, Michael, editor. | Fernández-Sebastián, Javier, 1952-
editor. | Leonhard, Jörn, editor.
Title: In search of European liberalisms : concepts, languages, ideologies /
edited by Michael Freeden, Javier Fernández-Sebastián and Jörn
Leonhard.
Description: First edition. | New York : Berghahn Books, 2019. | Series:
European conceptual history ; volume 6 | Includes bibliographical
references and index.
Identifiers: LCCN 2019014410 (print) | LCCN 2019980640 (ebook) | ISBN
9781789202809 (hardback) | ISBN 9781789202816 (ebook)
Subjects: LCSH: Liberalism--Europe--History.
Classification: LCC JC574.2.E85 I6 2019 (print) | LCC JC574.2.E85 (ebook) |
DDC 320.51094--dc23
LC record available at https://lccn.loc.gov/2019014410
LC ebook record available at https://lccn.loc.gov/2019980640

British Library Cataloguing in Publication Data
A catalogue record for this book is available from the British Library

ISBN 978-1-78920-280-9 hardback
ISBN 978-1-80073-635-1 paperback
ISBN 978-1-78920-281-6 ebook

https://doi.org/10.3167/9781789202809

Contents

Introduction

European Liberal Discourses

Conceptual Affinities and Disparities

Michael Freeden and Javier Fernández-Sebastián

❖

The term 'liberal' occupies a special place in European culture. Its detractors and opponents may rail about its paternalism, its elitism, its oft-deplorable colonial record and, occasionally, its monadic individualism, but liberalism has been associated with emancipation, openness, reform, tolerance, legality, political accountability, the removal of barriers to human interaction and, above all, humanism, values on which most Europeans pride themselves – despite the horrendous events that struck at the heart of European civilization during the twentieth century. If that account may seem too starry-eyed, one has also to recall that many liberals themselves approached their creed from other, extra-humanist angles: the lifting of material economic constraints, a passport to modernization and a constitutional guarantor of a stable, conservatively inclined polity. Nor is that all when a conceptual story of Europe is undertaken. It is not only that many non-European societies have embraced and developed these liberal ideas further; contrary to the perspective adopted by many historical studies, as Javier Fernández-Sebastián demonstrates in his chapter, these ideas were preceded or paralleled in parts of Hispanic America, occasioning an early two-way transmission of liberal languages across the Atlantic.

For many thinkers, liberalism is neither just an ideology nor a philosophical-political theory like any other, such as socialism, anarchism or conservatism, but rather a set of basic cultural postulates that opens the possibility of debate among all modern ideologies. In that sense, liberalism has often been equated with the mainstream of modern Western civilization and even with modernity as such. Just as it has been said in the sphere of contemporary art that 'Cubism is not just one "ism" among many, but the condition for all the others', in the political arena one might also say that 'liberalism is not just one "ism" among many, but the condition for all the others'. Whether that is indeed the case, or whether liberalism is nonetheless a (multi-)provincial construct is for its students to judge.

Conceptualizing and Reconceptualizing: The Liberal Maze

In this book we have chosen to put aside our own definitions in order to explore some of the descriptions, interpretations and conceptual constellations of liberalism that have been advanced by a number of historical actors, mostly liberals, in Europe over the past two centuries. Instead of the usual question 'What is Liberalism?',[1] as posed by politicians and academics, we will attempt to answer two alternative questions. The first question is central to the practice of conceptual history: 'What did they mean by liberal or liberalism?', when 'they' refers to a transgenerational collective of historical agents who lived in different European countries, from the beginning of the nineteenth century to the end of the twentieth century. As far as we know, this question was first posed in a traditionalist Spanish newspaper in 1813,[2] since which time it has been periodically rephrased. The second question has in recent years been included within the remit of conceptual history: 'Which diverse conceptual collocations and cognates have imparted and fine-tuned the competing and coalescing meanings that liberalism has exhibited throughout its history?' This reflects the multiple dimensions that have generated a loosely shared body, or family, of liberal languages, yet one that interacts with continuously changing political vocabularies. These languages have drawn sustenance from a common substratum, and their mutation not infrequently reveals mutual exchanges, linguistic borrowings and grafts. The concept of liberalism is thus liberated from the misleading confines of a uniform definition, since no definition is capable of delivering a satisfactory account of all aspects of such a vast and complex ideology-cum-movement. In parallel, the study of conceptual morphology indicates the inevitability of selective choices among different conceptions of any political concept, given the inescapable incompatibility of many of these conceptions with one another.[3]

Our volume restricts itself to the terms 'liberal' and 'liberalism', though – particularly in Franz L. Fillafer's chapter on liberalism under the Habsburgs – it acknowledges liberalism's immediate European prehistory as it emerged in a swirl of Enlightenment and religious argumentation at the end of the eighteenth century. We cannot of course cover the conceptual history of the past 200 years in any given chapter, nor can we do justice to all European countries. Together, these studies proffer a measured spatial and temporal cross-cut of the conceptual history of European liberalism in each of the selected countries, through diverse, dedicated analyses of broad segments of that history: as initiating periods, as periods of maturing complexity or as turning-points. In so doing, they reflect the various layers and conceptions that have fermented and matured in liberalism's embrace from its inception as liberalism two centuries ago, and whose continuous internal jostling has produced a powerful and imaginative dynamic. In the tug-of-war between space, time and context, 'liberal' and 'liberalism' have undergone such remarkable mutations that it becomes a challenge to determine whether we are dealing with the same concepts or whether seismic shifts have occurred beneath the surface of the words. If this indicates nothing else, it dismisses the abstract universalism that many political philosophers have conferred on liberalism, even though, unsurprisingly, the contents of that universalism are themselves contested among such philosophers.

Historiographically, too, we are beginning to understand that the idealized concept of 'Western liberalism', so frequently invoked by the historians who have contributed to that grand narrative, is in fact highly dependent on the archetypal story of the origins of liberalism invented and promoted by the first European liberals themselves almost 200 years ago in order to give their political programme a prestigious prehistory and intellectual pedigree. We are aware that in order to analyse the conceptual indeterminacy of ideologies adequately, it is necessary to break with the inertia characterizing old-style histories of political thought. We wish to investigate historically how specific political forces came to be through the use of particular languages and concepts, giving themselves at the same time an ad hoc intellectual and political past. Our starting point is the history of actually existing liberals, although we must bear in mind that the concepts used by liberals were in no way exclusively theirs; as is well known, one of the characteristics of political modernity in linguistic terms is that, to a great extent, adversaries use the same concepts, interpreted in a discordant and often antagonistic manner.

Yet although the incipient epistemic entity called liberalism gradually converted into an increasingly variegated set of interconnected currents, it contains sufficiently intertwined semantic elements for those to be considered components of the 'same' concept. Beyond the concrete movements, ideologies and political parties labelled 'liberal', it is possible to identify liberalism as a great current of thought, with some imbricated – and partially contradictory – features, mutating over time. Consequently, we have opted to use the phrase *European liberalisms* in the plural in order to emphasize the multifaceted spectrum of understandings nested under the liberal umbrella and to offer an 'empirical-conceptual' approach to those liberalisms.

The comparative perspective endorsed in this volume underlines the claim that the study of liberalism passes through multiple heuristic filters: not only as a concept or cluster of concepts, but as a political vocabulary, a colloquial language, an ideology, an array of practices, a compendium of human values and a plethora of concrete experiences. Nor is liberalism solely about politics; its reach also encompasses morality, the economy, culture and religion. All this raises profound methodological issues. For as one attempts to engage with the divergent universe of meanings that 'liberal' and 'liberalism' have accrued in Europe, meanings that mix with local understandings wherever they alight – both within the continent and far beyond its physical borders – one is led to reflect on the paths that a conceptual history of liberalism should tread. Should we locate its concepts and collocations in certain cultural practices, in linguistic and rhetorical verbal usage, in vernacular discourse, in the political theories of eminent individuals, in religious faiths and cultural dispositions, in the institutions of political parties, in the diverse disciplinary traditions of politics, economics and philosophy, in a social transition from small scale human conduct – being personally 'liberal' – to large-scale social phenomena, an ideology of liberalism? Does liberalism have a prehistory that conceptual historians need to take into account? Do the uppercase 'L' and the lowercase 'l' indicate a distinction of importance or is there – as in so many other instances – a permeable boundary problem?

Liberal Pluralities and Academic Viewpoints: A Medley of Abundance

The approaches in this volume illustrate the fruitfulness that a conceptual history of European liberalisms can display. It can focus on a geocultural story of origins. Its diverse exemplars can indicate clear cross-cultural impact, semi-coincidental parallelisms or the equivalence of 'false friends'. It confronts the question of whether the regional subgroupings recognize and acknowledge each other, though often with universal pretensions, airs and graces, or whether the flow of perceived influence is disrupted through the discourses and activities of distanced observers and misinterpreters – in which case, the broader continental parochialism that is liberalism may be transformed into a series of even smaller discrete national parochialisms. And a conceptual history of European liberalisms needs to engage with the manner in which the imaginations and fantasies of the past stamp their imprint on what liberals can think, utter and write, as well as with determining whether liberals possess a distinct facility for projecting the future and subscribing to a distinctive horizon of expectations.

The various chapters in this volume touch, collectively if not individually, on most of the above issues. The contributors all share a deep-seated interest in the historical analysis of the concepts, discourses and ideological features that have characterized European liberalisms, and their chapters are all linked by the common purpose of finding the key concepts that mattered in particular cases. At the same time, they offer a broad sample of approaches, reflecting on the one hand the multiple historical understandings of the concept of liberalism that past discourses and thinkers have employed, and revealing on the other hand the methodological plurality that today inhabits the domain of conceptual history. The authors have been encouraged to exercise their freedom to focus on their own research and understandings, and their analyses provide a differently weighted set of perspectives the student of liberalism might adopt. Their chapters range across different timespans, affording the reader windows into diverse European experiences of liberalism over more than 200 years, although most chapters focus on the nineteenth and early twentieth centuries.

As will be seen, some of the following chapters are closer to the history of political thought, while others are closer to the history of concepts. Furthermore, within this latter modality, there are authors more attentive to vocabularies, while others try to take into account practices and even, as in Michael Freeden's final chapter, attempt to reduce the motley outlook and morphological complexity of British/European liberalisms to a repertoire of historical layers. While it is certainly not easy to combine the historical-conceptual approach with the methodology of ideal types, Freeden's endeavour to delineate the major temporal strata of liberalism offers a heuristic tool to find a middle way between idiographic and nomothetic perspectives, a proposed method for synthesizing and dissecting the changing conceptual constellations historically present in liberal ideologies into a circumscribed range of types and strata. In sum, we see this book as an opening gambit in developing a rich and intricate understanding of European liberalism's conceptual history, in the hope that it will encourage further studies in this field.[4]

A central aim of this book is to restore the historicity and substantivity of European liberalisms rather than framing them in some grand enterprise of evolutionary momentum or philosophical truth, which all too often results in flattening the differences and varieties of liberalism. The usual approaches, especially when referring to nineteenth-century European liberalism, tend to reduce it to only one version: that of so-called 'classical liberalism', which is often equated with a short list of British political philosophers. At worst, this perspective could lead to the absurdity of maintaining that, until the twentieth century, the only relevant form of liberalism was that in Britain. Ironically, the words 'liberal' and 'liberalism' when applied to a party were first employed in other countries of Mediterranean Europe, whereas in Britain it was initially perceived as a foreign term, and entered British political discourse only later and with difficulty.

Despite the many differences between the cases examined here, some basic similarities emerge from this comparison. In the final chapter in this volume, Freeden offers an overall morphological-evolutionary view that, although referring mainly to British liberalism, *mutatis mutandis* could serve as a general scheme and as a counterpoint to other particular cases. These prepolitical similarities emanate from a common cultural and semantic substratum that, long before liberalism took shape as a political 'ism', and even before the first of the five layers identified by Freeden had completed their sedimentation, was already shared in large areas of Europe. Thus, the excellence of the virtue of liberality, essentially understood as generosity and open-mindedness, was recognized almost everywhere. This enduring substratum accounts for the frequent practice of numerous liberals throughout the last two centuries – as emphasized by several authors in their respective chapters – of invoking the echoes of the ancient moral virtue of liberality, echoes that still resonate in our day. Moreover, the fact that the term 'liberalism' refers to such an overarching nonspecific concept surely has much to do with the ambiguity and polyvalence of the concept of freedom, on which liberalism ultimately rests. As Portuguese historian Oliveira Martins demonstrated in 1881, and as most of the contributors to this volume note, freedom is one of the most complex, contested and difficult-to-grasp concepts of the entire political vocabulary. This is evident in the Polish case, as Maciej Janowski shows in Chapter 8, and in Chapter 11, where Freeden illustrates some of its changing interpretations.

Entering the Age of the 'Isms'

Within the 'great age of "isms"' that was the nineteenth century, its first decades saw the advent in the West of the initial and most important political 'isms'. If we take up the much-discussed Koselleckian notion of *Sattelzeit*, the first half of the nineteenth century could be described from this perspective as a crucial extension of the threshold period of entry into full modernity, during which a special type of neologisms crystallized, relating to 'concepts of movement' (*Bewegungsbegriffe*). The rapid coinage in English of terms such as liberalism, radicalism, socialism, conservatism, nationalism and communism in a short period of time allows us to date the critical phase of that advent as occurring between 1819 and 1840.[5]

This chronological enumeration of half a dozen of those key modern 'isms' shows that liberalism was the forerunner of the great ideologies, and therefore the most durable 'ism', because through many ups and downs, it continues to accompany us today. And, given that in the series of which this book is a part, other volumes dedicated to different 'isms' may be published in the near future, let us pause a moment to consider a little more closely the place occupied by liberalism in the context of the political 'isms'.[6]

We suggested at the beginning of this introduction that this first political 'ism' of modernity could be seen as a prototype and precondition of all others, if only because of its ability to ignite public debate about the best policies for society in different spheres, thus opening up a struggle between ideologies that would never be extinguished. In any case, there is no shortage of critics of all stripes that affirm that the other ideologies harbour to some extent a development and a sequel of liberal principles – either by extension and deepening or by negation and rejection. It is not uncommon for the harshest critics of incipient liberalism to accompany their attacks with a diatribe against 'isms' in general.

As a political 'ism', liberalism emerged precisely at the pivotal moment of the turn from religious 'isms' – most of them derogatory – that had proliferated since the Reformation towards the new ideological-political 'isms' oriented towards the future.[7] In fact, in the second decade of the nineteenth century, when the word 'liberalism' was coined, the majority of the most common 'isms' still remained religious and philosophical in nature.[8] No wonder, then, that the earliest discussions on the meaning of the word liberalism – originating from publicists hostile to that emerging 'ism' – hesitated to label it as a heresy or as a new political faith.[9]

Two scholars who have recently written on this topic remark that when analysing 'isms', it is advisable to examine the root and the suffix, since 'the ism suffix often adds a particular claim of "ownership" to the use of a concept due to the generalising and universalising effect of the suffix'.[10] The semantic effects of this suffixation were already noticed and passionately discussed in the mid nineteenth century by Prince Metternich in an exchange of letters with the Marquis of Valdegamas on the occasion of the publication of the latter's *Ensayo sobre el catolicismo, el liberalismo y el socialismo* (1851). In that correspondence, Metternich strongly states his 'aversion to isms, when I see them applied to any noun that expresses a quality or a right'. According to the Austrian politician, when the suffix 'ism' is added to abstract names such as God, reason, constitution, society or common to turn them into deism, rationalism, constitutionalism, socialism and communism, that simple 'grammatical transmutation' perverts the meaning of the original concepts and lends the new isms thus formed a 'dangerous elasticity'. Donoso responds by acknowledging the evils derived from the 'abuse of that termination', although he excludes Catholicism from that will of appropriation and falsification that characterizes most of the 'isms'. On the other hand, liberalism would be for Donoso, and years later was still for his disciple Tejada, a dangerous and condemnable falsification of freedom, the true source from which all modern errors spring.[11]

It is interesting to note in this regard the obsessive aversion of antimodern authors to political 'isms', and also the fact that the debate to which we have just referred was triggered by the publication of a book very critical of liberalism such as Donoso's *Essay*, widely circulated among reactionary groups throughout Europe. The strong dislike of these groups for liberalism stems from their belief that liberalism was ultimately the origin of all other political 'isms' – including socialism – and responsible for all evils of modernity (an 'accusation' that, incidentally, would reappear in the second half of the twentieth century under very different circumstances, when some well-known authors – several of them German Jewish intellectuals who took refuge in the United States – blamed the Enlightenment and liberalism for incubating the serpent's egg of totalitarianism). While this accusation is clearly exaggerated, there is no doubt that fundamental elements of liberal ideology have permeated and have been absorbed by other ideologies to variable effect. Moreover, some of these ideologies present their own projects as the true fulfilment of some of the unfulfilled promises of liberalism. On the other hand, it is evident that liberalism has powerfully contributed to shaping many modern practices and institutions in Europe and beyond.

The enormous breadth that the semantic field of liberalism has come to exhibit over time is best understood if one takes into account that the concept fits into each and every one of the six categories proposed by Höpfl to classify 'isms', namely: doctrines, traditions, rhetorics, attitudes, ethos and movements.[12] The same can be said about most types of 'isms' according to the classification proposed by Cuttica, inspired by Höpfl. Liberalism would fit into at least four of these types: 'isms' referring to group conduct; generated in ideological conflicts, be they politico-religious or politico-intellectual; and adapted to scholarly use.[13]

A final aspect that deserves special consideration in this section is the position of liberalism in the context of the 'isms' of the nineteenth and twentieth centuries. The variable relations of opposition, affinity, competition or complementarity that it has maintained with the other great 'isms' of modernity reveal much about the evolution of the liberal mainstream. Its antagonists have been changing over time, successively labelled in various contexts and circumstances as absolutism, servilism, conservatism, democratism (or simply democracy), socialism, communism, authoritarianism, collectivism, statism, totalitarianism, fundamentalism, republicanism or communitarianism. These and other purportedly antiliberal positions that constitute the broad array of what we might call the 'counter-isms' of liberalism – as the political spectrum was expanded and new political 'isms' emerged on its right, and especially on its left – also account for why, in certain places and moments, liberalism could be conflated with, and sometimes be opposed to, radicalism, utilitarianism, Jacobinism, internationalism, conservatism, progressivism and ultimately identity particularisms.

That is not all. To add complexity to this analysis, we must bear in mind that, under the umbrella term 'liberalism', there is room for not a few other 'isms'. From this perspective, the word 'liberalism' can be seen as a hyper-nym that shelters a cluster of more specific hyponyms under its broad aegis, several of which may in turn take the form of minor, sectorial 'isms' (though no less abstract and complex). Contractualism, constitutionalism, parliamen-tarism, *librecambismo* (free trade), individualism, iusnaturalism, rationalism, egalitarianism and developmentalism are some of those subordinate 'isms' that at one time or another have been part – totally or partially – of the liberal creed. Just as Freeden has shown how the variable weight and disposition of some core, adjacent and peripheral concepts, as well as their diverse ways of decontestation, explain different ideological constellations, we could say that the emphasis on, or demoting of, some of those 'isms' with which liberalism intersects provides a good indication of the predominance of one aspect or another of liberal ideology at a given moment.

The Phases of European Liberalisms

While liberalism was still a vague and diffuse term, and its early meanings were under construction, the apostles of that first liberalism could under-stand the concept as a vast international movement. This explains why in the first decades of the nineteenth century, a number of political actors talked of European, American (referring mainly, *pace* Hartz,[14] to Spanish American countries) and even universal liberalism.[15] However, as the term 'liberalism' was applied to more diverse realities and circumstances and was loaded with particular expectations, the meanings of the word became ever more diversi-fied. Over time, the concept was adapted to the peculiar contexts and specific problems of each society, allowing us to witness a certain 'nationalization' of liberalisms.[16] The dissemination and internationalization of the concept increased its presence in a variety of political arenas and thus led by the same token to its growing nationalization. However, it is no less true that some authors and currents of liberalism – mainly British and French – achieved a great international impact in much of Europe. Jeremy Bentham, Benjamin Constant, François Guizot, Alexis de Tocqueville, John Stuart Mill, Herbert Spencer and Leonard Hobhouse, among others (also, later on, the Austrians Ludwig von Mises, Friedrich von Hayek and Karl Popper), were widely known and read beyond the borders of their respective countries. And, as the reader will see in several chapters of this volume, the French *doctrinaires* and British new liberalism are two currents that circulated widely in Europe, the former in the first half of the nineteenth century and the latter since the end of that century. (Ironically, as we will see later, French doctrinarism came to be considered by some critics as a systematization of Whig principles.)

As the nineteenth century unfolded, the concept and language of liberalism gradually gained ground, expanding its semantic field. This expansion and increasing complexity has left its mark on some lexical and grammatical changes. Phrases such as 'liberal ideas', 'liberal constitution', 'liberal party', 'liberal system' and so on became more frequently used and acquired conceptual and intellectual thickness as new experiences and expectations impacted on them. The word/concept 'liberal' and its cognates went through a series of phases that were not necessarily sequential and, indeed, partly overlapped. Six such phases may be identified from the late eighteenth century to the early twentieth century.

The Emergence and 'Substantivization' of the Word

The transfer of the liberal adjective from the realm of morality to that of politics occurred conspicuously in France, coinciding with the Brumaire coup of Napoleon Bonaparte, although that rhetorical move was preceded in the 1790s by a heated discussion in Britain about the extent to which the French revolutionaries' way of conducting themselves was or was not consistent with 'liberal principles'. This transfer metaphorically shifted positive connotations usually associated with certain noble and generous acts and conduct – usually attributed to eminent individuals and to God himself – to a handful of abstract ideas. Conversely, qualifying certain ideas and principles as 'liberal' gave them a presumption of magnanimity and concern for the common good that could not but arouse the respect and sympathy of the majority of the public. This moral sympathy then reverted to the bearers of such ideas, who could be presumed to have attitudes of altruism, benevolence, inclusiveness, moderation and patriotism. The emergence of the word 'liberal' in politics was followed shortly afterwards by its transformation from adjective into noun: in addition to 'a liberal mind' or 'a person with liberal ideas', it was possible to say 'a liberal' when referring to a person who possessed a particular ideology – in mainland Europe chiefly a supporter of constitutionalism,[17] but also one advocating reform and individual liberty, as in Britain. It is worth noting that this small grammatical leap – from adjective to noun – that, as far as we know, took place around 1809–10 almost simultaneously at two extremes of the continent – in Sweden and in Spain – heralded a considerable change in the evolution of the concept. This change involved nothing less than the application of human agency to liberal political conceptions, which could thus descend from the lofty world of ideas to materialize in the political praxis of flesh-and-blood human beings. The emergence of a new political identity attributable to real actors – the liberals, the liberal movement and the liberal party – made it more difficult for further developments of the concept and its diversification to be conceived as mere speculative games of disincarnated ideas, detached from the concrete actions of that ideology's supporters. The passage from the old moral virtue of liberality – with strong classical and Christian undertones – to a new liberal political identity could be described as a circular process: the adjective began by qualifying a personal virtue to a series of ideas and principles, and from there it descended again, substantivized, towards people, which made it possible to speak of *liberals* as a new kind of political label. That political label began to appear from 1812, usually referring to Spanish *liberales*, with increasing frequency in European and American newspapers.

Ideologization, Temporalization and Transformation into an 'Ism'
The movement here is from 'liberal' to 'liberalism'. The 'ismization' of the word 'liberal' was in all likelihood the work of its enemies. They were the ones who urgently needed to encapsulate in a denigrating shorthand the whole set of 'liberal' people, doctrines and practices they were preparing to fight. In any case, since the 'friends of freedom' did not reject the name imposed on them by their adversaries – thus converting, as has happened so many times, a derogatory hetero-designation into a self-designation borne with pride – this move made it possible for the vague 'liberal ideas' to be later ordered and assembled into an initially relatively structured system of political thought by some ideologists. Once the term 'liberalism' was coined, one can observe – beyond divergences among some liberal groups and others – various attempts to determine the principles of the new doctrine/ideology more or less systematically. One of the first attempts of this kind occurred in 1820. A Spanish journalist, citing the opinions of the French politician Carrion-Nisas, wrote that 'liberals across Europe' agree on half-a-dozen basic points, namely: individual freedom, respect for property, freedom of expression, equality before the law, equitable distribution of taxes and equal access to public office based on personal merit. Out of those six principles that constituted one of the first definitions of European liberalism, the first and the third refer to freedom, the second to individual possession and the last three to equality or fairness. Hence – the journalist concluded – any representative government founded on such principles, whether monarchical or republican, is liberal.[18] Alongside these 'constitutionalist' definitions, which broadly coincide with layer one as suggested by Freeden in Chapter 11 below, we find other definitions that insist instead on the temporal dimension of liberalism, understood both as a

political ideology and a set of institutions capable of ensuring the progress, development and continuous improvement of the individual and of society[19] (Freeden, layer three, see Chapter 11). Little by little, other definitions would be added. However, as is the case with all the great abstract political concepts, no definition of liberalism could ever settle the then initiated discussion about its 'true meaning'. Its meanings were and are multiple, changing and controversial. Conceptual historians, instead of adding another definition, try to exhume, gather and systematize these meanings so that the current reader can better understand the parameters of politics and thought of past times. In the previous section, we have alluded to the vanguard location of liberalism within the emerging 'isms' of modernity. In this sense, we could regard the word liberalism as a *mot-témoin* ('word-witness')[20] whose appearance testifies to a profound shift taking place in the mentality of an entire epoch, a shift referred to above as the entry into the age of the 'isms'. It is revealing, in this respect, that in little more than a decade – around 1820, a decisive date that marks the irruption in the European scene of that new actor called 'liberalism' – the first books and pamphlets containing the word 'liberalism' in their title began to be published in various European languages.[21] In some of those books, several of them frankly hostile to liberalism, this brand new 'ism' appears as a personified acting subject, endowed with a will and purposes of its own, as if it were an entity capable of planning and performing autonomous actions.

Partisanship and Pluralization

The term 'liberal party' now appeared. However, since initially the idea of a party was loaded with negative connotations and was not easily accepted, liberals presented themselves as defenders of the common good, claiming to speak on behalf of the whole nation. The party frequently split into several tendencies or wings, moderate and radical, conservative and progressive. Often the very word 'liberalism' became a disputed and controversial label, as each (sub)group claimed its own interpretation for itself and each understood it as the only 'true liberalism', while accusing its rivals for the liberal label of being 'false liberals'. In addition to a coherent set of political principles – which nonetheless would change markedly, depending on time and place – liberalism also reflected a series of shared political and personal experiences. Some countries hosted several parties that, under different names, regarded themselves as liberal. In several of these countries – Britain, the Netherlands, Portugal, Spain, Sweden and Denmark – the majority, or at least a good part of the groups represented in their parliaments, considered themselves liberal in one way or another. Yet far from settling disputes over meaning, it enlivened them. At any given moment, each country witnessed several

lines of fracture between conservative and progressive liberals, beginning
with the varying degrees of radicalism and the speed of the reforms that each
group intended to introduce. The attitudes of the various liberal subgroups
to revolutionary tactics were often a bone of contention that led to the rupture
between different factions. Thus, the close association of the term 'liberalism'
with the revolution explains that in some countries, as in the Netherlands,
liberalism continued to be a radical and threatening term even in the 1830s.[22]
From a very early stage, these differences of valuation became evident with
respect to the French Revolution – the origin of liberalism for some and
a perfect example of illiberalism for others. As early as the last decade of
the eighteenth century, Burke, Jovellanos and other European conservative
intellectuals had branded the French revolutionaries as illiberal. In 1814,
M. Lorenzo de Vidaurre, an official of the Spanish Crown in Peru, carefully
distinguished between two very different meanings of the noun 'liberal'.
Vidaurre willingly declared himself to be a liberal, if that name was understood as a synonym for 'constitutional' and 'defender of civil rights', but
roundly refused to be so if liberal was understood to entail 'a supporter of the
revolution'.[23] In the light of the new rhetoric, the split between a moderate
and a revolutionary liberalism could be seen as a duplication or rupture of
the concept, which was divided into a good and a bad version.[24] These types
of fissure were to occur again and again throughout the history of liberalism,
giving rise to numerous subdivisions.

However, the greater or lesser radicalism of the proposed reforms is not
the only reason for the internal rupture and diversification of liberalisms. The
multiplicity of spheres (political, economic and religious) to which liberal
thinking could be applied is also an important factor in this pluralization. It
also signals, as is evident in the case of the Habsburg lands, the existence of
different political sensibilities arising from the mixture of liberal ideology
with nationalist tendencies.[25]

Historicization and Canonization

In the 1820s, a number of writers and publicists began to articulate a grand
narrative of the origins of liberalism (a current they equated with Western
civilization), accompanied by a tentative list of great thinkers held to have
contributed historically to shaping the liberal doctrine. This canon of those
considered to be the founders of liberalism and the authors of its classics
grew with the passage of time to include newer names of nineteenth-century
theorists and also – retrospectively – of the early modern period. 'European
Liberalism' could thus be understood largely as a historical-intellectual narrative constructed by liberal actors and later endorsed by historians of political
thought. Comparing the various lists of theorists and presumed forefathers

of liberalism drawn up in the same country at different times (or even the alternative assessments of the same episodes and characters offered at a given time by different segments of liberalism),[26] as well as between different countries and continents, is a very instructive exercise. It says much about the national and international processes of historical – and historiographical – construction of liberalism and the gradual establishment and 'negotiation' of the prevailing canon in the West, a canon that today is above all enshrined in, and reinforced by, the list of classical 'liberal' authors studied in history of political theory syllabi in Western universities. We will return to this point below.

The crystallization of the liberal canon is of course partly a product of shared intellectual traditions, but also of the 'elective traditions' that result from selecting those elements of the past that best fit the needs of present predicaments and the expectations of a particular group or community.[27] Hence, alongside the grand narrative of liberalism as the backbone of Western civilization, liberals also generally constructed a series of national historical accounts, starting at least in the Middle Ages, in which the most significant advances of freedom in their respective countries were glorified. In several countries, liberals even argued that their original freedoms were reminiscent of a kind of national ancient constitution. Needless to say, the so-called Whig interpretation of history is the most perfect example of this kind. Especially controversial was the historicization of the Enlightenment, which in many countries – as, for instance, in Austria – went hand in hand with the historicization of liberalism. It gave rise to political-intellectual conflicts among rival groups, each of which claimed to be the legitimate heir of the legacy of an Enlightenment tailor-made to their political requirements.[28]

Systematization and the Crisis of Bourgeois Liberalism

From the 1830s onwards, several theorists began to realize that a system characterized as liberal extended over much of European society: "The new system by which people have been working for three centuries in order to replace the previous one is that based on freedom. It is the truly liberal system which, conceived by philosophy, later applied to the reform of Church and State, has now been extended to almost all spheres of social activity."[29] One of these spheres emerged as the economy: economic liberalism became an increasingly employed formulation (Freeden's layer two, see Chapter 11), to the extent that over time some would fallaciously identify 'classical' liberalism with the doctrine of laissez-faire. In that respect, it is revealing that the word 'liberalism' gradually began to make an appearance in encyclopaedias in various European languages and countries. By the middle of the century, following the Revolution of July 1830 in France and even more after 1848, liberalism began to be seen by its left-wing critics as a bourgeois movement. The so-called 'social question' posed a challenge to liberal governments, parties and theorists who were wondering how to tackle the serious problems of the emerging working class in a society undergoing profound transformations, such as industrialization, secularization, and urbanization. Under these conditions, as Helena Rosenblatt shows in her chapter, liberalism came to be described by some of its enemies, in a sense completely contrary to its original meaning, as a 'pernicious form of individualism' wholly devoid of generosity.[30]

Renovation and Resemantization

By the end of the nineteenth century, a fundamental shift took place in the way in which liberalism was understood, especially in relation to the role of the state in the economy, the expansion of fundamental human rights and the widespread enablement of human opportunity. New liberalisms emerged, aware of social responsibilities towards individuals in tandem with the protection of their liberties, and paving the way for the modern welfare state (Freeden, layer four, see Chapter 11). Among the different versions of this reinvented progressive liberalism – *solidarisme*, *Kathedersozialismus*, *krausoinstitucionalismo* and social liberalism – that distanced itself from the old elitist liberalism of notables and middle class and was further extended in the twentieth century, undoubtedly the most influential was the British new liberalism.[31] L.T. Hobhouse's book *Liberalism* (1911), in particular, was translated into Swedish, Spanish and other languages, and achieved a significant impact on the continent (in the Netherlands, Sweden, Poland, Portugal[32] and Spain,[33] though not in other countries, such as Denmark).

The six phases add internal complexity, both accumulative and selective, to liberalism that results in a remarkable diversification of the concept. Interestingly enough, as we move away from the origins, the line of demarcation between the political facets of the concept and the tendentially academic uses that some authors make of it becomes more and more blurred. For example, Hobhouse and other representatives of the new liberalism – like Posada, Almagro or Elorrieta – were both rigorous scholars and public intellectuals, and it is difficult to say whether, when they wrote about liberalism and its history, they did so as politically active citizens or as scientists (the two vocations on which Weber famously lectured in those same years). Most of the time, they did so on the basis of their dual status as teachers and ideologues. The result, then, is that at least since the beginning of the twentieth century, it has become increasingly difficult to distinguish between liberalism as an ideological concept and as an analytical tool.

Academic and Philosophical Traditions

The academic and philosophical understandings of liberalism deserve separate attention. They have played, and still play, a major part in a somewhat different conceptual trajectory – a parallel orbit of 'liberalism' that nonetheless intersects frequently with more colloquial and vernacular discourses. In that intellectualized and university-supported domain, a divergence of opinions and definitions abounds in no less intensity than in other contestations over the term 'liberalism'. It has commanded a pronounced presence of its own in Europe, while also interacting with, and being receptive to, American academic debate. A few instances are chosen here to represent some of the nodal points of contention displayed by major philosophical and ideational claims about liberalism, magnified by the reputation of their authors and the widespread readership of their analyses. That prominence singles them out as important events in liberalism's conceptual history. Guido de Ruggiero's *Storia del liberalismo europeo* (1925) was for many years the seminal history of its subject matter, particularly in its 1927 English translation as *The History of European Liberalism*. In the preface, its translator, the noted British philosopher R.G. Collingwood, observed that the 'aim of Liberalism is to assist the individual to discipline himself and achieve his own moral progress', leading to a view of the state 'not as the vehicle of a superhuman wisdom or a superhuman power, but as the organ by which a people expresses whatever of political ability it can find and breed and train within itself'.[34] While alert to the 'diversity of [liberalism's] national forms' within Europe, de Ruggiero believed to have identified 'a process of mutual assimilation, gradually building up a European Liberal consciousness pervading its particular manifestations without destroying their differences.'.[35] He held liberalism to consist, first and foremost, of 'the recognition of a fact, the fact of liberty'. To that was added a method, 'a capacity to reconstruct within oneself the spiritual processes of others', a 'higher synthesis' of political life combining 'resistance and movement, conservation and progress', and 'the continual exercise and impartial discipline of governing'. Significantly here, liberalism is endowed with spirituality and an ethical and humanist vision that aspired to transcend the partisanship of politics.

This strand of Italian political theory is also evident in the work of Benedetto Croce, who, as Pombeni argues,[36] entertained a transcendental, spiritual idea of liberalism. With strong Hegelian undertones reflecting the ethical purpose of the state and the dialectical progress of humanity away from authoritarianism, Croce's grandiose interpretation of liberalism is encapsulated in a chapter in his *Politics and Morals* entitled 'Liberalism as a Concept of Life'.[37] By contrast, Isaiah Berlin, the best known of the mid twentieth-century British liberals, espoused a more restricted notion of liberalism in his famous essay 'Two Concepts of Liberty', arguing approvingly that 'the fathers of liberalism – Mill and Constant ... demand a maximum degree of non-interference compatible with the minimum demands of social life'. Berlin thus beat a retreat from the ideational positions earlier occupied by Hobhouse and Hobson.[38] Controversially, in 1949, and with merely perfunctory regard for its nuances and variations, Berlin had portrayed liberalism in terms even more unitary than those of de Ruggiero, as verging on the universal:

> The language of the great founders of European liberalism – Condorcet, for example, or Helvétius – does not differ greatly in substance, or indeed in form, from the most characteristic moments in the speeches of Woodrow Wilson or Thomas Masaryk. European liberalism wears the appearance of a single coherent movement, little altered during almost three centuries ... In this movement there is in principle a rational answer to every question.[39]

From different ends of the ideological spectrum, one may select Harold J. Laski and Friedrich Hayek as symptomatic of two modes of criticizing liberalism. In his 1936 book, Laski reflected the sustained attack on liberalism from the socialist left, as he berated liberalism from a Marxist perspective: 'Liberalism ... has always refused to see how little meaning there is in freedom of contract when it is divorced from equality of bargaining power.' Liberalism's language of 'the common well-being, the maintenance of order, the preservation of civilized life' masked the 'destruction of the liberal spirit', while in effect pursuing profit-making.[40] As for Hayek, boxing from the other corner, his 1973 entry for the *Enciclopedia del Novecento* argued that Mill's mature writings had already abandoned many principles and characteristics of liberalism. He contended that by the end of the nineteenth century, liberalism had thrown in the towel and surrendered to the social reform of the new liberalism – simply socialism in disguise. The entry tellingly begins with the statement: 'The term [liberalism] is now used with a variety of meanings which have little in common beyond describing a openness to new ideas, including some which are directly opposed to those which are originally designated by it during the nineteenth and the earlier parts of the twentieth centuries' – those original concepts having been liberty under the rule of law, with its concomitant idea of just procedures. From the late nineteenth century onwards, Hayek claimed that liberalism had entered into decline. Mill's sympathy for 'socialist aspirations' began the transition towards a moderate socialism, and the welfare policies of the British Liberal government prior to the First World War (layer four of Freeden's schema, see Chapter 11) prompted 'new experiments in social policy which were only doubtfully compatible with the older liberal principles'.[41] No wonder that Hayek saw himself as a liberal suspended in time as he conspired to stall liberalism's conceptual history. However, the textual evidence of his writings points to his conservatism. The lesson here for conceptual history is that a concept cannot be evaluated without taking into account its cultural and ideological milieus. By failing to acknowledge the conceptual mutation that occurs beneath the surface of a word, its users will find that they are stranded on the shores of a fast-receding tide.

Towards the Politicization of a Term

To begin with, 'liberal' arose out of a culture of civility, of social norms that could be associated with those equipped either with the religious inclination or the financial means to show generosity to others. We find this semantic usage across most of Western Europe. For example, as Rui Ramos and Nuno Monteiro note in their chapter, an eighteenth-century Portuguese book already referred to 'liberality as a moderate virtue of the human affection of giving and receiving human riches' associated with nobility.[42] Edmund Burke, too, wrote of a civilization he believed produced 'power gentle, and obedience liberal' and regarded it as the result of two principles: 'the spirit of a gentleman and the spirit of religion'.[43] That, rather than the quasi-paternalistic attitude of toleration – which too has religious origins, as can be seen in the writings of John Locke, and is also related to later liberal tenets – seems to be the animating social etiquette that inspired a nonegocentric, nonmonadist view of human relationships from which liberalism could draw. In Germany, however, as Jörn Leonhard observes, 'liberal' indicated not a quasi-aristocratic and gentlemanly culture of manners and good bearing, but the possession of an ethical sensitized and enlightened mind.[44]

It is of course possible to relate the liberality of a civil, polite society to its subsequently unfolding political and ideological connotations. Open-mindedness, the love of liberty, consideration for others and a sense of common interests, both cultural and economic, lay the ground for a distinctive political mindset, and controlled and regulated public conduct that incorporated a protective dimension into legal relationships, promoting some of the components of constitutionalism. These could then attract a disparate range of tenets and practices to give depth and breadth to the mutating and developing conceptualizations that thickened 'liberal' and later 'liberalism' in their journey towards political salience and status. The self-constraint, respect and unassailability required by 'natural rights', the social orderliness fortified by the assurances and predictability of a 'social contract', and the socioeconomic harmony underpinned by an 'invisible hand' were retrospectively assembled as showpieces of the liberal arsenal that melded philosophical, legal and economic insights. To these should be added the political constraints of constitutionalism, the religious injunctions of tolerance, and the moral imperatives of responsible human and social development. All these were forged in spheres of thought that, notwithstanding a degree of interdependence, possessed their own logic. It follows that a historical-conceptual dynamic necessitates taking into account both the particular semantics of certain concepts as they relate to those specialized spheres, and the changes that took place in their broader social conditions and 'extra-linguistic' sociopolitical contexts.

Notably, while the older meaning of 'liberal' as generous or accommodating had received general and positive assent, its entry into the vocabulary of politics was accompanied by strong negative appraisals almost from the start, particularly through its rejection by conservatives, alarmed by its radical potential. Scholars disagree over when the terms 'liberal' and 'liberalism' became specifically political, the issue often being that of identifying liberalism as a party-political label or as demarcating an intellectual and ideological current or movement. That divergence is also evident in the different foci of some of the chapters in this volume, be they weighted more towards institutional political history or the history of political ideas. Spain may claim the earliest use of the noun, as Fernández-Sebastián maintains, while France may have seen the initial distinct politicization of the adjective 'liberal'. Thus, Rosenblatt identifies the 'idées libérales' promoted by Napoleon in his attempt to secure the legacy of the French Revolution, while Leonhard tracks the dissemination of the phrase to Germany and Italy ('liberale Ideen', 'le idee liberali') following French imperial expansionism, where they took root in different national contexts.[45]

By the late 1820s, the newer connotations of the word – whether derogatory, laudatory or plainly informative – had begun to spread across much of the continent with considerable rapidity over a short period. French liberal language was quickly adapted to German debates, in which French understandings of liberalism predominated, as Leonhard shows. In parallel, Fernández-Sebastián highlights the pronounced ideational activism of Spanish 'liberales' that saw their ideas traversing their national boundaries and creating early liberal offshoots in European capitals such as London and Paris. The conceptual trajectory of liberalism increasingly fluctuated between broad agreement on its principles and characteristics, a basic consensus on a thin framework (but little else) and strong and divisive contention over which attributes liberalism exhibited. Notably, the numerical preponderance of early assaults on liberalism contributed significantly to the circulation of the term in countries such as Spain and Britain. This again serves to remind us that liberalism is not a default ideational position of the human condition, as some universalizing ethicists appear to hold, but an ideology crafted in a constant struggle with other creeds and *Weltanschauungen*, often besieged and on the defensive, and frequently reflecting a minority taste.

Word and Concept

A related problem is that many of the attributes of liberalisms long preceded the word that eventually included them. Purists among conceptual historians may have a case in contending that the history of the word 'liberalism' rules out the rather clumsily named notion of 'proto' liberalisms. But inasmuch as the concept 'liberalism' contains many interrelated concepts under its aegis – concepts such as liberty, tolerance and the rule of law – we ought at least to recall that their older history is inextricably intertwined with the story of liberalism itself. Conceptual histories need to stray occasionally from their chosen word in order to reflect the richness it accrues in constant dialogue and interaction with social and political ideas and language. It is therefore incumbent on historians to take note of instances where the absence or disuse of the word 'liberalism' is assumed to indicate the lack of the concept. John Stuart Mill employed the word 'liberalism' only exceptionally, and Benjamin Constant, as Rosenblatt observes, never did. The tendency to shrink the concept to the word is present both in historical discourses within the political and intellectual classes and constitutes a trend – though to a lesser degree – within the discipline of conceptual history itself. Three issues follow. First, the obverse of the retrospective construction of liberal narratives is the practice of many intellectual historians to trace liberal ideas back to a time when the word was unknown in political discourse. Rights, individualism, constitutionalism and private property often serve in such 'ersatz' roles, and they are co-opted, sometimes erroneously, to indicate milestones in a long and durable liberal trajectory. Second, that process is sometimes accompanied by a contemporary misrecognition of the contours and layers of liberal thinking: the strong similarities between French *solidarisme* and British left-liberalism in the late nineteenth century are a case in point, despite the prevailing exclusion of the former from the category of 'liberal' by French analysts and commentators. In Britain, 'radical' and 'progressive' frequently substituted for, or intersected with, 'liberal', and variants of social democracy have shared much of their conceptual content with liberalism – an overlap also notable in Sweden – even when it is politically inconvenient to draw attention to such conceptual overlaps. Third, as noted above, the rather crude references to a concept such as liberalism as if it constituted an integrated block or mass undervalue the subtle, intricately bound, mutating and often fragile liberalisms – the conceptions that cohabit or feud under the umbrella term.

Constitution, Individual, Social: Three Liberal Strands

From the outset, some time before liberalism became a more complex and multifaceted concept, it initially displayed two different strands. One commenced from a constitutional order that set boundaries and established proper spheres of sociopolitical conduct for governments and individuals alike. The other focused on the virtues of individuality: of personal freedom and growth as constitutive of both private and public wellbeing, rather than on self-centred individualism, and often with augmented democratic undertones that affirmed the worth of each and every person.

The early association of liberalism with a constitutional order is striking, which may account for its relative collocationary absence in British liberal languages, where constitutionality was considered to be given, unwritten and, indeed, not particular to a liberal order. Thus, in the Netherlands, as Henk te Velde observes, liberalism entailed constitutionalism and that preoccupation with order propelled it into a more conservative orbit, while in Portugal, liberalism demarcated the common terrain of liberals and conservatives under a constitutional monarchy and was linked to the Constitutional Charter of 1826. In Italy, a liberal constitutionalism, as Paolo Pombeni emphasizes, was propped up by the aura of authority and, indeed, power that the state claimed as it assimilated features of community under its wing. In Germany, the 'Rechtsstaat' epitomized the legal cognate of liberalism and its initial compatibility with constitutional monarchy: the prominence of the state could not be ignored in that national context, though liberalism became progressively susceptible to challenges from radical democrats.

Constitutionalism also entailed the civil rights enshrined in constitutions, but the broader liberal notion of human rights needs to be elaborated and parsed. In some European societies, Russia included, it referred more modestly to legal protection for individuals or, as in France, a protection that emphasized civil equality. In others – such as the United Kingdom – it expanded to include the development of individuality as a core liberal objective.[46] Ultimately, liberalism as a theory, or ideology, dedicated to pursuing the individual good in common with others, of opposing harm and preventable suffering, and of the public justification of its principles began to dominate in philosophical and legal circles more than in political ones.[47] Liberty became the means to fulfilment and self-expression, while torture and the death penalty eventually became red lines that liberals would not cross.[48]

The uneasy and often tortuous relationship between liberalism and democracy is among the better-known aspects of nineteenth-century political thought. A reluctant coming to terms of the two concepts in countries such as Spain and Britain slowly saw each propelled, at least in part, into the other's orbit, but the distrust of the newly empowered masses took a while to clear across much of Europe. In Britain, liberals had to overcome a fear of majoritarianism and of political mediocrity before they embraced political – and, later, social – reform. Democracy was often associated with Jacobinism in countries that had experienced the political and intellectual impact of the French Revolution. In Dutch liberal discourse, prior preferences for constitutionalism over democracy eventually made way for a hesitant liberal relationship with democratic progressivism. In Germany and France, the semantic antagonism between liberalism and democracy remained resilient for a long time. Though liberalism was initially aligned with democracy against monarchical proclivities, it was increasingly perceived as distant from democracy's radical social perspectives, while republican democracy was out of step with the constitutional and bourgeois identity of many liberals. A similar gap between liberalism and social democracy can be seen in Poland. In Sweden and Denmark, liberals emphasized parliamentary democracy and citizens' responsibility as against the far greater emphasis of the Social Democrats on industrial and economic democracy; yet, in Sweden in particular, effective forms of liberal social democracy were emerging by the twentieth century, as was the case in Britain. It was only well into the twentieth century that self-styled liberals and democrats ceased to circle each other warily, though in recent years new antagonisms have once again surfaced under the contentious banner of 'illiberal democracy'.

As the nineteenth century began to draw to a close, a third liberal strand became gradually more prominent: the incorporation of human sociability into liberalism in such a way that individuality and personal flourishing became partly dependent on state-directed social policies. These strands are notable in Britain, in Sweden (though not in Denmark, as Jussi Kurunmäki and Jeppe Nevers explain in their chapter), in Portugal and Spain,[49] and to some extent in Poland, where – as Maciej Janowski points out – a new social liberalism relying on state activity was mooted. In Sweden, liberalism accrued a reformist, politically radical and social democratic character before the Social Democrats secured a distinct identity. In Britain, the association of liberalism with the organic interdependence of free individuals was to be enabled by a state that was both benevolent and democratic. The promotion, in certain circumstances, of private alongside collectively held property partly replaced the earlier ethos of free trade and entrepreneurial individualism. It gave rise to the welfare state – a notably liberal achievement that placed British liberalism well towards the left of the political spectrum. In Denmark, however, as Kurunmäki and Nevers observe, liberalism was a once-rural, antiregulatory concept directed against state absolutism and located to the right of the political spectrum. By contrast, the mid twentieth-century emergence of 'Ordoliberalism' in Germany envisaged a market economy presided over by the state.[50] In general, the positive or negative role ascribed to the state turned out to be one of the sharpest divisions in the European family of liberalisms, a theme central to Olga Malinova's analysis of recent Russian liberalism.[51] This division was superimposed on disjunctures between property and morality, or between an economic liberalism and a social or humanistic one.

Liberalism as a Doctrine

An intriguing question is the extent to which liberalism was perceived as a distinct political doctrine. One may well ask why Mill frequently referred to 'socialism' in his economic works and in his posthumous *Chapters on Socialism*, yet this eminent liberal thinker never produced an equivalent *Chapters on Liberalism* and did not label his own political theory as liberal. In British political discourse and in a culture where ideologies were fluid rather than sharply defined, liberalism was not considered to be a doctrine (except by some of its ideological opponents), but a far looser set of ideas and dispositions, not least because of the association of doctrine with a formally structured, even coded, set of principles, and its frequent emanation from above, be that party, state or church. The *Oxford English Dictionary* refers to 'doctrine' as 'a body of instruction or teaching', 'That which is taught or laid down as true concerning a particular subject or department of knowledge, as religion, politics, science, etc.; a belief, theoretical opinion; a dogma, tenet' and 'A body or system of principles or tenets; a doctrinal or theoretical system'[52] – none of which would have resonance with British liberal thinking.

By contrast, the collocation of 'liberalism' and 'doctrine' is familiar in some other European countries, occasionally for the very reason that would have been discredited in the United Kingdom. The 'French Doctrinaires' such as Guizot and Royer-Collard combined royalist respect for a constitutional monarchy with the association of liberty with abstract reason and truth, anchored in law. This prompted Mill to draw a telling juxtaposition: 'in England few, except the very greatest thinkers, think systematically, or aim at connecting their scattered opinions into a consistent scheme of general principles'. Hence, 'no person has been able to tell what Whiggery is, or what a Whig believes'. The Whigs – at the time the party of reform – 'were united … by a common spirit, and a general disposition to take similar views of most political questions as they arose, but not by any definite creed or profession of faith'. However, in France, 'the Doctrinaires … took the phrase "Whig principles" *au pied de la lettre* … the Doctrinaires are the authors of the only

Whig *code* in existence'.[53] In the Netherlands too, Thorbecke was considered a doctrinaire due to his emphasis on the rigorous juridical and constitutional reorganization of the state. This ideology also achieved considerable success in Portugal and Spain. From the 1830s, doctrinaire liberalism was received with hostility by the radical admirers of the Constitution of 1812 (*liberales exaltados*) as a foreign conservative fashion, but it then took root strongly and became one of the most enduring and influential ideologies of modern Spain.[54]

Another sense of doctrine also pervaded liberal economic discourses. In Portugal, although liberalism did not signify a specific doctrinal current, Ramos and Monteiro illustrate some initial attempts to see it as 'as a unified doctrine, based on ethical individualism and free trade economics'.[55] In Sweden, Kurunmäki and Nevers observe that the older 'laissez-faire' of liberal economics was regarded as a doctrine, and in France, the doctrines of the liberal economists were separately rejected as a 'theology of material interests', as Rosenblatt demonstrates.[56] Social issues were consigned to the margins of French liberalism and by the mid nineteenth century the label 'liberalism' had become increasingly contaminated, a process exacerbated later in the century as socialist concerns for social justice put French liberal reformism in the shade. Over a century later, in Russia, liberals were perceived as cultivating a doctrinal image by sidelining social needs in favour of economic ones.[57]

Liberal Futures and Horizons

A further compelling theme is the conceptualization of futures enabled through liberal languages and – to invoke Reinhart Koselleck's own interests – the variable horizons of expectations they produce.[58] This can be investigated on a number of levels. The first level concerns theories of growth, improvement and progress. When liberalism is closely linked to a diverse and free individuality, as in the writings of W. von Humboldt and Mill in Germany and Britain respectively, it becomes a spiritual ideal, a vehicle of intellectual and spiritual maturation along the path to culture, or *Bildung*, and civilization. Among the Spanish intelligentsia and its press, an optimism relating to the universal march of liberalism shone through. Though often presented as 'open-ended' – a horizon that gently recedes as one approaches it – there is nonetheless a sense of entering an advanced stage of personal and, particularly, social development that has permeated the attitudes of liberals towards their own societies as well as towards colonies and non-Western societies, as if each nation were located on a single evolutionary trajectory. Inevitably, one could invoke Mill's famous – or notorious – plea to secure a movement from barbarism to civilization by employing all expedient means in the 'spirit of improvement'.[59] Concurrently, an ingrained reformism was perceived as the key to a steady liberal movement over time, although political upheavals instigated by liberals, whether 'constitutional' or 'revolutionary', were necessitated in order to unblock hindrances to such gradual progress when these persisted in conservative or reactionary societies.

The second level is the association of liberalism and modernization that also reflects a commitment to a path of development, but in a narrower institutional and technological sense. Especially in Eastern Europe, liberalism was entrusted with a rather different task: providing the ideological arguments and incentives that would enable nations such as Poland and Russia to be propelled as full and equal members into the company of economically and politically confident states. This was not merely a question of prosperity, and even less one of individual development, but of displaying the centralized apparatus of a well-ordered society. In Poland, as Janowski maintains, this aspiration charged the state with the duty to counter the country's evident 'backwardness' by promoting legal reforms and public policy that would underpin economic growth and wealth as well as individual liberty. In Russia, as Malinova contends, liberalism was regarded as a 'civilizational choice', but in a more material sense than that imagined by Mill. Here the modernizing alternative was slanted towards 'Westernism' and against nationalism or Slavophilism, though it encountered strong national cultural resistance.[60]

A third level concerns Koselleck's 'horizon of experience', referring here in the main to its discursive and ideational dimensions. As liberalism gradually acquired new semantic layers over time, interpretations of the past were reformulated. Alongside changes in the standpoint from which, at any moment in time, liberals cast a historical/retrospective gaze on their own past, their accepted canon of authors was also altered. New names were added and granted greater or lesser significance, according to the liberal variant that a particular interpreter of liberalism felt obliged to defend in set circumstances at a given moment.

By the turn of the twentieth century, various salient liberal groups had been able, in spite of their discrepancies, to construct a canonical account with a considerable degree of consensus. A narrative had been woven by several authors, perfected in the interwar period, in the midst of a dramatic crisis of liberalism, and consolidated with some modifications in the second postwar period. This narrative, which identified the sources of liberalism in early European modernity, and even found its deepest roots in Greco-Roman antiquity, saw liberal democracy as the natural destination of a long historical process. And in that teleological vision, nineteenth-century liberalism appeared as a necessary, if inevitably flawed, imperfect stage towards the fully fledged Western democracies of the twentieth century. Such interpretations, however, stripped the late eighteenth-century revolutions and the liberalisms of the central decades of the nineteenth century of their genuine historical substance, by understanding those revolutions, movements and ideologies as mere intermediate stations, as if they were but stages in a necessary transition from the Enlightenment to the model of parliamentary democracy triumphant in the West after the Second World War. In order to restore the historicity and substance of these processes, several chapters of this volume pay special attention to the nascent liberalisms in the first decades of the nineteenth century.

Liberalism: The Differential Weighting of a Concept

Even when the term 'liberalism' became a regular fixture in the ideological and political firmament, it is more appropriate to regard its internal elements as possessing a Wittgensteinian 'family resemblance', as a fluctuating cluster of collocations and partner concepts. Notably, in that analogy, Wittgenstein explains that although every member will share some overlapping features with many or most other members, there still may be a few members who have very little in common with some others. Recently, this has markedly been the case with neoliberalism, which may share elements with a range of economic liberalisms, while being unable to correspond to constitutional or social liberalisms, or even to the ethical calling pursued by some nineteenth century free-traders. The European liberalisms that constitute the focus of this volume possess obvious similarities and greater affinity with each other than with neoliberalism, but additional refinement is necessary. There is a clear distinction between: first, the self-description of a polity as a liberal state or society; second, the centrality or marginality of liberalism in a given European society as a set of substantive ideas and practices; and, third, the relative weight of liberalism's internal conceptual components in each instance. The conceptual history of liberalism is coloured by those factors that affect its variable paths.

On the first topic, Portugal, the Netherlands, Denmark and Britain offer different lessons. In Portugal, as Ramos and Monteiro note, liberalism attained hegemonic status in the mid 1830s, and all political groups claimed the label. In the Netherlands, as te Velde argues, the term 'liberaliteit', incorporating freedom and tolerance, had an accepted cultural connotation singling out a Dutch national identity, but liberalism as a political creed suffered from an association with bourgeois economic values, endowing it with a conservative tinge. Hence, when its progressive adherents attempted to enter the territory of social legislation, they were hampered by the label 'liberal'. Indeed, as te

Velde notes, no one in the Netherlands has called liberal democracy 'liberal'. In Denmark at the end of the nineteenth century, as Kurunmäki and Nevers maintain, the absence of liberal ideology itself meant that no one seriously claimed the term 'liberal'. In Britain, according to Freeden, 'liberal' as an intellectual identifier of a political ideology and movement became far more acceptable, particularly in the half-century following Mill's death. Liberal ideas and, to some extent, the liberal language of individual rights and personal liberty percolated beyond party divides both into conservative and social-democratic/Labour camps, but as a party name Liberalism had a more restricted life.

The location of liberalism on a European map of political languages as well as liberal principles is more complex. The radical, even utilitarian, roots of British liberalism coalesced with a historically ingrained narrative of individual human rights that defined the relationship between individual and state. There was little need to import such ideas from other European countries, though German ideas of *Bildung*, as informed personal flourishing, found ready ears in Britain.[61] Austria-Hungary did not endow liberalism with public salience, but nonetheless displayed a brand of tolerance that revealed a liberalism focusing on coexistence in a pluralist social structure – something quite at odds with the unifying organic vision of the British new liberals. In Portugal, however, the terminological dominance of 'liberalism' as a common political label was generally acknowledged, and because Spain, as Fernández-Sebastián indicates, uniquely straddled Europe and the Hispanic world, liberalism accrued an unusually broad resonance as a political concept. Indeed, the spread of liberalism in intricate interchanges with other continents through colonial powers, not least in India, should not be forgotten.[62] In Eastern Europe, recent variants emerged that add important nuances to the historical mutation of the concept of liberalism. The experience of living under totalitarian governments, pursuing an ostensibly socialist and collectivist vision, created a reaction to the statist and welfare functions with which the term 'liberalism' had been associated in some West European liberal varieties. The concept now marked a rift between the flight from the oppressive state and the rediscovery of liberty in civil society on the one hand, and the lure of the material benefits liberal markets seemed to hold out on the other.[63] In Russia, Malinova demonstrates that, following the collapse of the Soviet Union, 'liberalism' indicated not just the defence of private property and free enterprise – as it had periodically been understood throughout its European history – but an ideological project for building a civilized capitalism. In view of Russia's previous Marxist ideology, this was a precious irony.

The cultural location of liberalism within a setting of religious beliefs and prescriptions is also vital to understanding its conceptual make-up.

Fillafer emphasizes the complexity of the Enlightenment's heritage in this regard, with Catholic liberals playing a part in mitigating a purely economic liberalism and imbuing it with moral import. This declined when rationalism, constitutionalism and popular sovereignty were extracted from the Enlightenment to become liberalism's hallmarks. In Italy, as Pombeni shows, Catholicism was all too often the foil against which liberals would contend, though Catholic thinking on the link between person and community significantly endorsed forms of pluralist democracy that liberals could accommodate. As a concept, liberalism was defined both through its negation by social Catholicism and by its susceptibility to socioreligious meanings on its ideological periphery. In Germany, Leonhard observes that Catholics increasingly associated liberalism with a strong anticlericalism. Indeed, as Rosenblatt remarks, French Catholic liberals resented those 'false liberals' who departed from the principle of nonintervention in religion through their exclusion of powerful Catholic orders.[64]

As for the varying internal conceptual arrangements of liberalism itself, one example may suffice. The liberty element of liberalism was differentially connected to groups rather than only to individuals. We have already mentioned the organic interconnections among people that suffused a welfare-oriented liberalism. But there was also a strong vein of national liberty at the heart of some regional European liberalisms. It should be distinguished from the prenationalist communitarianism that was found either in its religious form – a Catholic community – or its jurisdictional corporate form, typical of the *ancien régime*, such as that occurring in Spain and Portugal in the context of their struggles against Napoleon in the early nineteenth century. Liberal nationalism was at the core of Mazzini's love of liberty and his advocacy of national self-determination that inspired the Risorgimento, as well as influencing Indian and Hispanic American debate.[65] As our purview moves eastwards, the nationalist connotations of liberalism become more pronounced. Under Habsburg rule, as Fillafer argues, the plurilingual patriotism of Czech and Hungarian national liberals countered Austro-German pressures to engineer a centralizing liberal nationalism, in each case appropriating rival interpretations of the Enlightenment. In Poland, tellingly, as Janowski maintains, personal liberty was not central to liberal discourse; rather, liberty was attached to ideas of ethnic national independence, a nationalism also stimulated by revolutionary Jacobin ideas.

There are also broader questions that, we submit, could serve as the focus of research. Has a perceived polarity between individual and society had a defining impact on what can be conceptualized as liberal? Are there Europe-specific cognates and clusters in whose 'force-fields' either 'liberal' or 'liberalism' can typically, or are more likely to, be found? How have variable colonial histories influenced and shaped the moulding of European liberalisms? Can one identify, within the melange of European political thinking, loci and eras of liberal inventiveness and influence that possess either greater significance or more manifest marginality, or, indeed, challenge conventional wisdoms on the matter? Conversely, is liberalism the product of a deeply held sense of European (or regional-European) superiority? Many of those questions have been addressed only indirectly in the chapters assembled in this volume, but the plurality of approaches and the diversity of perspectives, periods and case studies attests to a new spirit of inquiry among the conceptual historians of Europe and, indeed, among the wider practitioners of conceptual history itself, as evidenced in the companion lead volume in this series.[66] We trust that this modest beginning will encourage others to explore these paths and to branch out into others.

Michael Freeden is Emeritus Professor of Politics, University of Oxford. His books include *The New Liberalism: An Ideology of Social Reform* (1978); *Liberalism Divided: A Study in British Political Thought 1914–1939* (1986); *Ideologies and Political Theory: A Conceptual Approach* (1996); *Ideology: A Very Short Introduction* (2003); *Liberal Languages: Ideological Imaginations and 20th Century Progressive Thought* (2005); *The Political Theory of Political Thinking* (2013); *Liberalism: A Very Short Introduction* (2015); and *Conceptual History in the European Space* (coedited with W. Steinmetz and J. Fernández-Sebastián, Berghahn Books, 2017). He is the founder-editor of the *Journal of Political Ideologies* and a Fellow of the Academy of Social Sciences.

Javier Fernández-Sebastián is Professor of History of Political Thought at the University of the Basque Country. He has published extensively on modern intellectual and conceptual history, with a particular focus on Spain and the Iberian world. He serves on the editorial board of various journals as well as the International Archives of the History of Ideas series with Springer Verlag. He has recently edited *Political Concepts and Time: New Approaches to Conceptual History* (2011) and *La Aurora de la Libertad: Los primeros liberalismos en el mundo iberoamerican* (2012).

Notes

1. D. Bell, 'What is Liberalism?', *Political Theory* 42 (2014), 1–34; M. Freeden, *Liberalism: A Very Short Introduction*, Oxford, 2015.
2. 'Liberalismo', *El Sensato* (Santiago de Compostela), 1 July 1813, 1553–59.

3. M. Freeden, 'The Morphological Analysis of Ideology', in M. Freeden, L.T. Sargent and M. Stears (eds), *The Oxford Handbook of Political Ideologies*, Oxford, 2013, 115–37.

4. To date, the only substantially detailed comparative treatment has been that of J. Leonhard, *Liberalismus: Zur historischen Semantik eines europäischen Deutungsmusters*, Munich, 2001, but our volume extends the geographical space explored.

5. R.R. Palmer, *A History of the Modern World*, 4th edn, New York, 1971, 472.

6. H. Höpfl, 'Isms', *British Journal of Political Science* 13 (1983), 1–17; C. Cuttica, 'Isms and History', in J.D. Wright (ed.), *Encyclopedia of the Social & Behavioral Sciences*, 2nd edn, 26 vols, Amsterdam, 2015, vol. 12, 289–93; J. Marjanen, 'Editorial: Ism Concepts in Science and Politics', *Contributions to the History of Concepts*, 13(1) (2018), v–ix; J. Kurunmäki and J. Marjanen, 'A Rhetorical View of Isms: An Introduction', *Journal of Political Ideologies* 23(3) (2018), 241–55.

7. Kurunmäki and Marjanen, 'A Rhetorical View', 247.

8. J. Kurunmäki and J. Marjanen, 'Isms, Ideologies and Setting the Agenda for Public Debate', *Journal of Political Ideologies* 23(3) (2018), 260.

9. Even if we leave aside the question of liberal Protestantism and Catholic liberalism, a religious imprint is present in liberalism in some cases well into the nineteenth century. Ramos and Monteiro report in Chapter 4 that in 1867, the Portuguese intellectual Alexandre Herculano still mentions 'the two opposing religions of absolutism and liberalism' and enumerates several 'liberal dogmas'.

10. Kurunmäki and Marjanen, 'A Rhetorical View', 243.

11. J. Donoso Cortés, *Obras*, 6 vols, ed. Gavino Tejado, Madrid, 1855, vol. 5, 177–84; G. Tejado, *El catolicismo liberal*, Madrid, 1875, 207f. Let us recall that in his 1864 encyclical *Quanta Cura*, followed by the *Syllabus* of 'the principal errors of our century', Pope Pius IX had unreservedly condemned liberalism and other modern 'isms', including socialism and communism.

12. Höpfl, 'Isms', 12.

13. Cuttica, 'Isms and History', 760f.

14. L. Hartz, *The Liberal Tradition in America*, New York, 1955. On the 'Americanization' of liberalism, see H. Rosenblatt, *The Lost History of Liberalism from Ancient Rome to the Twenty-First Century*, Princeton, 2018, 245–64.

15. Most of the chapters of this volume contain more or less relevant samples of this type of universalist discourse. In the second half of the nineteenth century, the echoes of liberal universalism were still heard from time to time on both sides of the Atlantic – for example, in President Lincoln's voice in the midst of the American Civil War (Rosenblatt, *The Lost History*, 168–75).

16. Leonhard, *Liberalismus*.

17. 'The adjective expresses our fears, the noun, our hopes.' M. Walzer, 'On Negative Politics', in B. Yack (ed.), *Liberalism without Illusions: An Introduction to Judith Shklar's Political Thought*, Chicago, 1996, 22.

18. 'Sobre las ideas republicanas', *El Censor*, no. 37, Madrid, 14 April 1821, 77–80. In a series of articles on a new 'dictionary' of politics, the following tentative

definition was included: 'Liberal: The wise publicists applied this word to the one who promoted in society the principles of civil and political liberty, deduced from the natural rights of man' (*Abeja Española*, no. 264, Cádiz, 2 June 1813, 18).

19. Thus, according to political essayist Juan de Olavarría, writing in 1820, 'true liberalism consists in the constant tendency towards the perfection of governments' according to 'the progress of human reason'. J. de Olavarría, *Reflexiones a las Cortes y otros escritos políticos*, edited by C. Morange, Bilbao, 2007, 181, 222f. In many other places in Europe, we find similar ideas that tend to identify liberalism with progress and the advance of freedom. See Chapter 2.

20. G. Matoré, *La méthode en lexicologie*, 2nd edn, Paris, 1973.

21. As far as we know, based on data provided by some contributors to this volume and some complementary bibliographic research, the first book or pamphlet published in Spanish that meets this condition dates from 1814. The first in French is 1819, in Portuguese in 1822, in English, German and Dutch in 1823, and in Italian in 1832.

22. See Chapter 7.

23. J. Fernández-Sebastián, 'Liberalismos nacientes en el Atlántico iberoamericano: "Liberal" como concepto y como identidad política, 1750–1850', *Jahrbuch für Geschichte Lateinamerikas* 45 (2008), 149–96, at 172.

24. N. Foxlee, 'Pivots and Levers: Political Rhetoric around *Capitalism* in Britain from the 1970s to the Present', *Contributions to the History of Concepts* 13(1) (2018), 78; C. Perelman and L. Olbrechts-Tyteca, *The New Rhetoric: A Treatise on Argumentation*, trans. J. Wilkinson and P. Weaver, Notre Dame, 1971, 411–59.

25. See Chapter 1.

26. See Chapter 1.

27. J. Fernández-Sebastián, 'Tradiciones electivas: Cambio, continuidad y ruptura en historia intelectual', *Almanack* 7 (2014), 5–26.

28. See Chapter 1.

29. 'Le systéme par lequel on a travaillé depuis trois siècles à remplacer le précedent est celui qui se fonde sur la liberté. C'est le *système libéral* proprement dit qui, conçu par la philosophie, appliqué ensuite à la réforme de l'Église et de l'État, a été étendu de nos jours à presque toutes les sphères de l'activité sociale.' H. Ahrens, *Cours de Droit naturel ou de Philosophie du Droit*, Brussels, 1838, vol. 2, 340f. Translated by Michael Freeden.

30. Quotation from Louis Blanc in the 1840s. See Rosenblatt, *The Lost History*, Chapter 5.

31. M. Freeden, *The New Liberalism: An Ideology of Social Reform*, Oxford, 1978.

32. See Chapters 7, 6, 8 and 4 respectively.

33. L.T. Hobhouse, *Liberalismo*, Barcelona, 1927. Throughout the first third of the twentieth century, several essays on this subject appeared in Spain. In these works one can perceive the intense circulation of ideas in those years and the eagerness for the renewal of the European liberal left. Among these works are: A. Posada, 'La noción de deber social', *La Lectura* 1 (1901), 1–7; A. Posada, 'Liberalismo y política social' ('Del viejo al nuevo liberalismo' and 'Las nuevas

corrientes políticas'), *La Lectura* 1 (1913), 366–78; M. Almagro Sanmartín, *El nuevo liberalismo*, Madrid, 1910; and T. Elorrieta Artaza, *Liberalismo*, Madrid, 1926. See also M. Suárez Cortina, 'El liberalismo democrático en España: de la Restauración a la República', *Historia y Política* 17 (2007), 121–50.

34. R.G. Collingwood, 'Preface', in G. de Ruggiero, *The History of European Liberalism*, Oxford, 1927, vii.
35. De Ruggiero, *The History*, 347.
36. See Chapter 9.
37. B. Croce, *Politics and Morals*, London, 1946, 78–87.
38. I. Berlin, *Four Essays on Liberty*, Oxford, 1969, 161. See also Freeden, Chapter 11 in this volume.
39. I. Berlin, *Four Essays*, 8.
40. H.J. Laski, *The Rise of European Liberalism*, London, 1962 [1936], 168, 171.
41. F. Hayek, *New Studies in Philosophy, Politics, Economics and the History of Ideas*, London, 1978, 119, 130, 141.
42. See Chapter 4.
43. E. Burke, *Reflections on the Revolution in France*, C.C. O'Brien (ed.), Harmondsworth, 1969, 173.
44. See Chapter 2.
45. See Chapters 5 and 2.
46. See Chapters 10, 5 and 11.
47. See e.g. G.F. Gaus, *Justificatory Liberalism*, Oxford, 1996.
48. See e.g. M. Freeden, 'The Elusiveness of European (Anti-)liberalism', in D. Gosewinkel (ed.), *Anti-liberal Europe: A Neglected Story of Europeanization*, New York and Oxford, 2015, 333–44.
49. M. Suárez Cortina, 'El liberalismo democrático en España: de la Restauración a la República', *Historia y Política* 17 (2007), 121–50.
50. For a recent assessment, see e.g. T. Beck and H-H. Kotz (eds), *Ordoliberalism. A German Oddity?*, London, 2017.
51. See Chapter 10.
52. *Oxford English Dictionary Online*, retrieved 17 February 2019.
53. J.S. Mill, 'French News', *Examiner*, 21 October 1832, in A.P. Robson and J.M. Robson (eds), *The Collected Works of John Stuart Mill*, 33 vols, Toronto and London, 1986, vol. 23, 513f.
54. See Chapters 3 and 4. Republican opponents of the liberal-conservative system in force in Spain during the last quarter of the nineteenth century and the first quarter of the twentieth century (called by historians 'the Restoration'), referred to that regime disparagingly with the label 'doctrinaire monarchy.' L. Díez del Corral, *El liberalismo doctrinario*, Madrid, 1956.
55. See Chapter 4.
56. See Chapters 6 and 5.
57. See Chapter 10.
58. R. Koselleck, *Futures Past: On the Semantics of Historical Time*, Cambridge, MA, 1985, 267–88.

59. J.S. Mill, *On Liberty*, London, 1910, 73.
60. See Chapters 8 and 10.
61. See Chapter 11.
62. See e.g. R. Bajpai, *Debating Difference: Group Rights and Liberal Democracy in India*, New Delhi, 2011.
63. M. Freeden, 'European Liberalisms: An Essay in Comparative Political Thought', *European Journal of Political Theory* 7 (2008), 9–30.
64. See Chapters 1, 9, 2 and 5.
65. C.A. Bayly and E.F. Biagini (eds), *Giuseppe Mazzini and the Globalization of Democratic Nationalism, 1830–1920*, Oxford, 2008; S. Recchia and N. Urbinati (eds), *A Cosmopolitanism of Nations*, Princeton, 2009.
66. W. Steinmetz, M. Freeden and J. Fernández-Sebastián (eds), *Conceptual History in the European Space*, New York, 2017.

Bibliography

Ahrens, H. *Cours de Droit naturel ou de Philosophie du Droit*, vol. 2. Brussels, 1838.

Almagro Sanmartín, M. *El nuevo liberalismo*. Madrid, 1910.

Bajpai, R. *Debating Difference: Group Rights and Liberal Democracy in India*. New Delhi, 2011.

Bayly, C.A., and E.F. Biagini (eds). *Giuseppe Mazzini and the Globalization of Democratic Nationalism, 1830–1920*. Oxford, 2008.

Beck, T., and H-H. Kotz (eds). *Ordoliberalism. A German Oddity?* London, 2017.

Bell, D. 'What is Liberalism?' *Political Theory* 42 (2014), 1–34.

Berlin, I. *Four Essays on Liberty*. Oxford, 1969.

Burke, E. *Reflections on the Revolution in France*, C.C. O'Brien (ed.). Harmondsworth, 1969.

Collingwood, R.G. 'Preface', in G. de Ruggiero, *The History of European Liberalism* (Oxford, 1927), vii–viii.

Croce, B. *Politics and Morals*. London, 1946.

Cuttica, C. 'Isms and History', in J.D. Wright (ed.), *Encyclopedia of the Social & Behavioral Sciences*, 2nd edn, vol. 12 (Amsterdam, 2015), 289–760.

De Olavarría, J. *Reflexiones a las Cortes y otros escritos políticos*, C. Morange (ed.). Bilbao, 2007.

De Ruggiero, G. *The History of European Liberalism*. Oxford, 1927.

Díez del Corral, L. *El liberalismo doctrinario*. Madrid, 1956.

Donoso Cortés, J. *Obras*, Gavino Tejado (ed.), 6 vols. Madrid, 1855.

Elorrieta Artaza, T. *Liberalismo*. Madrid, 1926.

Fernández-Sebastián, J. 'Liberalismos nacientes en el Atlántico iberoamericano: "Liberal" como concepto y como identidad política, 1750–1850'. *Jahrbuch für Geschichte Lateinamerikas* 45 (2008), 149–96.

Fernández-Sebastián, J. 'Tradiciones electivas: Cambio, continuidad y ruptura en historia intelectual'. *Almanack* 7 (2014), 5–26.

Foxlee, N. 'Pivots and Levers: Political Rhetoric around *Capitalism* in Britain from the 1970s to the Present'. *Contributions to the History of Concepts* 13(1) (2018), 75–99.

Freeden, M. 'The Elusiveness of European (Anti-)liberalism', in D. Gosewinkel (ed.), *Anti-liberal Europe: A Neglected Story of Europeanization* (New York and Oxford, 2015), 333–44.

———. 'European Liberalisms: An Essay in Comparative Political Thought'. *European Journal of Political Theory* 7 (2008), 9–30.

———. *Liberalism: A Very Short Introduction*. Oxford, 2015.

———. 'The Morphological Analysis of Ideology', in M. Freeden, L.T. Sargent and M. Stears (eds), *The Oxford Handbook of Political Ideologies* (Oxford, 2013), 115–37.

———. *The New Liberalism: An Ideology of Social Reform*. Oxford, 1978.

Gaus, G.F. *Justificatory Liberalism*. Oxford, 1996.

Hartz, L. *The Liberal Tradition in America*. New York, 1955.

Hayek, F. *New Studies in Philosophy, Politics, Economics and the History of Ideas*. London, 1978.

Hobhouse, L.T. *Liberalismo*. Barcelona, 1927.

Höpfl, H. 'Isms'. *British Journal of Political Science* 13 (1983), 1–17.

Koselleck, R. *Futures Past: On the Semantics of Historical Time*. Cambridge, MA, 1985.

Kurunmäki, J., and J. Marjanen. 'A Rhetorical View of Isms: An Introduction'. *Journal of Political Ideologies* 23 (3) (2018), 241–55.

———. 'Isms, Ideologies and Setting the Agenda for Public Debate'. *Journal of Political Ideologies* 23 (3) (2018), 256–82.

Laski, H.J. *The Rise of European Liberalism*. London, 1962 [1936].

Leonhard, J. *Liberalismus: Zur historischen Semantik eines europäischen Deutungsmusters*. Munich, 2001.

'Liberalismo'. *El Sensato* (Santiago de Compostela) (1 July 1813), 1553–59.

Marjanen, J. 'Editorial: Ism Concepts in Science and Politics'. *Contributions to the History of Concepts* 13(1) (2018), v–ix.

Matoré, G. *La méthode en lexicologie*, 2nd edn. Paris, 1973.

Mill, J.S. *The Collected Works of John Stuart Mill, Volume XXIII: Newspaper Writings August 1831–October 1834 Part II* [1831], A.P Robson and J.M. Robson (ed.). Toronto, 1986.

———. *On Liberty*. London, 1910.

Oxford English Dictionary Online. Retrieved 17 February 2019 from https://enox forddictionaries.com.

Palmer, R.R. *A History of the Modern World*, 4th edn. New York, 1971.

Perelman, C., and L. Olbrechts-Tyteca. *The New Rhetoric: A Treatise on Argumentation*, trans. J. Wilkinson and P. Weaver. Notre Dame, 1971.

Posada, A. 'La noción de deber social'. *La Lectura* 1 (1901), 1–7.

———. 'Liberalismo y política social' ('Del viejo al nuevo liberalismo' and 'Las nuevas corrientes políticas'). *La Lectura* 1 (1913), 366–78.

Recchia, S., and N. Urbinati (eds). *A Cosmopolitanism of Nations*. Princeton, 2009.

Rosenblatt, H. *The Lost History of Liberalism from Ancient Rome to the Twenty-First Century*. Princeton, 2018.

Steinmetz, W., M. Freeden and J. Fernández-Sebastián (eds). *Conceptual History in the European Space*. New York, 2017.

Suárez Cortina, M. 'El liberalismo democrático en España: de la Restauración a la República'. *Historia y Política* 17 (2007), 121–50.

Tejado, G. *El catolicismo liberal*. Madrid, 1875.

Walzer, M. 'On Negative Politics', in B. Yack (ed.), *Liberalism without Illusions: An Introduction to Judith Shklar's Political Thought* (Chicago, 1996), 17–24.

Chapter 1

Habsburg Liberalisms and the Enlightenment Past, 1790–1848

Franz L. Fillafer

❖

This chapter establishes a dialogue between two areas of research that rarely speak to each other. The first is recent scholarship that critically tackles the old notion of a monolithic eighteenth-century Enlightenment; today the eighteenth century teems with sentimental empiricists, republican hacks, defenders of enlightened kingship and Anglican Newtonians – some scholars even speak of 'rival Enlightenments'.[1] In the second field, several studies have begun to view afresh the varieties of European liberalism in the nineteenth century beyond the binary opposition between a laissez-faire agenda and a republican model predicated on either political participation, civic virtue or both.[2]

Both approaches are important, but they rarely make contact. If the Enlightenment is no longer seen as a robustly uniform set of idioms and imperatives, we also need to rethink its 'end'. The conventional tale about its abrupt dissolution or fragmentation around 1800 can no longer offer convincing guidance, and nor can the story about Enlightenment's 'almost imperceptible'[3] transformation into liberalism. Both accounts invite scrutiny and they prompt us to rethink three large-scale problems. What happened to rival Enlightenment vocabularies and practices on their way into the nineteenth century? In what ways did their conceptual refurbishment impinge on the Enlightenment's becoming historical, on the emergence of an Enlightenment past? What role did liberals play in this process, and what does this mean for the architectonic traits of liberal 'languages'?

What Enlightenment? What Liberalism?

As the following pages will try to show, the study of the relationship between the Enlightenment and liberalism is also a fertile line of enquiry because it offers valuable material for a redescription of the Enlightenment. The study of the stages of conceptual engineering by which liberals made the Enlightenment part of their political pedigree permits us to reconstruct how the Enlightenment became what it seems today: rationalist, predicated on natural law, deist, anticlerical and imbued with the idea of popular sover-eignty. The Enlightenment was now regarded as a result of the Reformation and it was believed to have culminated in the French Revolution. Liberals remade the Enlightenment in their image, and the study of this process tells us a lot both about the eighteenth-century Enlightenment and about the emergence of liberalism.

These problems are directly relevant to the comparative study of liberal-isms. Some students of liberal 'languages' have noted the deceptive similarity of purportedly equivalent semantic patterns across European contexts.[4] Nevertheless, it is far from clear how a comparison of liberalisms can avoid glossing over the asymmetries and dislocations that existed among them. This point is directly related to the interaction and conceptual transfer between different strands of liberalism. The study of these phenomena must take into account frictions, transmission losses and the repercussions that intellectual change at the ostensibly 'peripheral' fringes had on what happened in the 'centres'.[5] The study of how liberals remade the eighteenth-century past can offer some relevant insights here.

The usual narrative on the intellectual history of the first third of the nineteenth century makes the Enlightenment shade into liberalism quite smoothly, yet few reliable studies exist on how exactly and by what means this happened. Little is known about the milieus, conceptual arbitrators and intermediaries that made this transition possible.[6] The approach advocated here can enable us to study the varieties of liberalism by exploring what Enlightenment resources it deployed and by seeing this activity in constant interplay with the concepts of the historical Enlightenment that a given strand of liberalism elaborated in order to embrace or to reject it.

This approach permits us to redescribe the 'genesis' of liberalism. In addressing this problem, the following pages will also raise some questions regarding method as the chapter permits us to look more closely at the scope, structure and durability of 'political languages'. The relationship between the Enlightenment and liberalism throws into relief some basic conceptual questions regarding the study of 'political languages' that I will turn to in the last section of this chapter. The specific formulation of the problem presented here is a response to the increasingly unsatisfactory older approach that simply antedated the development of liberalism by identifying 'anticipations' of liberalism and 'protoliberal' sentiments in the eighteenth century. It is precisely at this point that close attention to the history of concepts, their usage and contestability, and to the historization of the Enlightenment can offer important insights.

Liberalism has long been defined on the basis of its British and French archetypes, yet both phenomena seem to disaggregate. The 'varieties of Whiggism' have become conspicuous in the British case, and we are in a good position to chart the divergences between Whigs and liberals regarding ethics and psychology that came to the fore once liberals had broken with the Newtonian notion of a creative mind that moulds inert and passive matter.[7] Liberals also deviated from the Smithian model of a self-adjusting equilibrium when they introduced scenarios of surpluses, slumps and business cycles, and they supplanted Smith's concept of labour, which relied on the measuring of amounts of value, with a definition of labour that rested on workers' toil, energy and time.[8] Liberals were also far from alone in laying claim to the Enlightenment's bequest: Edmund Burke's defence of a free enterprise system in an Anglican environment, protected by a mixed constitution and chivalric manners, resonated with early nineteenth-century readers. David Hume's and Adam Smith's sceptical Whiggism bred a distinctive brand of enlightened Toryism that emphasized the personal security of property in a society of ranks and led to protectionist arguments, schemes of entail reform and proposals for more effective poor laws.[9] To complicate matters further, evangelical revivalism whose strength grew after 1800 shared the basic premises of economic deregulation, although evangelicals derided liberals' distributional paradigm of natural gratification, sweetness and light. Instead, they saw the competitive economy as a divinely ordained moral trial, a framework of rewards and reprimands whose adverse effects could be soothed by self-help once the theology of special providence had been abandoned.[10]

The same variegation applies to France, where a similar system of vertical conceptual corridors that led from the eighteenth to the nineteenth century emerges. Studies of French liberalism have discovered various solvents under an ostensibly solid crust.[11] In France, 'republican' arguments of frugality and civic ethos have been shown to persist after 1800, now replete with lessons learned from the deprivation of politics under the *ancien régime* and under Napoleon's dictatorship.[12] This republican strand existed beside an 'aristocratic liberal' tradition. Aristocratic liberals rebelled against bourgeois *enrichessement*, which led to smug and philistine self-gratification and destroyed the moral personality of the citizen. Aristocratic liberals deplored 'individualism' because it led to a loss of civil consciousness and was accompanied by the destruction of constitutional intermediary powers.[13] This tradition ran from Montesquieu to Tocqueville, and it tilted lances against the third contender to the title 'liberal', the statist liberalism of the *juste milieu* most fully embodied by François Guizot after the 1830s.[14]

'National' varieties of liberalism can only be understood if one applies a new grid of similarities, imbrications and elective affinities in which forms of European liberalism can be assorted. What also deserves to be highlighted here is the uneasy relationship of liberal aims in different sectors of public life that becomes obvious: 'liberal' attitudes to sociopolitical, economic and religious issues were not necessarily compatible. In the British case, for instance, economic liberals were often High Churchmen or evangelicals who resisted Catholic emancipation and poor relief, while social and economic interventionists were liberals in terms of religion. Hence, Liberal Anglicans, Whigs and High Tories supported a generous treatment of Dissenters, but refused to believe that the economic order inculcated an authorized, natural version of social morality.[15]

Liberalism thus seems quite brittle, and scholars are becoming sceptical of its unity across time and across sectors of intellectual activity and enquiry. The older idea that liberals defended an agenda based on an unfettered market economy, associational psychology, rational individualism and an anthropology that maintained the satisfaction of given ends without a moral hierarchy among them melts into the air. Thereby, the British variety of liberalism is being progressively dislodged from its previous privileged position as a set of standard values against which liberals elsewhere were measured. This leapfrogging liberalism that united the triumvirate of Locke, Smith and Bentham never existed, and it has ceased to loom as large over Europe as it once did.[16] Once this apparently coherent pattern of thought comes apart in Britain, its absence elsewhere can no longer signify the nonexistence of proper 'liberalism' in these regions.

The Habsburg Case

The main part of this chapter focuses on the Habsburg lands between 1790s and the 1850s. The findings of the history of concepts seem unambiguous here: as in other European places, the term 'liberal' denoted 'generosity' in the languages of the Habsburg lands after 1800 and came to change from this meaning of magnanimity into a substantive '-ism' that bristled with the energy of a 'concept of movement' (*Bewegungsbegriff*) in the 1820s and 1830s.[17] The intellectual roots of liberalism are usually traced back to the sources nineteenth-century liberals themselves proudly advertised: the reforms of Joseph II. The textbook account suggests that the Habsburg monarchy was jolted out of torpor by Joseph II. He broke with his mother Maria Theresa's method of cautious change and set off an avalanche of ill-prepared reforms.[18] Joseph enacted toleration of all Christian religions and of the Jews, prepared a civil code that was to ensure equality before the law, and abolished serfdom and bondage in his lands. Joseph's roughshod ride over inherited rights and privileges led to outbursts of popular disaffection that brought the monarchy to the brink of disaster.

The conventional account of the emergence of liberalism is heavily coloured by the work of nineteenth-century liberal historians. It runs like this: after Joseph was forced to rescind much of his legislation on his deathbed in 1790, Leopold II managed to restore order. Leopold was succeeded by his son, Francis II/I, whose reign made the monarchy sink into obscurantism and reaction. The repressive regime of Prince Metternich continued until 1848, when the Revolution blew the *Vormärz* system into pieces. The year 1848 saw the election of an imperial parliament whose plenary hall teemed with delegates from all Habsburg kingdoms and duchies with the exception of the Hungarian and Croatian lands. This was the dawn of constitutionalism in the Habsburg monarchy. The standard account suggests that this was the success of liberals who had clung to Joseph's reformist project and handed down his legacy over the decades. This implies that liberalism surreptitiously continued the aims and concepts of the Enlightenment the governments of Francis II/I and Ferdinand I had sought to suppress.[19] Yet liberals' legacy-building obliterated two key aspects: first, the reactionary regime that liberals rebelled against in the name of Joseph II continued to rely on Joseph's designs in law, civic administration, religious toleration and economic politics; and, second, mid nineteenth-century liberals also drastically abridged and shrunk the Enlightenment in retrospect. According to liberal historians and politicians, the Enlightenment had been eradicated under Francis II/I, thereby becoming the very antipode of pre–1848 reaction and a legacy for liberals to piously appropriate.

Liberals' remaking of their Enlightenment patrimony belittled the claims of collateral heirs to that estate.[20] Conservatives and radicals were excluded from this legacy. Liberals neatly patterned their constitutional aims on the epoch before 1848.[21] This led to an all-inclusive approach to liberalism, making it an umbrella term for all forms of pre–Revolutionary criticism of the regime, an approach which truncated the variety of pre–1848 political life. I shall turn to this problem in a moment when I survey selected Enlightenment conceptual resources and how early nineteenth-century liberals made use of them. Before I explore this issue in more detail, I will turn to the question of liberal nationalisms in the pluricultural and pluriconfessional Habsburg monarchy.

The liberal refashioning of the Enlightenment past offers rich insights for a better understanding of the various national revivals in the Habsburg lands, but also for the differences between distinct strands of liberalism in the region. The early nineteenth century was the epoch of 'national renascences' in the Habsburg lands.[22] These revivals have been long seen as rambunctiously romantic movements that ran up to their preordained destinations, namely national independence. Enlightenment patriotism in particular has been treated as a convenient signpost on this road, as a mere premonition of full-fledged nineteenth-century aims. Hence, the Enlightenment has been reduced to a mere precursor of more fully and stridently articulated nineteenth-century demands. This is a deeply problematic account that recent scholarship on philology, aesthetics, bourgeois associations, patriotic science and collecting has done much to correct.[23] In fact, enlightened *Landespatriotismus*, a plurilingual form of patriotic sentiment tied to the respective land within the larger monarchy, persisted well into the nineteenth century and was not simply replaced or gobbled up by nationalism proper.[24] We are also in a better position now to appreciate that the role of the Enlightenment in the history of the respective nations was disputed from the 1820s to the 1840s. Contemporaries debated whether their national renascence was a result of Catholic Baroque patriotism or of the Enlightenment. In these debates, the Enlightenment was remodelled to serve as a precursor of liberalism, as anticlerical and constitutionalist, but this did not go undisputed. Liberals neither succeeded in styling themselves as the sole and pioneering protagonists of the revival, nor did they manage to convince their contemporaries that they were the only ones permitted legitimately to lay claim to the Enlightenment past as its proper legatees. Yet this discourse reveals more and finer differences once it comes to the place that Joseph II and his legacy occupied here.

Here it is revealing to look at the nuances of the historical and political attitudes towards enlightened absolutism in the early nineteenth century, because they also shed light on the variegation of liberalism in the Habsburg lands. It is helpful to begin with an observation on the region's plurilingualism. From the perspective of the history of concepts, it is quite revealing to study the strategic uses both of the concept 'liberalism' and of the Enlightenment past in multilingual regions like the Habsburg lands. If we bear in mind the polyglotism of the Empire's educated elites, it becomes possible to monitor the development of national discursive spheres in which asymmetrical counterconcepts and ascriptions of 'liberalism' and 'radicalism' emerged. These concepts often bore the imprint of memories and reappraisals of enlightened absolutism. It is in the first half of the nineteenth century that we find the term *Aufklärung*, the German term for Enlightenment, used in various texts side by side with its cognates in other vernaculars (*osvícenství, felvilágosodás*) that were about to re-emerge as literary languages.[25] Such multilingual spheres of communication also offer revealing material on contemporaries' awareness of asynchronic conceptual changes in the languages their filter screen of semantic developments registers.

By juxtaposing cognates of these terms in different languages, the authors of the time also alluded to different historical frames of reference. This combination could imply that enlightened absolutism and *Aufklärung* constituted a heritage best left to self-proclaimed centralist liberals who operated within the dominant Germanophone linguistic framework and were suspected of streamlining unification and hostility towards the Monarchy's nations. At the same time, the issue of liberals' indebtedness to enlightened absolutist imperatives created friction among the discourse controllers of various 'national revivals'. Conservative revivalist clerics criticized liberal revivalists' radicalism and tarred them as closet admirers of the proto-liberal saccharine hero Joseph II, whom Catholic revivalists viewed as a draconian martinet.[26] According to clerical revivalists, liberals jeopardized the regeneration of the nation that was to be based on its respective pristine faith. It is important to note that this negative image of Joseph II united conservatives of different stripes, persuasions and mother tongues within the monarchy, whereas conflicts over Joseph's reputation drove a wedge between liberals with different national agendas.[27]

In the 1830s and 1840s, liberals in the Czech and Hungarian contexts rejected their Austro-German counterparts' claim that Enlightenment and Josephinism were two sides of the same coin. They conceded that elements of Josephinian rule had been beneficial to their respective nation's development, and it was particularly in the domain of church reform, toleration and the abolition of serfdom that they sided with Austro-German liberals' praise of the emperor and acknowledged his Enlightenment credentials. Yet what Austro-German liberals saw as a valid and timeless treasure that the Emperor had bequeathed to posterity – German culture as the overarching framework to unite the Monarchy – seemed an inexcusable blemish to Czech and Hungarian liberals. Many enlightened patriots around 1800 had also praised Joseph's reforms of the church, of peasant property and of taxation, but they judged Joseph's language politics much less harshly than their later-born liberal successors.[28] Priorities were to change in the coming decades. In the 1830s and 1840s, when Austro-German liberals saw the existing regime of Francis I and Ferdinand I as the outright refutation of everything Joseph II stood for, Hungarian and Czech liberals emphasized the elements of continuity between Joseph's reign and those of his successors. Joseph's 'Germanizing' designs were now perceived by many national liberals from the Bohemian lands and Hungary as repellent enough to overshadow his other achievements. Joseph's neglect of the Enlightenment's national dimensions discredited his reign as the remnant of a bygone age. What won Austro-German liberals' praise seemed a symptom of reaction to their Czech and Hungarian counterparts.[29]

Austro-German liberals around the middle of the nineteenth century made Enlightenment and Josephinism coterminous: Enlighteners and admirers of Joseph II seemed to be cut from one cloth. Inaccurate as this conflation is, it nevertheless continued to serve as a basic premise of much historiography on the eighteenth century. This conflation had a second effect: it made liberalism seem tantamount to the admiration of Joseph II. Yet while it is true that Austro-German liberals draped themselves with the mantle of Joseph II,[30] the situation is much more complicated if one turns to their fellow liberals from Lombardy and Venetia, as well as from the Bohemian and Hungarian lands. If one seeks to recover the conditions under which the equation between liberalism and Josephinian Enlightenment was forged, one quickly detects strategies of dissociation and self-affirmation. Most Austro-German liberals ardently believed in the blessings of universal German culture for the less educated nations of the monarchy. The invocation of Joseph's Enlightenment legacy permitted Austro-German liberals to perform three tasks in the middle of the 'confusion of ideas'[31] that was rampant in 1848: first, it allowed them to stamp their fellow pre–1848 malcontents as illiberals; second, it made them gloss over the difficulties they had with the 'old Josephinians' among the bureaucracy who refused to endorse what liberals made of Joseph's legacy;[32] and, third, the appropriation of this heritage permitted Austro-German liberals to brand Bohemian, Italian and Hungarian liberals as self-seeking and myopic 'nationalists'. This attitude was to persist in politics until 1900 and it continues to exert influence on historiography up to the present day.[33]

Enlightenment Conceptual Resources and Liberal Scholarship

In the second section of this chapter, I wish to briefly discuss three domains of liberal thought. This will throw into relief what liberals made of Enlightenment conceptual resources in the early nineteenth-century Habsburg lands. The three fields I have selected are law, religion and political economy. This approach will also prove important for a better and more refined understanding of the varieties of liberalism.

Habsburg Natural Jurisprudence and the Rediscovery of Roman Law
Enlightened natural law was enshrined in the 1811 Civil Code promulgated for the Austro-Bohemian part of the monarchy.[34] Yet the intellectual horizon

of Habsburg jurists did not remain confined to natural law. New ideas and practices soaked in, and political aims and theoretical predilections changed. In the early nineteenth century Habsburg lands, liberal paradigms were predicated on natural law or historicist agendas, the latter were either aimed at the conceptual remodelling of Roman law or they strove to unearth the respective 'national spirit' in the history of law. A third strand of Young Hegelian jurists emerged since the 1830s. Enlightened natural law with its contractualist foundation of society, and its use of the contract to explain various dimensions of legal life from the acquisition and prescription of land over allodification to the state's monopoly on retribution and coercion, was attacked and jettisoned by many liberal legalists.[35] In the sphere of public law, many liberals were disenchanted with contractualism; they found historical institutions located in the distant past of their respective nation (electoral kingship, rulers as chief magistrates, popular assemblies and jury courts) more promising for the realization of their vision of accountable power.

Historicist and Young Hegelian liberals saw the contract as unable to safeguard personal autonomy, as well as incapable of explaining the moral foundations necessary for the security of society. This criticism impinged on different material legal structures, among them on joint property, replevin, demurrage, paterfamilial control and custodial supervision of gilt-edged and collateralized loans.[36] Interestingly and importantly, the reconstruction of historical precedents and formats of law championed by these jurists did *not* contradict Enlightenment proclivities; Montesquieu's and Mascov's medievalist works loomed large here as sources of inspiration.[37] The significant point here is the early nineteenth-century obliteration of the fact that these segments belonged to the Enlightenment.[38] By disentangling a 'rationalist' epistemology, which many liberals rejected, from a vaguely defined, lofty Enlightenment past, a conceptually reified legacy was created that lastingly impoverished our understanding of the eighteenth century.

The Revolution of 1848 constituted a watershed in the development of Habsburg legal culture. In its aftermath, new schools of Austrian and Hungarian liberal jurists, the so-called Pandectists,[39] turned to Roman law in remodelling the past and present of Habsburg jurisprudence.[40] This led to drastically abridged and distorted accounts of pre–1848 intellectual life. According to the Pandectists, pre–1848 jurists had been intellectually imprisoned by the Civil Code and its principles of natural law. The Pandectists indeed turned natural law into a scapegoat, denouncing it as both unscientific *and* crypto-revolutionary in order to boost their own reputation as politically innocuous innovators. Reworking the culture of interpretation of the 1811 Civil Code, Joseph Unger's Austrian Pandectists suffused the code with their own concepts, and in particular the will theory, which they regarded as much more suitable for the modern acquisitive society than the old theory of trust.[41]

This refashioning did not go undisputed: adherents of enlightened natural law joined forces with practitioners of historical-legal scholarship, of old Slavic law in particular, and attacked the Pandectist design engrafted on the Civil Code. While striving to rehabilitate much-abused pre-1848 legal scholarship, they simultaneously rebelled against the new curriculum. The new Roman law curriculum came with a heavy dose of German legal and imperial history, which Bohemian and Hungarian jurists found particularly jarring.[42] To some of these rebels against Pandectism, textbooks based on enlightened natural law seemed much better suited to a plurilingual monarchy than those of the Pandectists with their Germanic complements and with their strict adherence to scholarship from the German lands, in particular to the works of F.C. von Savigny and F. Puchta.[43]

Catholic Liberalism

A strong case has been made for English popular liberalism's debt to eighteenth-century religious dissent and nonconformism,[44] while very little is known about the religious pedigree of liberalism in Catholic Europe.[45] As a result of the culture wars, the educated European publics of the later nineteenth century came to view Catholicism as the very counterpart of the Enlightenment.[46] The Catholic Enlightenment fell into oblivion and Catholic liberalism shared this fate. The standard account suggests that the Catholic restoration sought to eradicate enlightened Catholicism, but that the Enlightenment turned into early liberalism quickly enough to survive.[47] Yet on closer inspection, this transition from Enlightenment to liberalism turns out to have been far from smooth and stringent.[48]

As it was made and remade after 1800, the Enlightenment legacy became an apple of discord in conflicts between Catholic liberals (e.g. Félicité de Lamennais, Jean Baptiste Lacordaire and Anton Günther) and late Enlighteners on the one hand, as well as between Catholic liberals and secularist liberals on the other.[49] Catholic liberals reduced the Enlightenment to a pastiche of rationalist deism and described it as a mainstay of 'absolutism', which muzzled the Church and made it unable to follow its patriotic and spiritual mission.[50] By equating the Enlightenment with the state church of the early nineteenth century, Catholic liberals effaced rival strands of enlightened theology such as sentimentalism and common sense.[51] Secularist liberals on the contrary invoked the Enlightenment as a noble agenda of worldly reason, civil rights and individual liberties.

Catholic liberals' dissociation from eighteenth-century thought was marked by a Pelagian, free-will refutation of Jansenism.[52] They simultaneously held a sympathetic attitude toward Jansenists' synodalist and antipapalist designs, but excoriated their regalism.[53] Catholic liberals of this hue strove for a 'free church in a free state'.[54] Catholic liberals sought to rehabilitate the role of Christianity in the history of Europe (the manumission of slaves, the personal status of legal inviolacy), which they regarded as distorted by the Enlightenment.[55] All this often went with speculative and providentialist modes of enquiry that placed the 'reason', around which the Enlightenment was taken to revolve, in a different epistemological setting.

The study of Catholic scholarship demonstrates with great clarity how the Enlightenment was realigned in the early nineteenth century. The Catholic restoration heavily relied on eighteenth-century sacred philology with its fine-grained study of Biblical subtexts, divine accommodation, implicatures, and its critique of verbal inspiration ($\alpha\dot{\upsilon}\xi\epsilon\varsigma\iota\varsigma$ and $\epsilon\kappa\beta\alpha\tau\iota\kappa\acute{\omega}\varsigma$). However, this philological method was played off against rationalism, with which the Enlightenment was retrospectively identified. Enlightened scholarly methods and procedures continued to be used, but their context of emergence was obliterated. Thereby, clerics of the restoration retained and restyled one strand of enlightened scholarship only to turn it into the Enlightenment's very antidote.[56]

A structurally similar redistribution of Enlightenment ancestries can be observed in the conflict between Catholic liberals and neoscholastic theologians. This confrontation also highlights the inner varieties of the restoration. Before the soaring success of neoscholastic theology in the 1840s and 1850s, the restoration had tried to accommodate both philological procedures and Kantian moral theology until it came under friendly fire from speculative theologians – in particular Anton Günther and his idealist circle – who wished to pave the way for the free church in a free state. Anton Günther's liberal Catholicism was ardently antischolastic; he accused scholasticism of pantheism and of a desiccated, rationalist conception of revelation. Instead, Günther took his cues from contemporary idealism, emphasizing the believers' capacity to progessively recognize their nature as god-created beings through reason and faith.[57] It is here that we can again observe the continuous usage of Enlightenment practices and the simultaneous collapsing of the Enlightenment's rival strands into a single past and intellectual patrimony. Despite Günther's critical engagement with eighteenth-century thought, his neoscholastic adversaries accused him of Enlightenment rationalism: This was a paradoxical claim as it was precisely these neoscholastics who relied on an arsenal of Wolffian concepts, postulated the noncontradiction among *verités du raison* and operated with the *principium rationis sufficientis*.[58] The conflict between neoscholastic clerics and Catholic liberals illustrates how closely connected the polemical reassignment of legacies, quarrels over method and the construction of the Enlightenment were in the 1830s and 1840s.

Mercantilists and Political Economists

Similar complications of liberals' Enlightenment heritage become obvious if one looks at the political economy. Adherents of Adam Smith and mercantilists developed quite different disciplinary genealogies and notions of Enlightenment in the early nineteenth-century Habsburg lands. Nevertheless, the standard accounts of the history of economic theory claim that the mercantilist school of Joseph von Sonnenfels (1732–1817) continued to provide the stable framework of economic thought in the Habsburg lands up to 1848.[59] This view relies on post–1848 sweeping condemnations of *Vormärz* intellectual life. Sonnenfels's textbook from the 1760s remained officially prescribed until 1848, but this does not mean that it caused intellectual gridlock and inertia.[60] On the one hand, a plethora of critical responses to Sonnenfels's doctrines had developed already in the first decade of the nineteenth century; on the other hand, we need to reassess the assumption that state-sponsored mercantilism acted as an obstacle to early liberalism prior to 1848.

Adam Smith's work already fell on fertile ground in the 1790s. There soon emerged a versatile elite of civil servants who opposed state subsidies, business privileges, the allocation of retail areas and the doling-out of eleemosynaries to the poor.[61] These liberals opposed many of the regulatory devises Sonnenfels had proposed. They openly rejected the protectionist tariffs system of the mercantilists in favour of free trade and broke with Sonnenfels's justification of a positive trade balance as one of its supreme aims.[62] These economic liberals also sought to develop monetary policies that would transcend mercantilists' warnings of capital drain and correct their insouciance about currency depreciation.[63] These civil servants creatively refashioned Sonnenfels's legacy: they harnessed his ideas about the natural 'confluence' of goods as well as about price formation, and combined these advances with the tools he provided to combat monopolies and cartels. So while liberal bureaucrats put the reciprocity of mutually reinforcing self-interest, of interactive greed, in the place of Sonnenfels's framework – the increase of production to meet the mounting domestic demand caused by successful populationist politics – their repertoire of action strongly resembled the one Sonnenfels himself had designed. Sonnenfels's thought was more of a springboard than a stumbling-block for early liberalism. The broad range of liberal measures and incentives prior to 1848 subverts the usual clichés about the stifling reaction of that period.[64] The relationship between Enlightenment mercantilism and liberalism was conflict-ridden, but liberals of the 1830s and 1840s chose to embroider the novelty of their approach and to make the rift between mercantilist doctrines and their own approach sharper than it had actually been.

The intellectual foundations of Smithian liberalism deserve a similar reappraisal. By the 1830s, Catholic liberals could draw on Smith's doctrines and combine them with a retributionist theology, a pattern of *parousia* that sharply diverged from the moderate Scottish emphasis on a fair natural distribution of the cake of domestic wealth.[65] In the view of these Catholic liberals, productive avarice, self-aggrandisement and prodigality should be balanced by cultivating man's divinely ordained energies of faith. Catholic liberals emphasized the positive experience of revelation and deliverance that would soften the pernicious moral effects of the system of economic self-gratification. Their sharp critique of absolutism hinged on this argument: by subjecting the Church to state tutelage and by retaining rationalist deism as official theology, the successive regimes since Joseph II continued to tamper with the spiritual life of Christian citizens. This produced depravity and venality. The state thwarted civic life, curbed free associations, hampered individual self-help and curtailed the development of adaptive skill profiles.

Economic liberals' engagement with Enlightenment mercantilism lastingly transformed its profile and properties for posterity. Catholic liberals in particular came to view mercantilism as rationalist and as a natural law-based doctrine. This dovetailed with the new account of the Enlightenment past predicated on natural law, deism and rationalism, but it was quite alien to the presuppositions of mercantilism. Producing a critical appraisal of political contractualism, Sonnenfels had dealt extensively with instinctual *appetitus societatis* and οἶκοςις.[66] Thus, apart from their significant remodelling of the Smithian prudent pursuit of artificial wants and virtuous rational self-interest, Catholic liberals also relegated Enlightenment mercantilism to the past by means of conceptual retrofitting. The deregulating agenda that economic liberals pursued was not necessarily tied to an advocacy of civil rights in the sense of constitutionally ensconced guarantees. As we have seen, the agenda of economic liberty could be based on a 'positive' institutional substructure, a spiritualized church freed from state interference as a supplier of moral guidance.

Conclusion

The Enlightenment was many before it became one. In the eighteenth century, it comprised diverse strands, physiocracy, mercantilism and Smithian political economy, Baroque rationalism and sensualist theology, Kantian chiliasm, natural law and legal-historical scholarship. It was in the nineteenth century that the Enlightenment acquired its ironclad coherence and unity and, equally importantly, its role as precursor of liberalism. The eight-eenth-century Enlightenment comprised conservative and Catholic varieties, both of which were factored out in the nineteenth century when liberalism began to appear as the rightful successor of the Enlightenment and conserva-tism as the descendant of the 'Counter-Enlightenment'.[67]

The plurality of the Enlightenment did not abruptly come to an end around 1800. Internal and external factors, intellectual transformations as well as the impact of the French Revolution began to change the ways in which one thought about the Enlightenment and situated oneself within it. Herein lies the source of the subsequent reconstruction of the Enlightenment, of its reduction to what we regard as its basic, quintessentially modern traits: rationalism, deism, natural law, constitutionalism and popular sovereignty. Here the Enlightenment acquired its historical, political and confessional trajectory: now it seemed to have led from its origins in the Reformation to its culmination in the French Revolution. We need to bear in mind that this is a conceptually refurbished Enlightenment, a patrimony constructed after 1800. In this chapter, I have tried to offer some cues regarding the difference between this heritage and the eighteenth-century Enlightenment it pretended to encompass.

It was in the early nineteenth century that the Enlightenment came to appear as rationalist, mechanist, deist and predicated on natural law. Liberals contributed to this reshaping, but they shied away from the conclusion their conservative and radical adversaries drew. Conservative and radical authors, working at cross-purposes in other respects, established a durable link between the Enlightenment and the French Revolution, and thereby contributed to the liberals' predicament: while radicals chided liberals for their cowardice, conservatives took them at their word and made liberals' admiration for the Enlightenment equivalent to Revolutionary zeal.

We need to break the ostensibly smooth transition from Enlightenment to liberalism up into smaller, more manageable units. In doing so, we realize that this process involved identifiable modes of conceptual engineering and retrofitting by which distinct groups of liberals interacted with identifiable variants of the Enlightenment. A sketch of interactions and transformations of this kind in the Habsburg lands has been provided above.

Liberals' self-assigned place as guardians of the Enlightenment pat-rimony became so convincing because it was predicated on two mutually reinforcing claims: during the first half of the nineteenth century, the legacy liberals embraced came to match the past conservatives wished to disclaim. There is much evidence to suggest that comparably stable liberal and con-servative political groups crystallized around distinct perceptions of the eighteenth-century past by the 1850s. This became possible only through a process that I have described as a progressive disentanglement between the political significance of the Enlightenment on the one hand, and the usage of Enlightenment arguments and practices on the other. This redistribution of legacies made varieties such as the conservative Enlightenment and the Catholic Enlightenment disappear. During the 1830s and 1840s the previous conflicts over the Enlightenment's content and genealogy began to give way to intentional disagreement over the beneficial or detrimental effects of a rationalist and deist Enlightenment on the state, Church and society.

A final remark with a methodological gist is necessary here. Much of the history of liberalism has suffered from the readiness with which similar 'liberal' responses to shared problems on a synchronic level were deduced from an imputed shared intellectual background, most notably 'the Enlightenment'. I have shown above how treacherous such similarities can be, and that liberal agendas were hardly all-encompassing in terms of subsidiary and necessarily connected political, economic, social and religious aims. This is one of the keys to the plurality of liberal languages that the present volume seeks to explore. The epistemological status of these 'political languages' continues to be rather rickety and controvertible: this applies as much to 'civic republicanism' as it does to other complexes treated as languages like 'natural law' if one thinks of primeval contracts, proselytizing, volition or primordial physiological drives and urges, as well as of the forfeiture of natural rights through the nonobservance of divinely ordained natural laws. It has by and large remained unclear what holds 'political languages' together across epochs, how small-scale changes in their lexicon, onomasiological fields and implicatures are aggregated to the level of languages' shared basic arguments, and how languages interact in a given text. It is important to bear this in mind because it is inaccurate to regard natural law as the chief trait of one 'language', namely liberalism, and to perceive the historical study of law as the basic characteristic of another, e.g. historicism. Natural law seems to have provided a repertory of arguments that different, rival forms of Enlightenment drew on and that was equally useful to rival strands of liberalism. Hence, I would argue that the historicality of traditions and legacies that became particularly conspicuous during the *Sattelzeit* seems an unjustly neglected, yet vitally important aspect of the emergence of nineteenth-century liberalism, but also of 'political languages' in general.

This applies both to liberals' remaking of their Enlightenment patrimony, but also to a plethora of more small-scale changes. As the previous pages have shown, the manipulation of past contexts was a recurrent procedure in conflicts over legacies, and over the routines and schemata they imparted. Recall how mercantilism and Enlightenment theology were placed in new contexts in the 1820s and 1830s, and how natural law was retrospectively invested by the Pandectists of the 1850s with a pre-eminence it had not possessed. To me it seems more profitable to explore the 'framing cues'[68] of such legacies than to enquire into the vertebrate traits of transtemporal 'political languages'.

In trying to provide a nutshell summary of the Enlightenment's political re-enlistment in the Habsburg lands up to the 1850s, I would like to distinguish two processes of conceptual engineering. For Austro-German liberals, the Josephinian reforms and the Enlightenment were cut from the same cloth. 'Josephinism' became the only acceptable ingredient and indicator of 'Enlightenment' across the Monarchy. Joseph's image as liberal anticlerical, Germanizer and peasant emancipator was carved out in the 1830s and 1840s by the Leipzig- and Hamburg-based brochure literature of 'Young Austria'. These texts became the treasure trove and cherished arsenal of Austro-German liberals, and the image they painted of Joseph II persisted for the rest of the century.

Czech and Hungarian liberals' engagement with the Josephinian sentiments of their enlightened predecessors had two argumentative components. They tended to factor out the pro-Josephinian sympathies of late enlightened *Gelehrtenpatrioten* and to style them as living precursors of the national revival. Quite often this happened despite the refusal of these late Enlighteners to acquiesce to the refashioning of their intellectual legacy. In order to enlist the respective late Enlighteners as preceptors of the early nineteenth-century national renascence, it was indispensable to demonstrate their disenchantment with Joseph and his reforming agenda. By this process, national-liberal legatees recruited a cast of venerable and legitimate ancestors.

Franz L. Fillafer is a historian of modern Europe whose research has chiefly focused on the Enlightenment and its posterities, as well as on the Habsburg Empire and its successor states. His most recent work is devoted to political Jansenism in its global contexts and to nineteenth-century forms of worldmaking like positivism and historicism that unfolded at the apogee of empire. After having held positions at the University of Cambridge, UCL London, the University of Konstanz and the European University Institute in Florence, he joined the Austrian Academy of Sciences in 2018 as a researcher at the Institute of Culture Studies. His recent publications include 'A World Connecting? From the Unity of History to Global History', *History and Theory* 56 (2017), 3–37; 'Whose Enlightenment?', *Austrian History Yearbook* 48 (2017), 111–25; and *The Worlds of Positivism: A Global Intellectual History, 1770–1930* (co-edited with J. Feichtinger and J. Surman, 2018).

Notes

1. J. Pocock speaks of families of Enlightenments in the plural, while J. Robertson delivered an eloquent defence of the unity of key Enlightenment concerns, procedures, social milieus and appeal to public opinion; c.f. J.G.A. Pocock, 'Clergy and Commerce. The Conservative Enlightenment in England', in ed. R. Ajello, *L'età dei lumi: Studi storici sul Settecento europeo in onore di Franco Venturi*, 2 vols, Naples, 1985, vol. 1, 523–62; J.G.A. Pocock, 'The Re-description of Enlightenment', *Proceedings of the British Academy* 125 (2006), 101–17; J.G.A. Pocock, 'Historiography and Enlightenment: A View of Their Relationship', *Modern Intellectual History* 5 (2008), 83–96; J. Robertson, 'The Enlightenments of J.G.A. Pocock', *Storia della storiografia* 39 (2001), 140–51; J. Robertson, *The Case for the Enlightenment. Scotland and Naples, 1680–1760*, Cambridge, 2005, 1–51; I. Hunter, *Rival Enlightenments: Civic and Metaphysical Philosophy in Early Modern Germany*, Cambridge, 2001; cf. S.A. Reinert, 'In margine a un bilancio sui Lumi europei', *Rivista storica italiana* 118 (2006), 975–86. J. Israel likewise emphasizes the unity of the Enlightenment, but presents a shaky distinction between pusillanimous and law-abiding 'moderates' on the one hand who at times do not seem to merit the epithet 'Enlighteners' any longer, and crypto-Spinozist radicals on the other. Israel portrays the latter as trailblazers of one-substance materialism, hylozoism, republicanism and protodemocratic leanings. At the core of Israel's work lies a preconceived *esprit de système*, a design of symmetry and subsidiarity: a materialist, Israel suggests, was by implication a political radical, a defender of the rights of women, etc, which makes radical leanings in one field count for similar attitudes in others. This tendency to extrapolate 'radicalism' and make it suffuse the entire historical oeuvre of any given 'crypto-Spinozist' is highly unsatisfactory and untenable in the light of eighteenth-century evidence; see J. Israel, *Radical Enlightenment: Philosophy and the Making of Modernity, 1650–1750*, Oxford, 2001; J. Israel, *Enlightenment Contested: Philosophy, Modernity, and the Emancipation of Man 1670–1752*, Oxford, 2006; J. Israel, *Democratic Enlightenment: Philosophy, Revolution, and Human Rights 1750–1790*, Oxford, 2011; G. Ricuperati, 'In margine al Radical Enlightenment di Jonathan I. Israel', *Rivista storica italiana* 115 (2003), 285–329; A. La Vopa, 'A New Intellectual History? Jonathan Israel's Enlightenment', *Historical Journal* 52 (2009), 717–38.

2. L. Siedentop, 'Two Liberal Traditions', in A. Ryan (ed.), *The Idea of Freedom: Essays in Honour of Isaiah Berlin*, Oxford, 1979, 153–74; G. Gángó, 'Egy "rettentő váz nevezet" jelentéstörténetéhez: Kit neveztek szabadelműnek, szabadelvűnek, és liberálisnak a reformkori Magyarországon?' ['On the Historical Semantics of a "Ghastly Skeleton": Who was Called Free-Minded, Libertarian and Liberal in the Hungarian Reform Age?'], *Holmi* 11 (1999), 327–42; Andreas Kalyvas, Ira Kaznelson, *Liberal Beginnings: Making a Republic for the Moderns*, New York, 2008.

3. F. Valjavec, *Die Entstehung der politischen Strömungen in Deutschland, 1770–1815*, 2nd edn, Königstein im Taunus, 1978, 28, 204 and 228; K. Epstein, *The Genesis of German Conservatism*, Princeton, 1966, 3–22.

4. See G. de Ruggiero, *Storia del liberalismo europeo*, Bari, 1925, 36, 87 and 198; J. Leonhard, *Liberalismus: Zur historischen Semantik eines europäischen Deutungsmusters*, Munich, 2001, 61–85; M. Janowski, 'Kecskék és tokhalak: A közép-kelet-európai liberalizmus sajátosságai a francia forradalom és az első világháború között' ['Goats and Sturgeons: The Characteristics of East-Central-European Liberalism between the French Revolution and World War I'], *Aetas* 14 (1999), 108–21; K.-G. Faber, '"Konservatorischer Liberalismus", "Umstürzender Liberalismus", "Konservatorischer Obskurantismus": Aus dem Briefwechsel zwischen Marschall und Allmendingen', *Nassauische Annalen* 78 (1967), 177–95.

5. See J. Fernández-Sebastián, 'Liberales y liberalismo en España, 1810–1850: La forja de un concepto y la creación de una identidad política', *Revista de Estudios Políticos (Nueva Época)* 134 (2006), 125–76.

6. This problem is explicitly addressed in a few studies; see J. Fernández-Sebastián, 'Du mépris à la louange : Image, présence et mise en valeur du Siècle des lumières dans l'Espagne contemporaine', in G. Ricuperati (ed.), *Historiographie et usages des Lumières*, Berlin, 2002, 133–58; S. Timpanaro, *Classicismo e Illuminismo nell'Ottocento Italiano*, 2nd edn, Pisa, 1969, 7; J. Klabouch, *Osvícenské právní nauky v českých zemích [Enlightenment Legal Scholarship in the Bohemian Lands]*, Prague, 1958, 230–33; B. Fontana, *Rethinking the Politics of Commercial Society: The Edinburgh Review, 1802–1832*, Cambridge, 1985: 65; S. Moravia, *Il tramonto dell'illuminismo: Filosofia e politica nella società francese, 1770–1810*, Bari, 1968, 22 and 76; R. Vierhaus, 'Aufklärung und Reformzeit: Kontinuitäten und Neuansätze in der deutschen Politik des späten 18. und frühen 19. Jahrhunderts', in Eberhard Weis (ed.), *Reformen im rheinbündischen Deutschland*, Munich, 1984, 287–301; S. Luzzatto, 'L'illuminismo impossibile. Alessandro Verri tra rivoluzione e restaurazione', *Rivista di letteratura italiana* 3 (1985), 263–90; H. Rosenberg, 'Theologischer Rationalismus und vormärzlicher Vulgärliberalismus', in H. Rosenberg, *Politische Denkströmungen im deutschen Vormärz*, Göttingen, 1972, 18–50; O. Briese, A. Liepert and E. Magdanz, 'Erfahrung des Wechsels: Wechsel der Erfahrung: Rekurrierten Vormärzliberale lediglich auf Aufklärung?', *Zeitschrift für Geschichtswissenschaft* 41 (1993), 781–91.

7. S. Collini, D. Winch and J. W. Burrow, *That Noble Science of Politics: A Study in Nineteenth-Century Intellectual History*, Cambridge, 1983, 91–126; P. Mandler, *Aristocratic Government in the Age of Reform: Whigs and Liberals, 1830–1852*, Oxford, 1990, 22f; J. W. Burrow, *Whigs and Liberals: Continuity and Change in English Political Thought*, Oxford, 1988; J.G.A. Pocock, 'The Varieties of Whiggism between Exclusion and Reform: A History of Ideology and Discourse', in J.G.A. Pocock (ed.), *Virtue, Commerce, and History. Essays on Political Thought and History, Chiefly in the Eighteenth Century*, Cambridge, 1985, 215–310.

8. Fontana, *Rethinking the Politics of Commercial Society*, 170–85; W. Thomas, *The Philosophical Radicals: Nine Studies in Theory and Practice, 1817–1841*, Oxford, 1979; D. Forbes, *Riches and Poverty: An Intellectual History of Political Economy in Britain, 1750–1834*, Cambridge, 1996, 377–89.

9. See e.g. M. Michie, *An Enlightenment Tory in Victorian Scotland: The Career of Sir Archibald Alison*, Montreal, 1997, 159–97; P. Mandler, 'Tories and Paupers. Christian Political Economy and the Making of the New Poor Law', *Historical Journal* 33 (1990), 81–103.

10. B. Hilton, *The Age of Atonement: The Influence of Evangelicalism on Social and Economic Thought, 1785–1865*, Oxford, 1988, 218–36. See the thoughtful comments of M. Berg, 'Progress and Providence in Early Nineteenth-Century Political Economy', *Social History* 15 (1990), 367–75; and M. Berg, *The Machinery Question and the Making of Political Economy*, Cambridge, 1980, 136–44.

11. For a realiable English-language guidebook to recent studies on French liberalism, see R. Geenens and H. Rosenblatt (eds), *French Liberalism from Montesquieu to the Present Day*, Cambridge, 2012.

12. See A. Jainchill, *Reimaginig Politics after the Terror: The Republican Origins of French Liberalism*, New York, 2008, 287–308; R. Whatmore, *Republicanism and the French Revolution: An Intellectual History of Jean-Baptiste Say's Political Economy*, Oxford, 2000; H. Rosenblatt, 'Re-evaluating Benjamin Constant's Liberalism: Industrialism, Saint-Simonianism and the Restoration Years', *History of European Ideas* 30 (2004), 23–37.

13. A. de Dijn, *French Political Thought from Montesquieu to Tocqueville: Liberty in a Levelled Society?*, Cambridge, 2008, 54–55, 170; C. Volpilhac-Auger, 'Tocqueville et Montesquieu: récrire l'histoire?', in F. Mélonio and J.-L. Diaz (eds), *Tocqueville et la littérature*, Paris, 2004, 221–32.

14. P. Rosanvallon, *Le moment Guizot*, Paris, 1985, 78 and 194; L. Jaume, *L' individu effacé ou le paradoxe du libéralisme française*, Paris, 1997, 67–124.

15. B. Hilton, *A Mad, Bad, and Dangerous People: England 1783–1846*, Oxford, 2006, 520–24. See also R. Brent, 'God's Providence: Liberal Political Economy as Natural Theology at Oxford, 1825–62', in M. Bentley (ed.), *Public and Private Doctrine: Essays in British History presented to Maurice Cowling*, Cambridge 1993, 85–107.

16. See e.g. J. Fernández-Sebastián, 'La Constitución de Cádiz: historiografía y conmemoración', in J. Á. Junco and J. M. Luzón (eds), *La Constitución de Cádiz: historiografía y conmemoración: Homenaje a Francisco Tomás y Valiente*, Madrid, 2006, 23–58; J. Dunn, 'The Politics of John Locke in the Eighteenth Century', in J. Yolton (ed.), *John Locke: Problems and Perspectives*, Cambridge, 1969, 45–80.

17. Gángó, 'Egy "rettentő váz nevezet" jelentéstörténetéhez', 333–34; G. Franz, *Liberalismus: Die deutschliberale Bewegung in der Habsburgischen Monarchie*. Munich, 1955, 7, 41 and 168. For the English dimension of this conceptual history, see D. Craig, 'The Language of Liberality in Britain, c.1760–c.1815', *Modern Intellectual History* (January 2018), 1–31. Retrieved 27 May 2019 from https://www.cambridge.org/core/journals/modern-intellectual-history/article/language-of-liberality-in-britain-c1760c1815/477C6709F627EC7FF161B442B5DF3ECA.

18. See D. Beales, *Joseph II, Vol. 2: Against the World: 1780–1790*, Cambridge, 2009, 239–332 and 477–554; on the Hungarian side, see É. H. Bálazs, *Hungary and*

the Habsburgs, 1765–1800: An Experiment in Enlightened Absolutism, Budapest, 1997.

19. E. Winter, *Frühliberalismus in der Donaumonarchie: Religiöse, nationale und wissenschaftliche Strömungen von 1790–1868*, Berlin, 1968, 103, claims that 'the transition from late Enlightenment to liberalism happened perfectly organically and without any rupture'. On Winter, compare F.L. Fillafer and T. Wallnig (eds), *Josephinismus zwischen den Regimen: Eduard Winter, Fritz Valjavec und die zentraleuropäischen Historiographien im 20. Jahrhundert*, Vienna, 2016. Critical revisions of Winter's account were formulated by K. Eder, *Der Liberalismus in Altösterreich: Geisteshaltung, Politik und Kultur*, Vienna, 1955, 72; and by C. Thienen-Adlerflycht, *Graf Leo Thun im Vormärz: Grundlagen des böhmischen Konservatismus im Kaisertum Österreich*, Graz, 1967, 3 and 98; cf. F.L. Fillafer, 'Die Aufklärung und ihr Erbe in der Habsburgermonarchie. Ein Forschungsüberblick', *Zeitschrift für historische Forschung* 40 (2013), 35–97.

20. For a conceptual reframing of the Enlightenment in the Habsburg lands in the light of stimulating recent studies, see F.L. Fillafer, 'Whose Enlightenment?', *Austrian History Yearbook* 48 (2017), 111–25.

21. See F. Engel-Jánosi, 'Zur Genesis der Revolution von 1848: Die Verfassungsfrage im deutschen Österreich, 1815–1848', *Zeitschrift für öffentliches Recht* 3 (1922/23), 571–82.

22. For the Czech case, see e.g. H. LeCaine Agnew, *Origins of the Czech National Renascence*, Stanford, 1994. For comparative perspectives, see F.L. Fillafer, 'Imperium oder Kulturstaat? Die Habsburgermonarchie und die Historisierung der Nationalkulturen im 19. Jahrhundert', in P. Ther (ed.), *Kulturpolitik und Theater: Die kontinentalen Imperien in Europa im Vergleich*, Vienna, 2012, 23–54; and E. Niederhauser, 'Problèmes de la conscience historique dans les mouvements de renaissance nationale en Europe Orientale', *Acta Historica Academiae Scientiarum Hungaricae* 18 (1972), 39–73.

23. See e.g. the excellent collection of S. Höhne and A. Ohme (eds), *Prozesse kultureller Integration und Disintegration: Deutsche, Tschechen, Böhmen im 19. Jahrhundert*, Munich, 2005; J. Rak, 'Koncepce historické práce Vlasteneckého muzea v Čechách' ['The Conception of Historical Research Activities of the Patriotic Museum of Bohemia'], *Časopis Národního Muzea – historické muzeum* 153 (1984), 98–111; I. Fried, 'Ein österreichischer Biedermeier-Dichter und die südslawische Volksdichtung', *Studia Slavica Hungarica* 20 (1974), 115–26.

24. S. Höhne and A. Ohme (eds), *Prozesse kultureller Integration und Desintegration*; A. Miskolczy, '"Hungarus Consciousness" in the Age of Early Nationalism', in G. Almási and L. Šubarić (eds), *Latin at the Crossroads of Identity: The Evolution of Linguistic Nationalism in the Kingdom of Hungary*, Leiden, 2015, 64–93.

25. On the phenomenon of multilingualism, compare P. Trost, 'Německo-česká dvojjzyčnost', 'Střídaní kódů', 'Česko-německý makaronismus' ['German-Czech Bilingualism, Code-Switching, Czech-German Macaronism'], in J. Povĕšíl (ed.), *Studie o jazycích a literatuře*, Prague, 1995; L. Sziklay, *Együttélés és többnyelvűség az irodalomban* [*Coexistence and Multilinguality in Literature*], Budapest, 1987;

F.L. Fillafer, 'Imperium oder Kulturstaat? Die Habsburgermonarchie und die Historisierung der Nationalkulturen im 19. Jahrhundert', in P. Ther (ed.), *Kulturpolitik und Theater: Die kontinentalen Imperien in Europa im Vergleich*, Munich, 2012, 23–53.

26. M. Hýsej, 'Dějiny t. zv. moravského separatismu' ['History of the So-Called Moravian Separatism'], *Časopis Matice moravské* 33 (1909), 24–51 and 146–72; J. Malíř, 'Morava na předělu: K formování národního vědomí na Moravě v letech 1848–1871' ['Moravia at the Crossroads: On the Formation of Moravian National Consciousness between 1848–1871'], *Časopis Matice moravské* 109 (1990), 345–63; J. Butvin, *Slovenské národno-zjednocovacie hnutie (1780–1848)* [*The Slovak Movement of National Unification (1780–1848)*], Bratislava, 1965, 220–78.

27. Á. Déak, 'Együttműködés vagy konkurencia. Az alsóausztriai, a csehországi és a magyarországi ellenzék összefogási kísérlete 1847–1848' ['Cooperation or Competition: An Attempt at Cooperation between the Lower-Austrian, Bohemian and Hungarian Opposition, 1847–1848'], *Aetas* 14 (1999), 43–61; B.G. Németh, 'A jozefinista illúzió fölvillanása 49 után' ['A Flash of the Josephinist Illusion after 1849'], in B.G. Németh (ed.), *Létharc és nemzetiség*, Budapest, 1976, 414–44.

28. F. Kazinczy, *Pályám emlékezete, 1759–1792* [*Autobiography, 1759–1792*], Budapest, 1956, 141; Compare J. Polišenský, *Aristocrats and the Crowd in the Revolutionary Year 1848: A Contribution to the History of Revolution and Counter-revolution in Austria*, Albany, 1980, 8–9; cf. A. Mészáros, *A marginalitás szelid bája* (*Arcképek a reformkori magyar filozófiából*) [*The Discreet Charm of Marginality (Portraits of Hungarian Philosophy of the Reform Age)*], Bratislava, 1994, 75–76; I. Fried, 'II. József, a jozefinisták és a reformerek: Vázlat a XVIII. század végének magyar közgondolkodásáról' ['Joseph II, Josephinists and Reformers: A Sketch of Hungarian Public Opinion at the Verge of the Eighteenth Century'], *Az Országos Széchényi Könyvtár Évlönyve* (1979), 563–91; J. Jeník z Bratřice, *Z mých paměti* [*From My Memoirs*], ed. J. Polišenský, Prague, 1947, 25–26 (where he says that Joseph II would have prevented the destruction of Bethlehem chapel, where Hus had preached, had he known of the plans to demolish it); cf. Z.V. David, *Realism, Tolerance, and Liberalism: Legacies of the Bohemian Reformation*, Baltimore, 2010, 52 and fn. 28, 272; ibid., 27 on Jeník's recollections of the Czech-speaking Prague of his youth; and E. Bass, *Čtení o roce osmačtyřicátém* [*Readings about 1848*], Prague, 1940; J. Polišenský and E. Illingova, *Jan Jeník z Bratřice* [*Jan Jeník of Bratřic*], Prague, 1989, 81–82, 85–86 and 90.

29. For the context, see Á. Déak, 'Pläne für die Neugstaltung der Habsburgermonarchie und Ungarns 1848–1852', *Ungarn-Jahrbuch* 24 (1998/99), 87–104.

30. See F. Engel-Jánosi, 'Kaiser Josef II. in der Wiener Bewegung des Jahres 1848', *Mitteilungen des Vereins für die Geschichte der Stadt Wien* 11 (1931), 53–72; P. Kurth and B. Morgenbrod, 'Wien 1848 und die Erinnerung an die Französische Revolution von 1789', in I. Götz von Olenhusen (ed.), *1848/49 in Europa und der Mythos der Französischen Revolution*, Göttingen, 1998, 114–33; D. Beales, 'The False Joseph II', *Historical Journal* 18 (1975), 467–95 debunked the Constantinople Letters, a concoction of mainly spurious letters by Joseph

produced in 1790 and taken as proclamations of his principles by liberals in the 1830s and 1840s.

31. Archduke Ludwig, who had been president of the state conference before the Revolution, wrote in a letter to his sister-in-law Archduchess Sophie, Francis Joseph's mother, of 6 November 1848: 'From now on one will have constantly to write new dictionaries wherein all the words previously known must acquire new meanings. The concept of anarchy for instance must be different from before, because I read with astonishment in all Viennese journals that there is no anarchy in Vienna but good order'; cf. G.C. Berger Waldenegg, 'Vaterländisches Gemeingefühl und nationale Charaktere: Die kaiserliche Regierung im Neoabsolutismus und die Erfindung einer österreichischen Nationalgeschichte', in H.P. Hye et al. (eds), *Nationalgeschichte als Artefakt: Zum Paradigma 'Nationalstaat' in den Historiographien Deutschlands, Italiens und Österreichs*, Vienna, 2009, 135–78. C. von Kübeck notes a similar dislocation 'where insanity, atrocious crime, desecration of right, fury, and blind passion [revel in] invoking and abusing holy liberty', C. Kübeck von Kübau *Tagebücher*, 2 vols., ed. by M. v. Kübeck, Vienna, 1909, vol II, 20–21.

32. H. Lentze, 'Andreas Freiherr von Baumgartner und die Thunsche Studienreform', *Anzeiger der Österreichischen Akademie der Wissenschaften, philosophisch-historische Klasse* 96 (1959), 161–79.

33. H.G. Ritter, 'Austrogerman Liberalism and the Modern Liberal Tradition', *German Studies Review* 7 (1984), 227–48; P.M. Judson, 'Die Liberalen und ihre interessierte Anti-Interessenpolitik', in S.P. Scheichl and E. Brix (eds), *'Dürfen's denn das?': Die fortdauernde Frage zum Jahr 1848*, Vienna, 1999, 127–40; V. Urfus, 'K vzájemnému poměru českého státoprávního programu a předbřeznové stavovské opozice v Čechách' ['On the Mutual Relationship between the Bohemian State Right Programme and the Bohemian Noble Opposition before 1848'], *Právněhistorické studie* 13 (1967), 85–103.

34. See J. Ofner (ed.), *Der Ur-Entwurf und die Berathungs-Protokolle des Österreichischen Allgemeinen bürgerlichen Gesetzbuches*, 2 vols, Vienna, 1889; W. Selb and H. Hofmeister (eds), *Forschungsband Franz von Zeiller (1751–1828): Beiträge zur Gesetzgebungs- und Wissenschaftsgeschichte*, Vienna, 1980; F. Eckhart, *A Jog- és Allatudományi Kar története* [A Királyi Magyar Pázmány Péter Tudományegyetem története, 2] [History of the Legal and Administrative Faculty], Budapest, 1936, 149–50, 184–85 and 330.

35. See K. Ebert, *Die Grazer Juristenfakultät im Vormärz: Rechtswissenschaft und Rechtslehre an der Grazer Hochschule von 1810 bis 1848*, Graz, 1969, 63, 82, 84, 97 and 99; V. Urfus, *Zdomácnění směnečného práva v českých zemích a počátky novodobého práva obchodního* [*The Introduction of Exchange Law in the Bohemian Lands and the Beginnings of Modern Commercial Law*], Prague, 1959, 257; G. Máthé, 'A jogegyenlőség és törvény előtti egyenlőség kérdései a reformkorban' ['Questions of Legal Equality and Equality before the Law in the Reform Age'], *Acta Facultatis Politico-Iuridicae Universitatis Scientiarum Budapestinensis de Rolando Eötvös Nominatae* 10 (1968), 341–61.

36. W. Brauneder, 'Von der moralischen Person des ABGB zur juristischen Person der Privatrechtswissenschaft', *Quaderni fiorentini per la storia del pensiero giuridico moderno*, 11/12 (1982–83), 265–317, 293; id., 'Privatrechtsfortbildung durch Juristenrecht in Exegetik und Pandektistik in Österreich', *Zeitschrift für Neuere Rechtsgeschichte* 5 (1983), 22–43; id., *Leseverein und Rechtskultur: Der juridisch-politische Leseverein zu Wien 1840 bis 1990*, Vienna, 1992, 92–93, 143–45, 105–10, 300 and 306; M. Schuster, *Theoretisch-praktischer Kommentar über das allgemeine bürgerliche Gesetzbuch*, vol. I, Prague, 1818, 344 and 348.

37. See A.C. Montoya, 'Medievalism and Enlightenment, 1647–1750: Jean Chapelain to Jean-Jacques Rousseau', *Romanic Review* (2009), 494–512.

38. See F.L. Fillafer, 'Escaping the Enlightenment: Liberalism and the Legacies of the Eighteenth Century in the Habsburg Lands, 1790–1848', Ph.D. dissertation (University of Konstanz, 2012).

39. Pandectism derives its name from the encylopaedic compendium of juristic writing put together under Emperor Justinian in the sixth century, the pandects (πανδέκτης), in English more commonly referred to as the Digest. The pandectists of the nineteenth century, chief among them J.F. Puchta, took their cues from F.C. von Savigny's historical school when trying to systematize the law in a conceptual grid and to make the Roman instruments suitable for bourgeois-acquisitive society; see A. Padoa-Schioppa, *A History of Law in Europe: From the Early Middle Ages to the Twentieth Century*, Cambridge, 2017, 585–616.

40. H. Lentze, 'Joseph Unger – Leben und Werk', in W.M. Plöchl and I. Gampl (eds), *Im Dienste des Rechtes in Kirche und Staat: Festschrift zum 70. Geburtstag von Univ.-Professor Prälat Dr. theol. et Dr. jur. Franz Arnold*, Vienna, 1963, 219–32; E. Pólay, 'A pandektisztika és hatása a magyar magánjog tudományára' ['The Pandectist School and its Impact on the Hungarian Science of Private Law'], *Acta Universitatis Szegediensis de Attila József nominatae, Acta politica et juridica* 23(6) (1976), 5–157.

41. J. Unger, *System des österreichischen allgemeinen Privatrechts*, 6 vols., Leipzig, 1856–64, vol. I: 67, 71, 240, ann. 22, 498; vol. II: 44–55 and 135; A. Exner, *Die Lehre vom Rechtserwerb durch Tradition*, Vienna, 1867: 259, ann. 10, 126, 176, 267, 270 and ann. 52; J. F. Stagl, 'Die Rezeption der Lehre vom Rechtsgeschäft in Österreich durch Joseph Unger', *Zeitschrift für europäisches Privatrecht* 1 (2007), 37–56.

42. G. Oberkofler, 'Die österreichische Juristentradition des Vormärz im Widerstreit mit den Reformen des Ministers Leo Thun', in G. Oberkofler (ed.), *Studien zur Geschichte der österreichischen Rechtswissenschaft*, Frankfurt am Main, 1984, 121–54; J. Morávek, 'K bojům Českých právníků 60. let XIX. století o orientaci České právní kultury' ['The Struggles of Czech Jurists from the 1860s for the Orientation of Czech Legal Culture'], *Právník* 107 (1968), 610–17.

43. F.L. Fillafer, 'Leo Thun und die Aufklärung: Wissenschaftsideal, Berufungspolitik und Deutungskämpfe', in C. Aichner and B. Mazohl (eds),

*Die Thun-Hohenstein'schen Universitätsreformen: Konzeption – Umsetzung –
Nachwirkungen*, Vienna, 2017, 55–75, 63–67.

44. G.S. Jones, *Languages of Class: Studies in English Working-Class History, 1832–
    1982*, Cambridge, 1983.

45. But see, most recently, M. Isabella, 'Citizens or Faithful? Religion and the Liberal
    Revolutions of the 1820s in Southern Europe', *Modern Intellectual History* 12
    (2015), 555–78.

46. See C. Clark and W. Kaiser (eds), *Culture Wars: Secular-Catholic Conflict in
    Nineteenth-Century Europe*, Cambridge, 2003. For an excellent case study, see
    K. Kaiserová, 'Die Barockzeit in den Schriften der Los-von-Rom-Bewegung', *O
    werthestes Vatter-Land! Kultur Deutschböhmens 17. – 19.Jh.* (Zprávy Společnosti
    pro dějiny Němců v Čechách – Mitteilungen für die Geschichte der Deutschen
    in Böhmen) 2 (2003), 29–33.

47. E. Winter, *Bernard Bolzano und sein Kreis: dargestellt mit erstmaliger Heranziehung
    der Nachlässe Bolzanos und seiner Freunde*, Prague, 1933.

48. Fillafer, 'Leo Thun und die Aufklärung'; M. Oubrechtová, 'Duchovní orien-
    tace děčínských Thun-Hohensteinů v době předbřeznové' ['The Religious
    Orientation of the Thun-Hohensteins of Děčín before 1848'], in Z.R. Nešpor
    and K. Kaiserová (eds), *Variety české religiozity v „dlouhém' 19. století (1780–
    1918)*, Ústí nad Labem, 2010, 254–69.

49. See the fine anthology of M. Prélot and F. G. Genuys (eds), *Le libéralisme
    catholique*, Paris, 1969; and also M. Sancipriano, *Lamennais in Italia: Autorità e
    libertà nel pensiero filosofico-religioso del Risorgimento*, Milan, 1973; H. Rosenblatt,
    'On the Need for a Protestant Reformation: Constant, Sismondi, Giuzot and
    Laboulaye', in Geenens and Rosenblatt (eds), *French Liberalism from Montesquieu
    to the Present Day*, 115–34, 129.

50. See P. Křivský, 'Papež Řehoř XVI. a vídeňský nuncius o panslavismu a husit-
    ství v Čechách v roce 1844' ['Pope Gregory XVI and the Viennese Nuncio
    on Panslavism and Hussitism in Bohemia in 1844'], *Husitský Tábor* 9 (1987),
    351–68; J. Rak, 'Dělníci na vinici Páně nebo na roli národní?' ['Workers in the
    Vineyard of the Lord or on a National Role?'], in Z.Hojda and R. Prahl (eds),
    Bůh a bohové: Církve, náboženství a spiritualita v českém 19. Století, Prague, 2003,
    128–38; Péter Zakar, 'Forradalom az egyházban? A radikális papság, 1848–49-
    ben' ['The Revolution and the Church: the Radical Priesthood in 1848–1849'], in
    C.M. Sarnyai (ed.), *Állam és egyház a polgári átalakulás korában Magyarországon:
    1848–1918*, Budapest, 2001, 53–62.

51. Compare e.g. J. Lorman, 'Rozum osvícený vírou: Poznámky k problematickému
    vztahu rozumu a zjevení na příkladech textů Johanna Augustina Zippeho a dalších
    soudobých morálních teologů' ['Reason Enlightened by Faith: Notes on the
    Problematic Relationship between Reason and Revelation in the Work of J.H. Zippe
    and Other Moral Theologians'], in J. Lorman and D. Tinková (eds), *Post tenebras
    spero lucem? Duchovní tvář českého a moravského osvícenství*, Prague, 2008, 252–70.

52. Jansenism (named after the Catholic theologian C. Jansen, † 1638) was a neo-
    Augustinian theological and political programme emphasizing human depravity

that strove for moral austerity and, particularly in its French variety, rejected the power claims of absolute monarchy. See D. van Kley, 'The Rejuvenation and Rejection of Jansenism in History and Historiography: Recent Literature on Eighteenth-Century Jansenism in French', *French Historical Studies* 29 (2006), 649–84.

53. See F.L. Fillafer, 'Il crepuscolo del giansenismo: La chiesa come repubblica durante l'età delle rivoluzioni – una prospettiva globale', in U. Taraborrelli (ed.), *Penitenza e Penitenzieria al tempo del giansenismo (secc. XVII–XVIII): Culture – Teologie – Prassi* (Rome, forthcoming, 2019).

54. H. Belovari, 'Christlicher Demokratismus und christlicher Sozialismus im Jahre 1848 in Wien', Ph.D. dissertation (University of Vienna, 1960); E. Weinzierl-Fischer, 'Die Kirchenfrage auf dem österreichischen Reichstag 1848/49', *Mitteilungen des Österreichischen Staatsarchivs* 8 (1955), 160–90.

55. C.F. von Hock, *Gebert, oder Pabst Sylvester II. und sein Jahrhundert*, Vienna, 1837, 198–213; F.J. von Buß, *Über den Einfluß des Christenthums auf Recht und Staat, von der Stiftung der Kirche bis auf die Gegenwart. Ein Versuch in drei Büchern*, 3 vols, Freiburg im Breisgau, 1841, vol. I, 96.

56. See Fillafer, 'Escaping the Enlightenment', 267–84; F. Cinek: *K národnímu probuzení moravského dorostu kněžského* [*The National Awakening among the Young Moravian Clergy*], Olomouc, 1934, 78 and 193.

57. A. Günther, *Süd- und Nordlichter am Horizonte spekulativer Theologie*, Vienna, 1832, 134–5; A. Günther, *Der letzte Symboliker: Eine durch die Werke Doctor J. A. Möhler's und Doctor C. F. Baur's veranlasste Schrift*, Vienna, 1834, 31 and 266.

58. J. Kleutgen, *Theologie der Vorzeit*, I, 2nd edn, Münster, 1867: 10; J. Kleutgen, *Theologie der Vorzeit*, vol. III, Münster, 1860, 224; A. Günther and J. H. Pabst, *Janusköpfe für Philosophie und Theologie*, Vienna, 1834, 338; M. Scattola, 'Die Geburt des katholischen Natur- und Völkerrechts aus dem Geist des Protestantismus im 19. Jahrhundert', in P. Cancik et al. (eds), *Auf der Suche nach konfessionell geprägten Denkmustern und Argumentationsstrategien in Recht und Rechtswissenschaft des 19. und 20. Jahrhunderts*, Frankfurt am Main, 2009, 95–120.

59. See J. Kautz, *Theorie und Geschichte der National-Oekonomik: Die geschichtliche Entwicklung und ihrer Literatur: Propyläen zum staats- und volkswirtschaftlichen Studium*, 2 vols, Vienna, 1858–60, vol. II, *Die geschichtliche Entwickelung der National-Oekonomik und ihrer Literatur*, 385; however, compare H. Matis, 'Sozioökonomische Aspekte des Liberalismus in Österreich, 1848–1918', in H.-U. Wehler (ed.), *Sozialgeschichte heute: Festschrift für Hans Rosenberg zum 70. Geburtstag*, Göttingen, 1974, 243–65; and R. Zuckerkandl, 'Beitrag zur Dogmen-Geschichte der Schutzzollidee', *Zeitschrift für Volkswirtschaft, Socialpolitik und Verwaltung* 1 (1892), 249–376.

60. J. von Sonnenfels, *Sätze aus der Polizey, Handlung und Finanz*, Vienna, 1765.

61. Austrian State Archives OeSta/ Haus-, Hof- und Staatsarchiv, Vienna, Kabinettsarchiv, Studienrevisionshofkommission, Faszikel 9, Protkoll Sitzung, 4 June 1799; On this commission, see H. Weitensfelder, *Studium und Staat: Heinrich*

Graf Rottenhan und Johann Melchior von Birkenstock als Repräsentanten der öster-reichischen Bildungspolitik um 1800, Vienna, 1996: 21–24, 137–46; cf. J. Krameš, *Kameralismus a klasická ekonomie v Čechách* [*Cameralism and Classical Economy in the Bohemian Lands*], Prague, 1998, 34; A. Csizmadia, 'Igazgatástudomány a XIX. század elején: Reviczky József' ['The Science of Administration in the Beginnings of the Nineteenth Century'], in A. Csizmadia (ed.), *Jogi emlékek és hagyományok: Esszék és tanulmányok*, Budapest, 1981, 245–61 and 246.

62. J. Kudler, *Die Grundlehren der Volkswirthschaftslehre*, 2 vols, vol. I, *Theoretischer Teil*, Vienna, 1846: iii–iv, 362 (usury), 46–47 and 51 (opinion and value); cf. P. Silverman, 'The Cameralist Roots of Menger's Achievement', in Bruce J. Caldwell (ed.), *Carl Menger and his Legacy in Economics*, London, 1990, 69–91.

63. A. Wagner, 'Zur Geschichte und Kritik der österreichischen Bankozettelperiode, Teil I', *Zeitschrift für die gesamte Staatswissenschaft* 17 (1861), 577–635.

64. See C. von Kübeck, *Tagebücher*, I/1: 192 (1807); F. von Pillersdorf, *Handschriftlicher Nachlaß des Freiherrn von Pillersdorf*, Vienna, 1863, 45–48; A. Brusatti, 'Die Staatsgüterveräußerungen in der Zeit von 1780–1848: Eine wirtschaftsgeschichtliche Untersuchung zum Problem des österreichischen Liberalismus', *Mitteilungen des österreichischen Staatsarchivs* 11 (1958), 252–74, at 264; I. von Beidtel and A. Huber, *Geschichte der österreichischen Staatsverwaltung, 1740–1848. Mit einem Anhange: Übersicht der österreichischen Kirchengeschichte von 1848–1861*, 2 vols, Innsbruck 1896–98, vol. 2, 41.

65. C. F. Hock, 'Die Grundlehren der Volkswirthschaftslehre, von Dr. Joseph Kudler', *Journal des Oesterreichischen Lloyd: Centralorgan für Handel, Industrie, Schiffahrt und Volkswirthschaft* 11 (1846), 93–95, 137–38 and 142–43.

66. See the excellent discussion in L. Sommer, *Die österreichischen Kameralisten in dogmengeschichtlicher Darstellung*, 2 vols, Vienna, 1920–25, vol. 2, 392–93; Hock, 'Die Grundlehren der Volkswirthschaftslehre, von Dr. Joseph Kudler', 93.

67. On the genealogy of the concept and the political freights it carries, see J. Mali and R. Wokler (eds), *Isaiah Berlin's Counter-Enlightenment*, Philadelphia, 2003.

68. E. Goffman, *Frame Analysis*, New York, 1974, 186; P. Burke, 'The Jargon of the Schools', in P. Burke and R. Porter (eds), *Languages and Jargons: Contributions to a Social History of Language*, Cambridge, 1995, 22–41.

Bibliography

Bálazs, É.H. *Hungary and the Habsburgs, 1765–1800: An Experiment in Enlightened Absolutism*. Budapest, 1997.

Bass, E. *Čtení o roce osmačtyřicátém* [*Readings about 1848*]. Prague, 1940.

Beales, D. 'The False Joseph II'. *Historical Journal* 18 (1975), 467–95.

———. *Joseph II, Vol. 2: Against the World: 1780–1790*. Cambridge, 2009.

Beidtel, I., and A. Huber. *Geschichte der österreichischen Staatsverwaltung, 1740–1848, mit einem Anhange: Übersicht der österreichischen Kirchengeschichte von 1848–1861*. 2 vols., Innsbruck, 1896–98.

Belovari, H. 'Christlicher Demokratismus und christlicher Sozialismus im Jahre 1848 in Wien', Ph.D. dissertation. University of Vienna, 1960.

Berg, M. *The Machinery Question and the Making of Political Economy*. Cambridge, 1980.

―――. 'Progress and Providence in Early Nineteenth-Century Political Economy'. *Social History* 15 (1990), 367–75.

Berger Waldenegg, G.C. 'Vaterländisches Gemeingefühl und nationale Charaktere: Die kaiserliche Regierung im Neoabsolutismus und die Erfindung einer österreichischen Nationalgeschichte', in H.P. Hye et al. (eds), *Nationalgeschichte als Artefakt: Zum Paradigma 'Nationalstaat' in den Historiographien Deutschlands, Italiens und Österreichs* (Vienna, 2009), 135–78.

Brauneder, W. *Leseverein und Rechtskultur: Der juridisch-politische Leseverein zu Wien 1840 bis 1990*. Vienna, 1992.

―――. 'Privatrechtsfortbildung durch Juristenrecht in Exegetik und Pandektistik in Österreich'. *Zeitschrift für Neuere Rechtsgeschichte* 5 (1983), 22–43.

―――. 'Von der moralischen Person des ABGB zur juristischen Person der Privatrechtswissenschaft'. *Quaderni fiorentini per la storia del pensiero giuridico moderno* 11/12 (1982–83), 265–317.

Brent, R. 'God's Providence: Liberal Political Economy as Natural Theology at Oxford, 1825–62', in M. Bentley (ed.), *Public and Private Doctrine: Essays in British History Presented to Maurice Cowling* (Cambridge, 1993), 85–107.

Briese, O., A. Liepert and E. Magdanz. 'Erfahrung des Wechsels – Wechsel der Erfahrung: Rekurrierten Vormärzliberale lediglich auf Aufklärung?'. *Zeitschrift für Geschichtswissenschaft* 41 (1993), 781–91.

Brusatti, A. 'Die Staatsgüterveräußerungen in der Zeit von 1780–1848: Eine wirtschaftsgeschichtliche Untersuchung zum Problem des österreichischen Liberalismus'. *Mitteilungen des österreichischen Staatsarchivs* 11 (1958), 252–74.

Burke, P. 'The Jargon of the Schools', in P. Burke and R. Porter (eds), *Languages and Jargons: Contributions to a Social History of Language* (Cambridge, 1995), 22–41.

Burrow, J.W. *Whigs and Liberals: Continuity and Change in English Political Thought*. Oxford, 1988.

Buß, F.J. *Über den Einfluß des Christenthums auf Recht und Staat, von der Stiftung der Kirche bis auf die Gegenwart. Ein Versuch in drei Büchern*, vol. I. Freiburg im Breisgau, 1841.

Butvin, J. *Slovenské národno-zjednocovacie hnutie (1780–1848)* [*The Slovak Movement of National Unification*]. Bratislava, 1965.

Cinek, F. *K národnímu probuzení moravského dorostu kněžského* [*The National Awakening among the Young Moravian Clergy*]. Olomouc, 1934.

Clark, C., and W. Kaiser (eds). *Culture Wars: Secular-Catholic Conflict in Nineteenth-Century Europe*. Cambridge, 2003.

Collini, S., D. Winch and J.W. Burrow. *That Noble Science of Politics. A Study in Nineteenth-Century Intellectual History*. Cambridge, 1983.

Craig, D. 'The Language of Liberality in Britain, c.1760–c.1815'. *Modern Intellectual History* (January 2018), 1–31. Retrieved 27 May 2019 from https://www.cam

bridge.org/core/journals/modern-intellectual-history/article/language-of-liber
ality-in-britain-c1760c1815/477C6709F627EC7FF161B442B5DF3ECA.

Csizmadia, A. 'Igazgatástudomány a XIX. század elején: Reviczky József' ['The
Science of Administration in the Beginnings of the Nineteenth Century'], in
A. Csizmadia (ed.), *Jogi emlékek és hagyományok: Esszék és tanulmányok* (Budapest,
1981), 245–61.

David, Z. V. *Realism, Tolerance, and Liberalism: Legacies of the Bohemian Reformation.*
Baltimore, 2010.

De Dijn, A. *French Political Thought from Montesquieu to Tocqueville: Liberty in a
Levelled Society?* Cambridge, 2008.

De Ruggiero, G. *Storia del liberalismo europeo.* Bari, 1925.

Déak, Á. 'Együttműködés vagy konkurencia. Az alsóausztriai, a csehországi és
a magyarországi ellenzék összefogási kísérlete 1847–1848' ['Cooperation or
Competition: An Attempt at Cooperation between the Lower-Austrian, Bohemian
and Hungarian Opposition, 1847–1848']. *Aetas* 14 (1999), 43–61.

———. 'Pläne für die Neugstaltung der Habsburgermonarchie und Ungarns 1848–
1852'. *Ungarn-Jahrbuch* 24 (1998/99), 87–104.

Dunn, J. 'The Politics of John Locke in the Eighteenth Century', in J. Yolton (ed.),
John Locke: Problems and Perspectives (Cambridge, 1969), 45–80.

Ebert, K. *Die Grazer Juristenfakultät im Vormärz: Rechtswissenschaft und Rechtslehre
an der Grazer Hochschule von 1810 bis 1848.* Graz, 1969.

Eckhart, F. *A Jog- és Allatudományi Kar története* [= A Királyi Magyar Pázmány Péter
Tudományegyetem története, 2] [History of the Legal and Administrative Faculty
(History of the Royal Hungarian Pázmány Péter University)]. Budapest, 1936.

Eder, K. *Der Liberalismus in Altösterreich: Geisteshaltung, Politik und Kultur.* Vienna,
1955.

Engel-Jánosi, F. 'Kaiser Josef II. in der Wiener Bewegung des Jahres 1848'.
Mitteilungen des Vereins für die Geschichte der Stadt Wien 11 (1931), 53–72.

———. 'Zur Genesis der Revolution von 1848. Die Verfassungsfrage im deutschen
Österreich, 1815–1848'. *Zeitschrift für öffentliches Recht* 3 (1922/23), 571–82.

Epstein, K. *The Genesis of German Conservatism.* Princeton, 1966.

Exner, A. *Die Lehre vom Rechtserwerb durch Tradition.* Vienna, 1867.

Faber, K.-G. '"Konservatorischer Liberalismus", "Umstürzender Liberalismus",
"Konservatorischer Obskurantismus": Aus dem Briefwechsel zwischen Marschall
und Allmendingen'. *Nassauische Annalen* 78 (1967), 177–95.

Fernández-Sebastián, J. 'Du mépris à la louange : Image, présence et mise en valeur
du Siècle des lumières dans l'Espagne contemporaine', in G. Ricuperati (ed.),
Historiographie et usages des Lumières (Berlin, 2002), 133–58.

———. 'La Constitución de Cádiz: historiografía y conmemoración', in J.Á. Junco
and J.M. Luzón (eds), *La Constitución de Cádiz: historiografía y conmemoración:
Homenaje a Francisco Tomás y Valiente* (Madrid, 2006), 23–58.

———. 'Liberales y liberalismo en España, 1810–1850 : La forja de un concepto y
la creación de una identidad política'. *Revista de Estudios Políticos (Nueva Época)*
134 (2006), 125–76.

Fillafer, F.L. 'Die Aufklärung und ihr Erbe in der Habsburgermonarchie. Ein Forschungsüberblick'. *Zeitschrift für historische Forschung* 40 (2013), 35–97.

———. 'Escaping the Enlightenment: Liberalism and the Legacies of the Eighteenth Century in the Habsburg Lands, 1790–1848', Ph.D. dissertation. University of Konstanz, 2012.

———. 'Il crepuscolo del giansenismo: La chiesa come repubblica durante l'età delle rivoluzioni – una prospettiva globale', in U. Taraborrelli (ed.), *Penitenza e Penitenzieria al tempo del giansenismo (secc. XVII–XVIII). Culture – Teologie – Prassi* (Rome, forthcoming, 2019).

———. 'Imperium oder Kulturstaat? Die Habsburgermonarchie und die Historisierung der Nationalkulturen im 19. Jahrhundert', in P. Ther (ed.), *Kulturpolitik und Theater: Die kontinentalen Imperien in Europa im Vergleich* (Vienna, 2012), 23–54.

———. 'Leo Thun und die Aufklärung: Wissenschaftsideal, Berufungspolitik und Deutungskämpfe, in C. Aichner and B. Mazohl (eds), *Die Thun-Hohenstein'schen Universitätsreformen: Konzeption – Umsetzung – Nachwirkungen* (Vienna, 2017), 55–75.

———. 'Whose Enlightenment?' *Austrian History Yearbook* 48 (2017), 111–25.

Fillafer, F.L., and T. Wallnig (eds). *Josephinismus zwischen den Regimen: Eduard Winter, Fritz Valjavec und die zentraleuropäischen Historiographien im 20. Jahrhundert.* Vienna, 2016.

Fontana, B. *Rethinking the Politics of Commercial Society: The Edinburgh Review, 1802–1832.* Cambridge, 1985.

Forbes, D. *Riches and Poverty: An Intellectual History of Political Economy in Britain, 1750–1834.* Cambridge, 1996.

Franz, G. *Liberalismus: Die deutschliberale Bewegung in der Habsburgischen Monarchie.* Munich, 1955.

Fried, I. 'Ein österreichischer Biedermeier-Dichter und die südslawische Volksdichtung'. *Studia Slavica Hungarica* 20 (1974), 115–26.

———. 'II. József, a jozefinisták és a reformerek: Vázlat a XVIII. század végének magyar közgondolkodásáról' ['Joseph II, Josephinists and Reformers: A Sketch of Hungarian Public Opinion at the Verge of the Eighteenth Century']. *Az Országos Széchényi Könyvtár Évlönyve* (1979), 563–91.

Gángó, G. 'Egy "rettentő váz nevezet" jelentéstörténetéhez: Kit neveztek szabadelműnek, szabadelvűnek, és liberálisnak a reformkori Magyarországon?' ['On the Historical Semantics of a "Ghastly Skeleton": Who was Called Free-Minded, Libertarian and Liberal in the Hungarian Reform Age?']. *Holmi* 11 (1999), 327–42.

Geenens, R., and H. Rosenblatt (eds). *French Liberalism from Montesquieu to the Present Day.* Cambridge, 2012.

Goffman, E. *Frame Analysis.* New York, 1974.

Günther A., and J.H. Pabst. *Der letzte Symboliker: Eine durch die Werke Doctor J. A. Möhler's und Doctor C. F. Baur's veranlasste Schrift.* Vienna, 1834.

L
66   *Franz L. Fillafer*

66   *Franz L. Fillafer*

————. *Janusköpfe für Philosophie und Theologie.* Vienna, 1834.
————. *Süd- und Nordlichter am Horizonte spekulativer Theologie.* Vienna, 1832.
Hilton, B. *The Age of Atonement: The Influence of Evangelicalism on Social and Economic Thought, 1785–1865.* Oxford, 1988.
————. *A Mad, Bad, and Dangerous People: England 1783–1846.* Oxford, 2006.
Hock, Dr [C.F.]. 'Die Grundlehren der Volkswirthschaftslehre, von Dr. Joseph Kudler'. *Journal des Oesterreichischen Lloyd: Centralorgan für Handel, Industrie, Schiffahrt und Volkswirthschaft* 11 (1846), 93–143.
————. *Gebert, oder Pabst Sylvester II. und sein Jahrhundert.* Vienna, 1837.
Höhne, S., and A. Ohme (eds). *Prozesse kultureller Integration und Disintegration: Deutsche, Tschechen, Böhmen im 19. Jahrhundert.* Munich, 2005.
Hunter, I. *Rival Enlightenments: Civic and Metaphysical Philosophy in Early Modern Germany.* Cambridge, 2001.
Hýsej, M. 'Dějiny t. zv. moravského separatismu' ['History of the So-Called Moravian Separatism']. *Časopis Matice moravské* 33 (1909), 24–51, 146–72.
Isabella, M. 'Citizens or Faithful? Religion and the Liberal Revolutions of the 1820s in Southern Europe'. *Modern Intellectual History* 12 (2015), 555–78.
Israel, J. *Democratic Enlightenment: Philosophy, Revolution, and Human Rights 1750–1790.* Oxford, 2011.
————. *Enlightenment Contested: Philosophy, Modernity, and the Emancipation of Man 1670–1752.* Oxford, 2006.
————. *Radical Enlightenment: Philosophy and the Making of Modernity, 1650–1750.* Oxford, 2001.
Jainchill, A. *Reimaginig Politics after the Terror: The Republican Origins of French Liberalism.* New York, 2008.
Janowski, M. 'Kecskék és tokhalak: A közép-kelet-európai liberalizmus sajátosságai a francia forradalom és az első világháború között' ['Goats and Sturgeons: The Characteristics of East-Central-European Liberalism between the French Revolution and World War I']. *Aetas* 14 (1999), 108–21.
Jaume, L. *L'individu effacé ou le paradoxe du libéralisme française.* Paris, 1997.
Jeník z Bratřice, J. *Z mých paměti [From My Memoirs]*, ed. J. Polišenský. Prague, 1947.
Jones, G.S. *Languages of Class: Studies in English Working-Class history, 1832–1982.* Cambridge, 1983.
Judson, P.M. 'Die Liberalen und ihre interessierte Anti-Interessenpolitik', in S.P. Scheichl and E. Brix (eds), *'Dürfen's denn das?': Die fortdauernde Frage zum Jahr 1848* (Vienna, 1999), 127–40.
Kaiserová, K. 'Die Barockzeit in den Schriften der Los-von-Rom-Bewegung'. *O werthestes Vatter-Land! Kultur Deutschböhmens 17. – 19.Jh.* (Zprávy Společnosti pro dějiny Němců v Čechách – Mitteilungen für die Geschichte der Deutschen in Böhmen) 2 (2003), 29–33.
Kautz, J. *Theorie und Geschichte der National-Oekonomik: Die geschichtliche Entwicklung und ihrer Literatur: Propyläen zum staats- und volkswirtschaftlichen Studium*, 2 vols. Vienna, 1858–60.

Kazinczy, F. *Pályám emlékezete, 1759–1792* [*Autobiography, 1759–1792*]. Budapest, 1956.

Klabouch, J. *Osvícenské právní nauky v českých zemích* [*Enlightenment Legal Scholarship in the Bohemian Lands*]. Prague, 1958.

Kleutgen, J. *Theologie der Vorzeit*, I, 2nd edn. Münster, 1867.

———. *Theologie der Vorzeit*, III. Münster, 1860.

Krameš, J. *Kameralismus a klasická ekonomie v Čechách* [*Cameralism and Classical Economy in the Bohemian Lands*]. Prague, 1998.

Křivský, P. 'Papež Řehoř XVI. a vídeňský nuncius o panslavismu a husitství v Čechách v roce 1844' ['Pope Gregory XVI and the Viennese Nuncio on Panslavism and Hussitism in Bohemia in 1844']. *Husitský Tábor* 9 (1987), 351–68.

Kübeck von Kübau, *Tagebücher*, ed. by M. von Kübeck, 2 vols. Vienna, 1909.

Kudler, J. *Die Grundlehren der Volkswirthschaftslehre*, 2 vols. Vienna, 1846.

Kurth, P., and B. Morgenbrod. 'Wien 1848 und die Erinnerung an die Französische Revolution von 1789', in I. Götz von Olenhusen (ed.), *1848/49 in Europa und der Mythos der Französischen Revolution* (Göttingen, 1998), 114–33.

La Vopa, A. 'A New Intellectual History? Jonathan Israel's Enlightenment'. *Historical Journal* 52 (2009), 717–38.

LeCaine Agnew, H. *Origins of the Czech National Renascence*. Stanford, 1994.

Lentze, H. 'Andreas Freiherr von Baumgartner und die Thunsche Studienreform'. *Anzeiger der Österreichischen Akademie der Wissenschaften, philosophisch-historische Klasse* 96 (1959), 161–79.

———. 'Joseph Unger – Leben und Werk', in W. M. Plöchl and I. Gampl (eds), *Im Dienste des Rechtes in Kirche und Staat: Festschrift zum 70. Geburtstag von Univ.-Professor Prälat Dr. theol. et Dr. jur. Franz Arnold* (Vienna, 1963), 219–32.

Leonhard, J. *Liberalismus: Zur historischen Semantik eines europäischen Deutungsmusters*. Munich, 2001.

Lorman, J. 'Rozum osvícený vírou: Poznámky k problematickému vztahu rozumu a zjevení na příkladech textů Johanna Augustina Zippeho a dalších soudobých morálních teologů' ['Reason Enlightened by Faith: Notes on the Problematic Relationship between Reason and Revelation in the Work of J.H. Zippe and Other Moral Theologians'], in J. Lorman and D. Tinková (eds), *Post tenebras spero lucem? Duchovní tvář českého a moravského osvícenství* (Prague, 2008), 252–70.

Luzzatto, S. 'L'illuminismo impossibile. Alessandro Verri tra rivoluzione e restaurazione'. *Rivista di letteratura italiana* 3 (1985), 263–90.

Mali, J., and R. Wokler (eds). *Isaiah Berlin's Counter-Enlightenment*. Philadelphia, 2003.

Malíř, J. 'Morava na předělu: K formování národního vědomí na Moravě v letech 1848–1871' ['Moravia at the Crossroads: On the Formation of Moravian National Consciousness between 1848–1871']. *Časopis Matice moravské* 109 (1990), 345–63.

Mandler, P. 'Tories and Paupers: Christian Political Economy and the Making of the New Poor Law'. *Historical Journal* 33 (1990), 81–103.

———. *Aristocratic Government in the Age of Reform: Whigs and Liberals, 1830–1852*. Oxford, 1990.

Máthé, G. 'A jogegyenlőség és törvény előtti egyenlőség kérdései a reformkorban' ['Questions of Legal Equality and Equality before the Law in the Reform Age']. *Acta Facultatis Politico-Iuridicae Universitatis Scientiarium Budapestinensis de Rolando Eötvös Nominatae* 10 (1968), 341–61.

Matis, H. 'Sozioökonomische Aspekte des Liberalismus in Österreich, 1848–1918', in H.-U. Wehler (ed.), *Sozialgeschichte heute: Festschrift für Hans Rosenberg zum 70. Geburtstag* (Göttingen, 1974), 243–65.

Mészáros, A. *A marginalitás szelid bája (Arcképek a reformkori magyar filozófiából)* [*The Discreet Charm of Marginality (Portraits of Hungarian Philosophy of the Reform Age)*]. Bratislava, 1994.

Michie, M. *An Enlightenment Tory in Victorian Scotland: The Career of Sir Archibald Alison.* Montreal, 1997.

Miskolczy, A. '"Hungarus Consciousness" in the Age of Early Nationalism', in G. Almási and L. Šubarić (eds), *Latin at the Crossroads of Identity: The Evolution of Linguistic Nationalism in the Kingdom of Hungary* (Leiden, 2015), 64–93.

Montoya, A.C. 'Medievalism and Enlightenment, 1647–1750: Jean Chapelain to Jean-Jacques Rousseau'. *Romanic Review* (2009), 494–512.

Morávek, J. 'K bojům Českých právníků 60. let XIX. století o orientaci České právní kultury' ['The Struggles of Czech Jurists from the 1860s for the Orientation of Czech Legal Culture']. *Právník* 107 (1968), 610–17.

Moravia, S. *Il tramonto dell'illuminismo: Filosofia e politica nella società francese, 1770–1810.* Bari, 1968.

Németh, B.G. 'A jozefinista illúzió fölvillanása 49 után' ['A Flash of the Josephinist Illusion after 1849'], in B.G. Németh (ed.), *Létharc és nemzetiség* (Budapest, 1976), 414–44.

Niederhauser, E. 'Problèmes de la conscience historique dans les mouvements de renaissance nationale en Europe Orientale'. *Acta Historica Academiae Scientiarum Hungaricae* 18 (1972), 39–73.

Oberkofler, G. 'Die österreichische Juristentradition des Vormärz im Widerstreit mit den Reformen des Ministers Leo Thun', in G. Oberkofler (ed.), *Studien zur Geschichte der österreichischen Rechtswissenschaft* (Frankfurt am Main, 1984), 121–54.

Ofner, J. (ed.). *Der Ur-Entwurf und die Berathungs-Protokolle des Österreichischen Allgemeinen bürgerlichen Gesetzbuches*, 2 vols. Vienna, 1889.

Oubrechtová, M. 'Duchovní orientace děčínských Thun-Hohensteinů v době předbřeznové' ['The Religious Orientation of the Thun-Hohensteins of Děčín before 1848'], in Z.R. Nešpor and K. Kaiserová (eds), *Variety české religiozity v „dlouhém' 19. století (1780–1918)* (Ústí nad Labem, 2010), 254–69.

Padoa-Schioppa, A. *A History of Law in Europe: From the Early Middle Ages to the Twentieth Century.* Cambridge, 2017.

Pillersdorf, F. von. *Handschriftlicher Nachlaß des Freiherrn von Pillersdorf.* Vienna. 1863.

Pocock, J.G.A. 'Clergy and Commerce: The Conservative Enlightenment in England', in R. Ajello (ed.), *L'età dei lumi. Studi storici sul Settecento europeo in onore di Franco Venturi*, vol. 1 (Naples, 1985), 523–62.

————. 'Historiography and Enlightenment: A View of Their Relationship'. *Modern Intellectual History* 5 (2008), 83–96.

————. 'The Re-description of Enlightenment'. *Proceedings of the British Academy* 125 (2006), 101–17.

————. 'The Varieties of Whiggism between Exclusion and Reform: A History of Ideology and Discourse', in J.G.A. Pocock (ed.), *Virtue, Commerce, and History: Essays on Political Thought and History, Chiefly in the Eighteenth* Century (Cambridge, 1985), 215–310.

Pólay, E. 'A pandektisztika és hatása a magyar magánjog tudományára' ['The Pandectist School and its Impact on the Hungarian Science of Private Law']. *Acta Universitatis Szegediensis de Attila József nominatae, Acta politica et juridica* 23(6) (1976), 5–157.

Polišenský, J., *Aristocrats and the Crowd in the Revolutionary Year 1848: A Contribution to the History of Revolution and Counter-revolution in Austria.* Albany, NY, 1980.

Polišenský, J., and E. Illingova. *Jan Jeník z Bratřice [Jan Jeník of Bratřic].* Prague, 1989.

Prélot, M., and F.G. Genuys (eds). *Le libéralisme catholique.* Paris, 1969.

Rak, J. 'Dělníci na vinici Páně nebo na roli národní?' ['Workers in the Vineyard of the Lord or on a National Role?'], in Z. Hojda and R. Prahl (eds), *Bůh a bohové: Církve, náboženství a spiritualita v českém 19. Století* (Prague, 2003), 128–38.

————. 'Koncepce historické práce Vlasteneckého muzea v Čechách,' ['The Conception of Historical Research Activities of the Patriotic Museum of Bohemia']. *Časopis Národního Muzea – historické muzeum* 153 (1984), 98–111.

Reinert, S.A. 'In margine a un bilancio sui Lumi europei'. *Rivista storica italiana* 118 (2006), 975–86.

Ricuperati, G. 'In margine al Radical Enlightenment di Jonathan I. Israel'. *Rivista storica italiana* 115 (2003), 285–329.

Ritter, H.G. 'Austrogerman Liberalism and the Modern Liberal Tradition'. *German Studies Review* 7 (1984), 227–48.

Robertson, J. *The Case for the Enlightenment: Scotland and Naples, 1680–1760.* Cambridge, 2005.

————. 'The Enlightenments of J.G.A. Pocock'. *Storia della storiografia* 39 (2001), 140–51.

Rosanvallon, P. *Le moment Guizot.* Paris, 1985.

Rosenberg, H. 'Theologischer Rationalismus und vormärzlicher Vulgärliberalismus', in H. Rosenberg, *Politische Denkströmungen im deutschen Vormärz* (Göttingen, 1972), 18–50.

Rosenblatt, H. 'On the Need for a Protestant Reformation: Constant, Sismondi, Giuzot and Laboulaye', in R. Geenens and H. Rosenblatt (eds), *French Liberalism from Montesquieu to the Present Day* (Cambridge, 2012), 115–34.

————. 'Re-evaluating Benjamin Constant's Liberalism: Industrialism, Saint-Simonianism and the Restoration Years'. *History of European Ideas* 30 (2004), 23–37.

Sancipriano, M. *Lamennais in Italia: Autorità e libertà nel pensiero filosofico-religioso del Risorgimento.* Milan, 1973.

Scattola, M. 'Die Geburt des katholischen Natur- und Völkerrechts aus dem Geist des Protestantismus im 19. Jahrhundert', in P. Cancik et al. (eds), *Auf der Suche nach konfessionell geprägten Denkmustern und Argumentationsstrategien in Recht und Rechtswissenschaft des 19. und 20. Jahrhunderts* (Frankfurt am Main, 2009), 95–120.

Schuster, M. *Theoretisch-praktischer Kommentar über das allgemeine bürgerliche Gesetzbuch*, vol. I. Prague, 1818.

Selb, W., and H. Hofmeister (eds). *Forschungsband Franz von Zeiller (1751–1828): Beiträge zur Gesetzgebungs- und Wissenschaftsgeschichte.* Vienna, 1980.

Siedentop, L. 'Two Liberal Traditions', in A. Ryan (ed.), *The Idea of Freedom: Essays in Honour of Isaiah Berlin* (Oxford, 1979), 153–74.

Silverman, P. 'The Cameralist Roots of Menger's Achievement', in B.J. Caldwell (ed.), *Carl Menger and His Legacy in Economics* (London, 1990), 69–91.

Sommer, L. *Die österreichischen Kameralisten in dogmengeschichtlicher Darstellung*, vol. 2. Vienna, 1920–25.

Sonnenfels, J. *Sätze aus der Polizey, Handlung und Finanz.* Vienna, 1765.

Stagl, J.F. 'Die Rezeption der Lehre vom Rechtsgeschäft in Österreich durch Joseph Unger'. *Zeitschrift für europäisches Privatrecht* 1 (2007), 37–56.

Sziklay, L. *Együttélés és többnyelvűség az irodalomban* ['Coexistence and Multilinguality in Literature']. Budapest, 1987.

Thienen-Adlerflycht, C. *Graf Leo Thun im Vormärz: Grundlagen des böhmischen Konservatismus im Kaisertum Österreich.* Graz, 1967.

Thomas, W. *The Philosophical Radicals: Nine Studies in Theory and Practice, 1817–1841.* Oxford, 1979.

Timpanaro, S. *Classicismo e Illuminismo nell'Ottocento Italiano*, 2nd edn. Pisa, 1969.

Trost, P. 'Česko-německý makaronismus' ['Czech-German Macaronism'], in id., *Studie o jazycích a literature*. ed. by J. Povĕšíl, Prague, 1995.

———. 'Nĕmecko-česká dvojjazyčnost', 'Czech-German Macaronism'], in id., *Studie o jazycích a literature*. ed. by J. Povĕšíl, Prague, 1995.

———. 'Střídaní kódů', ['Code-Switching'], in id., *Studie o jazycích a literature*. ed. by J. Povĕšíl, Prague, 1995.

Unger, J. *System des österreichischen allgemeinen Privatrechts*, 6 vols. Leipzig, 1856–64.

Urfus, V. 'K vzájemnému poměru českého státoprávního programu a předbřeznové stavovské opozice v Čechách' ['On the Mutual Relationship between the Bohemian State Right Programme and the Bohemian Noble Opposition before 1848']. *Právněhistorické studie* 13 (1967), 85–103.

———. *Zdomácnění smĕnečného práva v českých zemích a počátky novodobého práva obchodního* [*The Introduction of Exchange Law in the Bohemian Lands and the Beginnings of Modern Commercial Law*]. Prague, 1959.

Valjavec, F. *Die Entstehung der politischen Strömungen in Deutschland, 1770–1815*, 2nd edn. Königstein im Taunus, 1978.

Van Kley, D. 'The Rejuvenation and Rejection of Jansenism in History and Historiography: Recent Literature on Eighteenth-Century Jansenism in French'. *French Historical Studies* 29 (2006), 649–84.

Vierhaus, R. 'Aufklärung und Reformzeit: Kontinuitäten und Neuansätze in der deutschen Politik des späten 18. und frühen 19. Jahrhunderts', in Eberhard Weis (ed.), *Reformen im rheinbündischen Deutschland* (Munich, 1984), 287–301.

Volpilhac-Auger, C. 'Tocqueville et Montesquieu: récrire l'histoire?', in F. Mélonio and J.-L. Diaz (eds), *Tocqueville et la littérature* (Paris, 2004), 221–32.

Wagner, A. 'Zur Geschichte und Kritik der österreichischen Bankozettelperiode, Teil I'. *Zeitschrift für die gesamte Staatswissenschaft* 17 (1861), 577–635.

Weinzierl-Fischer, E. 'Die Kirchenfrage auf dem österreichischen Reichstag 1848/49'. *Mitteilungen des Österreichischen Staatsarchivs* 8 (1955), 160–90.

Weitensfelder, H. *Studium und Staat: Heinrich Graf Rottenhan und Johann Melchior von Birkenstock als Repräsentanten der österreichischen Bildungspolitik um 1800.* Vienna, 1996.

Whatmore, R. *Republicanism and the French Revolution: An Intellectual History of Jean-Baptiste Say's Political Economy.* Oxford, 2000.

Winter, E. *Bernard Bolzano und sein Kreis: dargestellt mit erstmaliger Heranziehung der Nachlässe Bolzanos und seiner Freunde.* Prague, 1933.

———. *Frühliberalismus in der Donaumonarchie: Religiöse, nationale und wissenschaftliche Strömungen von 1790–1868.* Berlin, 1968.

Zakar, P. 'Forradalom az egyházban? A radikális papság, 1848–49-ben' ['The Revolution and the Church: the Radical Priesthood in 1848–1849'], in C.M. Sarnyai (ed.), *Állam és egyház a polgári átalakulás korában Magyarországon: 1848–1918* (Budapest, 2001), 53–62.

Zuckerkandl, R. 'Beitrag zur Dogmen-Geschichte der Schutzzollidee'. *Zeitschrift für Volkswirtschaft, Socialpolitik und Verwaltung* 1 (1892), 249–376.

Chapter 2

Formulating and Reformulating 'Liberalism'

Germany in European Comparison

Jörn Leonhard

Introduction: Liberalism as an Exhausted Concept?

Speaking to a conference of German liberals in December 1948, Theodor
Heuss, later the President of the Federal Republic, asked his audience
whether the label 'liberal' could still be used to identify a political party that
regarded itself as part of political liberalism's tradition in Germany. The fact
that the conference voted in favour of 'Free Democratic Party' instead of
'Liberal Democratic Party' as its official party name indicated a widespread
scepticism: the very concept of 'liberalism', representing the ambivalent
experiences of the nineteenth century, seemed too much associated with
the German liberals' *Kulturkampf* of the 1870s and capitalism, which, in the
eyes of so many, had prevented liberals from a more progressive social policy
that could have bridged the gap between bourgeois liberalism and social
democracy before 1914 and especially after 1918.[1]

   In 1950, Thomas Mann, one of the most prominent representatives of
the German educated bourgeoisie and its political culture, went even further. Reflecting upon the fate of liberalism after the experience of European
fascism from American exile, Mann pointed out that the concept 'liberal'
seemed exhausted and had become void and meaningless. Against the background of the fascist challenge and European liberals' inability to prevent
its rise, Mann demanded a redefinition of how liberty and equality could be
reconciled. In contrast to what he regarded as the liberal primacy of liberty,
Mann pointed to equality as the 'leading idea of the current epoch'. What all
postwar societies needed was, in Mann's eyes, a social emancipation distinct

from the totalitarian model. While liberalism seemed to represent political emancipation, constitutions and political institutions as the legacy of the nineteenth century, 'social emancipation' could no longer be defined by a simple reference to a concept that seemed semantically exhausted. Mann pointed to the necessity to transform the paradigm of bourgeois revolution into 'social democracy'. If Goethe, at the end of his life, had declared that every reasonable individual was actually a 'liberal', Mann underlined that at present every reasonable human being was to be a socialist.[2]

Was there really a crisis of liberalism, reflecting the exhaustion of liberal political agendas after 1945?[3] Was it a particularly German response to the experience of liberals' electoral decline after 1918 and their failure to prevent the rise of fascism? Or was it a general European and transatlantic trend that needs careful explanation? Any attempt to approach these questions will have to take into account the semantic transformations of 'liberal' and 'liberalism' in the long nineteenth century from the perspective of a European comparison. The starting point of such an operation is the apparent triumph of liberalism in nearly all European societies of the 1870s and the perception of 'liberal' and 'liberalism' as both a universal trend of progressivism and a national narrative. Thus, Matthew Arnold in his 'Culture and Anarchy' of 1869 defined the success of the English liberal idea as 'the legislation of middle-class parliaments ... the local self-government of middle-class vestries ... the unrestricted competition of middle-class industrialists ... the dissidence of middle-class Dissent and the Protestantism of middle-class Protestant religion'?[4] Towards the end of the century, Gladstonian liberalism seemed to have become not just a personalized style of politics, but also a symbol of the British nation as the most progressive power in the world. Benjamin Jowett, Vice-Chancellor of Oxford University, commented on Gladstone's role in the Irish Home Rule debate by pointing to the triumph of an evolutionary reform strategy by which liberals seemed to have stimulated even their conservative counterpart for the good of the country: 'Liberals have, to a great extent, removed the impression they had created in England that they were the friends of disorder. Do you know, I cannot help feeling that I have more of the Liberal element in me than of the Conservative? This rivalry between the parties, each surprising the other by their liberality, has done a great deal of good to the people of England.'[5]

What seemed to be a natural progression towards 'liberalism' as an accepted key concept of the later nineteenth century becomes much more complicated and ambivalent if we focus on the actual diachronic varieties of 'liberal' and 'liberalism' and the historical change of meaning attached to these concepts in European comparison. In the late 1960s, the German historian Reinhart Koselleck developed a model of semantic change that he applied to key concepts of modern political and social vocabularies. According to him, these developed in a particular 'saddle epoch' (*Sattelzeit*) between 1750 and 1850.[6] However, this model primarily focused on German sources and left out particular semantic changes and impulses, differences and exchanges among European cases. More recent approaches have tried to develop the German tradition of *Begriffsgeschichte* into a transnational comparative analysis.[7] The following is an attempt to illustrate the potential for such an operation by looking at the comparative semantics of 'liberal' and 'liberalism' with a special focus on Germany.[8]

From Prepolitical Meanings to the Multifaceted European Semantics of 'Liberal' after 1800

For the history of this key concept, one can discern four subsequent processes as ideal types that characterise the semantic transformation from the eighteenth century to the nineteenth century.[9] The first is the prepolitical stage of semantics: in the case of 'liberal', this is the period dominated by the pre–1789 uses of 'liberal 'or 'liberality' in different contexts. In a society that, in comparison to Germany or France, was much less characterized by formal criteria, the English phrase 'as a gentleman be liberal' signified a social distance defined by cultural criteria.[10] Munificence and tolerance presupposed economic independence and a classical education. The persistence of this aristocratic meaning of 'liberal' cannot be overestimated; it dominated the prepolitical meaning of the concept 'liberal' for a long time, and even when a new political semantic was imported from the continent in response to the consequences of the French Revolution, the traditional prepolitical connotation of 'liberal' as a social attribute of an educated gentleman was never totally eliminated. Even in 1818 a contemporary dictionary attributed 'liberal habits' to 'persons of good birth'. The expression 'liberal attitude' indicated an individual, not a political programme. It depended on tolerance, an open and unprejudiced state of mind, and the will to take responsibility for one's own opinion in public. Whereas 'liberal' in England had either a more aristocratic connotation in expressions like 'liberal gentleman' or 'liberal education', or was used in the religious sphere, 'liberal' in Germany indicated, at least since the late 1750s, an individual quality of an advanced enlightened *Gesinnung*, which not only meant a cast of mind or a basic conviction, but also denoted a moral quality. *Liberale Gesinnung* pointed to the fundamental idea of the responsible individual who was of higher moral and ethical value on account of his unprejudiced state of mind. This meaning persisted in the later history of the political concept 'liberal' in Germany. The moral quality of the *liberale Gesinnung* or *Liberalität* went far beyond mere political denominations. Immanuel Kant's distinction between 'liberalitas sumptu-osa', mere munificence in the tradition of the Roman emperors' 'liberalitas', and 'liberalitas moralis' as an unprejudiced state of mind and independence of one's own opinion, deeply influenced the later history of *liberale Gesinnung*.[11] As in the case of Kant's 'Liberalität dei Denkungsart'[12] or Sieyès' 'éducation libérale'[13] of the Third Estate in France, the concepts reflected an enlightened educational ideal without a fixed political or social meaning.

This was followed by a second type: a fermentation of traditional and new semantic elements, caused by new political, social and cultural experiences, newly articulated interests and new expectations against the background of the French Revolution. Prepolitical and politicized meanings began to over-lap, starting with the invention of the *idées liberales* in France in 1799 and their subsequent translation into *liberale Ideen* in Germany and *idee liberali* in Italy,[14] but also with the emergence of *liberales* and *serviles* as party names in Spain and the export of this nomenclature to other European countries. The third period was characterized by the politicization of concepts as contro-versial through changing connotations of traditional concepts and the devel-opment of new concepts. In this phase, speakers attempted to structure the semantic field using canonical definitions and semantic clarity. At this point, the import of concepts such as the French *idées liberales* created a framework for the articulation of new experiences and stimulated conceptual debates, thereby testing the semantic field. Finally, an ideological polarization devel-oped, with bipolar or multipolar semantic structures resulting in a wider field of political and social nomenclatures and their use in arguments. In the case of 'liberal', the semantic field became defined by symmetric counterconcepts such as 'radical', 'conservative' or later 'socialist'.

For the politicization of 'liberal' in continental European societies, the confrontation with the French Revolution and Napoleon played a fundamen-tal role. French expansionism led to a direct confrontation with the French *idées libérales* as Bonaparte's programmatic formula of the results of 1789.[15] In his Proclamation of the 18th Brumaire 1799, justifying the coup d'état, Bonaparte's *idées libérales* stood for a defensive strategy to safeguard the rev-olution's legacy by ending both political instability and social anarchy: 'Les idées conservatrices, tutélaires, libérales, sont rentrées dans leurs droits par la dispersion des factieux qui opprimaient les conseils.' ('The conservative, protective, liberal ideas have been brought back to their rights by dispersing the political factions which oppressed the councils.').[16] Napoleon's invention of the *idées libérales* became part of his short-lived but influential imperial ideology. As the 'héro des idées liberales', he proclaimed himself to be both the only legitimate heir of 1789 and the only 'garant' of the Revolution's positive achievements, as incarnated by the Civil Code and the idea of the nation's sovereignty.[17] By referring to the imperial understanding of the *idées libérales*, Napoleon claimed to fulfil the Revolution's original and legitimate objects. On the other hand, turning the transpersonal principle of the *idées libérales* against Napoleon's military despotism after 1810 integrated the opposition of the new political movement of the anti-Napoleonic *libéraux* around Benjamin Constant and Madame de Staël.[18] This explained why the *idées libérales* survived the Emperor's defeat in 1815. As a result, the *idées libérales* had by 1815 become a universal concept for continental authors. In Germany and Italy, it was possible to distance them from their Napoleonic origin and use the expression to articulate new constitutional, social and national expectations.

Whereas the English denomination of parties had originated in the seventeenth century and immunized the country's political discourse against continental imports, which meant that 'liberal' was only slowly and reluctantly integrated into an already-existing political nomenclature, the semantic import of 'liberal' coined by the French Revolution and Napoleon was essential for German contemporaries.[19] In the member states of the Confederation of the Rhine, a new language policy was directed by the French authorities, by which the *idées libérales* and the *constitution libérale* found their way into German journals and newspapers. The *idées libérales*, after 1815 translated into *liberale Ideen* as a semantic basis for 'liberalism' after 1820, indicated the overall demand for both national unity and constitutional progress in Germany. When German authors looked at French debates, their translation changed from a mere imitation of the concept to its application to a particular situation outside France. An excellent example for the importance of interpretative adaptation was Johann Christoph von Aretin's translation of a contemporary French article on 'Les idées libérales' published in 1814.[20] In his translation, Aretin applied the French concept to his own German background and the political and national situation of the German states at the end of the Napoleonic Wars.[21] He paid particular attention to the idea of a constitution as the incarnation of a new balance between monarchy and people. Where the French text spoke of *civilisation* as the main criterion behind liberty, Aretin used the German *Bildung*, which had a much more socially exclusive meaning. In the same way, the concept of 'nation' had very different connotations in France and Germany at that time. Whereas French semantics oscillated between the nation's revolutionary sovereignty and the nation as represented by a constitutional monarch, the German expectation was to establish a constitutional nation-state that by 1815 already existed in France.[22] Similarly different connotations lie behind the concept of *gouvernement*. Whereas the French author explicitly acknowledged the existence of an institutionalized opposition in a national parliament, Aretin could only focus on public opinion as a source of political legitimacy and an instrument with which to counterbalance the dangers of despotic rule, since a German parliament did not exist in 1814/15.[23]

France was not the only birthplace of the new concept; again, it was through a complex process of translations that Spanish *liberales* influenced the modernization of other European vocabularies. The political meaning of 'liberal' as a party denomination originated from the first Spanish Constitution of 1812. The adherents of this new constitution called themselves *liberales* and spoke of their opponents who supported the principles of absolute monarchy as *serviles*.[24] It was with regard to the political situation in Spain that the new political adjective found its way into the English political vocabulary. The British example illustrated the limits of translations and the factors that sheltered one political discourse against conceptual imports from outside, because the British import of the Spanish concept was a negative semantic adaptation. In 1816, Lord Castlereagh thought of a purely revolutionary party in the tradition of the French Jacobins when he spoke of the Spanish *liberales*, although their origin had been the fight against French occupation during Napoleon's reign.[25] Until 1818/19, English authors made use of the new political concept – often in the foreign spelling – to describe the domestic political situation of continental countries, thereby underlining its un-English origin. When speaking of British politics, authors continued to refer to the historical party names 'Whig' and 'Tory' or 'radical'. The reluctant import of the new concept 'liberal' pointed back to the experiences of the seventeenth century and the existence of premodern party names, at least until the early 1830s. Only then, the semantic transformation was defined by the complex translation from 'Whig' to 'liberal'.[26] In that way, the history of 'liberal' signified distinct *ancien régimes*.

The British example illustrated an imitating, not an adapting, translation.[27] The continental context dominated the meaning of 'liberal' when used in English political texts well after 1815. Only very reluctantly did the concept appear after 1815, indicating a different tone in British politics. In 1816, Robert Southey spoke of the 'British "liberales"', mixing the Spanish spelling of the party name with an application to the English political scene and stigmatizing the political opponent by the use of the continental adjective.[28] For many Tory authors, 'liberal' served as a negative label with which they could relate their opponents to the revolutionary experiments in France, Spain, Italy or Greece. For them, 'liberal' represented Jacobin terror and Napoleonic despotism under the guise of an apparently progressive label. The import of *libéral* or *liberales* in the British case for a long time indicated a confrontation with continental revolutionary experiences and provoked political resistance.

Only reluctantly was the concept's un-English connotation overcome, making the semantic application of 'liberal' to English politics possible. An important catalyst for the integration of 'liberal' into the English political vocabulary was the founding of Leigh Hunt's *The Liberal, or Verse and Prose from the South* journal in 1822, the short-lived but influential literary journal of the Byron circle that contained articles by Byron and Shelley, often in a critical tone, not only focusing on political developments in the South of Europe but also criticizing the politics of George III and Lord Castlereagh. The title already anticipated the programme: the South of Europe with its revolutionary movements for national independence and political liberty, such as in Italy, Greece and Spain, constituted the background, but Leigh Hunt in his preface of the first edition also pointed to the traditional meaning of 'liberal' in the context of classical education, relating the political implications to the ideal of Roman and Greek literature as the framework of humanity and political liberty.[29] In the course of the public controversy about the new journal, its opponents reacted to the title by publishing a satirical antidote: *The Illiberal! Verse and Prose from the North!!*[30]

The blockade of public debate about reform in British politics, defended until 1815 because of the necessary concentration of national forces in the fight against France, was gradually lifted in 1815. The shift of political attention from foreign affairs to domestic problems provided a fertile ground for the semantic transformation of 'liberal' from an apparently un-English adjective with revolutionary and continental implications into an integral concept of Britain's political language, especially for the reform-oriented Whigs inside and outside Parliament. This included a new context in which the foreign concept's translation helped to develop a new framework for political reforms. The changing atmosphere of public opinion, now considered an important factor in the nation's political life, was reflected in the slow adaptation of 'liberal'. In a letter to John Wilson Croker in 1820, Robert Peel observed:

> Do not you think that the tone of England – of that great compound of folly, weakness, prejudice, wrong feeling, right feeling, obstinacy, and newspaper paragraphs, which is called public opinion – is more liberal – to use an odious but intelligible phrase, than the policy of the Government? Do not you think that there is a feeling, becoming daily more general and more confined – that is independent of the pressure of taxation, or any immediate cause – in favour of some undefined change in the mode of governing the country?[31]

In 1827, Henry Brougham, a leading member of the moderate Whigs among the Edinburgh Reviewers, reflected on the 'State of parties' since the beginning of the 1820s. He made extensive use of 'liberal' to denote a new principle in British politics. Behind the progress of 'liberal opinions' he identified a new concept of foreign policy, advocating national independence abroad and opposing the restorative objects of the Holy Alliance. Already before the transformation of the traditional party names 'Whig' and 'Tory' into 'Liberal' and 'Conservative', a long-term semantic process that was not completed before the 1840s, Brougham concluded that the main ideological antagonism in British politics could no longer be expressed by traditional political labels. These party names had either originated from the seventeenth century, reflecting the factions of the Civil War ('Court' versus 'Country'), the political antagonists of the Glorious Revolution ('Whig' versus 'Tory') or indicating the aspirations of the Stuarts ('Loyalist' versus 'Jacobin') during the eighteenth century or, pointing to the continent, the new party names coined in the course of the French Revolution: 'A new casting also of political sects has taken place; the distinctions, and almost the names, of Loyalist and Jacobin, Whig and Tory, Court and Country Faction, are fast wearing away. Two great divisions of the community will, in all likelihood, soon be far more generally known; the Liberal and the Illiberal, who will divide, but we may be sure most unequally, the suffrages of the Nation.'[32] Unlike most continental party names that had originated from the post–1789 period, 'liberal' as a postrevolutionary concept in Britain must be interpreted with regard to the ideological polarization since the absolutist experiments of the seventeenth century, pointing to a distinct British saddle epoch. This was reproduced in the subsequent premodern party names that did not have an equivalent in continental discourses.

The post–1815 period in continental societies showed a different history of 'liberal' in political vocabularies. Following the Revolution and the Napoleonic Empire, French contemporaries observed an inflation of political party names, reflecting different layers of experiences and polarization with regard to the legacies of the past. Following the establishment of a constitutional monarchy under Louis XVIII in 1814/15, 'liberal' became a tool used to structure the political landscape's complexity. But already in 1819, the distinctive quality of 'liberal' was indirectly questioned when compared to the meaning of 'democratic ideas'. One observer distinguished between two political extremes: those 'known under the name of ultra-royalist' and those under the name of *libéraux*. But since this denomination seemed more 'of an accolade than a qualification ... because there can nonetheless be liberality in the doctrines', the author referred to the concept *démocratique* to highlight the ideological antagonism between what he regarded as the two main political parties of France: 'I would prefer to call democratic the party whose views are opposed to those of the first; because from liberalism – as it is understood – to democracy there is a gentle slope and a quite slippery track.'[33] In France, this semantic connection between 'liberal' and 'democratic' mirrored the consequences of a polarizing revolutionary legacy, which would influence French political culture well after 1815. Identifying with or distancing from the restored monarchy served as a dividing line and allowed the political camps to be structured by a clear antagonism that put 'liberal' close to 'democratic ideas':

> Here we have the two parties that exist and will exist in France like in England: the royalist party, which supports the monarchical ideas and the aristocratic ideas which are inseparable from them; the liberal party, that supports the democratic ideas ... We counted four parties in France, or rather in parliament; the two liberal varieties composed of the more or less pronounced partisans of the democratic ideas, and which are designated under the name of the left and the centre-left; the two royalist varieties, composed of the more or less pronounced partisans of the monarchical and aristocratic ideas, that is to say the right and the centre-right.[34]

This relation between 'liberal' and 'democratic' continued to be of fundamental importance for the future meaning of 'liberalism'. While 'liberal' in France became identified with the constitutional opposition and bourgeois values against a restorative monarchy in the course of the 1820s, it also became increasingly identified with political institutions and not paying enough attention to the meaning of social processes. Towards the end of Napoleon III's Second Empire, Émile Ollivier, the key figure in the transformation from the *empire autoritaire* into the *empire libéral*, used *democratie et liberté* as a programmatic motto to describe the change in the regime's political course during the 1860s.[35] A few months before the empire's collapse, he advocated the strength of a government based on the will of the people as proven in plebiscites: 'Who would rise against such a democratic, liberal, progressive government?'[36] However, being a truly democratic voter could still mean opposing the focus on the social question, which many identified with a democratic party: 'The liberal party confines itself a little too much to the study of pure politics, while the democratic party confines itself to the study of a false social economics.'[37]

The Semantics of 'Liberal' and the Relationship between State and Society in Germany after 1815

In Germany, the import of the new concept 'liberal' provoked resistance after 1815, reflecting the change from politicization to ideological polarization. For Metternich and the German Confederation, 'liberal' denoted a revolutionary direction. Public confidence in the *Liberalität der Regierung*, the 'government's liberality', for instance during the Prussian reform era or in the South German constitutional states of Baden, Württemberg and Bavaria, became increasingly disillusioned after the reactionary change in the political atmosphere following the murder of August von Kotzebue and the Carlsbad Decrees in 1819/20.[38] When it became clear that there would be no further constitutional progress and no more parliaments in the German states, 'liberal' changed into an opposition-label that defined the progressive forces in society. Now the use of the term reflected the widening gap between state and society. At the end of the 1820s, 'liberalism' in Germany signified an uncontested belief in the progress of reason, while the restorative governments represented backwardness and anachronistic forces in history. The 'liberal party' stood for a 'movement party' (*Bewegungspartei*), representing natural progress in history.[39]

Translations from French into German in that period meant an ongoing, implicit confrontation with France. In contrast to the optimistic self-estimation of what 'liberal' should stand for, early definitions of the concept in Germany also reflected a specific uncertainty about the political and social implications of a concrete programme. According to most contemporaries, *wahrer Liberalismus*, 'true liberalism', had to be defended against radical forces in the tradition of the French revolutionary terror.[40] At least until the French July Revolution of 1830, the history of 'liberal' in Germany was a history of interpreting the French Revolution and its consequences in the German states.

When the original connection with a 'liberal government' came under increasing pressure after 1815, the debate within the political opposition intensified. When 'liberal ideas' changed into 'liberalism', the new concept was associated with an ideal of constitutional reform, if possible in cooperation with reform-oriented and enlightened governments. But at the same time, other divisions became visible.[41] The early signs of conflicts between Roman Catholics and liberals anticipated many of the conflict lines of the later Kulturkampf of the 1870s. Although 'Catholicism' and 'liberalism' were not yet deadly antagonistic concepts, ultramontane and Protestant liberals began to oppose each other. Many liberals strongly attacked the traditional alliance between throne and altar and the clergy's antiliberal influence on the people, and increasingly supported a strong anticlericalism.[42] As Paul Pfizer put it in the *Staats-Lexikon*, which was the most important encyclopaedia of South German liberalism prior to the Revolution of 1848:

Indeed liberalism has no need of religion in order to give legally untenable arrogance a false justification. Against the so-called rights of God – a misused term – it has to set a right of truly divine origin, that is the right of reason, in whose claims God will as certainly announce himself as in the positive revelations, which can gain their final justification for a thinking being only by their correspondence with the laws of his reason.[43]

In contrast to Britain, 'liberalism' in Germany neither represented religious minorities, except the Jews, though with significant modifications, nor did it fight for political rights of those groups.

Many of the liberal premises of the second half of the nineteenth century developed between 1820 and 1848. German liberals believed that the future involved a somewhat natural ascent towards liberty and progress.[44] Accordingly, in 1840, Paul Pfizer defined liberalism as 'nothing ... but the transition from the state of nature to the state founded on the rule of law which becomes necessary at a certain stage in human development'.[45] Liberalism would direct 'the state back to what the whole nation in its rational interest wants or must want'.[46] Even if 'institutions and laws might temporarily step backwards ... the ideas of the law of reason will always awake again ... For liberty has now become a necessity and no human power can hope to suffocate these world-shaking ideas, which will find their way through all impediments and barriers until they have passed through all the stages which have been determined by a higher hand'.[47] Sitting in regional parliaments but excluded from political practice and forming governments, early liberals often regarded their movement as the promoter of ideas and not of practical agendas: 'There is in the movements of our time a predominately spiritual quality, a battle of ideas.'[48]

On the other hand, a key element in definitions of 'liberalism' in Germany was the idea of the concrete *Rechtsstaat*, a state founded on the rule of law. In terms of practical reforms, it was identified with constitutional monarchy and not with a republic, a crucial fact that after 1830 distinguished constitutional liberals from democratic radicals.[49] Paul Pfizer placed constitutional monarchy in the middle between radical concepts and mere conservatism, opposing both the 'most horrible radicalism' and the 'untrue and misunderstood liberalism', and at the same time rejecting the 'affected idolatry of the status quo or of things which have already died out'.[50] In a constitutional monarchy, liberals hoped to find a compromise between the 'law of reason and historical law' in order to realize the 'most perfect form of the state according to our historical conditions'. Consequently, 'liberalism' was identified with a written constitution as the basis of the 'idea of the true state', which should exclude 'all arbitrary use of power from above' and below and would found 'the civic relationships on the stable and unchangeable law of morality'.[51] Hence, many observers in Germany did not identify 'liberalism' with the aim to minimize the power of the state, but to establish liberty within the state and through its support. Consequently, the constitution became the centre of all strategies of political reform. According to Carl Rotteck, a people without a constitution was 'in the noble sense of the word no people ... but a sum of subjects'.[52] He argued that 'the constitutional system establishes ... the equal participation in all civic welfare, the equal (legal and juridical) distribution of individual liberty and of legal property and acquisition for all, the equal claim of all who are capable of position and authority and finally the equal obligation to obey the law'.[53] The idea of the state founded on the rule of law implied both political change and the preservation of traditional elements, but no revolutionary concept.

However, this self-positioning of 'liberalism' came under pressure during the 1830s when fierce controversies over the concept's meaning developed against the background of the July Revolution in France and the Hambach Festival in 1832, which demonstrated the split between liberals in regional parliaments and democrats outside parliaments. Despite its territorial fragmentation, the 1830s and 1840s witnessed the evolution of distinct party names in German political discourse, reflecting a broadening spectrum of ideological camps and competing visions of political and social order. In 1843, Karl Rosenkranz pointed to the fact that these new names no longer marked personal or corporatist positions, but different political agendas that allowed mobilization and identification in a changing society. Now 'liberals' formed only one group within this spectrum:

> It is only with such an awareness that the dependence of the individual on the nepotism of the party or family, on the egoism of the guild, the corporation or the estate disappears. The designations of the parties themselves are generalized. Instead of the accidental names of their founders, designations expressing a concept emerge. One speaks of democrats and oligarchs, of republicans and royalists, of liberals and serviles, of radicals and conservatives.[54]

Against this background of ideological polarization and political pluralization during the 1840s, 'liberalism' provoked systematic criticism from the left, coupled with a positive connotation of a 'democratic party' and *Demokratismus*. Arnold Ruge developed one of the most influential critiques of 'liberalism' in 1843.[55] For him, the German people's fight against Napoleonic occupation and military repression before 1815 was the real birthplace of a democratic party in Germany, the predecessor of the 'radicals' in Ruge's own days: 'In the Wars of Liberation a nucleus of the new Germany was present: the radical democrats, whose great effectiveness is evident in the regeneration of Prussia and the whole popular uprising against Napoleon.'[56] Following the course of polemic against constitutional liberals around 1830, especially on the occasion of the Hambach Festival in 1832, Ruge defined 'liberalism' as a bourgeois movement, oriented towards constitutions and political compromises, still hoping for a reform-oriented state to prevent a social revolution, a repetition of violent events as in France, but too narrow to understand the dynamics of the growing proletariat and to respond adequately to the challenges of pauperism as the social question of the day. According to Ruge, 'liberalism' was outdated and had no future if it was not prepared to accept the new ideal of free man and free people.[57] If liberals of the 1840s still insisted on an integrative understanding of liberalism, a movement and a habitus that would embrace all reasonable political trends, avoiding extremes and a revolutionary conflict with existing governments, Ruge demanded liberalism's transformation into a primarily democratic ideology, 'in one word the dissolution of liberalism into democratism [*Demokratismus*]'.[58]

Prior to 1848, the very term 'liberal party' in Germany represented a far-reaching community of ideas and values. Early liberals wanted to maintain their individual independence from any closer organizational structures, which was one major reason for the variety of individual definitions of 'liberalism'. In 1833, Heinrich Laube wrote: 'I am a liberal, but I do not ever want to belong to those who call themselves liberal.'[59] These self-images and the definitions of what 'liberalism' stood for were challenged by the experience of 1848/49. In Germany, the revolution failed to achieve its main aims – constitutional government and national unity – because of a complex interaction of factors, but in the long term, the revolutionary experience intensified a substantial process of progressive politicization, which had a fundamental impact on the meaning of 'liberalism'. The heterogeneity of interests and strategies in different parts of society led to a disintegration and fragmentation of the temporary homogeneity of an oppositional movement in the spring of 1848, resulting in the split between moderate and constitutional 'liberalism' and democratic 'radicalism', and weakening the forces against counterrevolutionary actions. The dual object of achieving political liberty and national unity, of state- and nation-building under increasing time pressures and against the background of Austrian and Prussian moves to open counterrevolution, proved to be a highly important cause for the reduction of political freedom of action after September 1848. But it also included an important political lesson: the gap between constitutional and national intentions on the one hand and the lack of executive power that would have made the Frankfurt Assembly more independent from cooperation with the state governments on the other hand demonstrated, at least in the eyes of many liberals, the widening gap between political ideals and a need to overcome mere opposition policy. Thus, *Realpolitik* could become such a key concept when defining 'liberals' and 'liberalism' in the postrevolutionary decades.[60]

Revolution and *Realpolitik*: The German Experience of 1848 and beyond

In 1848, most moderate and constitutional liberals did not regard themselves as revolutionaries. They halted a movement, which had started on the strects, by legalizing and channelling it through a national parliament. Their temporary freedom of action was based on revolutionary legitimacy in March 1848, but their political strategy rather pointed back to the pre-March experience. Many constitutional liberals focused on the state as motor and guarantee of gradualist reform. Given the experience of 1848, the move towards *Realpolitik* was not inevitable, but, given Otto von Bismarck's successes in overcoming the framework of the German Confederation in 1864 and 1866, it became an ever more attractive option. The promise to overcome mere opposition politics was fundamental in the context of Prussian political successes in the 1860s, based on military victories. But to reduce the semantics of 'liberalism' to the split between 'National Liberals' and 'Progressive Liberals' following the Prussian victory of Sadowa in 1866 would be simplistic. Already in 1865, the *National-Zeitung*, the major Berlin liberal newspaper, argued that the party's way had to be from unity to freedom. It was not a simple sacrifice of freedom, but a different priority of political objects that distinguished the 'liberalism' of 1848 from that of 1866. Those who felt that it was necessary to compromise with Bismarck's government in order to achieve the nation-state first and then reform it according to liberal principles referred to *Regierungsfähigkeit*, the ability to take part in a government, as Hermann Baumgarten explained in 1866.[61] *Realpolitik* expressed the need to accept that ideals bereft of the power to control the executive forces, the government, the bureaucracy and the military, were senseless. The National Liberals, who finally supported Bismarck's Indemnity Bill with which the constitutional crisis over the Prussian military reforms of the 1860s ended, did not act from a position of weakness. They regarded themselves, and indeed were regarded, as the strongest popular force in favour of the national unification which took place in 1871.

The most important and long-term consequence of the Revolution of 1848/49 in Germany points to an intensified semantic antagonism between 'liberalism' and 'democracy', between liberal variations of constitutional monarchy and connotations of social democracy.[62] The dividing line between liberals and democratic radicals was a leitmotif inside and outside parliaments. 'Liberalism' was defined as the only movement capable of finding the middle ground between the extremes of absolutism and democratic self-government.[63] In Heinrich Laube's description of the German National Assembly of 1848, the antagonism between liberals and democratic radicals was the most profound aspect: 'For at least a year the liberals of Germany, the liberals of education and patriotism, were not only internally, but also externally separated from the radicals, to whom an abstract concept called democracy, republic or whatever else had priority.'[64] *Radikale* or *Demokraten* became associated with ideals such as popular sovereignty, solidarity among European peoples, national unity, universal suffrage and social rights. *Demokraten* changed into a positive self-description after 1848/49. In that way, Lorenz von Stein referred to social equality symbolized by universal suffrage as the most relevant trend in politics and society, a process most advanced in France. For Stein, 'social democracy' was a fact transcending the difference between constitution and administration as he saw it in the French Second Republic.[65]

What made the semantic gulf between 'liberal' and 'democratic' still wider had to do with the influence of Karl Marx and Friedrich Engels. For them, real democracy could be found only in communism, and the Revolution of 1848/49 signified a merely temporary alliance between workers and petty bourgeois democrats, as demonstrated in France. In their eyes, the concept of 'democracy' also allowed self-positioning in the historical process; hence, 'pure democracy' would be transformed into 'social democracy' and later into the dictatorship of the proletariat, which would then embody democracy in a communist society.[66] This interpretation proved to be influential for the concept's perception among the workers' movement. In 1863, Ferdinand Lassalle wrote about the separation between 'democracy' and 'liberalism': 'Democracy was the unifying bond between the bourgeoisie and the working class. By shaking off and renouncing this name, this unifying bond was cut from this side, and the banner was no longer planted in a democratic, but in a liberal bourgeois, movement.'[67] After this separation from liberalism, the working class could be the sole basis of democracy.

In contrast to this understanding of 'democracy' on the political left, National Liberals and Progressive Liberals maintained a negative connotation of 'democracy' after 1848/49. The concept became increasingly identified with Socialists and Social Democrats after the foundation of the Second German Empire in 1871. The supposed internationalist orientation of Social Democrats and Roman Catholics seemed to challenge the new nation-state's existence. For liberals who regarded themselves as the natural political force behind the emergence of the German nation-state of 1871, the Kulturkampf as well as the antisocialist stereotype influenced their understanding of the concept. A strong indication of this negative perception was the fact that neither 'democracy nor 'democratic' was used for the official party name of liberal parties, nor was either a key aspect in liberals' party programmes before 1918 – with the one exception of a democratic connotation in the South

German 'Deutsche Volkspartei', later the 'Fortschrittliche Volkspartei', which was presented as a fusion between liberals and democrats.[68]

Reformulating 'Liberalism' prior to and after the First World War

However, from the 1880s onwards, discussions over a necessary reformulation of 'liberalism' intensified.[69] Confronted with the consequences of dynamic industrial development and the emergence of an independent and strong party representing the working classes' interests, the circle around Friedrich Naumann and his 'Nationalsozialer Verein' sought to bridge the ideological gap between liberalism and the Social Democratic Party (SPD). Naumann openly criticized the fact that German liberals, through their primary focus on constitutional and legal agendas, had never really developed a positive response to modern industrial society and the need to integrate the industrial workers positively. In Naumann's eyes, this also explained the crisis of liberalism's legitimacy, which became obvious around 1900 due to continuously decreasing electoral support in general elections. A merely political, constitutional or legal definition of progress, which had dominated the liberal paradigm of the pre- and post–1848 period, would not gain liberalism any popularity.[70] Naumann's premise was derived from his experiences of Christian Socialism, which, under the influence of Germany's dynamic industrial development in the 1870s and 1880s, had sought reconciliation between the social classes. As a young theologian under the influence of Johann Adolf Wichern and later as a Protestant minister, Naumann had noticed the social consequences of rapid industrialization. His initial response was not to attack the concept of private property, but a vague anticapitalism, which sought to go beyond both traditional paternalism and to respond positively to the rise of the SPD after the end of antisocialist legislation.[71]

Given the agenda of German National Liberalism and Progressive Liberalism under Eugen Richter in Wilhelmine Germany, there was little common ground between Naumann's position and that of organized party liberalism. For Naumann, German liberalism in general and Eugen Richter's Progressive Liberals in particular represented an inflexible and old-fashioned liberalism of notables ('Honoratiorenliberalismus'), staunchly opposed to any idea of social or economic state intervention. The contemporary criticism of German 'Manchester liberals' referred to the fact that the social expectation of most National or Progressive Liberals was still grounded in the earlier nineteenth century: the bourgeois model of a harmonious middle class in which all members would sooner or later, and as the result of a natural process, become property owners and hence be qualified for active political participation.[72] This model ruled out even modest attempts at social reforms, not to mention the implementation of compulsory social insurance schemes. Despite certain tendencies from the 1890s onwards, which indicated at least the start of a progressive reformulation of 'liberalism', intellectually stimulated by Lujo Brentano and politically fostered by Theodor Barth,[73] social liberalism still provoked widespread resistance among many liberals in Germany. Even in 1896, Ludwig Bamberger could still not see any fundamental difference between the regulation of working hours in bakeries and a state's trade monopoly, as they seemed to stand for the same false principle.[74]

Confronted with the intransigent position of the Protestant churches in Germany, Naumann gave up his Christian Socialist beliefs and began to focus on party politics. His 'Nationalsozialer Verein', modelled after the 'Nationalverein' of the late 1850s, was meant to work as a political stormtrooper, balancing between the political representatives of the working classes and the established parties of Germany's political spectrum. At the same time, Naumann supported Max Weber's nationalist and imperialist position, as formulated in Weber's Freiburg inauguration lecture.[75] Naumann linked the idea of a necessary German expansion to the concept of social reforms in order to redefine 'liberalism'. Liberal imperialism could therefore be directed against the contemporary antisocialist integration policy, the so-called *Sammlungspolitik*. The result was a very ambivalent programme: support of navy armaments and demands of an unrestricted right of workers to form coalitions; an aggressive colonial policy against Britain; and a democratic franchise in all regional and local elections. However, in terms of party politics, this progressively oriented social imperialism had no chance. Naumann's 'Nationalsozialer Verein' remained without major influence among the liberal electorate.[76] Naumann argued that liberalism and socialism were inextricably related to each other by the relevance of democracy in modern industrial societies and strongly advocated a fusion between social liberalism and democracy. What he called in 1901 the 'innovation of liberalism' had to be founded on universal suffrage as a bridge between liberals and Social Democrats. Naumann also demanded a social opening of liberalism that should go hand in hand with Social Democracy becoming a national and integrative party in the German Empire's political system.[77]

These attempts to overcome the semantic antagonism between 'liberalism' and 'democracy' marked an important ideological discourse before the First World War, but they did not change the nature of German politics as represented by political parties in the Reichstag.[78] It took many more years and the experience of the First World War before this trend was taken up again. When war broke out in the summer of 1914, the cultural war between European intellectuals concentrated on different understandings of political cultures, but it was no longer 'liberalism' that served as a key concept in this context, but a negative image of Western 'democracy'. The German 'ideas of 1914' were identified with a particular understanding of culture and community and positioned against the French 'ideas of 1789', associated with mass politics, a fragile republican democracy and a decadent civilization, or against Britain's materialism and cultural decline.

Only after 1918 and against the background of the German Empire's collapse and the need to define a framework for the republic were new attempts made to overcome the semantic antagonism between 'liberalism' and 'democracy'. The German theologian and political observer Ernst Troeltsch offers a particularly interesting example of the attempts to reformulate a German political culture in a radically different political and social context.[79] A staunch supporter of the German 'ideas of 1914' in the summer of 1914, he became much more sceptical during the war. In 1919 and during the debates on drafting a new republican constitution, he insisted that this transformation was more than just the consequence of defeat and revolution in Germany. Instead, it reflected structural processes that had been catalysed by the events of late 1918: 'Democracy is the natural consequence of modern population density combined with the popular education, industrialisation, mobilisation, military reinvigoration and politicisation necessary for its sustenance.' Strongly opposed to the prospect of an October Revolution in Germany, a radical social revolution following the Bolshevik model, Troeltsch took up earlier approaches to reformulate 'liberalism' before 1914 and demanded the acceptance of social democracy as a historical fact – this relates his understanding of the concept to Arnold Ruge's definition in the 1840s and Friedrich Naumann's position around 1900. For Troeltsch, 'democracy' seemed to be 'the only means to lead the reverse class rule, the rule of the proletariat, into the course of a healthy and just state formation and to save the healthy nucleus of a state-preserving socialism'.[80] Democracy, according to him, was not the result of a mere political doctrine, but the consequence of a social process, which had been revealed by war and defeat.

Conclusion: German Semantics of 'Liberalism' in European Comparison

The ideological controversies that characterized the debates about the semantics of 'liberal' and 'liberalism' in early nineteenth-century Germany were a consequence of the fight for political institutions that had been in existence in France or were about to be reformed in Britain at the same time. In Germany, the discussion about 'liberal' and 'liberalism' accompanied the foundation of a political landscape with different political groups that later would become political parties, whereas in France and Britain, this landscape already existed, marked by new party names as developed during the Revolution and the post-Napoleonic period in France, or traditional party denominations as in Britain. The evolutionary transition of this ideological landscape was anticipated by the transformation from 'Whig' to 'liberal', illustrated by John Stuart Mill's juxtaposition between an aristocratic Whig and a utilitarian middle-class understanding of 'liberal'.[81]

In Germany, on the other hand, the attempt to hold on to the concept 'liberal' as the expression of reasonable progress in cooperation with the reform-oriented state stood in contrast to revolutionary violence as exemplified in the eyes of many who accepted the concept 'liberal' as a self-description by France since 1789. This constellation illustrated the disintegration of the German opposition movement after 1830. The lack of concrete political participation in many states of the German Confederation before 1848, and in Prussia in particular, postponed the outbreak of this conflict until 1848, but the semantic distinction between *liberal* and *radikal* already anticipated different strategies and the polarization of semantics. In spite of the optimistic meaning of *liberal* at the end of the 1820s, it was no longer possible to integrate all political interests of a society in transition under this label – this led to ever more reformulations of 'liberalism' vis-à-vis the experience of revolution in 1848, of nation-state-building in the 1860s and 1870s, the problem of imperial expansion and social integration before 1914, and the challenge of war, defeat and the democratic republic after 1918.

In a long-term perspective, the *Weltanschauung* of progress in history and political reason as an enlightened response to 1789 did not fill the ever-widening gap between political and social interests. This led to a far-reaching ambivalence in the history of the concept in Germany in European comparison: ongoing optimism and the belief in natural progress, and the actual defence of 'liberal' and 'liberalism' in the face of conservative and radical groups overlapped. This constellation would continue in the later decades of the nineteenth century and the early twentieth century.

This simultaneous overlapping of noncontemporaneous semantic aspects crystallized the transformation of political language in Germany and distinguishes it from other European examples.[82] The German example with its various historical layers of meanings, of controversies and reformulations, illustrates why Theodor Heuss in 1948 was so sceptical in applying the concept 'liberal' to the name of a new political party whose members saw themselves in the tradition of German liberalism. The concept seemed to be exhausted by its own history. What this sketch of different semantic transformations in European comparison shows is that there is no linear history towards a universal meaning of 'liberal' and 'liberalism'. Instead, the focus on comparison and entanglement between the European variations of conceptual history leads to a complex representation of political landscapes, based on specific experiences of the past and expectations of the future.

Jörn Leonhard is Full Professor in Modern European History at the History Department of Freiburg University. From 2007 to 2012, he was one of the Founding Directors of the School of History of the Freiburg Institute for Advanced Studies (FRIAS). In 2015, he was elected as a member of the Heidelberg Academy of Sciences. His main publications include *Liberalismus: Zur historischen Semantik eines europäischen Deutungsmusters* (2001); *Bellizismus und Nation. Kriegsdeutung und Nationalbestimmung in Europa und den Vereinigten Staaten 1750–1914* (2008); *Pandora's Box: A History of the First World War* (German edn 2014, English edn 2018); and *Der überforderte Frieden: Versailles und die Welt* (2018).

Notes

1. T. Heuss, 'Speech at the Party Founding Conference, 10th/11th December 1948', in Bundesvorstand der Freien Demokratischen Partei (ed.), *Zeugnisse liberaler Politik: 25 Jahre F.D.P.*, Bonn, 1973, 13–15; see also H. Kaack, *Zur Geschichte und Programmatik der Freien Demokratischen Partei*, 3rd edn, Meisenheim, 1979, 12.
2. T. Mann, 'Meine Zeit' (1950), in *Gesammelte Werke*, vol. 11, *Reden und Aufsätze*, part 3, Frankfurt am Main, 1990, 322–23.
3. J. Leonhard, together with A. Doering-Manteuffel, 'Liberalismus im 20. Jahrhundert – Aufriss einer historischen Phänomenologie', in A. Doering-Manteuffel and J. Leonhard (eds), *Liberalismus im 20. Jahrhundert*, Stuttgart, 2015, 13–32.
4. M. Arnold, *Culture and Anarchy* (1869), J. Dover Wilson (ed.), Cambridge, 1971, 63; see also M. Arnold, 'Irish Catholicism and British Liberalism', *Fortnightly Review* 30 (1878), 26–45; M. Arnold, 'The Future of Liberalism', *Nineteenth Century* 8 (1880), 1–18; M. Arnold, 'The Nadir of Liberalism', *Nineteenth Century* 19 (1886), 645–63.
5. B. Jowett, quoted in M. Asquith, *Autobiography*, London, 1936, 110–11.
6. R. Koselleck, 'Richtlinien für das Lexikon politisch-sozialer Begriffe der Neuzeit', *Archiv für Begriffsgeschichte* 11 (1967), 81–99; R. Koselleck, 'Einleitung', in O. Brunner, W. Conze and R. Koselleck (eds), *Geschichtliche Grundbegriffe: Historisches Lexikon zur politisch-sozialen Sprache in Deutschland*, vol. 1, Stuttgart, 1972, xiii–xxvii. For a general overview over the approach of 'Begriffsgeschichte', see W. Steinmetz, 'Vierzig Jahre Begriffsgeschichte: The State of the Art', in H. Kämper and L.M. Eichinger (eds), *Sprache – Kognition*

– *Kultur: Sprache zwischen mentaler Struktur und kultureller Prägung*, Berlin, 2008, 174–97.

7. J. Leonhard, 'Grundbegriffe und Sattelzeiten – Languages and Discourses: Europäische und anglo-amerikanische Deutungen des Verhältnisses von Sprache und Geschichte', in R. Habermas and R. von Mallinckrodt (eds), *Interkultureller Transfer und nationaler Eigensinn: Europäische und anglo-amerikanische Positionen der Kulturwissenschaft*, Göttingen, 2004, 71–86

8. J. Leonhard, *Liberalismus: Zur historischen Semantik eines europäischen Deutungsmusters*, Munich, 2001; J. Leonhard, 'From European Liberalism to the Languages of Liberalisms: The Semantics of Liberalism in European Comparison', *Redescriptions. Yearbook of Political Thought and Conceptional History* 8 (2004): 17–51; J. Leonhard, 'Europäisches Deutungswissen in komparativer Absicht. Zugänge, Methoden und Potentiale', *Zeitschrift für Staats- und Europawissenschaften* 4(3) (2006), 341–63; J. Leonhard, 'Erfahrungsgeschichten der Moderne: Von der komparativen Semantik zur Temporalisierung europäischer Sattelzeiten', in H. Joas and P. Vogt (eds), *Begriffene Geschichte – Beiträge zum Werk Reinhart Kosellecks*, Frankfurt am Main, 2011: 423–48; J. Leonhard, 'Language, Experience and Translation: Towards a Comparative Dimension', in J. Fernández-Sebastián (ed.), *Political Concepts and Time: New Approaches to Conceptual History*, Santander, 2011, 245–72; J. Leonhard, 'Conceptual History: The Comparative Dimension', in W. Steinmetz, M. Freeden and J. Fernández-Sebastián (eds), *Conceptual History in the European Space*, New York, 2017, 175–96.

9. J. Leonhard, 'Translation as Cultural Transfer and Semantic Interaction: European Variations of Liberal between 1800 and 1830', in Martin J. Burke and Melvin Richter (eds), *Why Concepts Matter: Translating Social and Political Thought*, Leiden, 2012, 93–108.

10. Quoted in *The Oxford English Dictionary*, 2nd edn, prepared by J.A. Simpson and E.S.C. Weiner, vol. 8, Oxford, 1989, 881–83.

11. I. Kant, *Metaphysik der Sitten: Metaphysische Anfangsgründe der Tugendlehre. I. Ethische Elementarlehre*, in Königlich Preußische Akademie der Wissenschaften (ed.), *Kant's gesammelte Schriften*, vol. 6, Berlin, 1907, 434; see also I. Kant, *Kritik der Urtheilskraft. 1. Theil: Kritik der ästhetischen Urtheilskraft, Kant's gesammelte Schriften*, vol. 5, Berlin, 1913, 268.

12. I. Kant, *Kritik der Urtheilskraft, 1. Theil: Kritik der ästhetischen Urtheilskraft, Kant's gesammelte Schriften*, vol. 5, Berlin, 1913, 268.

13. E. Sieyès, *Qu'est-ce que le tiers état? (1789), précédé de l'Essai sur les privilèges. Édition critique avec une introduction par Edmé Champion*, Paris, 1888, 42.

14. See e.g. P. Vergani, *Le Idee Liberali: Ultimo rifugio dei nemici della religione e del trono*, Genoa, 1816, 2nd edn 1817, 3rd edn Turin, 1821; see J. Leonhard, 'Italia liberale und Italia cattolica: Historisch-semantische Ursprünge eines ideologischen Antagonismus im frühen italienischen Risorgimento', *Quellen und Forschungen aus italienischen Archiven und Bibliotheken* 80 (2000), 495–542.

15. J. Leonhard, '"1789 fait la ligne de demarcation": Von den napoleonischen idées libérales zum ideologischen Richtungsbegriff libéralisme in Frankreich bis 1850', *Jahrbuch zur Liberalismus-Forschung* 11 (1999), 67–105.

16. 'Proclamation du général en chef Bonaparte'. Le 19 brumaire, 11 heures du soir, *Le Diplomate* xvi, Tridi 23 Brumaire, an VIII de la République française (13 November 1799); see also P.J.B. Buchez and P.C. Roux, *Histoire parlementaire de la Révolution française ou journal des assemblées nationales depuis 1789 jusqu'en 1815*, vol. 38, Paris, 1838, 257.

17. [L.A.F. de Bourrienne] *Mémoires de M. de Bourrienne, ministre d'état; sur Napoléon, le directoire, le consulat, l'empire et la restauration*, vol. 3, Paris, 1829, 28.

18. See X. Martin, 'Libéral/Illibéral: Sur l'emploi de ces mots dans les *Travaux préparatoires du Code civil* (1801–1804)', in *Dictionnaire des Usages socio-politiques (1770–1815)*, vol. 2, *Notions-concepts*, Paris, 1987, 45–53.

19. J. Leonhard, 'Von den idées libérales zu den liberalen Ideen: Historisch-semantischer Kulturtransfer zwischen Übersetzung, Adaption und Integration', in M. Schalenberg (ed.), *Kulturtransfer im 19. Jahrhundert*, Berlin, 1998, 13–45.

20. 'Les Idées libérales', in *Le Nouvelliste Français ou Recueil Choisi de Mémoires* xii, Pesth, 1815, 273–82.

21. [J.C. Freiherr von Aretin] 'Was heißt Liberal? Zum Theil mit Benützung eines französischen Aufsatzes in dem *Nouvelliste français*', *Neue Allemannia* i (1816), 163–75.

22. 'Les Idées libérales', 278–79.

23. [Aretin], 'Was heißt Liberal?', 171; 'Les Idées libérales', 279–80.

24. See J.F. Fuentes and J. Fernández-Sebastián, 'Liberalismo', in J.F. Fuentes and J. Fernández-Sebastián (eds), *Diccionario político y social del siglo XIX español*, Madrid, 2002, 413–28.

25. Speech of 15 February 1816, *The Parliamentary Debates from the Year 1803 to the Present Time*, First Series (1803–1820), T.C. Hansard (ed.), vol. 37, 602.

26. J. Leonhard, '"True English Guelphs and Gibelines": Zum historischen Bedeutungs- und Funktionswandel von *whig* und *tory* im englischen Politikdiskurs seit dem 17. Jahrhundert', *Archiv für Kulturgeschichte* 83 (2002), 175–213.

27. J. Leonhard, '"An Odious But Intelligible Phrase": Liberal im politischen Diskurs Deutschlands und Englands bis 1830/32', *Jahrbuch zur Liberalismus-Forschung* 8 (1996), 11–41.

28. *The Life and Times of Henry, Lord Brougham*, vol. 2, London, 1871, 325.

29. [L. Hunt] 'Preface', *The Liberal, or Verse and Prose from the South* (1822), viii–ix.

30. [W. Gifford] *The Illiberal! Verse and Prose from the North!! Dedicated to My Lord Byron in the South!! To be continued occasionally!! As a supplement to each number of 'The Liberal'*, London [1822].

31. Letter of Robert Peel to John Wilson Crocker, 23 March 1820, in *The Correspondence and Diaries of the Late Right Honourable John Wilson Crocker*, vol. 1, Lewis J. Jennings (ed.), New York, 1884, 155–56.

32. [H. Brougham] 'State of Parties', *Edinburgh Review* 46 (1827), 431.

33. *De l'état des partis et des affaires, à l'ouverture de la session de 1819*, Paris, 1819, 2–3.
34. Ibid., 27 and 173.
35. É. Ollivier, *Démocratie et liberté (1861–1867)*, Paris, 1867.
36. É. Ollivier, 'Speech Given on 4th April 1870', in *Annales parlementaires: Annales du Corps législatif*, vol. 3, 309.
37. *Mon Programme: Par un électeur nantais démocrate, anticommuniste, antisocialiste, antiautoritaire*, Nantes, [1869], 20.
38. 'Über Völkerbestimmung', *Allemannia* 7 (1816), 51–52.
39. See e.g. T. Mundt, *Moderne Lebenswirren*, Leipzig, 1834, 33.
40. See W.T. Krug, *Der falsche Liberalismus unserer Zeit: Ein Beitrag zur Geschichte des Liberalismus und eine Mahnung für künftige Volksvertreter*, Leipzig, 1832.
41. J. Leonhard, 'Coexistence and Conflict: Structures and Positions of Nineteenth Century Liberalism in Germany', in P. van Schie and G. Voerman (eds), *The Dividing Line between Success and Failure: A Comparison of Liberalism in the Netherlands and Germany in the 19th and 20th Centuries*, Berlin, 2006, 9–35.
42. R. Muhs, 'Deutscher und britischer Liberalismus im Vergleich: Trägerschichten, Zielvorstellungen und Rahmenbedingungen (ca. 1830–1870)', in D. Langewiesche (ed.), *Liberalismus im 19. Jahrhundert: Deutschland im europäischen Vergleich*, Göttingen, 1988, 223–59, at 242.
43. C. von Rotteck and C.T. Welcker (eds), *Staats-Lexikon oder Enzyklopädie der Staatswissenschaften, in Verbindung mit vielen der angesehensten Publicisten Deutschlands*, vol. 9, 2nd edn, Altona, 1845–48, 717.
44. T. Nipperdey, *Deutsche Geschichte 1800–1866*, 2nd edn, Munich, 1984, 287; see also J. Leonhard, '"Die Zukunft der Geschichte"? – Carl von Rotteck und die Widersprüche des deutschen Frühliberalismus', in S. Gerber, W. Greiling, T. Kaiser and K. Ries (eds), *Zwischen Stadt, Staat und Nation: Bürgertum in Deutschland*, vol. 1, Göttingen, 2014, 373–89.
45. Rotteck and Welcker (eds), *Staats-Lexikon*, vol. 9, 710.
46. Ibid., 714.
47. Ibid., 710.
48. C. von Rotteck, *Gesammelte und nachgelassene Schriften mit Biographie und Briefwechsel*, H. von Rotteck (ed.), vol. 1, Pforzheim, 1841, 157–60.
49. P. Wende, *Radikalismus im Vormärz*, Frankfurt am Main, 1975.
50. Quoted in D. Langewiesche, *Liberalismus in Deutschland*, Frankfurt am Main, 1988, 21.
51. K.H.L. Pölitz, *Die Staatswissenschaften im Lichte unserer Zeit* (Leipzig, 1827), in *Restauration und Frühliberalismus 1814–1840*, Hardtwig Brandt (ed.), Darmstadt, 1979, 176–77.
52. C. von Rotteck, 'Ein Wort über Landstände', in *Schriften*, vol. 2, 407.
53. Rotteck and Welcker (eds), *Staats-Lexikon*, vol. 3, 767.
54. K. Rosenkranz, *Über den Begriff der politischen Partei. Rede zum 18. Januar 1843, dem Krönungsfeste Preußens: Gehalten in der Königl. Deutschen Gesellschaft*, Königsberg, 1843, 18.
55. See Leonhard, *Liberalismus*, 442–57.

56. A. Ruge, 'Selbstkritik des Liberalismus' (1843), in *Sämtliche Werke*, vol. 4, 2nd edn, Mannheim, 1847, 76–116, at 81.
57. Ibid., 116.
58. Ibid.
59. Quoted in O. Ladendorf, *Historisches Schlagwörterbuch*, Strasbourg, 1906, 194.
60. See L.A. von Rochau, *Grundsätze der Realpolitik, angewendet auf die staatlichen Zustände Deutschlands*, Stuttgart, 1859.
61. H. Baumgarten, 'Der deutsche Liberalismus. Eine Selbstkritik', *Preußische Jahrbücher* 18 (1866), 455–515, 575–629.
62. Leonhard, *Liberalismus*, Chapter VI.2 and especially 463–67; see also J. Leonhard, 'Semantische Deplazierung und Entwertung – Deutsche Deutungen von liberal und Liberalismus nach 1850 im europäischen Vergleich', *Geschichte und Gesellschaft* 29(1) (2003), 5–39.
63. See W. Pretzsch, 'Liberalismus', in R. Blum (ed.), *Volksthümliches Handbuch der Staatswissenschaften und Politik. Ein Staatslexicon für das Volk*, vol. 2, Leipzig, 1851, 37.
64. H. Laube, *Das erste deutsche Parlament*, vol. 1, Leipzig, 1849, 118.
65. L. von Stein, *Geschichte der sozialen Bewegung in Frankreich von 1789 bis auf unsere Tage*, Gottfried Salomon (ed.), vol. 3, Munich, 1921, 406.
66. K. Marx, 'Der achtzehnte Brumaire des Louis Bonaparte', 1852, in K. Marx and F. Engels, *Werke*, vol. 8, Berlin [Ost], 1960, 141.
67. F. Lassalle, 'Speech of 19th May 1863', in *Gesammelte Reden und Schriften*, vol. 3, Berlin, 1919, 273; see also W. Conze, R. Koselleck, H. Maier, C. Meier and H.L. Reimann, 'Demokratie', in *Geschichtliche Grundbegriffe*, vol. 1, 821–99, at 869 and 891.
68. F. Naumann, 'Fortschrittliche Volkspartei' (1910), in *Politische Schriften*, Theodor Schieder (ed.), vol. 5, Cologne, 1964, 448.
69. J. Leonhard, 'Progressive Politics and the Dilemma of Reform: German and American Liberalism in Comparison, 1880–1920', in M. Vaudagna (ed.), *The Place of Europe in American History: Twentieth Century Perspectives*, Turin, 2007, 115–32.
70. F. Naumann, 'Der Niedergang des Liberalismus: Vortrag auf der 6. Vertretertagung des Nationalsozialen Vereins zu Frankfurt am Main 1901', in *Politische Schriften*, vol. 4, 215–36.
71. P. Theiner, 'Friedrich Naumann und der soziale Liberalismus im Kaiserreich', in K. Holl, G. Trautmann and H. Vorländer (eds), *Sozialer Liberalismus*, Göttingen, 1986, 72–83; P. Theiner, *Sozialer Liberalismus und deutsche Weltpolitik. Friedrich Naumann im Wilhelminischen Deutschland*, Baden-Baden, 1983.
72. L. Gall, 'Liberalismus und "bürgerliche Gesellschaft": Zu Charakter und Entwicklung der liberalen Bewegung in Deutschland', *Historische Zeitschrift* 220 (1975), 324–56; W.J. Mommsen, 'Der deutsche Liberalismus zwischen "klassenloser Bürgergesellschaft" und "Organisiertem Kapitalismus": Zu einigen neueren Liberalismusinterpretationen, *Geschichte und Gesellschaft* 4 (1978), 77–90.

73. L. Brentano, 'Die liberale Partei und die Arbeiter', *Preußische Jahrbücher* 40 (1877), 112–23; I. Jastrow, *Sozialliberal: Die Aufgaben des Liberalismus in Preußen*, 2nd edn, Berlin, 1894; T. Barth, *Neue Aufgaben des Liberalismus: Nach einer in München am 28. Januar 1904 gehaltenen Rede über Liberalen Revisionismus*, Berlin, 1904; T. Barth, *Was ist Liberalismus? Eine Gegenwartsfrage!*, Berlin, 1905; L. Haas, *Die Einigung des Liberalismus und der Demokratie*, Frankfurt am Main, 1905; *Der Liberalismus und die Arbeiter: Seinen Arbeitskollegen gewidmet von einem Arbeiter*, Berlin, 1906; F. Naumann, *Gegenwart und Zukunft des Liberalismus*, Munich, 1911.
74. Theiner, 'Naumann', 73, and Langewiesche, *Liberalismus*, 195–98.
75. M. Weber, 'Der Nationalstaat und die Volkswirtschaftspolitik' (1895), in J. Winckelmann (ed.) *Gesammelte Politische Schriften*, 3rd edn, Tübingen, 1971, 2–25; W.J. Mommsen, *Max Weber und die deutsche Politik 1890–1920*, 2nd edn, Tübingen, 1974.
76. D. Düding, *Der Nationalsoziale Verein: Der gescheiterte Versuch einer parteipolitischen Synthese von Nationalismus, Sozialismus und Liberalismus*, Munich, 1972, 47–52; Theiner, 'Naumann', 73–74.
77. F. Naumann, 'Niedergang des Liberalismus', quoted in Lothar Gall and Rainer Koch (eds), *Der europäische Liberalismus im 19. Jahrhundert: Texte zu seiner Entwicklung*, vol. 4, Frankfurt am Main, 1981, 254–76, at 258–60 and 262.
78. See e.g. L. Haas, *Die Einigung des Liberalismus und der Demokratie*, Frankfurt am Main, 1905; T. Curti, *Die Reaktion und der Liberalismus: Rede, gehalten in der polizeilich aufgelösten Sitzung des Frankfurter Demokratischen Vereins vom 1. Juli 1878*, Munich, 1912.
79. See J. Leonhard, '"Über Nacht sind wir zur radikalsten Demokratie Europas geworden": Ernst Troeltsch und die geschichtspolitische Überwindung der Ideen von 1914', in F.W. Graf (ed.), *'Geschichte durch Geschichte überwinden': Ernst Troeltsch in Berlin*, Gütersloh, 2006, 205–30.
80. E. Troeltsch, 'Demokratie', August 1919, in *Kritische Gesamtausgabe*, vol. 15, G. Hübinger (ed., in cooperation with J. Mikuleit), Berlin, 2002, 207–24, at 211 and 215.
81. [J.S. Mill] 'Tories, Whigs, and Radicals', *Westminster Review* xxv (1836), 293.
82. See W. Hardtwig, 'Der deutsche Weg in die Moderne: Die Gleichzeitigkeit des Ungleichzeitigen als Grundproblem der deutschen Geschichte 1789–1871', in W. Hardtwig and H.-H. Brandt (eds), *Deutschlands Weg in die Moderne: Politik, Gesellschaft und Kultur im 19. Jahrhundert*, Munich, 1993, 9–31.

Bibliography

Arnold, M. *Culture and Anarchy* (1869), J. Dover Wilson (ed.). Cambridge, 1971.
———. 'The Future of Liberalism'. *Nineteenth Century* 8 (1880), 1–18.
———. 'Irish Catholicism and British Liberalism'. *Fortnightly Review* 30 (1878), 26–45.
———. 'The Nadir of Liberalism'. *Nineteenth Century* 19 (1886), 645–63.
Asquith, M. *Autobiography*. London, 1936.

Barth, T. *Neue Aufgaben des Liberalismus: Nach einer in München am 28. Januar 1904 gehaltenen Rede über Liberalen Revisionismus.* Berlin, 1904.

———. *Was ist Liberalismus? Eine Gegenwartsfrage!* Berlin, 1905.

Baumgarten, H. 'Der deutsche Liberalismus: Eine Selbstkritik', *Preußische Jahrbücher* 18 (1866), 455–515.

Brentano, L. 'Die liberale Partei und die Arbeiter'. *Preußische Jahrbücher* 40 (1877), 112–23.

Buchez, P.J.B., and P.C. Roux. *Histoire parlementaire de la Révolution française ou journal des assemblées nationales depuis 1789 jusqu'en 1815*, vol. 38. Paris, 1838.

Conze, W., R. Koselleck, H. Maier, C. Meier and H.L. Reimann. 'Demokratie', in O. Brunner, W. Conze and R. Koselleck (eds), *Geschichtliche Grundbegriffe*, vol. 1 (Stuttgart, 1972), 821–99.

Curti, T. *Die Reaktion und der Liberalismus: Rede, gehalten in der polizeilich aufgelösten Sitzung des Frankfurter Demokratischen Vereins vom 1. Juli 1878.* Munich, 1912.

De l'état des partis et des affaires, à l'ouverture de la session de 1819. Paris, 1819.

Der Liberalismus und die Arbeiter: Seinen Arbeitskollegen gewidmet von einem Arbeiter. Berlin, 1906.

Düding, D. *Der Nationalsoziale Verein: Der gescheiterte Versuch einer parteipolitischen Synthese von Nationalismus, Sozialismus und Liberalismus.* Munich, 1972.

Fuentes, J.F., and J. Fernández-Sebastián. 'Liberalismo', in J.F. Fuentes and J. Fernández-Sebastián (eds), *Diccionario político y social del siglo XIX español* (Madrid, 2002), 413–28.

Gall, L. 'Liberalismus und "bürgerliche Gesellschaft": Zu Charakter und Entwicklung der liberalen Bewegung in Deutschland'. *Historische Zeitschrift* 220 (1975), 324–56.

Haas, L. *Die Einigung des Liberalismus und der Demokratie.* Frankfurt am Main, 1905.

Hansard, T.C. (ed.), *The Parliamentary Debates from the Year 1803 to the Present Time*, First Series. London, 1803–20.

Hardtwig, W. 'Der deutsche Weg in die Moderne: Die Gleichzeitigkeit des Ungleichzeitigen als Grundproblem der deutschen Geschichte 1789–1871', in W. Hardtwig and H.-H. Brandt (eds), *Deutschlands Weg in die Moderne: Politik, Gesellschaft und Kultur im 19. Jahrhundert* (Munich, 1993), 9–31.

Heuss, T. 'Speech at the Party Founding Conference, 10th/11th December 1948', in Bundesvorstand der Freien Demokratischen Partei (ed.), *Zeugnisse liberaler Politik: 25 Jahre F.D.P.* (Bonn, 1973), 13–15.

[Gifford, W.] *The Illiberal! Verse and Prose from the North!! Dedicated to My Lord Byron in the South!! To be continued occasionally!! As a supplement to each number of 'The Liberal'.* London, [1822].

Jastrow, I. *Sozialliberal: Die Aufgaben des Liberalismus in Preußen*, 2nd edn. Berlin, 1894.

Jennings, L.J. (ed.) *The Correspondence and Diaries of the Late Right Honourable John Wilson Crocker*, vol. 1. New York, 1884.

Kaack, H. *Zur Geschichte und Programmatik der Freien Demokratischen Partei*, 3rd edn. Meisenheim, 1979.

Kant, I. *Kritik der Urtheilskraft, 1. Theil: Kritik der ästhetischen Urtheilskraft*, *Kant's gesammelte Schriften*, vol. 5. Berlin, 1913.

———. *Metaphysik der Sitten: Metaphysische Anfangsgründe der Tugendlehre. I. Ethische Elementarlehre*, in Könglich Preußische Akademie der Wissenschaften (ed.), *Kant's gesammelte Schriften*, vol. 6. Berlin, 1907.

Koselleck, R. 'Einleitung', in O. Brunner, W. Conze and R. Koselleck (eds), *Geschichtliche Grundbegriffe: Historisches Lexikon zur politisch-sozialen Sprache in Deutschland*, vol. 1 (Stuttgart, 1972), xiii–xxvii.

———. 'Richtlinien für das Lexikon politisch-sozialer Begriffe der Neuzeit', in *Archiv für Begriffsgeschichte* 11 (1967), 81–99.

Krug, W.T. *Der falsche Liberalismus unserer Zeit: Ein Beitrag zur Geschichte des Liberalismus und eine Mahnung für künftige Volksvertreter*. Leipzig, 1832.

Ladendorf, O. *Historisches Schlagwörterbuch*. Strasbourg, 1906.

Langewiesche, D. *Liberalismus in Deutschland*. Frankfurt am Main, 1988.

Lassalle, F. *Gesammelte Reden und Schriften*, vol. 3. Berlin, 1919.

Laube, H. *Das erste deutsche Parlament*, vol. 1. Leipzig, 1849.

Leonhard, J. '"1789 fait la ligne de démarcation": Von den napoleonischen idées libérales zum ideologischen Richtungsbegriff libéralisme in Frankreich bis 1850'. *Jahrbuch zur Liberalismus-Forschung* 11 (1999), 67–105.

———. '"Die Zukunft der Geschichte"? Carl von Rotteck und die Widersprüche des deutschen Frühliberalismus', in S. Gerber, W. Greiling, T. Kaiser and K. Ries (eds), *Zwischen Stadt, Staat und Nation: Bürgertum in Deutschland*, vol. 1 (Göttingen, 2014), 373–89.

———. 'Coexistence and Conflict: Structures and Positions of Nineteenth Century Liberalism in Germany', in P. van Schie and G. Voerman (eds), *The Dividing Line between Success and Failure: A Comparison of Liberalism in the Netherlands and Germany in the 19th and 20th Centuries* (Berlin, 2006), 9–35.

———. 'Conceptual History: The Comparative Dimension', in W. Steinmetz, M. Freeden and J. Fernández-Sebastián (eds), *Conceptual History in the European Space* (New York, 2017), 175–96.

———. 'Erfahrungsgeschichten der Moderne: Von der komparativen Semantik zur Temporalisierung europäischer Sattelzeiten', in H. Joas and P. Vogt (eds), *Begriffene Geschichte: Beiträge zum Werk Reinhart Kosellecks* (Frankfurt am Main, 2011), 423–48.

———. 'Europäisches Deutungswissen in komparativer Absicht: Zugänge, Methoden und Potentiale'. *Zeitschrift für Staats- und Europawissenschaften* 4(3) (2006), 341–63.

———. 'From European Liberalism to the Languages of Liberalisms: The Semantics of Liberalism in European Comparison'. *Redescriptions. Yearbook of Political Thought and Conceptional History* 8 (2004), 17–51.

———. 'Grundbegriffe und Sattelzeiten – Languages and Discourses: Europäische und anglo-amerikanische Deutungen des Verhältnisses von Sprache und

Geschichte', in R. Habermas and R. von Mallinckrodt (eds), *Interkultureller Transfer und nationaler Eigensinn: Europäische und anglo-amerikanische Positionen der Kulturwissenschaft* (Göttingen, 2004), 71–86.

―――. 'Italia liberale und Italia cattolica: Historisch-semantische Ursprünge eines ideologischen Antagonismus im frühen italienischen Risorgimento'. *Quellen und Forschungen aus italienischen Archiven und Bibliotheken* 80 (2000), 495–542.

―――. 'Language, Experience and Translation: Towards a Comparative Dimension', in J. Fernández-Sebastián (ed.), *Political Concepts and Time: New Approaches to Conceptual History* (Santander, 2011), 245–72.

―――. *Liberalismus: Zur historischen Semantik eines europäischen Deutungsmusters*. Munich, 2001.

―――. '"An Odious But Intelligible Phrase": Liberal im politischen Diskurs Deutschlands und Englands bis 1830/32'. *Jahrbuch zur Liberalismus-Forschung* 8 (1996), 11–41.

―――. 'Progressive Politics and the Dilemma of Reform: German and American Liberalism in Comparison, 1880–1920', in M. Vaudagna (ed.), *The Place of Europe in American History: Twentieth Century Perspectives* (Turin, 2007), 115–32.

―――. 'Semantische Deplazierung und Entwertung: Deutsche Deutungen von liberal und Liberalismus nach 1850 im europäischen Vergleich'. *Geschichte und Gesellschaft* 29(1) (2003), 5–39.

―――. 'Translation as Cultural Transfer and Semantic Interaction: European Variations of Liberal between 1800 and 1830', in Martin J. Burke and Melvin Richter (eds), *Why Concepts Matter: Translating Social and Political Thought* (Leiden, 2012), 93–108.

―――. '"True English Guelphs and Gibelines": Zum historischen Bedeutungs- und Funktionswandel von *whig* und *tory* im englischen Politikdiskurs seit dem 17. Jahrhundert'. *Archiv für Kulturgeschichte* 83 (2002), 175–213.

―――. '"Über Nacht sind wir zur radikalsten Demokratie Europas geworden": Ernst Troeltsch und die geschichtspolitische Überwindung der Ideen von 1914', in F.W. Graf (ed.), *'Geschichte durch Geschichte überwinden': Ernst Troeltsch in Berlin* (Gütersloh, 2006), 205–30.

―――. 'Von den idées libérales zu den liberalen Ideen: Historisch-semantischer Kulturtransfer zwischen Übersetzung, Adaption und Integration', in M. Schalenberg (ed.), *Kulturtransfer im 19. Jahrhundert* (Berlin, 1998), 13–45.

Leonhard, J., and A. Doering-Manteuffel. 'Liberalismus im 20. Jahrhundert: Aufriss einer historischen Phänomenologie', in A. Doering-Manteuffel and J. Leonhard (eds), *Liberalismus im 20. Jahrhundert* (Stuttgart, 2015), 13–32.

'Les Idées libérales', in *Le Nouvelliste Français ou Recueil Choisi de Mémoires* xii (1815), 273–82.

The Life and Times of Henry, Lord Brougham, vol. 2. London, 1871.

Mann, T. 'Meine Zeit', in *Gesammelte Werke*, vol. 11, *Reden und Aufsätze*, part 3. Frankfurt am Main, 1990.

[Bourrienne, L.A.F. de] *Mémoires de M. de Bourrienne, ministre d'état; sur Napoléon, le directoire, le consulat, l'empire et la restauration*, vol. 3. Paris, 1829.

Martin, X. 'Libéral/Illibéral : Sur l'emploi de ces mots dans les *Travaux préparatoires du Code civil* (1801–1804)'. in *Dictionnaire des Usages socio-politiques (1770–1815)*, vol. 2, *Notions-concepts*. (Paris, 1987), 45–53.

Marx, K. 'Der achtzehnte Brumaire des Louis Bonaparte', in K. Marx and F. Engels, *Werke*, vol. 8, (Berlin [Ost], 1960), 111–207.

Mommsen, W.J. 'Der deutsche Liberalismus zwischen "klassenloser Bürgergesellschaft" und "Organisiertem Kapitalismus": Zu einigen neueren Liberalismusinterpretationen'. *Geschichte und Gesellschaft* 4 (1978), 77–90.

———. *Max Weber und die deutsche Politik 1890–1920*, 2nd edn. Tübingen, 1974.

Mon Programme: Par un électeur nantais démocrate, anticommuniste, antisocialiste, anti-autoritaire. Nantes, [1869].

Muhs, R. 'Deutscher und britischer Liberalismus im Vergleich. Trägerschichten, Zielvorstellungen und Rahmenbedingungen (ca. 1830–1870)', in D. Langewiesche (ed.), *Liberalismus im 19. Jahrhundert: Deutschland im europäischen Vergleich* (Göttingen, 1988), 223–59.

Mundt, T. *Moderne Lebenswirren*. Leipzig, 1834.

Naumann, F. 'Der Niedergang des Liberalismus. Vortrag auf der 6. Vertretertagung des Nationalsozialen Vereins zu Frankfurt am Main 1901', in *Politische Schriften*, ed. by Theodor Schieder, vol. 4 (Cologne, 1964), 215–36.

———. 'Fortschrittliche Volkspartei', in *Politische Schriften*, ed. by Theodor Schieder, vol. 5 (Cologne, 1964), 448.

———. *Gegenwart und Zukunft des Liberalismus*. Munich, 1911.

———. 'Niedergang des Liberalismus', in Lothar Gall and Rainer Koch (eds), *Der europäische Liberalismus im 19. Jahrhundert: Texte zu seiner Entwicklung*, vol. 4 (Frankfurt am Main, 1981), 254–76.

Nipperdey, T. *Deutsche Geschichte 1800–1866*, 2nd edn. Munich, 1984.

Ollivier, E. *Démocratie et liberté (1861–1867)*. Paris, 1867.

———. 'Speech Given on 4th April 1870', in *Annales parlementaires: Annales du Corps législatif*, vol. 3 (Paris, 1870), 309.

Oxford English Dictionary, 2nd edn, prepared by J.A. Simpson and E.S.C. Weiner, vol. 8, Oxford, 1989.

[Hunt, L.] 'Preface'. *The Liberal, or Verse and Prose from the South* (London, 1822), viii–ix.

Pölitz, K.H.L. *Die Staatswissenschaften im Lichte unserer Zeit* (Leipzig, 1827), in Hardtwig Brandt (ed.), *Restauration und Frühliberalismus 1814–1840* (Darmstadt, 1979), 176–77.

Pretzsch, P. 'Liberalismus', in R. Blum (ed.), *Volksthümliches Handbuch der Staatswissenschaften und Politik: Ein Staatslexicon für das Volk*, vol. 2 (Leipzig, 1851), 37-8.

'Proclamation du général en chef Bonaparte', *Le Diplomate* xvi, Tridi 23 Brumaire, an VIII de la République française (13 November 1799).

Rochau, L.A. von. *Grundsätze der Realpolitik, angewendet auf die staatlichen Zustände Deutschlands*. Stuttgart, 1859.

Rosenkranz, K. *Über den Begriff der politischen Partei: Rede zum 18. Januar 1843, dem Krönungsfeste Preußens. Gehalten in der Königl. Deutschen Gesellschaft.* Königsberg, 1843.

Rotteck, C. von. *Gesammelte und nachgelassene Schriften mit Biographie und Briefwechsel*, H. von Rotteck (ed.). Pforzheim, 1841.

Rotteck, C. von, and C.T. Welcker (eds). *Staats-Lexikon oder Enzyklopädie der Staatswissenschaften, in Verbindung mit vielen der angesehensten Publicisten Deutschlands*, vol. 9, 2nd edn. Altona, 1845–48.

Ruge, A. 'Selbstkritik des Liberalismus', in *Sämtliche Werke*, vol. 4, 2nd edn (Mannheim, 1847), 76–116.

[Brougham, H.] 'State of Parties', *Edinburgh Review* 46 (1827), 415–32.

Sieyès, E. *Qu'est-ce que le tiers état? (1789), précédé de l'Essai sur les privilèges : Édition critique avec une introduction par Edmé Champion.* Paris, 1888.

Stein, L. von. *Geschichte der sozialen Bewegung in Frankreich von 1789 bis auf unsere Tage*, Gottfried Salomon (ed.), vol. 3. Munich, 1921.

Steinmetz, W. 'Vierzig Jahre Begriffsgeschichte: The State of the Art', in H. Kämper and L.M. Eichinger (eds), *Sprache – Kognition – Kultur: Sprache zwischen mentaler Struktur und kultureller Prägung* (Berlin, 2008), 174–97.

[Mill, J.S.] 'Tories, Whigs, and Radicals', *Westminster Review* xxv (1836), 281–300.

Theiner, P. 'Friedrich Naumann und der soziale Liberalismus im Kaiserreich', in K. Holl, G. Trautmann and H. Vorländer (eds), *Sozialer Liberalismus* (Göttingen, 1986), 7–83.

———. *Sozialer Liberalismus und deutsche Weltpolitik: Friedrich Naumann im Wilhelminischen Deutschland.* Baden-Baden, 1983.

Troeltsch, E. 'Demokratie', in *Kritische Gesamtausgabe*, vol. 15, ed. by G. Hübinger in cooperation with J. Mikuleit (Berlin, 2002), 207–24.

'Über Völkerbestimmung'. *Allemannia* 7 (1816), 51–52.

Vergani, P. *Le Idee Liberali: Ultimo rifugio dei nemici della religione e del trono.* Genoa, 1816.

[Aretin, J.C. Freiherr von] 'Was heißt Liberal? Zum Theil mit Benützung eines französischen Aufsatzes in dem *Nouvelliste français*'. *Neue Allemannia* i (1816), 163–280.

Weber, M. 'Der Nationalstaat und die Volkswirtschaftspolitik', in J. Winckelmann (ed.), *Gesammelte Politische Schriften*, 3rd edn (Tübingen, 1971), 2–25.

Wende, P. *Radikalismus im Vormärz.* Frankfurt am Main, 1975.

Chapter 3

'Friends of Freedom'

First Liberalisms in Spain and Beyond

Javier Fernández-Sebastián

❦

The aim of this chapter is to provide an overview of the nascent liberalisms in Spain and in the Iberian-American world during the early decades of the nineteenth century, that is, at a crucial moment of the launch of that ideology in Europe and America.

I shall begin by showing how that liberalism in the making was not introduced into the region like an exotic plant, but was more a case of the Euro-American territories of Iberian origin constituting fertile soil for its germination. Employing a range of sources from the time, I will then illustrate the decidedly transnational – and, in the Spanish case, specifically Europeanist – nature of that emerging liberalism, which I will analyse above all as a political movement. I will then go on to describe some aspects of the incipient ideology that inspired it and will characterize those who were constructing that ideology – in other words, the first so-called liberals. It will become clear that the liberal political identity and the word 'liberalism' were initially highly polemic. Therefore, the approach to the meaning of both terms has to be less through the interpretation of doctrinal texts on liberal political theory than via a diversity of sources of different leanings. Hence, we should pay as much or more heed to what was said and written at the time by the adversaries, the antiliberals, as to the writings and actions of the advocates of liberalism themselves (who also displayed a certain degree of eclecticism and doctrinal heterogeneity). By way of conclusion, I will underline two characteristics of that early liberalism that, at first glance, might seem contradictory: on the one hand, the universalism of the first Iberian liberals; and, on the other, the peculiar idiosyncrasy of a movement whose ideology – which in some aspects resembled a fledgling democracy – does not always conform to the conventional vision of nineteenth-century classical liberalism, an ideal type generally inspired by a limited number of Anglophone and Francophone thinkers.

An Early, Diverse and Little-Known Liberalism

The cycle of Iberian revolutions (1808–40) represents the third great wave of Atlantic revolutions after the North American and French upheavals at the end of the eighteenth century (and the Haitian Revolution, connected with the French). However, for reasons not unrelated to the reductionist vision predominant in Western historiography, these are far less well-known or studied historical processes. To form an idea of the magnitude of these events, it is worth recalling that at the beginning of the process of emancipation, the Spanish and Portuguese dominions, inhabited by around 30 million people of differing tongues and races, spread far and wide over immense areas between the Atlantic and the Pacific – from Madrid and Lisbon to California, Chile and the Philippines. This revolutionary cycle began with the crisis of the two Iberian monarchies in 1807/8, accentuated by the Napoleonic invasion of the Peninsula, and might be regarded as over by the late 1830s, with the establishment of representative and constitutional governments, monarchic or republican, in the new states that resulted from the collapse of both empires. Hispanic historiography has conceptualized these processes as a 'liberal revolution'.

Such an intensive sequence of construction of states was unprecedented. Never before had so many republics been established and so many nations designed in so short a space of time.[1] If Spain and Portugal had been the forerunners of European expansion overseas and of modern empire-building, it might be said that Spanish America and Brazil, in the wake of the North American Revolution, were in the vanguard of the processes of dismantling empires and constructing states and republics. Indeed, the Latin American republics are older than nearly all the European ones. Oddly enough, not only is this precociousness in the shaping of liberal and republican languages, institutions and practices rarely acknowledged in the canonical accounts of Western modernity, but the Iberian world – and Latin America in particular – also appears in these narratives as the antimodel and the epitome of backwardness.[2] In fact, as a result of prolonged political instability during much of the nineteenth century, which is often regarded as endemic, by the beginning of the twentieth century, the liberalism of those countries was viewed through a well-established and very negative image, sometimes designated with offensive expressions such as *banana republic*. Joseph Conrad's novel *Nostromo* (1904) provides an accurate reflection of this disdainful evaluation of liberal experiences in the region.

One of the most frequent explanations for this disappointing evaluation is that of those who claimed that liberalism was an exotic plant and that the untimely attempt to transplant these misplaced ideas to the region was always doomed to failure. How could an ideology invented in Europe, conceived by and for Europeans, serve to govern such different, complex, multi-ethnic and mixed societies as the Spanish and Portuguese Americas?

However, some revealing data seems to question this simplistic explanation. Is liberalism really an exclusively European and North American ideology? We know, for instance, that amongst the founders of the first so-called 'liberal party' – formed in the Cortes in Cadiz in 1810 – there were quite a few Hispanic Americans, and the word *liberal*, as the name of a newspaper, appeared earlier in the Cadiz and Lima press than in that of Paris, London, Boston, New York or Philadelphia.[3] We also know that liberal language was widely employed in the Hispanic Atlantic before it became popular in most of Europe, and that even the indigenous communities of New Spain (now Mexico) or certain Afro-American groups in South America made considerable use of constitutionalism and electoral practices to reinforce local self-government or to formulate their wishes and claims. In different regions of Spanish America, one can speak of a flourishing *popular liberalism*, essentially egalitarian and closely linked to people of colour, during much of the nineteenth century (it is a telling fact that the liberals were pejoratively termed *negros* by the most extreme conservatives, both in Colombia and, for different reasons, in Carlist Spain).[4]

Moreover, the development of a global historiography is revealing of unexpected connections. We have been aware for some time of the projection of the Cadiz Constitution in various European and American countries.[5] What we did not know until recently is that in 1822, one of the fathers of liberalism in India, the Bengali Rammohan Roy, 'hosted dinners in the Calcutta Town Hall to celebrate the Iberian constitutions' and provided economic assistance for the Hispanic American emancipation movements. As Bayly has noted, 'India's dawning interest in European concepts of freedom and constitutional government was reciprocated. When Spanish reformers reissued the original 1812 Cadiz constitution', the Spanish Philippine Company gave him a copy of this constitutional text; it was dedicated as follows: 'Al liberalismo del noble, sabio y virtuoso Brahma Ram-Mohan Roy' ('To the liberalism of the noble, wise and virtuous Brahma Ram-Mohan Roy').[6] It was then that 'liberalism' became visible to diverse informed observers, in very distant parts of the world, as a transnational movement that, along with the French flag and the Marseillaise, had elevated the mythical Hispanic constitution to the category of universal symbol of an expansive 'democratic party'. A party formed by 'liberal missionaries' was capable of extending – as a certain author ironically suggests – the thaumaturgic virtues of the Cadiz Magna Carta not only to the American continent, but also to Africa and the Far East.[7] After all, as José M. Portillo has shown, this Spanish charter 'was conceived as a universal constitution, general to all the space that could fall into an idea of a Catholic nation'.[8] This universalist rhetoric – against a Catholic background, one hears the echoes of philanthropy and enlightened cosmopolitanism – had appeared at the time of the beginnings of the uprising of the Spanish against Napoleon.[9] Soon, the first *liberals* would be described by sympathetic members of the press as 'friends of humanity',[10] and one of the leaders of Spanish liberalism called upon the 'Governments of the entire globe' in the name of the 'universal interest of Nations' to seek a just solution to the disputes between peninsular Spaniards and Spanish Americans.[11] 'The true lover of his country is the lover of all countries and all men. He who isolates this love for a people or a nation does not understand his true interests.'[12] 'The universal love of men is a principle of liberalism', we read in a Madrid newspaper of the second constitutional period. The development of sciences and civilization would hopefully permit a significant advance in 'the great task of establishing harmony between nations', gradually eroding 'religious or natural hatred'.[13]

The universal scope of the Spanish liberal cause was especially evident after the intervention of the Holy Alliance in the spring of 1823 to abort the constitutional experiment in the Peninsula. Various voices, both Spanish and foreign, were heard reclaiming the freedom and peace supposedly under threat across the globe. General Quiroga, for instance, declared in a proclamation delivered in Lugo on 6 May 1823 that the Spanish battlefields will be 'the theatre where weapons must decide the great question of the freedom of the World'. Something similar had been said a little earlier by the British MP J. Macdonald in a parliamentary debate. And, indeed, diverse groups of auxiliary troops and militia formed by French, Italians, British, etc. fought on Spanish soil in defence of the constitutional regime, making up what was then called the Liberal Foreign Legion.[14]

In spite of this irenic and humanitarian discourse, the case of this first liberalism is a good example of the dysfunctions caused by the implantation of the emancipatory language of freedom and independence in so vast, multi-ethnic and socially variegated a monarchy as that of Spain.[15] How could the inequality of status, dependence or even slavery be reconciled with the egalitarian language of citizenship? Terms like 'liberalism', 'emancipation' and 'human rights' soon revealed their enormous illocutionary power and almost unlimited expansive capacity, thus becoming concepts of historical movement capable of generating indefinitely new expectations of liberation amongst increasingly broader sections of society. Perhaps this was why, as a Spanish civil servant in Manila noted years later, shortly after a bloody indigenous uprising on the archipelago, the small minority of 'Philippine Spaniards' living there would be 'prevented by circumstances from adopting the liberal system ... with regard to these ... natives'; 'it is essential to avoid', he concluded, 'the formation of liberals, because, in a colony, liberal and insurgent are one and the same word'.[16]

Liberalism in Spain

'What does liberalism mean?' was the rhetorical question asked by an adversary of this incipient ideology in a Spanish newspaper of 1813. The answer could not have been more hostile: 'A system invented in Cadiz in the twelfth year of the nineteenth century, founded upon ignorance, absurd, anti-social, anti-monarchic, anti-Catholic and destroyer of national honour.' Before attempting to argue this denigrating pseudo-definition point by point, the writer lists a series of heretic sects – from Antiquity to Jansenism, not forgetting Lutherans and Calvinists – and concludes that 'Liberalism' is the new heresy of his age.

Not without irony, the anonymous author acknowledges that:

> the word [liberalism] is somewhat pompous, though obscure, for it does not hint at who might have been the inventor of the new sect. But as there is no evidence of such an expression across the centuries, until the Semanarists, Concisos, Gallardos, etc. declared themselves liberals, openly glorying in their liberalism, to them must be attributed this exquisite novelty. However, to avoid errors in the future, it would be more reasonable to call them Quintanistas or Gallardinos [in reference to Quintana and Gallardo], the two patriarchs of this great system.[17]

Thus, according to this journalist – in all probability a provincial cleric of clearly traditionalist leanings – liberalism was a sect and a doctrinal system that was just taking its first steps. It was a 'party' and a political-religious ideology disseminated from Cadiz by a group of parliamentarians, writers and journalists sufficiently skilled in propaganda to attract a considerable number of followers in a short space of time.

Whilst not denying the expertise of the brand new liberal party in the art of accumulating converts, the fact is that the antagonistic propaganda was not far behind. Thousands of articles and pamphlets published in Spain between 1810 and 1814 directed their assaults against liberals and liberalism (in fact, their opponents were those who contributed most towards spreading the word 'liberalism'). Most of these antiliberal texts were written on the defensive and advocated a kind of alliance between the throne and the altar.

They attacked the supporters of the reforms with a belligerence comparable to that employed against the enemy – it should not be forgotten that much of the peninsula was occupied by Napoleon's armies – and sometimes did not hesitate to liken the Spanish revolutionaries to the French, portraying them as a fifth column infiltrated within the patriotic ranks.

All in all, the caricaturesque vision transmitted by this highly partisan literature presents the liberals as a group of frivolous and inexperienced youths, chatterboxes and regular customers of coffee houses, most of them members of the middle classes, fond of imitating foreign customs and institutions, and barely religious, godless even. They could be identified, above all, by the emphatic use of a characteristic vocabulary: 'liberty', 'nation', 'despotism', 'constitution' and 'citizen' were some of their favourite words. Their intellectual leaders, rather than genuine scholars and men of letters, were literary hacks and superficial writers who were more accustomed to reading and writing newspapers and leaflets of little importance than treatises and works of real substance. In a manner not totally coherent with this line of argument, these same liberals were contemptuously branded by their opponents as 'new philosophers', whose political proposals would have been inspired by reading the better known works of Montesquieu, Rousseau and the *philosophes*.[18] According to these critics, Spanish liberalism was but a pale reflection and a late echo of the *Lumières* and the French Revolution, and the Constitution of 1812 was a barely disguised copy of the French Constitution of 1791.

This was not the impression, needless to say, which the liberals themselves had of their group. One of the writers mentioned, Manuel J. Quintana, founder of the principal political newspaper of the time (*Semanario Patriótico* (*Patriotic Weekly*)) and leader of the liberal revolution in Spain, admitted years later in a letter to his friend Lord Holland that 'for me liberty is an object of action and instinct, and not of arguments and doctrine; and when I see it being deposited in the realm of metaphysics I am immediately fearful lest it turn into smoke'.[19] Without forgetting to praise a few 'native philosophers' such as Feijoo, Mayans, Isla, Campomanes and Jovellanos, some foreign observers made similar remarks about the 'enthusiasm of liberty' in Spain as 'a natural sentiment', which has little to do with bookish ideas.[20]

In any case, the analysis of the political texts produced in the Iberian world during these years suggests that we are not talking about an intellectual and speculative liberalism, but rather an ideology of combat, forged in haste to construct an alternative legitimacy in the difficult circumstances affecting both monarchies (and that of Spain in particular). The very actors who carried out the revolution were in turn improvised theorists, albeit that they naturally wove their theories on the basis of traditional political culture, with recourse in addition to certain texts that were widely read throughout the

Atlantic, and drawing inspiration from earlier revolutionary experiences in
Europe and America.

The core of this emerging ideology lay in the notions of liberty and
independence – or national sovereignty – understood as the struggle of individuals and above all of peoples against external and internal despotism.[21] In
Spanish America, especially during the revolutions of independence, homeland liberals were often accused of being insufficiently liberal/generous in
terms of the parliamentary representation of the American population in the
Cortes.[22]

The uses of this ideology-concept very often revolved around the great
metaphors of slavery and emancipation. Thus, the Caracas republican Simón
Rodríguez – Bolívar's tutor – equates the meaning of the nouns *liberal* and
liberator (*libertador*) when he succinctly defined liberalism as 'the set of
opposite ideas to servitude'. According to Rodríguez, *a liberal* is someone
who 'advocates liberty', understood as nondependence, and suggests that the
origin of the concept might have been the *generosity* of those who '*release* or
liberate [someone] from an uncomfortable dependence'.[23]

Although the spokesmen for the counterrevolution maintained, as we
know, that the philosophers of the Enlightenment were ultimately responsible
for the great upheavals of the age – beginning with what occurred in France
in 1789 – and the revolutionaries themselves fuelled this interpretation, the
fact is that historiography has recently questioned this alleged relationship
of cause-effect between the diffusion of certain ideas and the outbreak of the
revolutions. Everything would appear to indicate that, rather than ideas, it
was political circumstances that set them off.[24]

'For European and American Liberty'

There is no doubt whatsoever that the disintegration of the Hispanic world
began with the implosion of its core, not with the explosion of the periphery.
It was the power vacuum in the homeland that triggered the emancipation
movements in the colonies, movements that would not have occurred so soon
or in the same manner without this catalyst and prior condition. More than a
series of nationalist uprisings, this was a complex and multifaceted 'imperial
revolution'.[25]

In this context, the emergence of a 'liberal party' in Spain in 1810 should
be regarded principally as the response to the need to tackle an extremely
serious political situation. The collapse of the monarchy as a result of the
king's captivity placed the notions of legitimacy, sovereignty and representation at the centre of political debate. The written word – multiplied by the
press – and the debates in *juntas* (committees), town councils (*ayuntamientos*)

and congresses spread far and wide a series of very contentious notions (constitution, rights and liberties, public opinion, etc.) that had previously been highbrow terms rarely subjected to public scrutiny.

The champions of more or less radical reforms that would lead to representative government used to refer to themselves as 'friends of freedom', and in Spanish sources they also appear under other labels, such as 'free party' or 'party of the free'. The noun *liberal* as a party designation was applied for the first time in Cadiz in the autumn of 1810. The public attending debates in the Cortes began to apply the word *liberales* to a group of reformist MPs, most of them young, who advocated the freedom of the press, often invoking 'liberal ideas and principles' (an expression already in vogue in much of Western Europe, particularly as a consequence of Napoleonic propaganda).[26]

Shortly afterwards, the liberals disseminated the derogatory term *serviles* (servile party), as an asymmetrical counterconcept that served to stigmatize their ideological adversaries. The poet Eugenio de Tapia, who coined this new political use of the old adjective *servil*, now used as a noun and separated the two syllables with a short hyphen (*ser-vil* = vile person), thus implicitly referred to the absolutists as *vile* people. There then ensued a bitter ideological struggle between both sides, a fierce confrontation that only a few strove to temper.[27] As a result of these propaganda campaigns, the designation *liberal* – and, much more rarely, the term *liberalism*[28] – spread rapidly across mainland Spain and, from there, to America[29] and the rest of Europe (José M. Blanco White, via his newspaper *El Español*, published in London, made a decisive contribution to the diffusion of the noun *liberal* as a new political designation on both continents).[30]

Henceforth, and following a long and intricate political process in which, in the case of Spain, the first constitutional phases (1810–14 and 1820–23) were followed by two restorations of absolutism (1814–20 and 1823–33), in the second half of the 1830s the liberals eventually managed to establish a constitutional regime that, while not without its ups and downs and moments of instability, would continue until well into the twentieth century. The main current of the liberalism that finally prevailed in Madrid in the mid nineteenth century, after a bloody civil war against the Carlists (1833–40), was of a conservative tendency, whilst to their left there emerged a series of diverse rival parties – *progresistas*, democrats, republicans, etc. – for whom the Constitution of 1812 was their principal ideal and political myth and who attained power only on a few occasions (usually by means of revolutions and for short periods of time).

Almost from the beginning, ideologically speaking, the liberals split into two groups. One, radical – composed of impassioned liberals, later known as *progresistas* (progressives) – inclined towards the use of insurrectional channels, was generally in favour of the existence of a single legislative assembly, open to the extension of the public sphere to include the middle and popular classes. Another, conservative – monarchic-constitutional, moderate – linked to the upper classes and to the intellectual elites, was more concerned with order and civil rights than with the extension of political liberties, respectful of tradition, in favour of bicameralism and anxious to put an end to the revolution.[31]

For several decades, both groups shared a handful of clichés – the spirit of the age, the advance of civilization or the need to reconcile liberty and order, for example – and a constellation of concepts. Furthermore, the concepts that integrated it were not only interpreted in different ways, but the significance that each group attributed to each conceptual item also varied considerably between conservatives and progressives. Whilst for the latter, the most frequently invoked notions were liberty and equality, independence, progress and national sovereignty, the conservatives preferred to insist upon negative liberty, property, law and order.

This distinction between two liberalisms, one positive, 'organizing' and respectable, which generally favoured the English model, and the other revolutionary – branded by its adversaries as disruptive and 'democratic' – which tended to be associated with French Jacobinism, would be at the root of endless polemics throughout the century. Needless to say, the advocates of both versions claimed to embody 'true' liberalism, attributing the 'false' one to their opponents. In Spain, this rupture took place during the 1820–23 Liberal Triennium, a moment that witnessed, via those returned from exile, most of them Francophiles (*afrancesados*), the systematic reception of the theories of Constant, Daunou, Guizot and the French doctrinaires (and also those of some English authors, especially the utilitarianism of Bentham, who in those days had numerous followers and correspondents in the Iberian worlds and beyond, thus contributing to the expansion of constitutional ideas throughout much of the world).[32]

It should be stressed that the experiences of exile – mainly in London and Paris, but also in Philadelphia, New York and other North American cities – were fundamental not only to the ideological evolution of the Iberian liberals (generally in a conservative direction), but also vis-à-vis the reinforcement of a kind of 'liberal internationalism'.[33] One detects the formation of a certain 'Iberian-American community' of liberals, sometimes invoked by several Atlantic figures of the age, such as Navarre's Javier Mina, the Guayaquilean Vicente Rocafuerte, the Veracruzan Manuel de Gorostiza and the Tucuman Bernardo de Monteagudo, to name but a few. The latter, in a posthumous essay published in Lima in which he proclaims the need for a General Federation of Hispanic-American States, appealed 'to all those who form the liberal party in both hemispheres' to fight together against European legitimism and in defence of the newly gained independences.[34]

At the same time, the departure into exile of thousands of liberals from all over the Hispanic world – many of whom sought refuge in London – contributed to the internationalization of a group of activists who described themselves as 'friends of European and American liberty' and tended to regard themselves as part of a broad epoch-making political movement – a sort of diasporic, transatlantic liberalism – immersed in an Atlantic rather than strictly national context.

In this sense, it is worth insisting on the high degree of internationalization of that first generation of so-called liberals, both in terms of their experiences and with regard to their objectives and their ideology. Following the gradual merging of political languages, a result of the growing interaction between the Atlantic empires (especially in the wake of the Seven Years' War), intellectual contacts and exchanges of every kind – translations, newspapers and pamphlets – prompted by the voluntary or forced travels of Europeans and Americans during those years in fact constituted one of the principal channels towards the internationalization of political vocabularies. Conceptual worlds that for a long time had remained relatively separated from one another seemed to be ever more closely interconnected.

At a time of growing political and intellectual globalization, terms such as 'colony', 'state', 'independence', 'nation', 'empire', 'constitution' and others had started to circulate via translations and a handful of widely read books (Raynal, Robertson, Vattel, de Lolme, de Pradt, Bentham and Paine on the one hand, and de Mier, Flórez Estrada, Blanco White, Roscio and Rocafuerte on the other). Although these words, and the languages and semantic constellations they formed, did not have the same meaning in every language, country or context, it is clear that most agents, be it in English, French or Spanish, tended to employ the same conceptual arsenal: a conceptual arsenal by means of which actors began to articulate several partially overlapping languages – contractualism, jusnaturalism, republicanism and liberalism – in order to express their claims and demands. That said, in light of the asymmetric intellectual flow between English-, French- and Spanish/Portuguese-speaking areas, and between the two Atlantic coasts, there can be little doubt as to the prevailing direction of these semantic transfers: from north to south and from east to west.

The first Spanish liberals were convinced that the 'ancient Spanish Constitution' – i.e. the old *fueros* (territorial laws) of the medieval peninsular kingdoms – had for centuries guaranteed the freedom of the vassals. However, the accession of a foreign dynasty (the Habsburgs) to the Spanish throne at the start of the sixteenth century had brought an end to this freedom and to the representative system upon which it was founded. In Spain, the true tradition, genuinely national, was freedom, whereas despotism was a foreign imposition. The Constitution of Cadiz, in this sense, actually put into effect once again the updated table of freedoms and rights that Spaniards had enjoyed in the Middle Ages. Many nineteenth-century Spanish progressives and democrats would subscribe to this interpretation of national history.[35]

One of the most radical newspapers at the time of the Cadiz Cortes categorically claims, for instance, that King Alfonso X of Castile, 'the father of our old legislation', had already affirmed in the code of the *Siete Partidas* (1265) such *modern* and *liberal* rights as the freedom of assembly.[36] Constitutionalist clerics such as Martínez Marina or Villanueva referred to Aquinas and to scholasticism – Suárez, Vitoria, Mariana, Vázquez de Menchaca, etc. – to construct a liberal political language based upon Catholicism, a language that had much in common with classical republicanism.[37] The republican language of virtue and patriotism appears then not only in combination with incipient liberalism, but is even seen to be compatible with monarchist sentiments.[38]

It should be added that many of the manifestos and proclamations that in those years justified the Spanish insurrection against Bonaparte were addressed in one way or another to Europeans as a whole. And, without underestimating the obvious influence of local factors at the start of the rebellion, the liberal leaders always claimed to have fought fiercely in that bloody war (1808–14) for 'the triumph of the European cause'. [39]

Iberian, European and Universal Liberalisms in the 1820s

In any case, the various forms of exchange, hybridization and conceptual convergence between different political and linguistic areas, the systematic collaboration between liberals from many different places and the confidence in the future generated by the new philosophies of history created a breeding ground for new political and historical-philosophical concepts that transcended national frontiers and traditional cultural and linguistic boundaries.

On 1 January 1820, Colonel Rafael del Riego rose up in arms in the south of Spain at the head of an expeditionary army and demanded that King Ferdinand VII re-establish the Constitution of 1812. The success of this rebellion would accelerate the independence processes in America, whilst lending considerable momentum to the liberal movements in Europe. The revolution, which would soon spread to Porto, Naples and Turin (also, later, to St Petersburg), exalted the Constitution of Cadiz,[40] and in 1821 was injected with further momentum by the Greek uprising against the Turks, which had a huge impact across all of Europe.

Some European and American liberals – several of them Hispanic – began to see themselves as part of a great transnational, multisecular movement and developed a historical narrative, epic in tone, aimed at reinforcing that progressive, triumphant identity. There now emerged such all-encompassing concepts as 'European liberalism', 'American liberalism' and even 'universal liberalism'. Conveniently historicized, blessed with a prestigious past and a promising future, liberalism began to identify itself during those years with the great march of Western civilization towards a degree of liberty and increasing perfection that would eventually embrace the whole of the planet.[41] We can read in a brochure from that period that: 'Liberal opinions form the spirit of our age.'[42]

The emphasis upon the deep indigenous roots of Spanish liberalism did not prevent its followers from seeing themselves as part of the great European liberal movement, even of the ecumenical current of 'universal liberalism'.[43] Various foreign refugees in Spain between 1820 and 1823 founded liberal newspapers of a clearly continental vocation, like *L'Écho de l'Europe* (Madrid, 1821) or *El Europeo* (Barcelona, 1823–24), which employed Spanish, Italian and English writers.

'The entire universe is energetically shaking the heavy chains of despotism', declared Torrijos in one of his last proclamations.[44] For the Spanish liberals of the period, many of whom shared exile – in London, Paris and other cities – with Iberian Americans and Europeans from diverse backgrounds (mostly, though not exclusively, from Mediterranean Europe), the Euro-American horizon could become more significant than the national scene.[45] The position of the Iberian countries is in this sense typically ambivalent, straddling two worlds; as José Joaquín de Mora suggests, Spain belongs to both the 'great European family' and the 'great Hispanic family'.[46] In Madrid in 1821, the Neapolitan General Guglielmo Pepe founded the European Constitutional Brothers, a secret society that years later would bond together the Spanish exiles in the English capital, where the European Constitutional Assembly and the Universal Centre, with branches in numerous countries, also had their headquarters.[47] The triple invocation to one's country, to Europe (or to America, if appropriate) and to humanity is typical in the proclamations of exiles, conspirators and liberal insurgents of those years, when 'European and American freedom' usually appear as an ideal shared by patriots. In his *Proclama a los españoles y americanos* (25 April 1817), the Navarran Javier Mina called for the establishment of 'liberal governments' on both sides of the Atlantic. As far as Europe was concerned, many activists believed that the struggle between the supporters of 'representative government' and those of 'absolute government', between the 'popular' and the 'aristocratic' party, transcended borders. This giant battle on a continental scale would only end, maintained Alcalá Galiano, 'with the triumph of freedom or the triumph of despotism'.[48] The Prefect of Basses-Pyrénées was of a similar mind. In a letter to the French Interior Minister, sent from Pau on 5 February 1820, the Prefet told him that 'the whole of Europe is divided between these two parties': *ultras* and *liberals*. Meanwhile, the royalist general Vicente Quesada addressed the inhabitants of Biscay from his exile in France, pointing out that 'in Europe there are only two nations: one composed of non-believers who under the vain pretext of freedom seek to destroy altars and thrones with the aim of upsetting the social order; the other composed of religious and loyal men, friends and defenders of their legitimate princes'.[49]

That crucial year, 1820, is seen by various political commentators as a genuine 'dawn of freedom':

> The exultation of the Liberals all over Europe was manifest in 1820, a year fruitful in revolutions, which merited it the name 'the first year of freedom's second dawn' ... This second dawn of freedom began with the Spanish, Portuguese, and Neapolitan revolutions, followed by the Piedmontese insurrection, by the irruption of Ypsilanti into Moldavia and Wallachia, by conspiracies in France, and by various insurrections in America. These events ... have all served to keep up the hopes and spirits of the great confederation of European Liberals.[50]

Finally, the revolutionaries declared, the dawn of a new age shone on the horizon. A new era of freedom and happiness commenced that would bury the old demons of despotism, ignorance and arbitrariness, quickly dispelling the shadows of a long night of oppression.[51] Unfortunately for them, these hopes were dashed once again, and in but a few years several thousand liberals were again imprisoned or cast into exile.

Within the ranks of emigrant conspirators in particular, there evolved a strong feeling of fraternity in relation to what came to be known as the 'struggle for European and American freedom'. Thus, the organizers of the failed constitutionalist conspiracy of El Palmar (1819) appealed to the 'new language of Enlightenment' (*nuevo idioma de la ilustración*) and to the 'language of universal liberalism', and, convinced that 'humanity forms one great society', advocated a 'great universal federation' of free nations.[52]

Not long afterwards, in one of the better of the nearly 700 newspapers published in Spain between 1820 and 1823, Alberto Lista wrote that 'liberalism is linked to the essence of European societies ... it is the consequence of all history, ancient and modern ... Freedom is the product of civilisation, of industry and of commerce'.[53] As can be seen, this historization of liberalism, which blindly trusted in the long-term triumph of that movement, went hand in hand with its transformation into a genuinely European (or, on occasions, Euro-American) phenomenon. It was not long before this kind of discourse made its way across the Atlantic: scarcely two years later, we find Lista's article reproduced in a Havana newspaper under the title 'Origin of Liberalism'.[54] This historization accompanied the 'discovery' of the Enlightenment as the necessary prologue to the development of liberalism: the liberal movement of the nineteenth century would have been prepared, ideologically speaking, by 'the enlightenment of the eighteenth century', when 'the first seeds of modern freedom' were sown.[55]

As opposed to the 'terrorism' of the ultra-liberals, equated by the journalists of *El Censor* to the French *jacobines*, the moderates argued that the true liberal was that 'friend of freedom who is at the same time the friend of that power which *suffices* to act as a guarantee of freedom, maintaining social order'. 'There is no freedom in disorder ... [nor] order without freedom', they claimed; liberalism would thus occupy a virtuous middle ground similarly distanced from the 'two vicious extremes': servilism and Jacobinism. Of the three competing parties – liberal, royalist and *exaltado* (radical) – the editors of *El Censor* were of the opinion that the radicals, blinded 'by the fear of tyranny', were promoting 'a kind of popular dictatorship' based upon an anachronistic vision of politics, completely unsuited to modern societies, whilst 'the bona fide *serviles* are thus due to their fear of anarchy'.[56]

In Portugal, there was a debate as to the meaning of the terms *liberal* and *liberalism* similar to the one that ten years earlier in Spain had divided supporters and opponents of this movement. In a leaflet published in the heat of this polemic, a certain journalist wrote that 'from Cadiz to St. Petersburg everybody understands the word *liberal*',[57] whilst his adversary bemoaned the fact that 'Portugal is divided into two sects: *Liberais* and *Corcundas* [hunchbacks]'. According to this traditionalist cleric, the Portuguese constitutionalists took their inspiration from libertinism and followed the ideas of Rousseau.[58]

When it came to compiling a list of the forerunners or founder fathers of liberalism, in the absence of an established canon, each sector offered its own proposals, giving rise to interesting variants. These alternative 'genealogies' depended, on the one hand, on the greater or lesser radicalism of those who traced them, but also on their country or continent of origin. Whilst for the Spanish, the intellectual roots of the Hispanic branch of liberalism invariable included such erudite names as Feijoo, Jovellanos, Aranda, Olavide and Campomanes[59] – alongside those of Montesquieu, Constant, Bentham, and others – the Hispanic-American politicians and intellectuals of the age tended to include in this canon a number of Anglo-American authors. Thus, Vicente Rocafuerte alluded in a leaflet of 1822 to 'the theories of liberalism revealed, explained and developed by Montesquieu, Mably, Filangieri, Constant, Franklin and Madison'.[60] The same author invited South Americans to imitate the 'liberal spirit of the United States' and argued that the promised land of 'true liberalism' must be the New World.

The collapse of the constitutional regime in Iberia in 1823 at the hands of a new French invasion organized by the Holy Alliance, far from slowing down these cosmopolitan tendencies, stimulated them. During the following decade, several thousand expatriate Spaniards, the vast majority of whom belonged to the middle classes – military officers, lawyers, priests, doctors, writers and traders – settled in London and in other English cities, which contributed enormously to the internationalization of Spanish liberalism. Their political, literary and journalistic initiatives played a significant role in the European and American diffusion of liberalism.[61] One of their most conspicuous adversaries complained that the 'liberal émigrés have neither stopped nor stop reproducing their ideas in Paris, London, New York, Bordeaux, Bayonne and elsewhere'.[62]

Juan de Olavarría and other Spanish exiles had high expectations regarding the progress of liberalism throughout the world, particularly in Hispanic America.[63] The historization/futurization of liberalism enabled its supporters – even in troubled times – to align themselves with this strong current, teleologically predestined to triumph, sooner rather than later, throughout the world. By prophetically equating liberalism with the progress of reason and the forward march of humanity, liberal intellectuals were assigning an unstoppable temporal direction to political action. Their rhetorical strategy led them doggedly to claim that reforms must be consistent with the 'spirit of the time' and thus satisfy the alleged needs of future generations. All this resulted in an unusual politicization of time and temporalization of politics. Whilst the supporters of liberalism were moving in the right direction – towards the future – those who opposed them were reactionaries who sought to return society to eras past.[64]

The schism between moderates and radicals (*exaltados*) would reappear in the mid 1830s, when the representative system was finally established in Spain, in the midst of a civil war against the supporters of the old regime. The two wings of liberalism – now called *moderados* and *progresistas* – would oppose one another in the elections of the summer of 1836. Various observers at the time remarked upon the struggle between 'two parties … both liberal', the difference between the two consisting in the fact that one or the other advocated 'more or fewer political rights, more or fewer social guarantees', and, above all, in the greater or lesser speed that each sought to assign to the reform process.[65] Unsurprisingly, the most advanced sector – at a time when liberalism was also triumphing in other European countries, like France, Belgium and Portugal – evinced an absolute faith in progress, set in a philosophy of seamless history: 'History walks towards freedom and there is nothing or nobody that can prevent humanity from reaching that goal.'[66]

Which Liberalism? Which Democracy?

If we compare the habitual usage in the mid eighteenth century of the term 'liberal', in Spanish and in Portuguese, with its dominant meaning one hundred years later, it is clear that in this period of time, a substantial change had taken place. Whilst in around 1750, the adjective 'liberal' generally referred to a generous and magnanimous person, a century later, a *liberal* was someone who advocated political freedom and representative government. This gradual movement *from liberality to liberalism* can be traced via a multitude of documents. All the evidence suggests that the transfer of the term from the moral to the political sphere was the result of a series of little steps rather than one big jump. So, when the adjective liberal no longer referred exclusively to people – be they rulers or commoners – but was also used to describe a government, a system or a constitution, the implication was that those institutions were magnanimously offering citizens the opportunity to act more freely and without hindrance; in other words, less restricted by impediments, ties and regulations.

We should bear in mind that, given that liberalism was not yet a minimally coherent political ideology anywhere in the world, in large parts of Restoration Europe, beginning with France, liberalism was little more than a flag of convenience under which distinct groups, unhappy with the legitimist order, gathered: for example, Jacobins and Bonapartistes, Carbonari and republicans. The contents and evaluation of the term varied enormously depending on the observer's point of view. Thus, the Spanish liberals could be accused, as they were by Lord Castlereagh in a parliamentary speech, of being 'a perfectly Jacobinical party, in point of principle',[67] whereas, also writing from a position hostile to liberalism, Chateaubriand and Vieusseux toned down this condemnation a few years later, alleging that at the end of the day, the Constitution of Cadiz had established a constitutional monarchy and not a republic.[68]

However, in Spain and the Hispanic world, liberalism presented certain distinguishing features that usually rendered it more respectable and moderate in the eyes of conservatives. To conclude, I shall briefly comment upon some of these features of the first Iberian liberalisms that, although divided into several branches and tendencies, share a certain family resemblance. Some of the principal traits are their extraordinary precocity, and the underlying experimentalism and instability, as well as their much more moral and political-constitutional than economic character.[69] Compared with other contemporary liberalisms in Western Europe, I would highlight in the first Iberian liberalisms, on the one hand, the greater weight of religion in the sphere of politics and, on the other, the lesser weight of individualism in law, economics and politics. The process of secularization, which was less intense in these societies than in Protestant countries, evolved over a considerably longer period of time, and the communitarian Catholic vision of the world deeply informed their political cultures. This influence is very apparent in the numerous confessional constitutions in force until well into the nineteenth century.

In the Spanish- and Portuguese-speaking territories, both the Enlightenment and the first liberalism and republicanism were unmistakably Catholic. In a world in which politics were not yet regarded as a completely separate sphere from religion, the Catholic faith was the most important sociocultural link within the populations of both monarchies, and continued to be the principal belief shared by nearly all the citizens of the new republics, which did not hesitate to proclaim Catholicism in their constitutions as the sole national religion.[70] One of the champions of Hispanic-American liberalism, Vicente Rocafuerte, maintained in this sense that, unlike the traditional pattern in Protestant Europe, whereas what began as the affirmation of freedom of consciousness later became political freedom, in the case of Hispanic America it appeared to follow a different course: the establishment of political freedom had come first, and one of its consequences would soon be religious tolerance.[71]

The first Hispanic liberalisms emerged in a traditional universe, in which for centuries the dominant legal culture had accustomed people to contemplating life collectively and acting in corporative and jurisdictional terms rather than on an individualist basis. The Constitution of Cadiz, on the other hand, lays more emphasis on the nation than on individuals, whose rights are confirmed precisely as a result of being members of the national community.[72] The appeal to the rights of the people would be a constant, which to a certain extent eclipsed the rights of individuals almost everywhere, when 1808 heralded the great Atlantic crisis that was at the root of the liberal and independence revolutions. Only later, from the mid 1800s onwards, and following considerable effort and re-adjustment, would the individual come to occupy a primary role in the imaginary and the practices of the Hispanic liberalisms (although invariably from a fundamentally statist perspective – in other words, more focused on state action than on the initiative of civil society).[73]

Furthermore, when comparing Iberian and Anglo-American political cultures, it is obvious that in the latter, there is considerably more presence of the individual and his/her rights at the core of the legal-political system.

It seems clear that the Iberian-American world at the time did not locate the individual at its centre, or at least not in the same way as might be the case in British and American society.[74]

Finally, I would like to highlight two other features of the first Iberian constitutionalisms. their emphasis on the need to guarantee the independence and sovereignty of states and, particularly in the case of Spanish liberalism, their close links with democracy.

The collapse of the monarchic state suffices to explain this strong desire to (re)build an alternative state constitutionalising independence. Thus, the first Hispanic Atlantic constitutionalism sought in general to construct the new institutions upon the sovereignty of the nation-state rather than upon individual rights.[75] This emphasis upon statehood, at a time when the modern concept of the state was itself under construction, explains the relevance of the law of nations (*ius gentium*) – one of the languages that contributed most towards moulding the new status quo during a period when international order tended to be regarded very differently on the old and the new continents.[76] However hard the constitutional monarchies tried to build a bridge between the two shores, the ideological-political distance between the legitimist postulates of the Congress of Vienna and the Pan-American republican ideals of the Congress of Panama of 1826 between the Holy Alliance and the so-called Monroe Doctrine was anything but easy to span. The discourse of dynastic legitimacy was at odds with the language of an incipient republican international law, where more or less 'popular' states were seen as moral persons, free and independent agents on the global stage.

A simple glance at the number of declarations of independence and constitutions produced throughout the world during that Atlantic stage of the 'age of revolutions' shows that there was a distinctly Hispanic initial phase in the implantation of the concepts of independence and constitution. Indeed, the vast majority of all the declarations of independence issued between 1776 and 1825 occurred in the Iberian American region and a very high percentage of the new constitutions, republics and representative governments were born there too.[77] In other words, the international launch of two such characteristic notions of Western political modernity as independence and constitution basically took place in the Iberian American area. As David Armitage observed, in relation to the first point, 'the practice of declaring independence gradually became routine for the wider world in large part because of events in Iberian America' so that 'in this regard, Iberian America's "age of imperial revolutions" anticipated some of the crucial processes in the making of the modern world'.[78]

The disintegration of the Spanish and Portuguese empires, and in particular the tide of revolution of 1820, gave rise to a decidedly internationalist type of political discourse. Although it is true that each of the national variations of 'European liberalism' reveals such clear differential characteristics that it is certainly preferable to speak in the plural of 'European liberalisms',[79] it is no less true that in the third decade of the nineteenth century, we often encounter – not only in the Iberian Atlantic – the notion that liberals throughout the world, especially the Europeans and Americans, form a part of a vast transnational movement, which begins to be known as 'European liberalism'. Whilst some conceived of this unitary movement simply as a more or less empirical 'confederation' of liberal parties,[80] others – above all amongst its supporters – favoured a more sophisticated philosophical inter-pretation of a teleological nature. This understanding considers liberalism to be the necessary result of the historical evolution of Europe from the days of ancient Greece to the most recent revolutionary period, via the Reformation and the Enlightenment.[81] However, theorists, politicians and publicists who wrote these accounts – which were to become increasingly common from the 1830s onwards – were in disagreement over which were the milestones that would mark this long process, particularly when it came to whether or not to include the French Revolution as one of the landmarks of this 'history of freedom'.[82] During the first decades of the nineteenth century, only the most radical political sectors in the Iberian world identified in the French Revolution a source of inspiration for liberal doctrines, practices and institutions. The French experience was generally regarded as an antimodel. However, with the passing of time, the interpretations of the revolutionary decade of 1789–99 in France– and especially of its moderate phases – became less hostile, leading to their integration in the canon of liberalism known as progressive.

With regard to political nomenclatures, in Hispanic America too, where the instability that began with the wars of independence lasted for decades, some factions recurred to asymmetrical counterconcepts of liberals and serviles – initially employed exclusively on the peninsula – to describe them-selves and stigmatize their opponents. This was the case in Mexico and other countries. In Colombia in the second half of the 1820s, the followers of President Santander called themselves *liberals* from legalist and 'civilist' positions, while reserving for their enemies, the supporters of Bolívar, the offensive term *servile* (those who backed Santander branded the Bolivarians as authoritarian and militarist).

While on the right, liberalism was presented as diametrically opposed to *servilism*, on the left, depending on strategies of reasoning and type of discourse, *democracy* could appear either as a concept akin to liberalism or as its antithesis. As the nineteenth century progressed, the names *liberal* and *democrat*, which might on occasions approach one another or even conflate – first, in their enemies' imaginations[83] and, later, in that of their most fervent supporters – began to interact in discourses as two rival but also partly complementary and convergent concepts. And since the first Spanish Constitution of 1812 was generally described in the European context of the age as democratic (owing to the broad franchise and the prevailing power of the legislative chamber), the *doceañista* liberal tradition throughout the century represented a kind of left-wing liberalism with a clear democratic and communitarian stamp. Although Spain's changing political circumstances and the reception of foreign political theories – French doctrinarism, utilitarianism and Krausism – introduced nuance to the relationship between *liberals* and *democrats* and rendered it more complex, [84] some mid-century lexicographers (like Ramón J. Domínguez in his *Diccionario Nacional*, 1846, in the definition of 'liberal') considered the two nouns to be practically synonymous. From the founding of the Spanish Democratic Party in Madrid in 1849 (as far as we know, one of the first parliamentary political groupings to adopt that title in Europe) at least until the Glorious Revolution (September 1868), an increasingly large number of democrats saw themselves as the only genuine liberals.[85] The radical socialist journalist Sixto Cámara argued, for instance, that the time had come for the venerable party 'that was once named liberal' to change its name to *democracy*, which was much more in keeping with the new times.[86] Nonetheless, as minister of Interior Escosura predicted not long afterwards in a speech before parliament, the disputes between rival political parties would not end easily, at least as long as liberalism and democracy continued to be two vague and 'badly defined' words.[87]

The study of the historical semantics of politics in the revolutionary age shows to what extent concepts and political identities – such as liberalism and democracy – were contingent and volatile entities in such a period of continual agitation.

The extreme fluidity of the interpretative models of political life and a certain 'experimentalism' typical of the period ensured that political language circulated with great rapidity from place to place. The dominant direction of this intellectual circulation was from the North Atlantic to the South, and from Europe to America; however, a history of concepts should deal with more than this simple schema and avoid, of course, narrow national scopes. In reality, the dynamic of many of these concepts – republic, liberalism, citizenship, democracy and many more – was clearly transnational. Furthermore, the reception and adaptation of these notions displays substantial variations depending on the different societies, places and times.

Notwithstanding the ultimate provenance of the 'ideas' and readings that occur in a given society, what a conceptual historian must understand is how agents use those ideas and readings, and the language employed within them, to interact with their political reality and mould it to respond to the challenges with which the continually agitated political situation presented them.

Liberalism, which traditional historiography has accustomed us to regarding as 'modern politics' par excellence, characterized by individualism, freedoms, the consent of the governed and the separation of powers, was in the first third of the nineteenth century a hesitant and ongoing concept, movement and ideology. As historians, we should strive to recover the vagueness and the contingency that characterized this notion for the actors of the era, avoiding as far as possible the retrospective attribution of the ideal-typical features of so-called 'classical liberalism'. Investigating what Europeans and Americans a century or two ago understood by 'liberal' and 'liberalism', in the different moments and contexts in which they found themselves, may provide us with a surprise or two. After all, for us – *qua* historians – 'liberalism' is a notion referring basically to the past, whilst for an important sector of the Euro-American elites in the first half of the nineteenth century, 'liberalism' was an imprecise and open concept guide, unequivocally oriented towards the future.

Javier Fernández-Sebastián is Professor of History of Political Thought at the University of the Basque Country. He has published extensively on modern intellectual and conceptual history, with a particular focus on Spain and the Iberian world. He serves on the editorial board of various journals as well as the International Archives of the History of Ideas series with Springer Verlag. He has recently edited the volumes *Political Concepts and Time: New Approaches to Conceptual History* (2011) and *La Aurora de la Libertad: Los primeros liberalismos en el mundo iberoamericano* (2012).

Notes

This text is part of the work of the Research Group, IT615–13 and the Research Project HAR2017–84032-P, financed by the Basque Department of Education, Universities and Research, and by the Ministry of Science and Innovation, Government of Spain (AEI, ERDF, EU), respectively. Several paragraphs in this chapter were previously published in J. Fernández-Sebastián, 'Liberalismo en España, 1810–1850: La construcción de un concepto y la forja de una identidad política', in J. Fernández-Sebastián (ed.), *La aurora de la libertad: Los primeros liberalismos en el mundo iberoamericano* (Madrid, 2012), 261–301.

1. F.-X. Guerra, *Modernidad e independencias: Ensayos sobre las revoluciones hispánicas*, Madrid, 1993; J.E. Rodríguez, *The Independence of Spanish America*, Cambridge, 1998.

2. M. Iarocci, *Properties of Modernity: Romantic Spain, Modern Europe, and the Legacies of Empire*, Nashville, 2006, 4–15.

3. J. Fernández-Sebastián, 'Liberalismos nacientes en el Atlántico iberoamericano: "liberal" como concepto y como identidad política, 1750–1850', in *Diccionario político y social del mundo iberoamericano: La era de las revoluciones, 1750–1850*, Madrid, 2009, vol. 1, 700.

4. A. Annino, 'Cádiz y la revolución territorial de los pueblos mexicanos', in *Historia de las elecciones en Iberoamérica, siglo XIX*, Buenos Aires, 1995, 177–226; J.E. Rodríguez (ed.), *The Divine Charter: Constitutionalism and Liberalism in Nineteenth-Century Mexico*, Lanham, 2007; V. Peralta, 'Los inicios del sistema representativo en Perú: Ayuntamientos constitucionales y diputaciones provinciales (1812–1815)', in M. Irurozqui (ed.), *La mirada esquiva: Reflexiones sobre la interacción del estado y la ciudadanía en los Andes (Bolivia, Ecuador y Perú), siglo XIX*, Madrid, 2005; S. Alda, *La participación indígena en la construcción de la república de Guatemala, s. XIX*, Madrid, 2002; J. Dym, *From Sovereign Villages to National States*, Albuquerque, 2006; R. Buve, 'La influencia del liberalismo doceañista en una provincia novohispana mayormente indígena: Tlaxcala, 1809–1824', in M. Chust and I. Frasquet (eds), *La trascendencia del liberalismo doceañista en España y en América*, Valencia, 2004, 115–35; J.E. Sanders, '"Citizens of a Free People": Popular Liberalism and Race in Nineteenth-Century Southwestern Colombia', *Hispanic American Historical Review* 84 (2004), 277–313; J.E. Sanders, *Contentious Republicans: Popular Politics, Race, and Class in Nineteenth-Century Colombia*, Durham, NC, 2004; M. Echeverri, 'Popular Royalists, Empire, and Politics in Southwestern New Granada, 1809–1819', *Hispanic American Historical Review* 91(2) (2011), 237–69; M. Lasso, *Myths of Harmony: Race and Republicanism during the Age of Revolution, Colombia, 1795–1831*, Pittsburgh, 2007.

5. I. Fernández Sarasola, 'La proyección europea e iberoamericana de la Constitución de 1812', in *La Constitución de Cádiz. Origen, contenido y proyección internacional*, Madrid, 2011, 271–336.

6. C.A. Bayly, 'The Age of Revolution in Global Context: An Afterword', in D. Armitage and S. Subrahmanyam (eds), *The Age of Revolutions in Global Context, c. 1760–1840*, Basingstoke, 2010, 213–14; C.A. Bayly, 'Rammohan Roy and the Advent of Constitutional Liberalism in India, 1800–1830', *Modern Intellectual History* 4 (2007), 26–28.

7. A. Vieusseux, *Essay on Liberalism; Being an Examination of the Nature and Tendency of the Liberal Opinions; with a View of the State of Parties on the Continent of Europe*, London, 1823, 110–12 and 209–10.

8. J.M. Portillo Valdés, 'La Constitución Universal', in J. Á. Junco and J. Moreno Luzón (eds), *La Constitución de Cádiz: historiografía y conmemoración*, Madrid, 2006, 99.

9. *Diario Mercantil de Cádiz*, 29 and 29 June 1808. During the ensuing years, various manifestos clearly intended for an international readership and issued by diverse actors and patriotic institutions from the Hispanic world (from the

Manifiesto a la Europa, February 1809, published by the Spanish Junta Central, drafted by Quintana, to the *Manifiesto al Mundo* in favour of the independence of Nueva España, by Manuel de la Bárcena, in 1821) bore testimony to the vigour and continuity of this universalist rhetoric.

10. *Abeja Española*, 16 December 1812.

11. Á. Flórez Estrada, *Examen imparcial de las disensiones de la América con la España, de los medios de su reconciliación y de la prosperidad de todas las naciones*, Cadiz, 1812, 283. English version by W. Burdon, *An Impartial Examination of the Dispute between Spain and Her American Colonies*, London, 1812.

12. Flórez Estrada, *Examen imparcial*, li–lii. This author had already indicated in the introduction to this text that its goal was 'the general good of the Nation and of all the men in the world' (ibid., 6).

13. *El Censor*, 17 November 1821, 83–84.

14. M.L. Meijide, *Contribución al estudio del liberalismo*, Sada, 1983, 156ff; *Gaceta de Madrid*, 3 August 1824, 390.

15. Article 1 of the Constitution of 1812 defined the Spanish nation as 'the reunion of all the Spaniards of both hemispheres' and in the Portuguese Constitution of 1822, we find an identical clause referring to the neighbouring nation.

16. S. de Mas, *Informe secreto sobre el estado de las islas Filipinas*, Madrid, 1843, 23ff.

17. 'Liberalismo', *El Sensato* (Santiago de Compostela), 1 July 1813, 1553–59. The allusions to Semanarists and Concisos refer to journalists of the *Semanario Patriótico* and to *El Conciso*, two of the better-known liberal newspapers, the former founded by Manuel J. Quintana. Bartolomé J. Gallardo was librarian in the Cortes and author of a famous anti-absolutist satire, the *Diccionario crítico burlesco*, Cadiz, 1811.

18. I have developed this theme in more detail in my article '*Liberales y liberalismo en España, 1810–1850: La forja de un concepto y la creación de una identidad política*', *Revista de Estudios Políticos* 134 (2006), 136–42.

19. Quoted by M. Moreno Alonso, *La forja del liberalismo en España: Los amigos españoles de Lord Holland, 1793–1840*, Madrid, 1997, 30.

20. Count Pecchio, *Anecdotes of the Spanish and Portuguese Revolutions*, London, 1822, 82.

21. C. García Monerris, 'El grito antidespótico de unos 'patriotas en guerra'', in R. Viguera Ruiz (ed.), *Dos siglos de Historia: Actualidad y debate histórico en torno a la guerra de la Independencia (1808–1814)*, Logroño, 2010, 233–56.

22. Fernández-Sebastián, 'Liberalismos nacientes', 708–10.

23. S. Rodríguez, *El Libertador del Mediodía de América y sus compañeros de armas, defendidos por un amigo de la causa social*, Arequipa, 1830.

24. R. Breña, *El imperio de las circunstancias: Las independencias hispanoamericanas y la revolución liberal española*, Mexico City, 2013.

25. J. Adelman, 'An Age of Imperial Revolutions', *American Historical Review* 113 (2008), 319–40.

26. J.M. Queipo de Llano, *Historia del levantamiento, guerra y revolución de España* (1835–37), Madrid, 1953, 303; V. Lloréns, 'Notas sobre la aparición de

liberal', *Nueva Revista de Filología Hispánica* XII (1958), 53–58; A. de Argüelles, *Examen histórico de la reforma constitucional que hicieron las Cortes Generales y Extraordinarias*, London, 1835, vol. I, 476–79.

27. 'Guerra político-literaria entre liberales y serviles, y preliminares de paz que propone un aventurero', *Semanario Patriótico*, 29 August 1811, 125–29; *El Amigo de los Sabios o Ilustración literaria: Quaderno núm. 2. En que es trata sobre el sistema de los Liberales y Anti-Liberales o Serviles, cuyos dos partidos tienen juego entre los individuos que forman nuestras Cortes*, Granada, 1813; *Catecismo liberal y servil, con la deducción de estas doctrinas en la juiciosa que conviene a la felicidad española: Dedicado a la Nación y al Rey*, Segovia, 1814; *Conseqüencias funestas del liberalismo en puntos de moral y religión: Carta a un condiscípulo*, Segovia, 1814; J. de San Bartolomé, *El liberalismo y la rebelión, confundidas por una tierna y delicada doncella*, Mexico City, 1817.

28. The word *liberalismo* began to be used in Spanish in 1811, in French in 1818 (*libéralisme*) and in English in 1819 (see 'liberalism' in the *Oxford English Dictionary*). During the early decades of the nineteenth century, the frequency of occurrences of the terms 'liberalism' and 'liberal party' was considerably greater in Spanish than in any other European language. See in this respect my work 'From Patriotism to Liberalism: Political Concepts in Revolution', in J. Muñoz-Basols et al. (eds), *The Routledge Companion to Iberian Studies*, New York, 2017, 305–18.

29. The brand new '-ism' did not take long to cross the Atlantic: in a Cuban newspaper of 1813, we read that *liberalismo* 'is the fashion and must be followed' (*El Filósofo Verdadero*, Havana, 4 October 1813, 25).

30. However, until well into the 1820s, the label 'liberal' was usually applied exclusively to Spanish and Portuguese activists. The counterrevolutionaries employed other specific nouns for similar left-wing groups in other European countries: French *jacobines*, English *radicals* and Italian *carbonari*. See *El monstruo más deforme, más feroz y venenoso que han visto jamás los siglos: descrito por un liberal desengañado. Carta del liberal arrepentido a su confesor*, Tortosa, 1824, 10.

31. F. Gómez Ochoa, 'El liberalismo conservador español del siglo XIX: La forja de una identidad política, 1810–1840', *Historia y Política* 17 (2007), 37–68.

32. G. Alonso, '"A Great People Struggling for Their Liberties": Spain and the Mediterranean in the Eyes of the Benthamites', *History of European Ideas* 41(2) (2015), 194–204; F. Rosen, *Bentham, Byron and Greece: Constitutionalism, Nationalism, and Early Liberal Political Thought*, Oxford, 1992.

33. As far as the Hispanic Atlantic is concerned, during the first third of the nineteenth century, certain cities served as meeting points for the exiles and centres of ideological radiation for those pioneers of liberalism. With regard to Europe, amongst the cities which placed a fundamental role in this type of political-cultural transfer, we should mention Cadiz from 1810 to 1814; Madrid, Barcelona and Lisbon from 1820 to 1823; London, from 1823 to 1830; and Paris, where many sought exile following the July Revolution (1830–33). See J.L. Simal, *Emigrados: España y el exilio internacional, 1814–1834*, Madrid, 2012; A. Bistarelli, *Gli*

esuli del Risorgimento, Bologna, 2011; M. Isabella, *Risorgimento in Exile: Italian Émigrés and the Liberal International in the Post-Napoleonic Era*, Oxford, 2009, as well as my chapter 'Liberales sin fronteras: Cádiz y el primer constitucionalismo hispánico', in F. García Sanz et al. (eds), *Cadice e oltre: Costituzione, Nazione e Libertà*, Rome, 2015, 465–90.

34. Bernardo de Monteagudo, *Ensayo: Sobre la necesidad de una Federación General entre los Estados Hispano-americanos y plan de su organización*, Lima, 1825.

35. Agustín de Argüelles, *Discurso preliminar a la Constitución de 1812*, L. Sánchez Agesta (ed.), Madrid, 1989, 67 and 96; F. Martínez Marina, *Teoría de las Cortes o grandes juntas nacionales de los reinos de León y Castilla*, Madrid, 1813; J. Varela, 'La doctrina de la Constitución Histórica: de Jovellanos a las Cortes de 1845', *Revista Española de Derecho Político* 39 (1995), 45–79.

36. *El Tribuno del Pueblo Español*, 15 December 1812, 178.

37. F. Martínez Marina, 'Discurso sobre el origen de la monarquía', introduction to *Teoría de las Cortes*, vol. I, 16; J.L. Villanueva, *Las angélicas fuentes o El tomista en las Cortes*, Madrid, 1849 [1811], 71; P. Fernández Albaladejo '"Observaciones políticas": Algunas consideraciones sobre el lenguaje político de Francisco Martínez Marina', in A. Iglesia Ferreirós (ed.), *Estat, Dret i Societat al segle XVIII: Homenatge al Prof. Josep M. Gay i Escoda*, Barcelona, 1996; O.C. Stoetzer, *The Scholastic Roots of the Spanish American Revolution*, New York, 1979.

38. Breña, *El imperio de las circunstancias*, 202–12; *Historia de la guerra de España contra Napoleón Bonaparte, escrita y publicada de orden de S. M.*, Madrid, 1818, xii–xiii; A. Alcalá Galiano, *Lecciones de Derecho Político* (1843–44), Madrid, 1984, 24.

39. J.M. Queipo de Llano, *Historia del levantamiento, guerra y revolución de España* (1835–37), Madrid, 1953, 525.

40. J. Moskal, '"To Speak in Sanchean Phrase": Cervantes and the Politics of Mary Shelley's *History of a Six Weeks' Tour*', in Betty T. Bennett and Stuart Curran (eds), *Mary Shelley in her Times*, Baltimore, 2000, 26–28. During all these events, 'European liberalism was evidence of a unity of visions and intentions'. C. Leynadier, *Histoire des peuples et des révolutions de l'Europe, de 1789 à 1849*, Paris, 1850–1, vol. IV, 292–93 and 300–1; J. Späth, *Revolution in Europa 1820–1823: Verfassung und Verfassungskultur in den Königreichen Spanien, beider Sizilien und Sardinien-Piemont*, Cologne, 2012; J. Ludwig, *Deutschland und die spanische Revolution 1820–1823*, Leipzig, 2013; I.-M. D'Aprile, 'Historias interconectadas de los medios de comunicación y el desarrollo de un discurso constitucional europeo en los albores del siglo XIX', *Ayer* 94 (2014), 49–69.

41. J. Fernández-Sebastián, '*Liberales y liberalismo* en España': 162–65.

42. M.N. Pérez de Camino, *La Opinión*, Bordeaux, 1820: 84.

43. C. Morange, *Una conspiración fallida y una Constitución non nata (1819)*, Madrid, 2006: 374ff. and 444.

44. 20 May 1831; A. Gil Novales, *Del Antiguo al Nuevo Régimen en España*, Caracas, 1986, 205. The Mexican Bernardo Couto claimed in 1835 that the upheaval in

his country formed part of the 'universal movement that today is shaking much of the earth': C.A. Hale, *El liberalismo mexicano en la época de Mora*, Mexico City, 1972, 149.

45. C. Charle, *Les intellectuels en Europe au XIXe siècle: Essai d'histoire comparée*, Paris, 2001, 131.

46. M.P. Asensio Manrique, 'Mora en Londres: Aportaciones al hispanoamericanismo', in D. Muñoz Sempere and G.A. García (eds), *Londres y el liberalismo hispánico*, Madrid, 2011, 112 and 115.

47. AHN, Estado, leg. 3.035-2. Gil Novales, *Del Antiguo al Nuevo Régimen en España*, 184; I. Castells, *La utopía insurreccional del liberalismo: Torrijos y las conspiraciones liberales de la década ominosa*, Barcelona, 1989, 38–40.

48. *DSC*, 10 November 1822.

49. ANF, F7 6642, f. 99. *La Ruche d'Aquitaine*, 14 March 1823. J.L. Simal, *Liberalismo internacional y exilio en Europa, 1814–1834*, Work document 2014/4, Seminario de Historia, Fundación José Ortega y Gasset, Madrid, 2012, 13 and 36. For many French politicians during the Restoration, the Spanish Revolution of 1820 was a re-enactment of the French Revolution, a new 1789 to the south of the Pyrenees; in the Chamber of Deputies, 'the two Frances identify themselves with the two Spains'. See S. Mellon, *The Political Uses of History. A Study of Historians in the French Restoration*, Stanford, 1958, 44–45.

50. Vieusseux, *Essay on Liberalism*, 103.

51. J. Fernández-Sebastián (ed.), *La aurora de la libertad: Los primeros liberalismos en el mundo iberoamericano*. Madrid, 2012, 20ff. See also J. Fernández-Sebastián, 'Las revoluciones hispánicas: Conceptos, metáforas y mitos', in Roger Chartier, Robert Darnton et al. (eds), *La Revolución francesa: ¿matriz de las revoluciones?*, Mexico City, 2010, 131–223 and 204–7; G. Paquette, 'Introduction: Liberalism in the Early Nineteenth-Century Iberian World', *History of European Ideas* 41(2) (2015), 153–65.

52. C. Morange, *Una conspiración fallida y una Constitución non nata*, Madrid, 2006, 374ff.

53. 'Origen del liberalismo europeo': *El Censor*, Madrid, 31 March 1821, 321–41.

54. 'Origen del liberalismo': *Amigo de la Constitución*, Havana, 28 February 1823.

55. *El Liberal Guipuzcoano*, 1 November 1822. 'Los partidos liberales en España', *La América. Crónica Hispano-Americana*, Madrid, 8 November 1857, 1.

56. *El Censor*, 31 March 1821, 341 and 18 August 1821, 7.

57. *Carta ao M. R. P. José Agostinho de Macedo sobre os Constitucionais e Liberais*, Lisbon, 1822, 8.

58. J.A. de Macedo, *O Liberalismo desenvolvido, ou Os chamados Liberais desmascarados e conhecidos como destruidores da nossa regeneraçao*, Lisbon, 1822, 12 and 29.

59. J. M. Blanco White, 'Spain', *Quarterly Review* 57 (April 1823), 240–76; A. Alcalá Galiano, 'Orígenes del liberalismo español', in *Obras escogidas*, Madrid, 1955, vol. 2, 440–45; J. de Olavarría, 'Defensa de las *Reflexiones a las Cortes*' (1820]), in Claude Morange (ed.), *'Reflexiones a las Cortes' y otros escritos políticos*, Bilbao, 2007, 207–44.

60. V. Rocafuerte, *Bosquejo ligerísimo de la revolución de México, desde el grito de Iguala hasta la proclamación imperial de Iturbide*, Philadelphia, 1822, vii.
61. V. Lloréns, *Liberales y románticos: Una emigración española en Inglaterra (1823–1834)*, Madrid, 1979.
62. J.C. Carnicero, *El liberalismo convencido por sus mismos escritos*, Madrid, 1830.
63. J. Fernández-Sebastián, 'Riding the Devil's Steed: Historical Acceleration in an Age of Revolutions', in J. Fernández-Sebastián (ed.), *Political Concepts and Time: New Approaches to Conceptual History*, Santander, 2011, 395–423.
64. For many Hispanic liberals at the time, 'true liberalism consists of the steady trend towards perfect government', in accordance with 'the progress of human reason'; J. de Olavarría, *Reflexiones a las Cortes y otros escritos políticos*, C. Morange (ed.), Bilbao, 2007, 222–23 and 314. According to this philosophy, time itself marches onwards to leave behind obsolete institutions, while the goal of liberalism is 'social improvement'; *El Nivel*, Mexico, 6 and 25 December 1825.
65. *El Nacional*, 14 July 1836; *La Ley*, 3, 4 and 5 June 1836; *El Liberal*, 30 June 1836.
66. *Eco del Comercio*, 20 April 1839.
67. Speech of 13 February 1816, quoted by J. Leonhard, *Liberalismus: Zur historischen Semantik eines europäischen Deutungsmusters*, Munich, 2001, 236.
68. F.-R. de Chateaubriand, 'Politique de l'Espagne', *Le Conservateur* VI (1820), 246–47; Vieusseux, *Essay on Liberalism*, 7–12. Once absolutism had been restored in Spain, comparisons appeared in the reactionary press between 'Spanish liberalism' and the other 'European liberalisms'; *El Restaurador*, 19 November 1823, 1122.
69. F.-X. Guerra, 'El apogeo de los liberalismos hispánicos: Orígenes, lógicas y límites', *Bicentenario. Revista de Historia de Chile y América* 3(2) (2004), 10.
70. J. Fernández-Sebastián, 'Toleration and Freedom of Expression in the Hispanic World between Enlightenment and Liberalism', *Past and Present* 211 (2011), 161–99.
71. V. Rocafuerte, *Ensayo sobre la tolerancia religiosa*, Mexico City, 1831, 17.
72. J.M. Portillo Valdés, *Revolución de nación: Orígenes de la cultura constitucional en España, 1780–1812*, Madrid, 2000; J.M. Portillo Valdés, *Crisis atlántica: Autonomía e independencia en la crisis de la monarquía hispana*, Madrid, 2006.
73. Guerra, 'El apogeo', 19–23.
74. However, see C. Bird, *The Myth of Liberal Individualism*, Cambridge, 2004.
75. Portillo Valdés, *Revolución de nación*.
76. J.C. Chiaramonte, *Nación y Estado en Iberoamérica: El lenguaje político en tiempos de las independencias*, Buenos Aires, 2004, 91ff.
77. A total of nineteen of the principal twenty-one declarations of independence throughout the world between 1800 and 1825 occurred in Hispanic-Portuguese countries; the only two exceptions were Haiti (1804) and Greece (1822).
78. D. Armitage, 'Declaraciones de independencia 1776–2011: del derecho natural al derecho internacional', in A. Ávila, É. Pani and J. Dym (eds), *Las declaraciones de independencia: Los textos fundamentales de las independencias americanas*, Mexico

City, 2013, 19–40. See also D. Armitage, *The Declaration of Independence: A Global History*, Cambridge, 2007.
79. Leonhard, *Liberalismus*.
80. According to Vieusseux, the year 1820 witnessed the activation of a kind of 'great confederation of European Liberals'; Vieusseux, *Essay on Liberalism*, 103.
81. A. Lista, 'Origen del liberalismo europeo', *El Censor*, Madrid, 31 March 1821, 321–41; W.T. Krug, *Geschichtliche Darstellung des Liberalismus alter und neuer Zeit: Ein historischer Versuch*, Leipzig, 1823; G.W.F. Hegel, *The Philosophy of History*, Ontario, 2001.
82. Thus, whilst a widely read French political dictionary openly declared that the French Revolution was 'an explosion of liberalism' and that 'the Principles of 89 are the code of the liberal Gospel of humanity' (A. Nefftzer, 'Libéralisme', in M. Block (ed.), *Dictionnaire général de la politique*, Paris, 1873–74, reproduced in L. Jaume, *L'individu effacé ou le paradoxe du libéralisme français*, Paris, 1997, 555–67 and 563–66), another work of the same period roundly denies that the French Revolution was of a liberal nature (G. de Molinari, *Napoléon III publiciste: sa pensée cherchée dans ses écrits, analyse et appréciation de ses oeuvres*, Brussels, 1861, 54ff). Vieusseux had already expressed the opinion that 'liberalism may be fairly stated to be the offspring of the French revolution' in *Essay on Liberalism*, 6. Twenty years earlier, that was not the opinion of G.M. de Jovellanos, the best-known representative of the Enlightenment in Spain. In his *Memoria sobre educación pública* (1802), de Jovellanos condemns the French revolutionaries, accusing them of having declared war on every 'liberal and benevolent idea'.
83. Thus, a counterrevolutionary manuscript published in Madrid on 12 May 1814 declared that in Spain 'democrats are called liberals' (BNE, ms. 12.931/27).
84. The conservative A. Lista, for example, condemned the 'democratic liberalism' associated with the 'anarchic' Constitution of 1812 as 'a masterpiece of 18th-century philosophical pedantry': *Gaceta de Bayona*, 15 September 1828 and 12 December 1828.
85. One of many examples: see N.M. Rivero, 'La legitimidad del Partido Democrático español', *La Discusión*, Madrid, 15 October 1858; J. Fernández-Sebastián and G. Capellán, "Democracy in Spain, 1780–1868: An Ever Expanding Ideal', in Joanna Innes and Mark Philp (eds), *Re-imagining Democracy in the Mediterranean*, New York, 2018.
86. *La Soberanía Nacional*, 25 November 1855.
87. *DSC*, 31 January 1856. Patricio de la Escosura had just been appointed Minister of Interior in the progressive leader Baldomero Espartero's cabinet.

Bibliography

Adelman, J. 'An Age of Imperial Revolutions'. *American Historical Review* 113 (2008), 319–40.
Alcalá Galiano, A. *Lecciones de Derecho Político*. Madrid, 1984.

————. 'Orígenes del liberalismo español', in *Obras escogidas*, vol. 2 (Madrid, 1955), 440–5.

Alda, S. *La participación indígena en la construcción de la república de Guatemala, s. XIX*. Madrid, 2002.

Alonso, G. '"A Great People Struggling for Their Liberties": Spain and the Mediterranean in the Eyes of the Benthamites'. *History of European Ideas* 41(2) (2015), 194–204.

Annino, A. 'Cádiz y la revolución territorial de los pueblos mexicanos', in *Historia de las elecciones en Iberoamérica, siglo XIX* (Buenos Aires, 1995), 177–226.

Armitage, D. 'Declaraciones de independencia 1776–2011: del derecho natural al derecho internacional', in A. Ávila, É. Pani and J. Dym (eds), *Las declaraciones de independencia: Los textos fundamentales de las independencias americanas* (Mexico City, 2013), 19–40.

————. *The Declaration of Independence: A Global History*. Cambridge, 2007.

Asensio Manrique, M.P. 'Mora en Londres: Aportaciones al hispanoamericanismo', in D. Muñoz Sempere and G.A. García (eds), *Londres y el liberalismo hispánico* (Madrid, 2011), 111–24.

Bayly, C.A. 'The Age of Revolution in Global Context: An Afterword', in D. Armitage and S. Subrahmanyam (eds), *The Age of Revolutions in Global Context, c. 1760–1840* (Basingstoke, 2010), 213–14.

————. 'Rammohan Roy and the Advent of Constitutional Liberalism in India, 1800–1830'. *Modern Intellectual History* 4 (2007), 26–28.

Bird, C. *The Myth of Liberal Individualism*. Cambridge, 2004.

Bistarelli, A. *Gli esuli del Risorgimento*. Bologna, 2011.

Blanco White, J.M. 'Spain'. *Quarterly Review* 57 (April 1823), 240–76.

Breña, R. *El imperio de las circunstancias: Las independencias hispanoamericanas y la revolución liberal española*. Mexico City, 2013.

Buve, R. 'La influencia del liberalismo doceañista en una provincia novohispana mayormente indígena: Tlaxcala, 1809–1824', in M. Chust and I. Frasquet (eds), *La trascendencia del liberalismo doceañista en España y en América* (Valencia, 2004), 115–35.

Carnicero, J.C. *El liberalismo convencido por sus mismos escritos*. Madrid, 1830.

Carta ao M. R. P. José Agostinho de Macedo sobre os Constitucionais e Liberais. Lisbon, 1822.

Castells, I. *La utopía insurreccional del liberalismo: Torrijos y las conspiraciones liberales de la década ominosa*. Barcelona, 1989.

Catecismo liberal y servil, con la deducción de estas doctrinas en la juiciosa que conviene a la felicidad española: Dedicado a la Nación y al Rey. Segovia, 1814.

Charle, C. *Les intellectuels en Europe au XIXe siècle: Essai d'histoire comparée*. Paris, 2001.

Chiaramonte, J.C. *Nación y Estado en Iberoamérica: El lenguaje político en tiempos de las independencias*. Buenos Aires, 2004.

Conseqüencias funestas del liberalismo en puntos de moral y religión: Carta a un condiscípulo. Segovia, 1814.

D'Aprile, I.-M. 'Historias interconectadas de los medios de comunicación y el desarrollo de un discurso constitucional europeo en los albores del siglo XIX'. *Ayer* 94 (2014), 49–69.

De Argüelles, A. *Discurso preliminar a la Constitución de 1812*, L. Sánchez Agesta (ed.). Madrid, 1989.

———. *Examen histórico de la reforma constitucional que hicieron las Cortes Generales y Extraordinarias.* London, 1835.

De Chateaubriand, F.-R. 'Politique de l'Espagne'. *Le Conservateur* VI (1820), 246–47.

De Jovellanos, G. M. *Memoria sobre educación pública* (1802), in De Jovellanos, G.M. de, *Obras completas: XIII Escritos Pedagógicos*, O. Negrín Fajardo (ed.) (Oviedo, 2010), 435–532.

De Macedo, J.A. *O Liberalismo desenvolvido, ou Os chamados Liberais desmascarados e conhecidos como destruidores da nossa regeneração.* Lisbon, 1822.

De Mas, S. *Informe secreto sobre el estado de las islas Filipinas.* Madrid, 1843.

De Molinari, G. *Napoléon III publiciste : sa pensée cherchée dans ses écrits, analyse et appréciation de ses œuvres.* Brussels, 1861.

De Monteagudo, B. *Ensayo: Sobre la necesidad de una Federación General entre los Estados Hispano-americanos y plan de su organización.* Lima, 1825.

De Olavarría, J. 'Defensa de las *Reflexiones a las Cortes*', in C. Morange (ed.), *'Reflexiones a las Cortes' y otros escritos políticos* (Bilbao, 2007), 207–44.

———. *Reflexiones a las Cortes y otros escritos políticos*, C. Morange (ed.). Bilbao, 2007.

De San Bartolomé, J. *El liberalismo y la rebelión, confundidas por una tierna y delicada doncella.* Mexico City, 1817.

Dym, J. *From Sovereign Villages to National States.* Albuquerque, 2006.

Echeverri, M. 'Popular Royalists, Empire, and Politics in Southwestern New Granada, 1809–1819'. *Hispanic American Historical Review* 91(2) (2011), 237–69.

El Amigo de los Sabios o Ilustración literaria. Quaderno núm. 2. En que es trata sobre el sistema de los Liberales y Anti-Liberales o Serviles, cuyos dos partidos tienen juego entre los individuos que forman nuestras Cortes. Granada, 1813.

El monstruo más deforme, más feroz y venenoso que han visto jamás los siglos: descrito por un liberal desengañado. Carta del liberal arrepentido a su confesor. Tortosa, 1824.

Fernández Albaladejo, P. '"Observaciones políticas": Algunas consideraciones sobre el lenguaje político de Francisco Martínez Marina', in A. Iglesia Ferreirós (ed.), *Estat, Dret i Societat al segle XVIII: Homenatge al Prof. Josep M. Gay i Escoda* (Barcelona, 1996), 691–714.

Fernández Sarasola, I. 'La proyección europea e iberoamericana de la Constitución de 1812', in *La Constitución de Cádiz: Origen, contenido y proyección internacional* (Madrid, 2011), 271–336.

Fernández-Sebastián, J. 'From Patriotism to Liberalism. Political Concepts in Revolution', in J. Muñoz-Basols et al. (eds), *The Routledge Companion to Iberian Studies* (New York, 2017), 305–18.

———. (ed.). *La aurora de la libertad: Los primeros liberalismos en el mundo iberoamericano.* Madrid, 2012.

————. 'Las revoluciones hispánicas: Conceptos, metáforas y mitos', in R. Chartier et al. (eds), *La Revolución francesa: ¿matriz de las revoluciones?* (Mexico City, 2010), 131–223.

————. 'Liberales sin fronteras: Cádiz y el primer constitucionalismo hispánico', in F. García Sanz et al. (eds), *Cadice e oltre: Costituzione, Nazione e Libertà* (Rome, 2015), 465–90.

————. 'Liberales y liberalismo en España, 1810–1850: La forja de un concepto y la creación de una identidad política', *Revista de Estudios Políticos* 134 (2006), 136–42.

————. 'Liberalismos nacientes en el Atlántico iberoamericano: "liberal" como concepto y como identidad política, 1750–1850', in *Diccionario político y social del mundo iberoamericano: La era de las revoluciones, 1750–1850*, vol. 1 (Madrid, 2009), 695–731.

————. 'Riding the Devil's Steed: Historical Acceleration in an Age of Revolutions', in J. Fernández-Sebastián (ed.), *Political Concepts and Time: New Approaches to Conceptual History* (Santander, 2011), 395–423.

————. 'Toleration and Freedom of Expression in the Hispanic World between Enlightenment and Liberalism', *Past and Present* 211 (2011), 161–99.

Fernández-Sebastián, J., and G. Capellán. 'Democracy in Spain, 1780–1868: An Ever Expanding Ideal', in J. Innes and M. Philp (eds), *Re-imagining Democracy in the Mediterranean* (New York, 2018), 53–76.

Flórez Estrada, Á. *An Impartial Examination of the Dispute between Spain and Her American Colonies*. London, 1812.

Flórez Estrada, Á. *Examen imparcial de las disensiones de la América con la España, de los medios de su reconciliación y de la prosperidad de todas las naciones*. Cadiz, 1812.

García Monerris, C. 'El grito antidespótico de unos "patriotas en guerra"', in R.V. Ruiz (ed.), *Dos siglos de Historia: Actualidad y debate histórico en torno a la guerra de la Independencia (1808–1814)* (Logroño, 2010), 233–56.

Gil Novales, A. *Del Antiguo al Nuevo Régimen en España*. Caracas, 1986.

Gómez Ochoa, F. 'El liberalismo conservador español del siglo XIX: La forja de una identidad política, 1810–1840', *Historia y Política* 17 (2007), 37–68.

Guerra, F.-X. 'El apogeo de los liberalismos hispánicos: Orígenes, lógicas y límites', *Bicentenario. Revista de Historia de Chile y América* 3(2) (2004), 7–40.

————. *Modernidad e independencias: Ensayos sobre las revoluciones hispánicas*. Madrid, 1993.

Hale, C.A. *El liberalismo mexicano en la época de Mora*. Mexico, 1972.

Hegel, G.W.F. *The Philosophy of History*. Ontario, 2001.

Historia de la guerra de España contra Napoleón Bonaparte, escrita y publicada de orden de S. M. Madrid, 1818.

Iarocci, M. *Properties of Modernity: Romantic Spain, Modern Europe, and the Legacies of Empire*. Nashville, 2006.

Isabella, M. *Risorgimento in Exile: Italian Émigrés and the Liberal International in the Post-Napoleonic Era*. Oxford, 2009.

Krug, W.T. *Geschichtliche Darstellung des Liberalismus alter und neuer Zeit: Ein historischer Versuch*. Leipzig, 1823.

Lasso, M. *Myths of Harmony: Race and Republicanism during the Age of Revolution, Colombia, 1795–1831*. Pittsburgh, 2007.

Leonhard, J. *Liberalismus: Zur historischen Semantik eines europäischen Deutungsmusters*. Munich, 2001.

Leynadier, C. *Histoire des peuples et des révolutions de l'Europe, de 1789 à 1849*. Paris, 1850–51.

Lloréns, V. *Liberales y románticos: Una emigración española en Inglaterra (1823–1834)*. Madrid, 1979.

————. 'Notas sobre la aparición de *liberal*', *Nueva Revista de Filología Hispánica* XII (1958), 53–58.

Ludwig, J. *Deutschland und die spanische Revolution 1820–1823*. Leipzig, 2013.

Martínez Marina, F. *Discurso sobre el origen de la monarquía*. Madrid, 1813.

————. *Teoría de las Cortes o grandes juntas nacionales de los reinos de León y Castilla* (1813), J.A. Escudero (ed.), 3 vols. Oviedo, 1996.

Meijide, M. L. *Contribución al estudio del liberalismo*. Sada, 1983.

Mellon, S. *The Political Uses of History: A Study of Historians in the French Restoration*. Stanford, 1958.

Morange, C. *Una conspiración fallida y una Constitución non nata (1819)*. Madrid, 2006.

Moreno Alonso, M. *La forja del liberalismo en España: Los amigos españoles de Lord Holland, 1793–1840*. Madrid, 1997.

Moskal, J. '"To Speak in Sanchean Phrase": Cervantes and the Politics of Mary Shelley's *History of a Six Weeks' Tour*', in B.T. Bennett and S. Curran (eds), *Mary Shelley in her Times* (Baltimore, 2000), 18–37

Nefftzer, A. 'Libéralisme', in M. Block (ed.), *Dictionnaire général de la politique*. Paris, 1873–1874. Reproduced in L. Jaume. *L'individu effacé ou le paradoxe du libéralisme français* (Paris, 1997), 557–567.

Paquette, G. 'Introduction: Liberalism in the Early Nineteenth-Century Iberian World', *History of European Ideas* 41(2) (2015), 153–65.

Pecchio, Count. *Anecdotes of the Spanish and Portuguese Revolutions*. London, 1822.

Peralta, V. 'Los inicios del sistema representativo en Perú: Ayuntamientos constitucionales y diputaciones provinciales (1812–1815)', in M. Irurozqui (ed.), *La mirada esquiva: Reflexiones sobre la interacción del estado y la ciudadanía en los Andes (Bolivia, Ecuador y Perú), siglo XIX* (Madrid, 2005), 65–92.

Pérez de Camino, M.N. *La Opinión*. Bordeaux, 1820.

Portillo Valdés, J.M. *Crisis atlántica: Autonomía e independencia en la crisis de la monarquía hispana*. Madrid, 2006.

————. 'La Constitución Universal', in J.Á. Junco and J. Moreno Luzón (eds), *La Constitución de Cádiz: historiografía y conmemoración* (Madrid, 2006), 85–100.

————. *Revolución de nación: Orígenes de la cultura constitucional en España, 1780–1812*. Madrid, 2000.

Queipo de Llano, J.M. *Historia del levantamiento, guerra y revolución de España*. Madrid, 1953.

Rivero, N.M. 'La legitimidad del Partido Democrático español', *La Discusión*, 15 October 1858.

Rocafuerte, V. *Bosquejo ligerísimo de la revolución de México, desde el grito de Iguala hasta la proclamación imperial de Iturbide*. Philadelphia, 1822.

———. *Ensayo sobre la tolerancia religiosa*. Mexico City, 1831.

Rodríguez J.E. (ed.). *The Divine Charter: Constitutionalism and Liberalism in Nineteenth-Century Mexico*. Lanham, 2007.

———. *The Independence of Spanish America*. Cambridge, 1998.

Rodríguez, S. *El Libertador del Mediodía de América y sus compañeros de armas, defendidos por un amigo de la causa social*. Arequipa, 1830.

Rosen, F. *Bentham, Byron and Greece: Constitutionalism, Nationalism, and Early Liberal Political Thought*. Oxford, 1992.

Sanders, J. E. '"Citizens of a Free People": Popular Liberalism and Race in Nineteenth-Century Southwestern Colombia', *Hispanic American Historical Review* 84 (2004), 277–313.

———. *Contentious Republicans: Popular Politics, Race, and Class in Nineteenth-Century Colombia*. Durham, NC, 2004.

Simal, J.L. *Emigrados: España y el exilio internacional, 1814–1834*. Madrid, 2012.

———. *Liberalismo internacional y exilio en Europa, 1814–1834*. Madrid, 2012.

Späth, J. *Revolution in Europa 1820–1823: Verfassung und Verfassungskultur in den Königreichen Spanien, beider Sizilien und Sardinien-Piemont*. Cologne, 2012.

Stoetzer, O.C. *The Scholastic Roots of the Spanish American Revolution*. New York, 1979.

Varela, J. 'La doctrina de la Constitución Histórica: de Jovellanos a las Cortes de 1845', *Revista Española de Derecho Político* 39 (1995), 45–79.

Vieusseux, A. *Essay on Liberalism; Being an Examination of the Nature and Tendency of the Liberal Opinions; with a View of the State of Parties on the Continent of Europe*. London, 1823.

Villanueva, J.L. *Las angélicas fuentes o El tomista en las Cortes*. Madrid, 1849.

Chapter 4

Liberalism in Portugal in the Nineteenth Century

Rui Ramos and Nuno Gonçalo Monteiro

The context for the rise of 'liberalism' in Portugal is to be found in the crisis of the intercontinental monarchy of the Braganças, precipitated by the French invasions of 1807–11. In 1820, a part of the country's administrative staff and the armed forces, accompanied by some important Lisbon businesspeople, were won over to the idea of constitutionalizing the monarchy, in line with the 'liberal' Constitution that had been adopted in Spain in 1812. Between 1820 and 1823, political power was concentrated in a unicameral parliament elected by a suffrage of adult citizens. The political driving forces behind this regime began to be identified as 'liberals', just as they were in Spain at the same time.

In this chapter, we shall focus on two aspects of the history of Portuguese liberalism. First of all, we shall look at the way in which historical liberalism in Portugal diverges from current conceptions of liberalism – for example, from an ideology of a 'minimal state'. In the 1820s, liberal rule triggered a process of intense political socialization in an extremely polarized environment, culminating in a violent civil war between 'liberals' and 'absolutists' (1832–34). This confrontation explains a fundamental characteristic of Portuguese liberalism: the concentration of power in the state, which sometimes took on authoritarian forms, and the use of this power to provoke social, economic and cultural transformations, justified as a means of undermining the influence of the opponents of liberalism (the Catholic Church, the court aristocracy, the provincial nobility and the municipal councils).

Second, we shall attempt to explain why 'liberalism' in Portugal did not correspond to the formation and activity of a Liberal party of the kind that defined nineteenth-century liberalism in some northern European countries such as Britain. After 1834, in the wake of the liberal victory in the civil war, 'liberalism' was adopted as a self-identification by all the political protagonists of the new constitutional monarchy of the Bragança. As such, at no time did liberalism ever signify a party or a specific and singular doctrinal current; in fact, most of the time, Portuguese 'liberals' were divided into opposing camps of radicals and moderates, such as the 'Septembrists' and 'Chartists' between 1836 and 1851. This political divide deteriorated into repeated bouts of violence and civil war, as happened in Spain between 'moderates' and 'progressists'. But even at the moment of greatest confrontation, all of these political groups professed to be acting in the name of 'liberalism' and claimed the inheritance of the liberal side in the 1830s civil war. It was a way of distinguishing themselves from the 'Miguelites', that is, those who defended the absolutist rule of King Dom Miguel (1828–34). Miguelites were the only political group to reject the designation of 'liberal' in mid nineteenth-century Portugal. After 1851, the new political situation of the 'Regeneration' insisted on maintaining the reference to liberalism as a common terrain for conservatives and progressives within the constitutional monarchy. Thus, at no time in the nineteenth century did a party or a political movement appear in Portugal to assume the cause of 'conservatism' or 'socialism' in opposition to 'liberalism'. And this remained the case throughout the entire period of the constitutional monarchy until 1910, so that all the parties, groups and leaders that, at one time or another, held power between 1834 and 1910 described themselves as 'liberals', claiming for themselves the memory of the victors of the civil war of 1832–34. The same applied to the Republicans who took power in 1910. Although influenced by contemporary French radicalism, they preferred to claim the inheritance of the first liberals of the early 1820s.

Liberal and Liberalism under the Absolute Monarchy before 1820

As was the case in most of the Iberian Peninsula and Latin America, liberalism as a political identity or as the description of public actors did not occur in Portugal before the 1810s. Throughout the eighteenth century and until 1820, the terms 'liberal' and 'liberalism' seem, in Portugal, to have remained almost immune to new uses and meanings. The spread of the term as a mark of political identity only began in the 1820s, through the importation of international references and in the context of massive political change.

In eighteenth-century Portuguese literature, the word 'liberal' and the virtue – 'liberality' – that was associated with it referred to a certain kind of disinterested generosity: 'modern philosophers have defined liberality as a moderate virtue of the human affection of giving and receiving human riches, solely for honest motives ... the Liberal is moved to spend riches without expecting to be paid anything in return for them'.[1] Liberality was therefore a virtue that was considered typical of princes and nobles. Thus, in his dictionary of the Portuguese language (1716), Raphael Bluteau defines 'Liberal' as 'Noble. Showing one self to be a person of quality. Having the characteristics of a prince'. According to the same dictionary, 'liberal' was also associated with the 'liberal arts', the only ones that were compatible with the nobility and that were defined through their contrast with the 'manual trades'. Manual trades were those that depended 'more on the body than on the spirit'. The liberal arts were therefore regarded as being in keeping with the ample notion of 'nobility' that prevailed in Portugal, to refer to almost anyone who could afford to live free of manual work, and thus lived like a nobleman.[2]

Beginning with the Marquis of Pombal (1699–1782), several late eighteenth-century Portuguese statesmen attempted to reform the institutions of the monarchy. But these reformers avoided a discussion of the basic premises of the political order, and instead concentrated on economic and civil topics. Although the Royal Academy of Sciences (1782) and new courses of studies at the University of Coimbra disseminated some topics of the European Enlightenment, this cultural opening was limited by a strict literary censorship and by the vigilance of the Intendência Geral da Polícia (General Police Intendancy). Thus, the culture and sociability of the Enlightenment seem to have been confined to upper social and political circles and to some limited middle urban sectors. There was nothing in Portugal to be compared with the 'societies of friends of the country' in Spain. Reformers such as Rodrigo de Sousa Coutinho (1755–1812), the minister of Prince Regent Dom João (Prince Regent, 1799–1816; King, 1816–26), defended the suppression of all the tax exemptions enjoyed by the clergy and the nobility, as well as their jurisdictional privileges. Rodrigo de Sousa Coutinho had read Adam Smith, whose *The Wealth of Nations* he recommended to several high officials, but he was not a 'liberal' in the political sense of the 1820s. Thus, he justified a proposal for a higher degree of commercial freedom in the Portuguese monarchy merely as a means to interest England in the consolidation and expansion of the Portuguese Empire in America. Otherwise, he opposed the summoning of the Cortes (parliament), despite his openly admitted admiration for the English political system.[3]

Even the more enlightened statesmen of the monarchy avoided any initiatives that might endanger the prerogatives of the king's government. Their supposed liberalism was associated, above all, with economic legislation and trade. Discussions about the political order were almost irrelevant, and the ideological conflicts between the more enlightened and the more conservative forces, which seem to have been extremely important in Spain, did not have much relevance in Portugal. Thus, in late eighteenth-century Portugal, the word 'liberal' still preserved much of its former meaning. In the *Diccionario da Lingua Portugueza composto pelo Padre D. Rafael Bluteau, reformado e accrescentado por Antonio de Moraes Silva* (Lisbon, 1789), 'liberal' was defined thus: 'adj. giving copiously, and spending, without avarice, or meanness; generous, § *Liberal art*, one that is not a mechanical or manual trade'.

In 1807, the French occupation did not provoke immediate political changes. Initially, the French enjoyed the cooperation of almost all of those high officials and court aristocrats who had not left for Brazil with the royal family, but only very few of them were to become truly 'afrancesados' (Frenchified). In 1808, some of them asked Napoleon for 'a constitution … similar to that of Warsaw', besides the introduction of relevant institutional changes, such as the equal status of all citizens before the law, the adoption of the Napoleonic Civil Code, and the sale of the assets and property of the monasteries and convents. But they formed only a very small group and no important changes took place. On the side of the anti-French forces, inspired by the Spanish revolt and helped to victory by the British intervention, the expression of any projects of political reform was negligible. There was no equivalent in Portugal to the 1812 Cádiz Cortes. However, the deportation to England of a number of people suspected of French sympathies contributed to the formation, after the war, of a nucleus of political émigrés who were decisive, through newspapers and pamphlets printed in London, in preparing the cultural environment for the 1820 constitutional revolution.[4]

The anti-Napoleonic propaganda during the war allowed for an unprecedented explosion of printed texts in Portugal, many translated from Spanish, but most the work of Portuguese authors. A common theme was the need to re-establish the traditional order, its accompanying values and the cult of the king, the nation and the Catholic religion. Enemies were described as 'francinotes' (Frenchies) and 'evil Jacobins', as well as 'insolent revolutionaries', but never as 'liberals'. Thus, while the basic topics of the antiliberal discourse were already present, the term 'liberal' in a political sense remained absent.[5]

Meanwhile, economic liberalism continued to develop, namely with the departure of the royal family to Brazil. Rodrigo de Sousa Coutinho justified that option by arguing that the monarchy of the Braganças was a multicontinental entity, in which Portugal was not 'the best and the most essential part', so that, given the circumstances of the European war, the only option remaining to the Prince Regent and the court was 'to go and create a powerful Empire in Brazil, from where they will return to reconquer what may have been lost in Europe'.[6] The establishment of the court in Rio de Janeiro in 1808 was accompanied by the opening of the ports of Brazil to the allied nations, which meant mostly Britain. This brought an end to the monopoly trading rights that Portugal and its traders enjoyed in the Brazilian market. In March 1810, the Prince Regent was to send a legal charter from Rio de Janeiro to Portugal, where the Anglo-Portuguese forces were confronting the French troops, in which he justified the measures taken in the following terms: 'I hereby order that the most clearly demonstrated principles of the healthy Political Economy be adopted, which are those of the freedom and openness of trade ... so that ... the farmers in Brazil might find the best consumption for their produce.' But he also added: 'the same principles of a Great and Liberal system of Trade are very much applicable to the Kingdom'. In this way, the royal government was proposing that the conditions should be created 'to ensure that your capital is usefully employed in Agriculture', ordering the governors of the kingdom to occupy themselves with reforming tithes and with reducing, fixing or even doing away with manorial rights altogether. This declaration, which was certainly drafted by Rodrigo de Sousa Coutinho, ended up having no effect, for practically the only measure that was in fact introduced was the opening of the ports. But it allowed political economy to have its brief moment of impact, namely in Brazil. Otherwise, it confirmed that in Portuguese public debate, 'liberal principles' at this time referred only to those of economic liberalism and not political liberalism. This, after all, was the new meaning that was to be found in Morais' 1813 *Dictionary* for the word 'liberal': 'Free, open: so that this *liberal navigation* was impeded by us (to the Moors).'

Further developments were determined by the impact, somewhat delayed over time but nonetheless decisive, of the Cádiz Cortes in Spain, and by the more immediate penetration of the Portuguese émigré press, edited and published in Paris and, above all, in London. This was a radically new phenomenon. The atrophy of the press had been one of the most distinctive features of the Portuguese monarchy in the second half of the eighteenth century. But in the aftermath of the war with the French, the first liberal political press was to appear in Portugal in a context of diffuse powers, which meant that there was little control over what was published.[7]

The émigré press had the support of Portuguese trading circles in London and, in some cases, also of the government in Rio de Janeiro itself, through the embassy. Despite their precautions, most of its authors ended up being persecuted by the Portuguese government, especially after the failed conspiracy of General Gomes Freire de Andrade in 1817. Yet, nothing could prevent the dissemination of the first émigré press in Portugal and in Brazil. The focus and tone of these publications varied over time, but there were two highly recurrent themes: the criticism of the 1810 treaty with England and the defence of the summoning of parliament. However, the condemnation of despotism and the apology for freedom, frequently associated with the

British regime, were not conceived as an apology for a liberal project. Only retrospectively, and many years later, was it claimed that 'it was the periodical press or Portuguese journalism in London that ... initiated the dissemination of liberal ideas in our country'.[8]

The Constitutionalization of the Monarchy in the 1820s

As we have seen, in the 1813 edition of Morais e Silva's *Dictionary of the Portuguese language*, 'liberal' had acquired a meaning associated with trade policies. As far as Morais e Silva's dictionary is concerned, it was only in the 1844 Lisbon edition that it was acknowledged that 'liberal' was 'also used to designate representative governments'.

This evolution was closely associated with the political history of the Portuguese multicontinental monarchy in the 1820s. In August 1820, a military uprising in Oporto forced the government to accept the summoning of the Cortes. In November, there was a confrontation between a so-called 'military party', which included army officers of different political shades, and the 'bachelors and judges' who manned the new government. The military party demanded that the 1812 Spanish Constitution of Cádiz should be immediately adopted in Portugal. They acknowledged that the Spanish Constitution required some 'convenient changes', but would not accept any adaptation that would make the Portuguese version 'less liberal'.[9] 'Liberal' had already acquired a clear political meaning. However, 'liberal' was not as widely used as words such as 'constitutional'. When it was applied to a political movement, it was generally through the pens of its political opponents.[10]

The Portuguese members of parliament elected in 1820 were deeply impressed by the Spanish example and by the absence of the king in Brazil. They soon showed their preference for a regime defined by the sovereignty of the nation in the shape of a one-chamber, all-powerful parliament. It was their loyalty to this constitutional model that best defined their politics and, as such, it was the word 'constitutional' that they chose to identify themselves. In the *Diário das Cortes* in 1821, the term 'liberal' was invoked less than two hundred times, whilst there were more than a thousand references to 'constitution' and to 'constitutional'. There were even fewer references to 'liberalism' – no more than thirty. The data obtained from the periodical press confirms this tendency. From a sample of 316 periodicals published in Portuguese between 1820 and 1834 (including some that were published in Brazil), there were almost thirty that included the words 'constitution' or 'constitutional' in the title, whereas only a dozen included the term 'liberal' (or 'liberals'). Some were royalist journals and the overwhelming majority were published after the concession of the Constitutional Charter of 1826.[11] All of this suggests that it was not the 'liberal' identity that best defined the political leaders of the period 1820–23.

It was certainly not by chance that the first references to the word 'liberal' in parliamentary debates occurred in relation to the Companhia das Vinhas do Alto Douro, a viticultural commercial monopoly created by the Marquis of Pombal. In the preamble to the bill presented to parliament in February 1821, it is stated that: 'Freedom enlivens the Arts, and mainly Agriculture; and that, on the contrary, monopolies weaken the industry, and Trade, being all the more harmful the more they accumulate: considering that the arbitrary system by which the Company is regulated is incompatible with the Liberal Constitution.' The economic dimension of liberalism seems to be still overwhelming.

In political terms, 'liberal' seems to have been used to compare institutions, as a matter of degree. Thus, one of the most distinguished members of parliament Manuel Fernandes Tomás (1771–1822) could promise in February of 1821 that 'it is not to be believed that, in the current circumstances, legislation will be made that is any less liberal than the one that we already have'.[12] Another member of parliament, Manuel Borges Carneiro (1774–1833), stated at the same time that 'as has been said, our Constitution does not have to be any less liberal than that of Spain'[13]. Furthermore, it is in the same sense that we find the first reference to liberalism, still in that very same month, uttered by the member of parliament Xavier Monteiro when discussing the establishment of two chambers and the king's veto: 'both the absolute veto and the two chambers are inadmissible in the Portuguese Constitution, since these are less liberal than the bases of the Spanish Constitution, whose liberalism of principles we cannot restrict without distancing ourselves from the Powers of Representation that the People entrust to us, and without our failing to fulfil what we have solemnly promised and sworn to do'.[14]

Even more significant is the use of the word 'liberalism' to counter the Brazilian claims to autonomy. When these demands were being discussed, in May 1822, the member of parliament Ferreira de Moura called into question the Brazilians' commitment to liberalism:

> We sent them the bases of the Constitution; these were applauded and cele-brated everywhere; oaths were sworn to them; and are they not in themselves a sufficient argument to finally convince them that we do not wish to colonise America? If the bases of the Constitution are not sufficient to undo such a miserable misunderstanding, then, in that case, America is lost, the union is broken; there is nothing that can convince those peoples of the principles of liberalism that we have adopted, and which we will always adopt in regard to America.[15]

The member of parliament Pinto da França was, in turn, to declare that 'we must finish the Constitution as soon as we possibly can; but I must remind you that the peoples of Brazil need this even more quickly than we do ... (and, for this reason, it is urgent) that the additional articles should be presented with the greatest possible brevity, in which the clearest spirit of liberalism and openness towards those peoples should shine through'.[16] In voting for the Constitution, Ferreira de Moura hoped that 'this would be opposed to the confused and frantic liberalism of the demagogues, who, against the general will of Brazil, demand an inopportune and premature independence'.[17]

The relative lack of definition of the word 'liberal' did not prevent the establishment of a link between 'liberalism' and 'liberty' or 'freedom', in opposition to 'despotism'. Once again, as was stated by the member of parliament Moura: 'I am greatly surprised to find that the greatest factors of Liberty and Liberalism are opposed to the existence of the Council of State, when I supposed that its existence was opposed to the principles of those who favour despotism.'[18]

The expression 'liberal party' is relatively rare. It appears in October 1821, in a speech by Manuel Borges Carneiro in which he refers the 'Members of parliament of the liberal party' in France. However, more significant than this is the use of the expression in 1822 in relation to the matter of voting rights, where it takes on a clearly social form of identification, in opposition to the so-called 'servile party':

> The nation (as we all know) is divided into two parties, the liberal and the servile, and since the traders and the artisans are a very worthy part of those who form the liberal party, if they should cease to vote, then the field is left almost completely open to the serviles; these will make the election exclusively by themselves and we will have a bad national representation, which, in the current circumstances, will be the greatest evil that could happen to us.[19]

The historical nature of constitutionalism – that is, the memory and tradition of the former Cortes of the monarchy – continued to be invoked insistently. For example, as early as February 1821, a moderate and conservative member of parliament such as Francisco Manuel Trigozo de Aragão Morato referred to 'our former Constitution', defining the current political process as a 'transition to the next Constitution'.[20] But the same ideas were also to be found among the more radical members of parliament, such as Manuel Borges Carneiro, addressing the opponents of the new order: 'you are the innovators, you are the revolutionaries who overthrew our former *Cortes* and the ancient principles of a temperate monarchy, in order to erect an absurd and despotic power, in whose shadow you will maintain your egoism and your prevarication'.[21]

The writer J.B.L. Almeida Garrett, who at that time was one of the main liberal journalists, insisted on that traditionalist conception of liberty: 'The *Cortes* of Lamego, whose existence can no longer be doubted, formed, within the cradle of the Portuguese Monarchy, its very own political Constitution … one of its most important declarations is that of our liberty; and the holiest and most unbreakable rule that is established, and conserved by so many years of glory, is that of the nation's representation through the *Cortes.*'[22] However, the idea that the new Constitution was perfectly in keeping with the historical tradition of the Portuguese monarchy did not prevent the constitutional assembly elected in 1820 – at the same time as they showed themselves to be moderate in their legislative production – from severely limiting the powers of the monarch (still absent in Brazil), going far beyond the Spanish Cádiz Constitution. Effectively, they adopted the principle of the 'sovereignty of the Nation' and only granted the king a suspensive veto over the decisions taken by the Cortes. They also made the Cortes the sole depositary of legislative power and adopted a single-chamber model, rejecting the census restrictions imposed on voting rights. Despite all this, those who supported the Constitution of 1821–22 always claimed to be recovering a medieval tradition that had lasted until the end of the seventeenth century (1698), when the last Cortes were convened (their historical knowledge of this subject was very limited – for instance, they were unaware that Brazil had sent representatives to the Cortes since 1653 or that these had met eight times between 1641 and 1698).

After the overthrow of the 1822 Constitution by another military coup in 1823, the pamphlet *A Revolução anti-constitutional em 1823, suas verdadeiras causas e effeitos* (*The Anti-constitutional Revolution in 1823, its True Causes and Effects,*[23] whose exact authorship remains unknown) identified the supporters of the 'constitutional cause' with the 'liberals', noting that 'the free masons have done great harm to the cause of Liberty, even though they all profess Liberalism'.

Two decisive and partly converging factors contributed to the words 'liberal' and 'liberalism' in Portugal finally acquiring their classic meaning and being used unreservedly to identify a political movement. The first of these was the granting of the Constitutional Charter by Dom Pedro, Emperor of Brazil, after the death of his father, Dom João VI, in 1826. The Charter, an adaptation of the Brazilian Constitution, eliminated the 1822 Constitution as the fundamental reference for those political movements that were opposed to absolutism. In the intermittent civil war that was waged in Portugal between 1826 and 1834, the different currents of opinion that sought shelter under the banner of the Constitutional Charter had no room for manoeuvre that would allow them to expound and further deepen their already-evident differences. The second decisive factor was the influence in Portugal of the French liberalism of the 1820s. Authors such as Benjamim Constant and François Guizot provided a moderate version of liberalism, very distinct from Jacobin radicalism, that allowed the term 'liberal' to gain a respectability that it did not previously have when it seemed associated with an extreme position. Thus, although 'constitutional' continued to be the term that was most frequently used to identify the defenders of the Constitutional Charter, there was a clear trend towards the use of the word 'liberal' to define the anti-absolutists, regardless of the different doctrines and philosophies that they espoused.

However, the reference to 'liberals' is perhaps still more recurrent in the counterrevolutionary literature than it is in the writings of those who actually claimed to be so. The traditional meaning still lingered – for instance, in 1828, Frei Mateus d'Assunção Brandão noted that 'it was only by offering a crown to someone to whom it did not belong that the liberals showed themselves actually to be liberal according to the old meaning of that word'. In 1833, the *Correio do Porto* had to remind its readers that 'the Constitutionals, the Liberals and the Free Masons' were all the same thing.[24] Likewise, in the 1831 edition of Morais e Silva's dictionary, the word 'liberalism' does not yet occur, while the only modern sense recorded for 'liberal' was the economic one: 'system of the governments that do not limit industry and trade, etc., nor restrict them with petty regulations, taxation and oppressive means'.[25]

The Portuguese 1822 Constitution had, as its starting point, the 1812 Cádiz Constitution, and the so-called '*Vintista* triennium' ended at practically the same time in the two Iberian countries. But, afterwards, despite their reciprocal influences, the political chronology of Portugal and Spain diverged. The 1826 Constitutional Charter, sent by Dom Pedro from Brazil, did not have any parallel in Spain, just as there was no correspondence for the second Portuguese liberal period from 1826 to 1828. There was also no Spanish equivalent to the absolutist government of King Dom Miguel, who seized power in 1828 and initiated the greatest political repression in Portuguese contemporary history; merely in the first year alone, between 20,000 and 30,000 people were imprisoned out of a population of three million inhabitants.

This extreme political radicalization was a factor that conditioned the implantation of liberalism in Portugal. It was in the midst of the civil war (1832–34) that José Xavier Mouzinho da Silveira (1780–1849), the Finance Minister of the Duke of Bragança, decreed most of the legislation that targeted the foundations of the *ancien régime* in Portugal: the abolition of entailed estates with a small income, the suppression of the *sisa* (sales tax), the administrative reforms (through which the judicial power was separated from the administrative power, and a centralist form of local administration was established, inspired by the Napoleonic model), the eradication of the central polysynodal tribunals, the suppression of ecclesiastical tithes and, finally, the abolition of manorial rights and of the system whereby these were awarded to the great aristocratic families and households. Subsequent legislation enacted in the same period would lead to the abolition of the religious orders, the craft guilds and, later, of most of the existing municipalities.

In no way did Mouzinho and the other liberal legislators claim to be enacting some predefined party programme. They seemed to believe that they were applying to Portugal what was generally accepted by all of enlightened Europe, in a context where any compromise with the Old Order was impossible. Further, it should be mentioned that in all this legislation, there were many more references to 'liberty' (*liberdade*) than to 'liberalism'. Liberalism seems to have been considered to be more a question of 'civil equality' than of a 'representative system', to use the terms that were in fashion at that time.

The civil war made it possible for liberals to use the power of the state to limit or destroy the social and cultural bases of political traditionalism. Mouzinho da Silveira had a clear notion that liberalism implied an unprecedented strengthening of the power of the state. In one of the few definitions made of the liberal state, he was to write:

> It has been said, and it is true, that liberalism is an ancient thing; and that absolutism is modern, but this truth needs to be clearly understood so that it does not make Europe look retrograde ... The liberalism of the ancients did not come from the strength of the opinion of the common people, nor from their knowledge; instead, it consisted in the spirit of privilege, and in the indomitable strength of character of the great classes.

But 'modern liberalism is a very different thing; it does not consist in the privileges of the cities, nor in the spirit of the corporations and guilds, but it is the result of the analysis that is applied to the deliberations of the government, and of the natural desire to improve their condition'.[26]

The 1830s and beyond: Why Did Liberalism Not Become the Reference for Just One Party?

The history of the constitutional monarchy in Portugal between 1834 and 1851 was shaped, just as in Spain, by the confrontation between 'moderate' and 'radical' liberals.[27] Radical liberals were known as 'Septembrists', a name they took from the revolution of September in 1836, which installed them in power until 1842, under a new Constitution (1838). Moderate liberals were called 'Chartists', from their defence of the 1826 Constitutional Charter, which they restored in 1842, initiating a period of predominance that lasted until 1851. The conflict between Septembrists and Chartists evolved through tense parliamentary debates, frequent political meetings, urban riots, military coups and recurring bouts of civil war, such as the one that took place in 1846–47. This struggle between political groups that had banded together in their fight against Dom Miguel before 1834, only to split and turn against each other afterwards, was to mark the development of 'liberalism' in the 1830s and 1840s, since all of them claimed to be the true liberals. Their polemics filled a profusion of newspapers published in Lisbon and many other cities.

The Portuguese clashes between Septembrists and Chartists echoed similar divisions in other European constitutional monarchies. The Septembrists were inspired by the arguments and rhetoric of the left-wing political factions of the July Monarchy in France (1830–48), a situation that the Septembrist leader Manuel da Silva Passos, better known as Passos Manuel (1801–62), made explicit when he assessed his government of 1836–37, quoting the Marquis de La Fayette: 'The Queen has no prerogatives, she has attributions: she is the first magistrate of the nation. I was the first in Portugal to implement the programme adopted (in July 1830) in the *Hotel de Ville* in Paris: I surrounded the throne with republican institutions.' Passos claimed that he had turned the Portuguese constitutional monarchy into the 'best of republics'.[28] He alluded to a political system that had the external form of a monarchy with an established Church, but in which sovereignty rested with parliament, local administration was entrusted to autonomous municipal chambers, the electoral franchise was low enough to allow for a quasi-universal suffrage, and there was complete freedom of speech and religion. Years later, the historian Alexandre Herculano (1810–77) defined the 1830s Septembrists as those who 'endeavoured to arrive, if not at a republic, at least at republican institutions'.[29] This republican conception of the regime was authorized through the way in which the constitutional monarchy could be understood, as Passos Manuel suggested in a speech in 1835, less as a form of monarchical government and more as one of 'mixed government', simultaneously displaying elements of both monarchy and republic.

In their turn, the Chartists came to adopt the ideas of the French 'doctrinaires', especially those of François Guizot, which made it possible to define liberalism in a conservative fashion, contrasting it with democracy.[30] Chartists discovered the advantages of traditional religion as a way of uniting and disciplining society, and the convenience of the joint exercise of power by the king and parliament, with the right to vote restricted to qualified citizens, as a way of preventing 'tyranny', that is, arbitrary power, which, according to them, could develop in a modern democracy as well as in an absolute monarchy. Liberty, which the Septembrists imagined 'in the Roman style', as the sovereignty of egalitarian assemblies of citizens, began to be conceived by the Chartists 'in the German style', associated with the spirit of independence of the nobility and of the medieval popular communities, as well as with the balance of powers deriving therefrom. Chartists exalted the role of the king as arbiter of the political life, defended the influence of government in municipal affairs, and saw Catholic priests, provided they identified with the Liberal state, as the most appropriate agents to involve the rural masses in an atmosphere of liberalism. Writers such as J.B.L. Almeida Garrett (1799–1854), an ex-Septembrist who converted to Chartism, and Alexandre Herculano (1810–77) expressed these ideas in a literary and erudite form. In his serialized feuilleton *Viagens na Minha Terra (Travels in My Homeland*, 1843), Garrett lamented the excesses of the liberal revolution. In his *História de Portugal (History of Portugal*, 1846), Herculano found in the medieval monarchy an archaic version of the conservative liberalism he thought was the best way for liberty to take roots in Portuguese society: a judicious combination of royal power and municipal institutions, with a Church preserved from ultramontane tendencies.

The division between Chartists and Septembrists never developed into a division between liberalism and another 'ism' (progressivism or conservatism, for example). The Septembrists claimed to be 'true patriots' and some of them did not hesitate to consider themselves 'incorrigible democrats'. The more radical factions among them laid claim to a political lineage arguably derived from French Jacobinism. However, they never renounced the liberal label and always maintained their commitment to the constitutional monarchy, even in its Chartist version, since, as one of them argued, 'while the statutes of the Charter were not the most liberal, they were also not the most restrictive'.[31] In the same way, the Chartists, despite their conservative 'doctrinairism', insisted on their title of 'liberals'. In fact, in relation to 'liberalism', both sides tried to reserve it for themselves and deny it to their adversaries: Septembrists accused Chartists of being too reactionary to be true liberals, and Chartists accused Septembrists of being more revolutionary than liberal. Thus, there never was in Portugal a distinction between 'democrats' and 'liberals', or 'liberals' and 'conservatives', since all political groups within the constitutional monarchy disputed the title of 'liberals'. After all, they had all been active in the campaign to establish representative institutions against Dom Miguel in the 1820s and early 1830s. Since 'liberalism' had become associated with that struggle, they all could claim its mantle with some justification. The meaning of the word 'liberal' registered in the 1844 Lisbon edition of Morais e Silva's dictionary – 'it is also used to designate representative governments'[32] – did not help to solve the dispute between the Chartists and Septembrists over who were the true liberals, since both claimed to support representative government.

Between 1842 and 1851, Portuguese political life was dominated by a ruthless Chartist leader, António Bernardo da Costa Cabral (1803–89). Cabral managed to build a strong basis of personal support in the army and in the court, and tried to exclude Septembrists not just from power, but also from the regime. Yet, in 1851, Cabral was finally overthrown by a military coup led by moderate Chartists. The leaders of the 'Regeneration', as the 1851 coup was called, sought to bring the Septembrists back into the regime.[33] Led by A.M. Fontes Pereira de Melo (1819–87), they developed a system of political alliances centred around a consensus on the Constitutional Charter, revised in 1852 to accommodate some Septembrists' demands (such as direct elections and a wider franchise), and a project of economic and social transformation of the country, based upon a programme of mass schooling and public investment in transport and communication infrastructures.[34] The period from the 1850s to the 1890s was the golden age of 'public works' in Portugal, with the building of a modern rail and road network, the expansion of the state administration and the creation of new public services. Fontes Pereira de Melo, whose political ascendancy lasted until his death in 1887, claimed he was free of the old partisan prejudices and acted in accordance with an 'experimental method'. As such, he and his followers insisted that there was no reason for party divisions such as those that had existed before 1851.[35]

This kind of politics, based on a profound renewal of the political personnel in the 1850s, succeeded in breaking up the former Chartist and Septembrist groupings. In the following decades, financial crises, such as those that occurred in 1868 and 1876, shook Fontes' control and allowed for occasional surges of democratic radicalism. Fontes responded to this challenge according to the principle of French 'political opportunism', doing his best to capture for himself the radical programme of the opposition. Thus, from 1878 onwards, he extended the right to vote, promoted administrative decentralization, limited the king's constitutional prerogatives and transformed the chamber of peers into an elective senate. According to Fontes, liberal politics should encompass all the ideas that were compatible with the framework of legality defined by the constitutional monarchy. Under Fontes, liberalism was never the doctrine of one party among others, but the common terms of reference for all those taking part in public debate out of a concern for the freedom and welfare of the nation, regardless of their particular doctrines.

Even the leaders of the Portuguese Republican Party, founded in 1876, considered themselves to be members of the liberal family. The same thing happened with some Catholic politicians, such as the Count of Samodães (1828–1918), the President of the influential Catholic Association of Porto (1872), although among more conservative Catholics, liberalism retained its counterrevolutionary association with freemasonry and anticlericalism.[36] Only the heirs of Miguelism continued, throughout the nineteenth century, to reject the qualification of 'liberal', although they eventually accepted the model of the constitutional state. Accordingly, unlike Spain, where the main parties of the 'rotation system' identified themselves from the 1870s onwards as conservative and liberal, their corresponding Portuguese parties (from the 1850s onwards) were known as the 'Party of the Regeneration' and the 'Historical Progressive Party' (later the 'Progressive Party'), and they both claimed the title of 'liberals'.

Could Portuguese liberalism be defined by the political system it established? In the second half of the nineteenth century, the liberal political elite corresponded to an urban class of high civil servants with a university or equivalent education. All the most important political leaders lived in Lisbon, then a city of some 200,000 inhabitants, and some in Porto, which maintained its own partly autonomous political life. Facing the liberals was a society overwhelmingly rural and illiterate (in 1878, 78 per cent of people aged seven or over could not read or write), despite the institution of state-sponsored compulsory free education in the 1830s. Very often, liberals invoked illiteracy to justify the strategy of using the clergy and the monarchy, in duly purged forms, as instruments of social control. Such an arrangement was possible because the Vatican saw in an agreement with the Portuguese state the best way of defending its interests in Portugal and because part of the royal family opted for the liberal cause in the 1820s. Thus, the liberals allowed themselves to give the state the structure of the former monarchy, with an official church and a monarchical constitution. Maintaining the balance of power was entrusted to the king, who was constitutionally endowed with the power to appoint the head of government and to control parliament (through the use of the royal veto and through dissolution). The royal prerogative preserved high politics from pressures from below. Changes in government were determined by the political intrigues of the liberal leaders around the king, and not directly through electoral results or through street protests. But the king's role was only justified insofar as it guaranteed the predominance of the liberals.[37] In fact, although the king was the arbiter of political life, liberals never promoted any sense of fidelity to the dynasty. All oppositions attacked the king in order to pressurize the monarch into rotating the members of his government. Every king from

1834 onwards was accused at one time or another of despotism and threatened with a 'revolution' by a section of the regime's political leaders. Thus, the competition for offices and positions among the liberal elite tended to endanger the structure of the state and to produce recurrent denunciations of its 'illiberal' character.[38]

The emphasis of government varied widely. In the second half of the nineteenth century, during the ascendancy of Fontes Pereira de Melo, it would be possible to identify at least three phases: a period of technocratic liberalism in the 1850s and 1860s, focused on public works, as in Napoleon III's France; an age of democratic liberalism in the 1870s, inspired by the Spanish 1868 Revolution and the French Third Republic, and materialized in recurrent constitutional and institutional engineering; and finally, in the 1880s, a move towards social liberalism, indebted to British 'new liberalism' and German social policies, with projects on work regulation, vocational training, healthcare and trade protectionism. This last phase of social liberalism was caused by some disillusionment with the democratic efforts of the 1870s. Progressive liberals had argued that the extension of the right to vote would be a form of civic education in itself: the simple responsibility of voting would convert the civically unworthy populations into exemplary citizens and would thus create a wide popular basis for the regime beyond the metropolitan elite and the court.[39] In 1878, this hope led to the vote being extended to all adult men who were heads of families.[40] Portugal thus acquired one of the largest electorates in Europe, comprising 72 per cent of adult men.[41] However, this broadening of the suffrage did not have the expected effects. On the contrary, the 1878 law was soon to be blamed for the ill-fated result of having drowned the vote of the truly 'independent' citizens in the uneducated sea of the 'dependent' masses, subject to the will of the 'caciques' (the influential local political bosses) and pressure from the state administration. The proof of this was in the fact that all governments, without exception, continued to win elections.[42] The disappointment with electoral democracy led many liberals, from the 1880s onwards, to concentrate on the role of the state in the creation of the social conditions of a democracy. Portuguese liberalism therefore reinforced a dimension that the contemporaries called 'socialist' and that was reflected in the increase of tariff duties, conceived of as a way of 'protecting national employment', although it also produced much-needed revenue for a fiscally unbalanced state.[43] Yet, this was not a real rupture with the liberal past. Ever since the 1830s, liberals had been concerned with social questions as much as with free enterprise. Progressive liberals had always been doubtful about laissez-faire and never ceased to demand state protection for the 'national industry'.[44] Even the more severe-minded economists accepted that man was not a simple economic agent, but also a 'moral being'.[45]

Nineteenth-century Portuguese liberalism was therefore never just a simple doctrine of laissez-faire.

The Problems of a Doctrinaire Formulation of Portuguese Liberalism: Alexandre Herculano and Oliveira Martins

Liberals had an enormous impact on the building of the structures of the modern state in Portugal and also in the formation of a new national culture. It was up to liberal authors, such as Almeida Garrett or Alexandre Herculano, from the 1830s onwards to develop the country's academic history, its literary canon and the study of its folklore. Between 1880 and 1898, at great civic festivities, liberals commemorated the centenaries of some of the great figures of Portuguese history, such as Camões (1880), the Marquis of Pombal (1882), Prince Henry the Navigator (1894) and Vasco da Gama (1898). Portuguese historical memory and national identity in the contemporary period were thus forged under the auspices of liberalism.[46] This was why, in 1891, a Portuguese diplomat could argue that Portugal 'was the most liberal country in the world'.[47]

But while liberals led the construction of a modern state and national culture in Portugal, did liberalism in Portugal ever correspond to a coherent set of ideas? At the end of his life, José Xavier Mouzinho da Silveira (1780–1849), Portuguese liberalism's most impressive legislator, recognized that his 1832 decrees had been a means of 'propaganda for liberalism'.[48] But it was only after the mid nineteenth century, reflecting the reading of the French doctrinaires, that the historian Alexandre Herculano committed himself to the defence and justification of the 1832 legislative legacy, identifying it with liberalism. For Herculano, liberalism embodied a point of view that was defined by its opposition to the *ancien régime*, but that was not to be confused with democracy.[49]

Among Herculano's essays defining liberalism, probably the most important is the one that, in 1852, he wrote in French on Mouzinho da Silveira. It opens with a quotation from Guizot and has, as its aim, to present 'an historical overview of the origins and the development of the liberal regime in this country'. For Herculano, 'before and after the events of the years between 1831 and 1834, the history of liberalism in Portugal was no more than an unsavoury charade'. The victory of the liberal forces in the civil war was not explained only by military success: ʹdefinitive triumph of the liberals had deeper and more general causes. Among these causes, Mouzinho's legislation was the most effective, since his decrees touched at the most serious social questions. Mouzinho abolished church tithes and feodal rights ... separated judicial functions from administrative functions... abolished the army reserve and the militias ... cut into the old and anti-economic institution of the entailment ... Convents and monasteries were shaken by secularization'. Mouzinho's legislation benefited the common people, 'those who own property and who work', from the business partner to the great landowner, from the small shopkeeper to the great trader and from the craftsman to the manufacturer, whom Herculano does not confuse with 'the plebs, who never think' – the great support base of the Miguelistes, of whom he says, 'I will leave them to the care of the democrats'.[50]

Right up until his very last writings, Herculano did not cease in his attempts to arrive at a definition of that specific identity of liberalism, which he contrasted with both absolutism and democracy. In 1867, he drew attention to the fact that, at the end of the civil war, those who had taken part were, as a general rule, 'people who had been baptised with fire and blood into the two opposing religions of absolutism and liberalism'. He contrasted liberalism with absolutism, but also with democracy, and he identified the reign of Dom Miguel between 1828 and 1834 as a kind of realization of a moment of 'popular sovereignty', in the sense of a regime supported by the common masses: 'liberalism found the general appearance of democracy to be quite unappealing. All that remained was popular sovereignty. This had been in operation for five years and had given a good account of itself'. But the times had changed:

> now that it has been found and demonstrated, by all accounts, that liberalism serves for nothing ... the dogma of popular sovereignty, proclaimed as a supreme entitlement, replaces the only absolute right that it has recognised: freedom and individual rights ... now civil equality, which was a consequence of the liberal dogma, is transferred to the political world ... the passion for freedom begins to fade, because it absorbs and transforms that of equality, the strongest, and almost the sole, passion of democracy.[51]

As has already been mentioned, despite the parting of waters attempted by Herculano, the label of liberal was not something that would have been rejected by any of the main Portuguese political movements in the second half of the nineteenth century, with the exception of the legitimists or Miguelistes. This fact was to influence the writer J.P. Oliveira Martins (1845–94), a future Finance Minister (1892), who in 1881 published what was to be the most influential history of Portuguese liberalism, *Portugal Contemporâneo*, a powerful narrative and analysis of Portuguese history between 1826 and the 1860s.[52]

In the two volumes of *Portugal Contemporâneo*, Oliveira Martins hesitated between two approaches to liberalism. In a first approach, manifested in the pages that he devoted to the reforms of Mouzinho da Silveira, he understood liberalism as the theory that was implicit in the great legislative transformations of the period 1832–34. According to Oliveira Martins, this theory was rooted in free trade and individualism, and rejected the traditional organicist conceptions of society. The main sources of liberalism would, according to Martins, have been Adam Smith and Jeremy Bentham. Oliveira Martins denied that such a free trade ideology had any social basis of support in Portugal. It was imposed on the country by a small enlightened elite that, in order to do so, resorted to force in 1832–34. Oliveira Martins agreed with Herculano: the liberal victory was a 'revolution' that had put an end to the 'Old Portugal'. But Oliveira Martins added that, after the abolition of the old institutions, the liberals had been incapable of organizing a viable society and state. According to Oliveira Martins, the original liberal impetus would have been continued through the free trade policy adopted by the Regeneration movement after 1851, which had reduced the country to being a producer of food and raw materials for the north of Europe and an exporter of emigrants to Brazil. For this reason, Oliveira Martins was to propose 'socialism' as a way of correcting the liberal revolution.

In his first approach to liberalism, Oliveira Martins treated it as a unified doctrine, based on ethical individualism and free trade economics. However, *Portugal Contemporâneo* included a second approach, which took liberalism as a much more complex phenomenon. Indeed, Oliveira Martins also drew attention to the fact that liberalism was represented, at the same time or successively, by public figures whose ideas diverged radically: according to him, in 1826, the Duke of Palmela, an influential notable of the courts of Dom João VI and Dona Maria II, attempted to promote an 'aristocratic' liberalism, based on a romantic admiration for the English constitutional monarchy'; in 1832, J.X. Mouzinho da Silveira, a minister of the liberal government in the Azores during the civil war, decreed major reforms based on utilitarian principles; in 1836, Passos Manuel, the leader of the 'September revolution', imposed a Jacobin, lay and democratic orientation on the country's government; in 1842, A.B. da Costa Cabral, leader of the 'Chartist restoration', established a form of government that was predominantly inspired by the religious and antidemocratic French 'doctrinairism'; and, finally, in 1851–52, the leaders of the Regeneration, such as A.M. Fontes Pereira de Melo, espoused 'Saint-Simonist' orientations and admitted some 'socialist' principles.

Now, as Oliveira Martins noted, all of these movements, despite their differences, had tried to pass themselves off as liberal: 'all of them, however different they may be, were always liberal'. And he explained: 'The very nature of liberalism itself, with its lack of any criterion except for the word *liberty* – a word and nothing more – was the cause of the multiplication of the different ways in which it was expressed.'[53]

But Oliveira Martins never reflected on the fact that in the midst of this variety, it would be difficult to find currents of thought and movements that subscribed entirely and exclusively to the first idea that he had given of liberalism, as an individualistic doctrine of economic freedom. Perhaps a firmer foundation for an historical definition of nineteenth-century Portuguese liberalism could be found in a reappraisal of the civic project that underlined all liberal efforts, either conservative or progressive, at different epochs from the 1820s: the restoration of the nation to its former glory through the foundation of a 'free State'. This did not simply consist of a legal structure, designed to guarantee the rights and freedoms of each individual, who in this way would be safe to lead an autonomous existence; rather, the 'free State' was the community of 'free men' – in other words, of individuals who cultivated the idea of an autonomous existence, to the extent of having transformed it into a collective ideal. The 'free man' was a 'citizen', but in the old sense of a 'governor': he did not exist in contrast to the state, but as someone who took part in its management. The condition of being a citizen depended on personal independence, defined by age, sex, income and education. The liberal citizen was thus, in political terms, not an abstract category that could encompass diverse individuals, but corresponded to a very concrete social type: the adult man with the necessary income to be independent, with a school education, and an interest in public affairs – in other words, the enlightened and patriotic gentleman-proprietor.[54] In this sense, it would be possible to argue that liberalism in Portugal referred to the rejection of the political order embodied by the traditional Catholic monarchy and to the projects of building a new political order where this type of free citizen could predominate, in the form of a constitutional monarchy.

Conclusion

In nineteenth-century Portugal, 'liberalism' referred first of all to the 'revolution' that brought an end to the absolute monarchy and to the 'ancient society' between 1820 and 1834. After 1834, liberalism became the hegemonic reference of Portuguese political life, with the various parties that accepted the constitutional monarchy, both on the right and on the left, claiming the mantle of liberalism, despite all the differences that existed between them. Perhaps for this reason, Portuguese liberalism was never established as a defined and stable doctrine, associated with just one party or one political movement, but instead tended to define the regime as a whole, while the label of 'liberals' was used to identify all those who agreed to participate in its legal political life, whether they were conservative or progressive, supporters of free trade or protectionists, defenders of the free market or of state-sponsored intervention, monarchists or republicans. Thus, although it is not easy to translate nineteenth-century Portuguese liberalism into the language of our modern-day political life, it would be possible to describe liberalism in a Portuguese context as identical with the culture of modern state reform and nation-building shared by the ruling elites of the constitutional monarchy.

In fact, the institutional reforms promoted throughout the nineteenth century, as well as the administrative bodies and the elites associated with them, had little to do with their objectives and social selection criteria with those prevailing in the *ancien régime*. And until the beginning of the twentieth century, alternatives to the regime were almost all conceived within the bounds of the legacy of 1834. It was only then that the frustrations with Portuguese realities began to be conceived as a global refusal of nineteenth-century Liberalism.

Rui Ramos is Senior Research Fellow at the Institute of Social Sciences, University of Lisbon. As an historian, he specializes in Portuguese political and cultural history in the nineteenth and twentieth centuries. He is the author of several books, including *A Segunda Fundação, 1890–1926* (*The Second Foundation*) (1994); *João Franco e o Fracasso do Reformismo Liberal, 1885–1908* (*João Franco and the Failure of Liberal Reformism*) (2001); and *História de Portugal* (*History of Portugal*) (2009), with B. de Vasconcelos and N.G. Monteiro. He was one of the editors of *A Monarquia Constitucional dos Braganças em Portugal e no Brasil, 1822–1910* (*The Constitutional Monarchy of the House of Bragança in Portugal and Brazil*) (2018); and of *Dicionário Crítico da Revolução Liberal Portuguesa, 1820–1834* (*A Critical Dictionary of the Portuguese Liberal Revolution*) (forthcoming).

Nuno Gonçalo Monteiro is a researcher and professor at the Institute of Social Sciences of the University of Lisbon. He has been a visiting professor at universities in France, Spain and Brazil, and has conducted around two hundred presentations and conferences in different countries. He coordinated several international research projects, among which are *Political Communication in Portuguese Intercontinental Monarchy (1580–1808): Kingdom, Atlantic and Brazil*, published (co-editor) as *Um reino e as suas repúblicas no Atlântico* (2017). He has published more than 150 titles on early modern history.

Notes

Translation by John Elliott with the support of ICS-UID/SOC/50013/2013.

Parts of this chapter have been previoulsly published in N.G. Monteiro and R. Ramos, 'El liberalismo en Portugal en el siglo XIX', in ed. J. Fernández-Sebastián, *La aurora de la libertad: Los primeros liberalismos en el mundo iberoamericano*, Madrid, 2012: 379–410.

1. D.L.F. Castro, *Politica moral, e civil* ..., Lisbon, 1749, 298f.
2. See N.G. Monteiro, *Elites e Poder: Entre o Antigo Regime e o Liberalism*, Lisbon, 2007.
3. See A. Mansuy-Diniz Silva, *Portrait d'un Homme d'État: D. Rodrigo de Sousa Coutinho, Comte de Linhares, 1755–1812*, Paris, 2002. On Portuguese politics in the early 1800s, see J. Pedreira and F. Dores Costa, *D. João VI*, Lisbon, 2005.
4. See R. Ramos, 'La revolución de 1808 y los origenes del liberalismo en Portugal: Una reinterpretación', in A. Ávila and P. Pérez Herrero (eds), *Las Experiencias de 1808 en Iberoamerica*, Mexico City, 2008, 251–78.
5. See F.D. Costa, 'Franceses e jacobinos: Movimentações populares e medidas de polícias em 1808 e 1809', *Ler História* 54 (2008), 95–132.
6. See V. Alexandre, *Os Sentidos do Império. Questão Nacional e Questão Colonial na Crise do Antigo Regime Português*, Oporto, 1993, 132.
7. See G. Boisvert, *Un Pionnier de la Propagande Libérale au Portugal: João Bernardo da Rocha Loureiro, 1778–1853*, Lisbon, 1974.
8. S.J. da Luz Soriano, *História da Guerra Civil e do Estabelecimento do Governo Representativo em Portugal*, Lisbon, 1881, vol. 2, 455.
9. On the 1820 constitutional revolution, see G. and J.S. da Silva Dias, *Os Primórdios da Maçonaria em Portugal*, Lisbon, 1980; V. Pulido Valente, *Os Militares e a Politica, 1820–1854*, Lisbon, 1997; Alexandre, *Os Sentidos*; and Pedreira and Costa, 'Franceses e jacobinos'.
10. T. Verdelho, *As Palavras e as Ideias na Revolução Liberal de 1820*, Coimbra, 1981.
11. M.A. Lousada, *O miguelismo (1828–1834): O discurso político e o apoio da nobreza titulada*, Lisbon, 1987.
12. *Diário das Cortes Constituintes e Extraordinárias...*, 13 February 1821, no. 14, 83.
13. Ibid., 84.
14. *Diário das Cortes Constituintes e Extraordinárias...*, 22 February 1821, no. 20, 137.
15. *Diário das Cortes Constituintes e Extraordinárias...*, 22 May 1822, no. 16, 228.
16. *Diário das Cortes Constituintes e Extraordinárias...*, 21 July 1822, no. 52, 760.
17. *Diário das Cortes Constituintes e Extraordinárias...*, 22 July 1822, no. 62, 894.
18. *Diário das Cortes Constituintes e Extraordinárias...*, 3 March 1821, no. 26, 198
19. *Diário das Cortes Constituintes e Extraordinárias...*, 7 September, 1822, no. 31, 875.
20. *Diário das Cortes Constituintes e Extraordinárias...*, 20 February 1821, no. 19, 125.
21. Quoted by Z. Osório de Castro, *Cultura e Política. Manuel Borges Carneiro e o vintismo*, 2 vols, Lisbon, 1989, vol. 2, 481.

22. J. Serrão (ed.), *Liberalismo, Socialismo, Republicanismo: Antologia de pensamento político português*, Lisbon, 1979, 57.

23. Anonymous, *A Revolução anti-constitutional em 1823, suas verdadeiras causas e effeitos*, London, 1825.

24. Lousada, *O miguelismo*, 41–43.

25. A. de Moraes e Silva, *Diccionario da lingua portuguesa*, 4th edn, Lisbon, 1844.

26. M. Halpern Pereira et al. (eds), *Obras de Mouzinho da Silveira*, 2 vols, Lisbon, 1989, vol. 1, 682.

27. On the history of the Portuguese 1830s and 1840s, see R. Ramos, 'A Revolução Liberal, 1834–1851', in R. Ramos, B.V. Sousa and N.G. Monteiro (eds), *História de Portugal*, Lisbon, 2009, 491–519; M. de Fátima Bonifácio, *D. Maria II*, Lisbon, 2006.

28. Quoted by J.P. Oliveira Martins, *Portugal Contemporâneo*, 2nd edn, 2 vols, Lisbon, 1883 [1881], vol. 2, 92, 119.

29. A. Herculano, *Introdução à Voz do Profeta* [1867], in *Opúsculos*, ed. J. Custódio and J.M. Garcia, Lisbon, 1982, vol. 1, 38.

30. See R. Ramos, 'Recordações românticas', an introduction to Prince Lichnowsky, *Portugal em 1842*, Lisbon, 1990, 7–19; and M. de Fátima Bonifácio, 'Costa Cabral no contexto do doutrinarismo europeu (1815–48)', *Análise Social* 123–24 (1993), 1043–91.

31. M. de Fátima Bonifácio, *Estudos de história contemporânea de Portugal*, Lisbon, 2007, 15, 26.

32. A. de Moraes e Silva, *Diccionario da lingua portuguesa*, 4th edn, Lisbon, 1844.

33. On the 1851 Regeneration, see R. Ramos, 'A Regeneração e o Fontismo, 1851–1890', in Ramos et al. (eds) *História de Portugal*, 521–48; M. de Fátima Bonifácio, *Um Homem Singular: Biografia Política de Rodrigo da Fonseca Magalhães*, Lisbon, 2013; J.M. Sardica, *A Regeneração sob o Signo do Consenso: A política e os partidos entre 1851 e 1861*, Lisbon, 2001.

34. On Fontes Pereira de Melo and the political tradition associated with him, see R. Ramos, *A Segunda Fundação, 1890–1926*, vol. 4 of J. Mattoso (ed.), *História de Portugal*, Lisbon, 2001; M.F. Mónica, *Fontes Pereira de Melo*, Porto, 1999.

35. J. Arroio, *Discursos Parlamentares*, Porto, 1885, 274f.

36. On the Catholic movements under the liberal regime, see M. Clemente, *Igreja e Sociedade Portuguesa do Liberalismo à República*, Lisbon, 2012; on the Portuguese Republican Party from the 1870s, see F. Catroga, *O Republicanismo em Portugal*, Coimbra, 1991.

37. R. Ramos, *João Franco e o Fracasso do Reformismo Liberal, 1884–1908*, Lisbon, 2001, 52–54.

38. On the debates on the monarchy under liberal rule, see R. Ramos, *D. Carlos, 1863–1908*, Lisbon, 2007.

39. See J.J. Lopes Praça, *Direito Constitucional Português: Estudos sobre a Carta Constitucional de 1826*, 3 vols, Coimbra, 1997, vol. 2, 120, 157.

40. In fact, the new electoral law did not completely break away from the previous mental frameworks. It was assumed that the capacity to maintain a family was

the sign of that 'independence' that until then had been proved through a person's income and level of education. See M.F. Mónica, 'As reformas eleitorais no Constitucionalismo Monárquico, 1852–1910', *Análise Social* 139 (1996), 1052.

41. P. Tavares de Almeida, *Eleições e Caciquismo no Portugal Oitocentista (1868–1890)*, Lisbon, 1991, 143.

42. Ramos, *D. Carlos*.

43. See R. Ramos, 'O país mais liberal do mundo: transformaciones y colapso del liberalismo en Portugal (1880–1910)', in Marcela García Sebastiani and Fernando del Rey (eds), *Los Desafíos de la Libertad: Transformación y Crisis del Liberalismo en Europa y América Latina*, Madrid, 2008, 97–119.

44. M. de Fátima Bonifácio, *Seis Estudos sobre o Liberalismo Português*, Lisbon, 1991, 241–79.

45. See, for example, J. Andrade Corvo, *Economia Política para Todos*, Lisbon, 1881.

46. R. Ramos, *A Segunda Fundação, 1890–1926*, vol. 6 of Mattoso (ed.), *História de Portugal*.

47. J. Batalha Reis, 'Conferência', *Revista de Portugal* 3 (1891), 375.

48. Halpern Pereira et al. (eds), *Obras de Mouzinho*.

49. On the ideas of Herculano, see A.J. Saraiva, *Herculano e o Liberalismo em Portugal*, Lisbon, 1977; and H. Bernstein, *Alexandre Herculano (1810–1877): Portugal's Prime Historian and Historical Novelist*, Paris, 1983.

50. A. Herculano, *Opúsculos…*, vol. 1, 293–311.

51. Ibid., 33–42.

52. On Oliveira Martins, see R. Ramos, 'Oliveira Martins e a Ética Republicana', *Penélope* 18 (1998), 167–87; and R. Ramos, 'A Prisoner of Liberalism: The Strange Case of J.P. Oliveira Martins', *Portuguese Studies* 16 (2000), 51–81; G. de Oliveira Martins, *Oliveira Martins*, Lisbon, 1999; C. Coelho Maurício, *A Invenção de Oliveira Martins: Política, Historiografia e Identidade Nacional no Portugal Contemporâneo*, Lisbon, 2005.

53. O. Martins, *Portugal Contemporâneo*, Lisbon, 1881, vol. 2, livro quarto: Chapter 3.

54. See R. Ramos, 'Portuguese, But Not Citizens: Restricted Citizenship in Portugal', in R. Bellamy and D. Castiglione (eds), *Lineages of Citizenship in Europe*, London, 2004, 92–112; and R. Ramos, 'A Tale of One City? Local Civic Traditions under Liberal and Republican Rule in Portugal', *Citizenship Studies* 11(2) (2007), 173–86.

Bibliography

A Revolução anti-constitutional em 1823, suas verdadeiras causas e effeitos. London, 1825.

Alexandre, V. *Os Sentidos do Império: Questão Nacional e Questão Colonial na Crise do Antigo Regime Português*. Oporto, 1993.

Almeida, P. Tavares de. *Eleições e Caciquismo no Portugal Oitocentista (1868–1890)*. Lisbon, 1991.

Arroio, J. *Discursos Parlamentares*. Porto, 1885.

Bernstein, H. *Alexandre Herculano (1810–1877): Portugal's Prime Historian and Historical Novelist*. Paris, 1983.

Bonifácio, M. De Fatima. 'Costa Cabral no contexto do doutrinarismo europeu (1815–48)'. *Análise Social*, 123–24 (1993), 1043–91.

Boisvert, G. *Un Pionnier de la Propagande Libérale au Portugal: João Bernardo da Rocha Loureiro, 1778–1853*. Lisbon, 1974.

Castro, D.L.F. *Politica moral, e civil …* Lisbon, 1749.

Catroga, F. *O Republicanismo em Portugal*. Coimbra, 1991.

Clemente, M. *Igreja e Sociedade Portuguesa do Liberalismo à República*. Lisbon, 2012.

Corvo, J. Andrade. *Economia Política para Todos*. Lisbon, 1881.

Costa, F.D. 'Franceses e jacobinos: Movimentações populares e medidas de polícias em 1808 e 1809'. *Ler História* 54 (2008), 95–132.

———. *D. Maria II*. Lisbon, 2006.

———. *Estudos de história contemporânea de Portugal*. Lisbon, 2007.

———. *Seis Estudos sobre o Liberalismo Português*. Lisbon, 1991.

———. *Um Homem Singular: Biografia Política de Rodrigo da Fonseca Magalhães*. Lisbon, 2013.

Dias, G., and J.S. da Silva. *Os Primórdios da Maçonaria em Portugal*. Lisbon, 1980.

E Silva, A. De Moraes. *Diccionario da lingua portuguesa*, 4th edn. Lisbon, 1844.

Herculano, A. *Opúsculos*. Ed. J. Custódio and J.M. Garcia, vol. 1, Lisbon, 1982.

Lousada, M.A. *O miguelismo (1828–1834): O discurso político e o apoio da nobreza titulada*. Lisbon, 1987.

Martins, G. De Oliveira. *Oliveira Martins*. Lisbon, 1999.

Martins, J.P. Oliveira. *Portugal Contemporâneo*, vol. 2. Lisbon, 1881.

Maurício, C. Coelho, *A Invenção de Oliveira Martins: Política, Historiografia e Identidade Nacional no Portugal Contemporâneo*. Lisbon, 2005.

Mónica, M.F. 'As reformas eleitorais no Constitucionalismo Monárquico, 1852–1910'. *Análise Social* 139 (1996), 1039–84.

———. *Fontes Pereira de Melo*. Porto, 1999.

Monteiro, N.G., and R. Ramos. 'El liberalismo en Portugal en el siglo XIX', in J. Fernández-Sebastián (ed.), *La aurora de la libertad: Los primeros liberalismos en el mundo iberoamericano* (Madrid, 2012), 379–410.

Monteiro, N.G. *Elites e Poder: Entre o Antigo Regime e o Liberalism*. Lisbon, 2007.

Osório de Castro, Z. *Cultura e Política. Manuel Borges Carneiro e o vintismo*, vol. 2. Lisbon, 1989.

Pedreira J., and F. Dores Costa. *D. João VI*. Lisbon, 2005.

Pereira, M. Halpern, Alexandre V. and Magda Pinheiro (eds). *Obras de Mouzinho da Silveira*, vol. 1, Lisbon, 1989.

Praça, J.J. Lopes. *Direito Constitucional Português: Estudos sobre a Carta Constitucional de 1826*, vol. 2. Coimbra, 1997.

Ramos, R. 'A Prisoner of Liberalism: The Strange Case of J.P. Oliveira Martins'. *Portuguese Studies* 16 (2000), 51–81.

———. 'A Regeneração e o Fontismo, 1851–1890', in R. Ramos, B.V. Sousa and N.G. Monteiro (eds), *História de Portugal* (Lisbon, 2009), 521–48.

———. 'A Revolução Liberal, 1834–1851', in R. Ramos, B.V. Sousa and N.G. Monteiro (eds), *História de Portugal* (Lisbon, 2009), 491–519.

———. *A Segunda Fundação, 1890–1926*, vol. 4 of J. Mattoso (ed.), *História de Portugal*. Lisbon, 2001.

———. *A Segunda Fundação, 1890–1926*, vol. 6 of J. Mattoso (ed.), *História de Portugal*. Lisbon, 2001.

———. *D. Carlos, 1863–1908*. Lisbon, 2007.

———. *João Franco e o Fracasso do Reformismo Liberal, 1884–1908*. Lisbon, 2001.

———. 'La revolución de 1808 y los origenes del liberalismo en Portugal: Una reinterpretación', in A. Ávila and P. Pérez Herrero (eds), *Las Experiencias de 1808 en Iberoamerica* (Mexico City, 2008), 251–78.

———. 'O país mais liberal do mundo: transformaciones y colapso del liberalismo en Portugal (1880–1910)', in M. García Sebastiani and F. del Rey (eds), *Los Desafíos de la Libertad: Transformación y Crisis del Liberalismo en Europa y América Latina* (Madrid, 2008), 97–119.

———. 'Oliveira Martins e a Ética Republicana'. *Penélope* 18 (1998), 167–87.

———. 'Portuguese, But Not Citizens: Restricted Citizenship in Portugal', in R. Bellamy and D. Castiglione (eds), *Lineages of Citizenship in Europe* (London, 2004), 92–112.

———. 'Recordações românticas', an introduction to P. Lichnowsky, *Portugal em 1842* (Lisbon, 1990), 7–19.

———. 'A Tale of One City? Local Civic Traditions under Liberal and Republican Rule in Portugal'. *Citizenship Studies* 11(2) (2007), 173–86.

Reis, J. Batalha. 'Características de Portugal na Europa – Conferência'. *Revista de Portugal* 3 (1891), 346–376.

Saraiva, A.J. *Herculano e o Liberalismo em Portugal*. Lisbon, 1977.

Sardica, J.M. *A Regeneração sob o Signo do Consenso: A política e os partidos entre 1851 e 1861*. Lisbon, 2001.

Serrão, J. (ed.). *Liberalismo, Socialismo, Republicanismo: Antologia de pensamento político português*. Lisbon, 1979.

Silva, A. Mansuy-Diniz. *Portrait d'un Homme d'État: D. Rodrigo de Sousa Coutinho, Comte de Linhares, 1755–1812*. Paris, 2002.

Soriano, S.J. da Luz. *História da Guerra Civil e do Estabelecimento do Governo Representativo em Portugal*, vol. 2. Lisbon, 1881.

Valente, V. Pulido. *Os Militares e a Política, 1820–1854*. Lisbon, 1997.

Verdelho, T. *As Palavras e as Ideias na Revolução Liberal de 1820*. Coimbra, 1981.

Chapter 5

The Rise and Fall of 'Liberalism' in France

Helena Rosenblatt

Recent scholarship has corrected the long-held misconception that France lacked a liberal tradition. A plethora of works now testify to the contrary, whether it be in the form of surveys of French political thought since the Revolution or monographs on individual thinkers.[1] This chapter aims to make a contribution to this growing body of scholarship on French liberalism. It will do so by adopting a relatively new approach.[2] Most existing work on the topic of liberalism starts with a preconceived notion of what 'liberalism' means and then proceeds to measure thinkers against that standard. In contrast, the aim here will be to comprehend what French thinkers themselves meant when they used the terms 'liberal' or 'liberalism'. Strong evidence now suggests that 'liberalism' was invented not in England or in America, but in France, and in reaction to the French Revolution. It was thereafter vigorously debated, adapted and transformed over the course of the nineteenth and twentieth centuries. By taking this approach, this chapter aims to correct some persisting misunderstandings of what liberalism actually meant during its so-called 'classical' period.

'Liberal' and 'Liberality' before 'Liberalism'

'Liberalism' emerged as a self-conscious political movement only in the nineteenth century, which is also when the word made its first appearances in dictionaries. Before then, however, the word 'liberal' had been in use for a long time. It stems from the Latin word *liber*, meaning both 'free' and 'generous', or *liberalis*, meaning 'befitting a free-born person' as opposed to a slave. Until the nineteenth century, the corresponding noun to the adjective 'liberal' was not 'liberalism', which did not yet exist, but 'liberality'. And 'liberality' referred to an ethical ideal and mode of conduct rather than a set of political principles.

Although the word 'liberal' did not point to any specific political policy or programme, it did have political implications and associations. In antiquity, the 'liberal arts' were meant to prepare free men for their freedom by teaching them the necessary virtues. The Roman Stoic philosopher Seneca (4 BCE–65 CE) defined 'liberal studies' (*studia liberalia*) as those 'worthy of a free-born gentleman'. He made sure to specify that such studies were *not* about preparing students for money-making or profit-bringing occupations; rather, they were about preparing them for virtue, with making them lofty, brave and great-souled.[3] The concept of the liberal arts was translated into French around 1210. There, as elsewhere, they were contrasted with the 'servile' or 'mechanical' arts, and thus dovetailed nicely with ideas about what it meant to be noble. Charles Loyseau's *Treatise on Orders* of 1610 explains that the:

> mechanical arts ... are so named to distinguish them from the liberal arts. This is so because the mechanical arts were formerly practiced by serfs and slaves, and indeed we commonly call mechanical anything that is vile and abject.[4]

The word 'liberal' also became overlaid with Christian meanings suggestive of charity and compassion. God, Christians were often told, was liberal in his mercy, as was Jesus in his love. French dictionaries from the Middle Ages on defined 'liberal' as 'he who likes to give; he who gives with ease and pleasure'.[5] This is the meaning of liberal found in Jacques-Benigne Bossuet's (1627–1704) famous *Funeral Orations*, in which liberal actions are described as charitable, generous and self-effacing ones, and 'liberality' is defined as 'giving not only with joy but with elevation of soul'.[6]

Such meanings had unmistakably aristocratic overtones in early modern France. The attribute 'liberal' indicated a generosity of spirit, a selflessness and a devotion to service that was at least supposed to be a noble attribute. As Jean-Baptiste Massillon (1663–1742) explained in one of his famous sermons, those 'born among the people' are 'less capable of liberality', while 'generosity, elevated sentiments, sensitivity to the unfortunate and ... *largesse*' are the marks of nobility. What could be more 'base' or 'common [*peuple*]', he asked, than being insensitive to human misery?[7] Indeed, a *Treatise on Nobility* published by the genealogist and court historiographer Gilles-André de la Rocque in 1678 identifies a number of different kinds of nobility, specifying that the 'liberal' variety was the one accorded to individuals who, 'moved by a laudable zeal, spend their wealth in defence of the state and fatherland'.[8] The same definition was repeated word for word in Diderot's and D'Alembert's *Encyclopedia* one hundred years later.[9] Thus, on the eve of the

French Revolution, 'liberal' signified the high-minded, magnanimous and patriotic ideals of a ruling class.

The Politicization of 'Liberal'

The French Revolution changed all of that. Its overall effect was to inflect the word 'liberal' in a decidedly political and populist direction. The word's connections with aristocratic values were loosened, while new connections with ideas of constitutionalism and natural rights were formed. The word 'liberalism' was born. But these innovations happened gradually and incompletely, and were contested every step of the way. Old notions of the word 'liberal' persisted alongside new ones. A French dictionary published as late as 1818 still attributed 'liberal habits' to 'persons of good birth'.[10]

Benjamin Constant (1767–1830) was one of the first in France to use the word 'liberal' to describe a political stance. In his early pamphlets, written during the Directory, he labelled his own politics 'liberal'.[11] 'Liberal opinions', 'liberal ideas' and 'liberal principles' were those of 'the friends of liberty and enlightenment', who defended the principal achievements of the Revolution.[12] To Constant, being liberal meant advocating civil equality and representative, constitutional government. During the Directory, it meant defending the Republic and the Constitution of 1795. Constant accused of 'illiberality' those who 'preach[ed] resistance to the necessary improvements', the men of 'retrograde' and 'narrow views', who wished to return to 'the triple edifice of royalty, nobility and priesthood'.[13] Constant's 'liberal' posture was one of self-conscious and deliberate centrism, moderation and pragmatism. To one correspondent, he wrote that he was against 'the extremes', whether they were right-wing 'Royalists' or left-wing 'Terrorists'.[14] He wished to consolidate constitutional government and to prevent a return to either the *ancien régime* or the Terror.

Using the word 'liberal' in this way was no doubt a bit of a rhetorical ploy – and one that certainly annoyed Constant's adversaries. Constant may well have hoped that employing a word that conjured up aristocratic values of *largesse*, Christian ideas of charity and compassion, and Roman notions of virtue and citizenship would help garner support for his cause. But his adversaries on the Right could not fail to notice the sleight of hand: he was in fact turning their own concept against them. He was using a word associated with aristocratic values against aristocratic privileges. Many of them felt that he was attacking Christian principles too. No wonder, then, that Constant was accused of being a liar and a hypocrite. To his enemies, his so-called 'liberal principles' were not liberal at all. What they stood for in reality was a 'revolutionary spirit' that threatened society with dissolution and anarchy.

Moreover, there was something foreign about these so-called 'liberal ideas' – something ominously 'Protestant'. Indeed, the counterrevolutionary theorist Joseph de Maistre (1753–1821) would later call Constant's principles 'political protestantism'.[15]

Such disagreements did not prevent others from continuing to link the word 'liberal' with what they regarded as the more 'generous' aspects of the Revolution. The word's positive connotations, combined with its still somewhat amorphous and malleable meaning, led Napoleon Bonaparte to adopt it for his own uses. In his famous proclamation of the 19th Brumaire (1799), in which he tried to explain his seizure of power in a reassuring way, he claimed to have acted in defence of 'conservative, protective [and] liberal ideas'.[16] A few days later, the newspaper *L'Ami des Lois* noted that 'from the mouth of Bonaparte, liberal ideas have another meaning than from the mouth of aristocrats'.[17] By his use of the word, Bonaparte was of course suggesting that he would safeguard the essential achievements of the Revolution. This is also why Madame de Staël (1766–1817), around the same time, could refer to him as 'the best republican in France … [and] the most liberal of Frenchmen'.[18] The idea that Napoleon was the 'hero of liberal ideas' thereafter became a central part of his propaganda.

It was probably through Napoleonic propaganda that the notion of 'liberal ideas' came to Spain. In the first known use of the word to designate a political party and platform, a group of delegates to the Spanish Cortes, meeting in Cadiz in 1812, adopted the term to designate a programme seeking to end feudal privileges and monarchical absolutism, and supporting civil equality and constitutional government instead. They called themselves 'Liberales' and their opponents 'Serviles'.[19] The *Liberales* supported principles such as national sovereignty, equality before the law, representative and elective government, and a number of individual rights, such as freedom from arbitrary arrest, freedom of the press and the protection of private property.[20] The constitution they produced consecrated these principles and was approved by the Cortes in 1812.

The connection of the word 'liberal' with constitutional government was thereafter reinforced by none other than Louis XVIII, who, in his famous declaration of Saint Ouen of 2 May 1814 issued upon his return from exile after the defeat of Napoleon, promised to 'give France a liberal constitution'.[21] Like its Spanish predecessor, this 'liberal constitution', also called the 'Constitutional Charter', instituted an elective, representative system of government and recognized a number of civil liberties, such as equality before the law, freedom of the press, freedom of religion and the inviolability of private property. After its proclamation, the word 'liberal' was sometimes used as a simple synonym for 'constitutional', or to designate supporters of the Charter.

Running for election as a member of what he now occasionally referred to as the 'liberal party', [22] Benjamin Constant promised to 'demand the exact execution of the Charter in its fullest scope'. He would protect 'the peaceful and gradual consolidation of our political institutions', 'strengthen our liberty' and fight for 'the rights and the happiness of all'.[23] Somewhat contradictorily, however, liberals like Constant also sometimes liked to claim that they were not really a 'party', since they saw themselves as above self-interested motives and as representing the best interests of the country as a whole. Liberals were those who wanted 'to be free under a truly representative government, in other words, only to submit to laws conforming to the good of all'.[24] As one journalist explained, a liberal was 'a friend of the public good; he [was] not a man of party'.[25] In fact, however, liberals *were* a party in the sense of being a loose coalition of like-minded members in the Chamber of Deputies, who voted in support of 'liberal' ideas and against reactionary ones.

Royalists and counterrevolutionaries objected to the new use of the word. They protested that it was being twisted and misused for self-interested and political reasons. As one of them complained: 'Today's political language is not yet fixed and words have as many meanings as the party spirit can find.'[26] Louis de Bonald (1754–1840), an important counterrevolutionary theorist and spokesman, noted that in the old days '[l]iberal, in good French, meant he who makes a noble use of his fortune'. Now people were using the word differently, speaking of 'liberal *ideas*'. This was to 'distort' the meaning in order to 'play a trick' on the country.[27] In *La Quotidienne*, one of the first reactionary newspapers of the Revolution that later returned during the Restoration, the attack on 'liberal ideas' continued:

> For some time there has been a lot of talk of liberal ideas. What is understood by that word? The Academy has not approved it in its Dictionary; Diderot and d'Alembert did not talk about it in the Encyclopedia. It is then evident that the word is very modern and that it was born during the revolution. The era of its origin must make it suspect.[28]

A barrage of articles and pamphlets lambasted the 'friends of supposedly liberal institutions' and the 'preachers of liberal ideas'. While claiming to be 'generous', they were really propagating a 'subtle poison' as 'dangerous' as it was 'seductive'. They had no sense of duty and respected no authority whatsoever;[29] they favoured 'the most absolute independence, the most unregulated liberty'. Motivated by 'vile egoism', the 'love of money' and 'insatiable ambition', they were the 'natural, and irreconcilable enemies of monarchy'.[30] How could liberals claim to defend the Charter, asked Louis de Bonald, when their principles were actually 'democratic'?[31]

In response, liberals produced campaigns and pamphlets of their own. The newspaper *La Minerve française*, to which Benjamin Constant contributed articles, went to great lengths to differentiate 'a constitutional and liberal system' from 'despotism' on the one hand and 'anarchy' on the other.[32] As for the invectives hurled against them, liberals showed that they could give as good as they got. They described ultraroyalism as 'a demeaning absurdity', a system favouring 'slavery', 'oligarchy' and 'despotism'.[33] But they also continued to claim the high ground, calling themselves 'the voice of the nation', fighting for 'the interests of the great majority' rather than those of 'a privileged caste'.[34] Reminding his readers of the Latin origins of the word, one liberal pamphleteer explained that 'a political idea is 'liberal'' when it:

> is directed toward the advantage of all, toward the public good and not toward the particular good of an individual or a class; when it favours generous, elevated, patriotic sentiments and not vanity, cupidity and weakness; when it is, in a word, worthy not of a clever courtisan, a mercenary adulator or a weak slave, but of a citizen of the State, an independent and active member of the political family.[35]

Liberals also liked to claim that only constitutional principles were in accordance with the forward march of history, while their adversaries were trying to take the country backwards. A short-lived newspaper called *The Liberal* declared that 'the era of liberal ideas' had finally arrived by 'the necessary course of things'.[36] Only a 'liberal regime' conformed to the current 'state of [French] *moeurs* and the enlightenment of the century'. Ultraroyalists responded that the so-called 'liberal ideas' would only bring destruction and disorder.

The Birth of 'Liberalism'

It was in this polarized context that the term 'liberalism' was coined. It seems highly likely that it was first employed by French ultraroyalists intending to discredit the 'liberal principles' of their adversaries. In one of the earliest uses of the word found in print, a virulent critic promises to expose the 'political lies built with words'. 'Liberalism', he writes, 'is supposed to signify all the generous sentiments, highminded wishes, love of true liberty, independence and nobility in the human heart.' It is also *supposed* to designate a 'profound respect for ... the equality of rights'. However, in fact, self-titled 'liberals' are 'the least liberal of all'. Their philosophy is nothing but 'selfishness', 'ambitiousness' and 'perfidy'. If liberals gained power in France, the inevitable result would be 'the most dreadful despotism'.[37]

Despite the insults being hurled back and forth, and the word games that were played, it *is* in fact possible to arrive at a fairly clear picture of what 'liberalism' meant during the Restoration. In the end, both sides agreed that it referred to the belief in limited, representative and constitutional monarchy, as well as civil equality and certain essential individual rights. And both sides agreed that liberals viewed the basic transformations to society brought about by the French Revolution as generally favourable ones, and wished to protect them.

Liberal Disagreements

In truth, however, there was a good deal of variation, disagreement and vagueness hidden behind the liberal label.[38] The word covered everything from old Jacobins and republicans to Bonapartists and constitutionalists of various political stripes. And while all liberals supported the 'principles of 1789' and the Constitutional Charter, they could interpret these differently. The Charter itself contained quite a few contradictions and ambiguities, and therefore invited disagreement among liberals on fundamental issues.

Liberals themselves were of course aware that their party was not homogeneous. An 1818 pamphlet distinguished between 'revolutionary', 'exaggerated' and 'royalist' liberals. 'Revolutionary' liberals were supporters of the more moderate principles of 1789, while 'exaggerated' liberals were supporters of the radical ideas of 1793, which included universal manhood suffrage. 'Royalist' liberals were recent converts to liberalism who supported constitutional monarchy under the Charter.[39] Such differences invariably created tensions over what reforms liberals should promote and how they should promote them. The pamphlet, *Advice to Liberals from a Liberal* (1818), censored certain liberals for being excessively critical of the current government and of royal power in general. Such a comportment risked turning the king into an enemy of the liberal party. Liberals should 'march with prudence and even slowness'.[40] Other liberals clearly disagreed. Some joined secret societies plotting to overthrow the government. One such secret society called itself 'The Liberal Union'.[41]

Much of Constant's work can be seen as an effort to educate and convince the French public as to *his* meaning of 'liberal principles'. The title of one of his most substantial publications, published in 1818–20, speaks for itself: *A Complete Collection of Works Published on Representative Government and the Present Constitution Constituting a Kind of Course in Constitutional Politics.* His reputation travelled as far as America, where, in 1820, the *National Gazette* called Constant the 'great leader' of the French 'liberals'.[42] At the same time, however, it should be known that Constant himself used the term

'liberal' very rarely and 'liberalism' not at all. He appears to have preferred
to call himself an 'independent'. Moreover, recent scholarship is proving that
Constant was quite a divisive figure, who never managed to coalesce a unified
party or even to generate a committed following, despite his ostensible popularity.[43] Late in life, Constant complained that no one was listening to him
and that he was sick of repeating himself.[44]

The truth is that prominent liberals disagreed on fairly substantive matters concerning principles, priorities and tactics. Constant and François
Guizot (1787–1874), for example, held very different views of the meaning
of representation, the legitimate location and extent of sovereignty, and the
role of the state. Liberals were also divided on the topic of religion, some
being atheist, others deist or Protestant, and some even being Catholic. Such
differences could and did translate into broad disagreements on religious and
educational policy. For example, there was no liberal consensus on the right
relationship between church and state.

Another area destined to become especially divisive among liberals was
that of political economy and, more specifically, the legacy of Adam Smith.
In late eighteenth and early nineteenth-century France, Smith was generally read as a deeply anti-aristocratic thinker very critical of the status quo.
During the Revolution, he was regarded as a friend of the poor and even a
closet republican, whose ideas justified radical constitutional change.[45] What
Smith was seen as advocating in *The Wealth of Nations* was the removal of
the economic prohibitions and restrictions that kept wealth and power in
the hands of the few at the expense of the many. In the nineteenth century,
several prominent French liberals were outspoken admirers of Smith's ideas
and they disseminated his ideas. Smith's 'liberal' economic principles complemented their liberal political principles: both aimed to put an end to the
unjust laws that propped up a regime based on special, inherited privileges.

Of course, Smith never called himself a 'liberal' or espoused anything
called 'liberalism', but he did use the word 'liberal' a handful of times in *The
Wealth of Nations*. Most tellingly, in Book IV, Chapter v on the Corn Laws,
he advocated a 'liberal system of free exportation and free importation',
which he contrasted with a 'mercantile one'. And in Book IV, Chapter IX, he
favoured 'allowing every man to pursue his own interest in his own way upon
the liberal plan of equality, liberty and justice'. Smith's 'liberal system', it is
clear, was 'in the interest of the public', while the mercantile one favoured the
'mean rapacity and monopolising spirit' of merchants and manufacturers in
cahoots with the landowning aristocracy.

Most prominent among Smith's early French disciples was Jean-Baptiste
Say (1767–1832), whose *Treatise on Political Economy* of 1803 clarified, sum-
marized and popularized Smith's ideas. Like Smith, Say strongly criticized

the tariffs and prohibitions that placed obstacles in the restraint of trade. In so doing, he displeased the life Consul, Napoleon, who demanded that Say make changes to his text or suffer censorship. When Say refused, he was prevented from publishing for the remainder of Napoleon's rule. Instead, Napoleon encouraged the publication of books favourable to mercantilism, such as François Ferrier's *On Government Considered in its Relationship with Commerce* of 1805. Ferrier (1777–1861) subsequently became Napoleon's Director of Customs. Defending the protectionist system of Colbert against the liberal one of Smith and his French disciples, Ferrier's book mocked their 'liberal principles', calling them the 'reveries' of 'anti-government writers' who fantasized about a 'liberal revolution' in commerce by which all nations would suddenly become friends.[46] Their false and 'absurd' ideas of freedom ran contrary to the lessons of history.

Immediately upon Napoleon's fall from power, Say published a new edition of his treatise on political economy, once again promoting 'liberal principles' of trade. However, despite his efforts, the Restoration ended up doing little to dismantle the established protectionist system. It seems that a laissez-faire approach to trade was never a realistic option for a regime that depended on the support of the very wealthy. Because of the regime's narrow basis of support, policy-makers could not avoid the prohibitions and tariffs demanded by special interests and its customs regime remained almost as restrictive as Napoleon's Continental System.[47] Evidence shows that there was also a good deal of support for prohibitions and protections among the middle and even lower classes,[48] which helps to explain the unrelenting educative efforts of Say and his disciples, who published streams of books and articles advocating the 'liberal' principles of trade.[49] Corrupt governments, Say warned, used prohibitions and tariffs to raise the money they needed to buy the votes required to stay in power.[50] Self-interested legislators colluded with avaricious businessmen against the public interest. It was necessary to educate the public directly, through articles, books and public lectures, about its true interests and about the true principles of political economy, to expose this 'vicious system' for what it was.

It is worth pointing out that Say's 'liberal' system, like that of Adam Smith, was not against all government intervention in the economy, although this is what some of his detractors claimed. He recognized explicitly that 'society is possessed of a natural right to regulate the exercise of any class of industry'. What he wished to abolish were 'arbitrary regulations' imposed 'under the pretext of the public good'. He argued that as a general rule, an enlightened government should be 'sparing' in its interference. But he also thought regulation 'useful and proper', when, for example, it aimed 'at the prevention of fraud or contrivance'. In matters of defence, the government clearly needed to play a major role. And public works were necessary, 'particularly roads, canals and harbours'. Say also believed that government should support 'academies, libraries, public schools and museums'. Finally, he made sure to state clearly that: 'Of all the means by which a government can stimulate production there is none so powerful as the perfect security of person and property, especially from the aggressions of arbitrary power.'[51]

Political economists like Say and his allies and disciples were in fact fighting a war on several fronts. They felt certain that liberal political institutions were not enough to produce a free and prosperous nation; liberal economic policies were vitally necessary as well. However, just as liberal politicians could disagree on basic principles and priorities, so could the liberal economists. Charles Comte (1782–1837) and Charles Dunoyer (1786–1862), editors of the journal *Le Censeur européen*, pushed government noninterventionism to extremes not found in either Smith or Say. Over time, they became disenchanted with politics and argued that liberal economic policies should be given *priority*, while further political reforms could wait. One recent scholar has rightly called them 'hard-core advocates of pure laissez-faire'.[52] But Jean-Charles-Léonard Sismondi (1773–1842), a close friend and collaborator of Constant, came to believe the opposite: in certain areas of the economy, the government should intervene *more* rather than less. In 1803, Sismondi had published *De la richesse commerciale*, in which he argued for the absolute freedom of commerce and industry. But in 1819, he published his *New Principles of Political Economy*, in which he changed his mind, urging the need to 'modify', 'complete' and 'develop' some of Smith's ideas in light of the new and shocking facts emerging about the conditions of workers in an industrializing economy.[53] It was time to focus not so much on wealth *creation*, but also on its *distribution*. Yet, despite these quite serious differences between the economists, they all remained within the 'liberal' camp, as defined at the time.[54] This becomes abundantly clear when we consider the tense years of the Restoration.

The Counterrevolutionary Attack Triggers the Revolution of 1830

In February of 1820, the ultraroyalist Duc de Berry, heir-presumptive to the French throne, was assassinated by a man named Louvel, who appears to have been mentally unwell. The murder triggered a wave of reaction across the country. Enraged royalists blamed liberals for the murder. One writer for the *Journal des Débats* declared: 'I have seen Louvel's dagger; it was a liberal idea.'[55] New election and press laws were now passed that made it more difficult for liberals to gain office, driving many of them underground, while ultraroyalists took control of the Chamber of Deputies. Laws to restore primogeniture, indemnify émigrés, limit press freedom further and make 'sacrilege' a crime punishable by death were proposed by the ultraroyalists, and were fought every step of the way by liberals. Tellingly, trade prohibitions were also imposed on the economy.

In July 1819, a French version of the British Corn Law of 1815 had been implemented in response to a decline in wheat prices. Beginning in the spring of 1821, the new ultraroyalist majority imposed an outright prohibition on the importation of foreign grain below a certain price. The Prime Minister and leader of the ultraroyalists in the Chamber, Joseph de Villèle, defended the measure on the grounds that it was necessary for the 'protection of agriculture'. The following year, another restrictive customs law was passed.

Benjamin Constant was one of the most vocal liberal critics of the measures. From the tribune he denounced – in his characteristically provocative and sarcastic manner – the 'enthusiasm for [the] high price [of grain]' among deputies who just happened to be large landowners as well. He called the proposed legislation 'cruel', 'unjust' and self-serving.[56] Clearly, the already-rich were using the government to enrich themselves further at the expense of the labouring poor. More controversially still, given the ultraroyalist mood of the Chamber, Constant defended the Revolution's equal inheritance laws: he said that the resulting division of property had been good for the country. He then published a book called *Commentary on the Work of Filangieri* to alert the public to the hoax being perpetrated on them. He blended economic and political arguments to combat the ultraroyalists and to educate the liberals. Beware of being hoodwinked, he said. Beware of governments who propose supposedly 'philanthropic projects'. Legislative improvements could not be expected from a government of the super-rich. 'Real progress', he urged, would only come from 'the progress of reason in the masses and from a truly representative government', which clearly did not yet exist in France. He urged liberals to keep their political spirit alive.[57] Under the present circumstances, France's government's economic role should be 'purely negative'. It should 'repress disorder, eliminate obstacles … [and] let the good take care of itself'. Given the state of France, the motto of its government should be 'Laissez faire et laissez passer'. It should be noted that despite his strong advocacy of government noninterventionism in this text, Constant also praised Sismondi's *New Principles* as being 'full of just and ingenious ideas and philanthropic views'.[58] And he insisted, in contrast to liberal political economists like Dunoyer, that constitutional issues remained vital. Constant knew very well that when it came to fighting the ultraroyalists, they were all on the same side.

Their adversaries responded angrily. François Ferrier's book deriding the 'liberal principles' of so-called 'anti-government writers' was reissued several times. Others used stronger language. Liberalism, they said, was 'a doctrine of hatred' not just against kings but also against landlords and all 'legitimate authority'.[59] Liberals were Jacobins in disguise who wanted to relaunch the Revolution. But as is now well known, the ultraroyalists in the Chamber misjudged the mood of the country. Their counterrevolutionary policies provoked a backlash across France and by 1827 the political pendulum had swung back in favour of liberals. Ultraroyalists now reacted in panic, eventually triggering the July Revolution of 1830. They attacked liberals for being:

> republican, anarchist and seditious gazeteers who, for more than twelve years, have relentlessly attacked all that is true and good ... [and who] long ardently for a new revolution, more complete than the first.[60]

In a certain sense, they were right: the expected Revolution came and was a clear victory for 'liberal principles'. The Charter was secured and absolutism was defeated. The new king, Louis-Philippe, accepted the principle of national sovereignty, replacing the white banner of the Bourbons with the Tricolour as France's national flag. But the celebrations would be short-lived. In power, liberals soon splintered into disputing factions unable to agree on fundamental issues. They argued over everything from the expansion of the suffrage to the size of the bureaucracy, the value of centralization, the advantages or disadvantages of associations, and on economic, foreign and religious policy. The 1830 Revolution was, indeed, a 'decisive moment for French liberalism',[61] as Pierre Rosanvallon has suggested, but it was not because French liberals opted for a large-state solution (as he and others have proposed), but because they could not agree on what they stood for.

'Liberal Disagreements ... Again'

An immediate fissure was one between those, like François Guizot and Charles de Rémusat (1797–1875), who saw the July Revolution as an essentially defensive or conservative one, and those, like the Marquis de Lafayette (1757–1834) and Odilon Barrot (1791–1873), who saw it as an opportunity to undertake more progressive reforms. Eventually the conservatives won, but not before major dissensions had arisen among those who wanted more 'movement' in the direction of democracy and those who stressed 'resistance' and 'order'. The French electorate was doubled in April 1831 from about 94,000 to 200,000, but this still meant that only the very wealthiest Frenchmen could vote and hold office. Some of those seeking movement merged with disgruntled republicans who also felt that the July Revolution had not gone far enough. They called for a regime based on universal male suffrage. Odilon Barrot argued that only 'liberal *and progressive*' reforms could guarantee the future of constitutional government.[62] The self-described 'liberal *and conservative*'[63] regime responded with laws restricting the right of association and freedom of the press. By a law of 29 November 1830, any journalist who attacked the dignity and constitutional prerogatives of the king, the order of succession to the throne, or the rights and authority of the legislative chambers was subject to prosecution and, if found guilty, to substantial fines and several months in prison. In 1835, it became illegal even to call oneself a republican. The liberals in power were now accused of betraying their own principles.

Economic policies also splintered and weakened the liberals while discrediting the regime in the eyes of the larger public. Barrot later recalled that the July Monarchy showed the same 'timidity, the same resistance to all change' in the economic realm as it had in the political realm.[64] Faced with a severe economic crisis that it could not or would not understand – it is said that Guizot would leave the room when the topic of conversation turned to economics – and the social problems that the crisis spawned, widespread unemployment and poverty, strikes, demonstrations and riots, compounded by a devastating cholera epidemic, the leadership responded in ways that were deemed callous, ineffective and even incoherent. Although, in government circles, economic liberalism dominated *theoretically*, in practice it yielded to pragmatic considerations, such as concerns about order and anxieties about the relatively slow pace of French economic modernization in comparison to England.[65] The government did very little to alleviate the suffering of the poor, while it intervened in ways that favoured the rich. It supported employers against workers, repeatedly sending out troops to suppress strikes and demonstrations. It maintained a high tariff regime that benefited wealthy producers over poor consumers and imposed taxes that hit the poor disproportionately hard. It heavily subsidized the construction of railroads and extended guaranteed loans to preferred industries. Continuing what was in fact long-established practice, the government pursued inconsistent interventionism that benefited only a small segment of the population.

Political economists voiced their dissatisfaction. They accused the '*so-called* liberal party' of fatal 'contradictions' and tried to lobby the government to change its policies.[66] In 1841, they founded a Société d'économie politique and launched the *Journal des économistes*.[67] They demanded '*truly liberal* legislation', in particular, a more 'liberal system of commerce', that they believed would lower the cost of living.[68] One of their most energetic and prolific journalists was Frédéric Bastiat (1801–50). Inspired by the British Anti-Corn

Law League, he tried to replicate its successes in France, but ultimately failed. As a group, French liberal economists became increasingly frustrated and doctrinaire. Dunoyer opposed governmental involvement in education, public works, mail delivery and even in the case of factory legislation to regulate child labour. The only legitimate role of the state, he insisted, was to provide internal and external security. Bastiat was only slightly less extreme. Early in 1831, he denounced the 'monstrous centralisation' of government perpetrated by Napoleon and perpetuated by the Restoration. Government had become a 'vast machine ... indefinitely expanding its sphere of action'.[69] Running for election fifteen years later, Bastiat explained what the word 'liberal' meant to him: it meant fighting to keep government within 'the most narrow limits' of its functions.[70] But the truth is that the liberal leadership was divided on the issue. While 'liberalism', to these political economists, came progressively to mean strict government 'noninterventionism', not all French 'liberals' were for it.

There continued to be liberals in the mould of Sismondi who wanted the government to intervene *more*, not less. Saint-Simonian and socialist movements emerged during the 1830s and 1840s, which defined themselves in direct opposition to laissez-faire, economic 'liberalism'. They decried it as a 'selfish' doctrine that reflected the 'political power of the bourgeoisie'.[71] Echoing arguments coming also from the right, socialists accused liberalism of 'fatalistic' economic policies that only led to 'pauperism', a new word increasingly used to refer the phenomenon of endemic urban poverty. Liberalism was now denounced as a pernicious form of 'individualism' *lacking* in 'generosity ... aim or scope, heart or feeling'.[72] Liberals, it was said, had served their purpose – they had helped bring down the *ancien régime*. They were good at destroying, but did not know how to build, and offered no solutions to the many new problems afflicting France. The socialist François Vidal claimed that 'the liberals of the old Restoration', while avant garde for their times, were now outmoded. Having once subscribed to liberal economic principles himself, he now thought them 'purely negative' and thus quite useless. Having made sense at a particular point in time, they now only served the good of a very small minority and had to be revised.

On that principle, another prominent liberal agreed. Charles Dupont-White (1807–78), friend and translator of John Stuart Mill, wrote in 1846 that '[t]he liberalism of the last fifteen years' would be but a 'vain theory' if it profited 'only a minority, that is, those who are rich, strong and intelligent'. The government needed to exercise its authority 'for the good of the majority'. It should protect the weak against the strong and ensure the working class a minimum of wellbeing and security. Dupont-White argued that liberal ideas about the government's role had to adjust to the profound changes that had taken place in France's economic, political and religious conditions. Although he too favoured free trade and denied that he was for 'an unjust and chimerical equality', Dupont-White insisted that 'there is no liberty without regulation'.[73]

A small but vocal group of Catholic liberals also became bitterly disappointed by the supposedly 'liberal' regime. Despite the fact that the constitution officially guaranteed freedom of religion, the July Monarchy maintained the state monopoly on teaching and state control of the Church. Many of its leading figures, and liberals in general, continued to be deeply mistrustful of Catholicism. Thus, the government decreased the amounts budgeted for the upkeep of the Church every year until 1836, and expelled religious orders such as the Carthusians, Trappists and Franciscans. Catholic liberals responded by denouncing the '*so-called* liberal party' for being insufficiently or falsely liberal – in other words, for betraying 'real liberalism'. 'The intervention of government in religious things is both absurd and illegal', wrote Lamennais in his new journal *L'Avenir*, which was launched less than three months after the July Revolution. 'What is a real liberal, a consistent liberal?' he asked. It is a man who supports freedom of religion, freedom of teaching, freedom of the press and of association. And yet the July Monarchy, beholden to a 'false liberalism', was denying French Catholics all of these. Once in power, the false liberals just wanted 'to sit on the debris of the imperial throne'; they insisted on maintaining the old and oppressive anti-Catholic legislation in order to further their own 'bourgeois' interests. *L'Avenir* also attacked the doctrines of the liberal political economists as nothing more than a 'theology of material interests' favouring the rich against the poor. It advocated a 'new liberalism', which it also called a 'young liberalism' or a 'true liberalism', and that would advocate all the essential freedoms denied by the 'false' liberals in power, along with universal manhood suffrage.[74]

Perhaps most debilitating of all for the liberals in power were the accusations of corruption levied against them. Many of these charges came, once again, from within the liberal camp. In 1838, Duvergier de la Hauranne published *On the Principles of Representative Government*, in which he accused the regime of making a sham of representative government. Contradicting the very principles of the July Revolution, the king had acquired too much power and was using it inappropriately. In 1846, he followed this up with an even harder-hitting pamphlet entitled *On Parliamentary and Electoral Reform*, in which he denounced the widespread and growing corruption. He went so far as to say that France no longer had a representative government, but only an 'administrative' one. A major problem was the large number of government officials who were simultaneously deputies, allowing the king and his ministers to manipulate the legislature.[75]

Faced with all this opposition and dissension within their ranks, it is no wonder that leaders like François Guizot and Adolphe Thiers increasingly avoided the liberal label. By 1841, Tocqueville would write with sadness that the 'liberal ... party, which alone suits me, does not exist'[76] – and he announced that he would have to be a 'new kind of liberal'. A *Dictionnaire politique* of 1842 began its entry on 'Liberalism' with the words: 'There are few words harder to define.'[77] On the eve of the 1848 Revolution, Tocqueville then delivered a speech in the Chamber that has since become famous. He declared that more than parliamentary reform was necessary to cure the 'disease' afflicting France; the 'very spirit of government' had to change. He added his name to the ever-growing list of liberals accusing France's leaders of 'indifference' and even 'selfishness' – a betrayal of 'liberal principles' indeed.[78] A few weeks later, the July Monarchy was overthrown, with the meaning of 'liberalism' in considerable disarray.

The 1848 Revolution was a major setback for liberals, whose disagreements had weakened and discredited them. Frightened by worker unrest and the sudden eruption of socialism, they were led to compromise – some would say abandon – their principles and accept the authoritarian rule of Napoleon III. Some said that liberalism was now 'over'. When the liberals eventually recovered and began to press for reforms, they continued to debate the meaning of 'true liberalism'; in fact, they continue to do so today.[79] Some would advocate laissez-faire. Others embraced 'solidarism' or what they also called 'liberal socialism'. In retrospect, we can see that, in so doing, they in fact conceded the label 'liberal' to free market advocates. If you meant something more open to government intervention, you were obliged to add a qualifying term like 'progressive' or 'reforming'. This is likely why today 'liberalism' in French colloquial parlance means 'small government', while in America it means 'big government'.[80]

Helena Rosenblatt is Professor of History and Professor of French at the Graduate Center of the City University of New York and the author, most recently, of *The Lost History of Liberalism from Ancient Rome to the Twenty-First Century* (2018). She is also the author of *Rousseau and Geneva from the* First Discourse *to the* Social Contract (1997) and *Liberal Values: Benjamin Constant and the Politics of Religion* (2008). She is the editor of the *Cambridge Companion to Constant* (2009) and co-editor (with Raf Geenens) of *French Liberalism from Montesquieu to the Present Day* (2012) and (with Paul Schweigert) *Thinking with Rousseau: From Machiavelli to Schmitt* (2017).

Notes

I expand further on some of the materials in this chapter in my book *The Lost History of Liberalism: From Ancient Rome to the Twenty-First Century*, Princeton, 2018.

1. Even a partial list should include the following: R. Geneens and H. Rosenblatt (eds), *French Liberalism from Montesquieu to the Present Day*, Cambridge, 2010; P. Nemo and J. Petitot (eds), *Histoire du libéralisme en Europe*, Paris, 2006, Part II; J.-P. Clément, *Aux Sources du libéralisme français : Boissy d'Anglas, Daunou, Lanjuinais*, Paris, 2000; A. Craiutu, *Liberalism under Siege: The Political Thought of the French Doctrinaires*, Lanham, MD, 2003; A. Craiutu, *A Virtue for Courageous Minds: Moderation in French Political Thought, 1748–1830*, Princeton, 2012; A. de Dijn, *French Political Thought from Montesquieu to Tocqueville: Liberty in a Levelled Society?*, Cambridge, 2008; A. Jainchill, *Reimagining Politics after the Terror: The Republican Origins of French Liberalism*, Ithaca, NY, 2008; L. Jaume, *L'Individu éffacé ou le paradoxe du libéralisme français*, Paris, 1997; J. Jennings, *Revolution and the Republic: A History of Political Thought in France since the Eighteenth Century*, Oxford, 2011; A. Kahan, *Alexis de Tocqueville*, New York, 2013; F. Mélonio, *Tocqueville et les Français*, Paris, 1993; K.S. Vincent, *Benjamin Constant and the Birth of French Liberalism*. New York, 2011; Pierre Rosanvallon, *The Demands of Liberty: Civil Society in France since the Revolution*, A. Goldhammer (trans.), Cambridge, MA, 2007; H. Rosenblatt, *Liberal Values: Benjamin Constant and the Politics of Religion*, Cambridge, 2008; C. Welch, *De Tocqueville*, New York, 2001; R. Whatmore, *Republicanism and the French Revolution: An Intellectual History of Jean-Baptiste Say's Political Economy*, Oxford, 2000.

2. Let me here acknowledge my indebtedness to the following trailblazers in the field of semantic and conceptual history: G. de Bertier de Sauvigny, 'Libéralisme : aux origines d'un mot', *Commentaire* 7 (1979), 420–24; R. Vierhaus, 'Liberalismus', in O. Brunner, W. Conze and R. Koselleck (eds), *Geschichtliche Grundbegriffe: Historisches Lexikon zur politisch-sozialen Sprache in Deutschland*, 8 vols, Stuttgart, 1982, vol. 3, 741–85; J. Leonhard, *Liberalismus: Zur historischen Semantik eines europäischen Deutungsmusters*, Munich, 2001. I would also like to acknowledge the work of Melvin Richter.

3. M. Nussbaum, *Cultivating Humanity: A Classical Defense of Reform in Liberal Education*, Cambridge, MA, 1998, 30.

4. C. Loyseau, 'Traité des ordres et dignitez', in K. M. Baker (ed.), *University of Chicago Readings in Western Civilization*, vol. 7, *The Old Regime and the French Revolution*, Chicago, 1987, 30.

5. *Le Dictionnaire de l'Académie françoise*, Paris, 1694, vol. 1, 644, quoting a medieval source. Unless otherwise indicated, all translations are my own.

6. *Oraisons funèbres de Bossuet*, Paris, 1886, 150.

7. *Oeuvres de Massillon*, Paris , 1833, vol 2, 504.

8. G.A.de la Rocque, *Traité de la noblesse: de ses différentes espèces*, Paris, 1678, i. The entry cites de la Rocque.

9. *Encyclopédie, ou dictionnaire raisonné des sciences, des arts et des métiers*, Samuel Faulche & Compagnie, vol. 9, Neuchatel, 1765, 460; see Leonhard, *Liberalismus*, 96–100.

10. Cited by J. Leonhard in 'From European Liberalism to the Languages of Liberalisms: The Semantics of *Liberalism* in European Comparison', *Redescriptions. Yearbook of Political Thought and Conceptual History* 8 (2004), 17–51, at 21.

11. See Vincent, *Benjamin Constant*; and K.S. Vincent, 'Benjamin Constant, the French Revolution, and the Origins of French Romantic Liberalism', *French Historical Studies* 23(4) (Fall 2000), 607–37.

12. Philippe Raynaud (ed.), *Des réactions politiques* in *De la force du gouvernement actuel de la France et de la nécessité de s'y rallier*, Paris, 1988, 111, 115 and 118.

13. Ibid., 119.

14. Benjamin Constant à la comtesse Ann-Marie-Pauline-Andrienne de Nassau (7 August 1795), quoted in Vincent, *Benjamin Constant*, 45.

15. Joseph de Maistre, quoted in K. Swart, '"Individualism" in the Mid-nineteenth Century (1826–1860)', *Journal of the History of Ideas* 23(1) (1962), 78.

16. Napoléon Bonaparte, *Correspondances de Napoléon 1er*, vol. 6, Paris, 1862, 5–6.

17. Quote found in G. de Bertier de Sauvigny, 'Liberalism, Nationalism, Socialism: The Birth of Three Words', *Review of Politics* 32 (1970), 151–52.

18. In a letter of 24 July 1797, quoted by J. von Leyden Blennerhassett in *Madame de Staël, Her Friends, and Her Influence in Politics and Literature*, J.E. Gordon Cumming (trans.), Cambridge, 2013 [1889], vol. 3, 429.

19. J. Marichal, 'Espana y las raices semanticas de l liberalismo', *Cuadernos. Congresso per la libertad de la cultura* (March/April 1955), 53–60; and L. Diez del Corral, *El liberalismo doctrinario*, Madrid, 1956, 423.

20. But not religious freedom. See J. Fernández-Sebastián, 'The Crisis of the Hispanic World: Tolerance and the Limits of Freedom of Expression in a Catholic Society', in Elizabeth Powers (ed.), *Freedom of Speech: The History of an Idea*, Lanham, MD, 2011, 103–32.

21. 'Déclaration de Saint-Ouen', reprinted in *La monarchie impossible: Les Chartes de 1814 et de 1830*, Paris, 1994, 90.

22. See 'Des elections, du ministere, de l'esprit public et du parti libéral en France', *La Minerve* 4(1) (1818), 379–84. Constant's considerable ambivalence towards the notion of a political party is discussed in J.A.W. Gunn, *When the French Tried to Be British: Party, Opposition, and the Quest for Civil Disagreement 1814–1848*, Montreal, 2009, Chapter 5.

23. *La Minerve francaise* 14(1) (4–5 November 1818), 14–22. The article was reprinted in *Cours de politique constitutionnelle*, Paris, 1819, vol. III, 53–58.

24. C. Comte and C. Dunoyer (eds), *Le Censeur européen, ou examen de diverses questions de droit public*, vol. I, Paris, 1817, 275–78.

25. *Le Censeur européen*, 1 November 1819, 1.

26. J. Fiévée, *Histoire de la session de 1815*, Paris, 1816, 2.

27. 'Sur les langues', in *Oeuvres de M. de Bonald*, vol. 7, Brussels, 1745, 455. On debates over the 'abus des mots', see S. Rosenfeld, *A Revolution in Language:*

The Problem of Signs in Late Eighteenth-Century France, Stanford, 2004. On the linguistic politics of the Revolution, see D. Bell, *The Cult of the Nation in France*, Cambridge, 2011, Chapter 6.

28. *La Quotidienne*, 23 August 1814, 3.

29. M.H.B., *De l'abus des mots, de leur fausse interprétation et de leur influence sur la destinée des peuples*, Paris, 1815, 14ff.

30. J.A. P., *De la Monarchie avec les philosophes, les révolutionnaires et les Jacobins*, Lyon, 1817, 29, 62, 29, 94.

31. L. de Bonald, *De la chambre de 1815*, in *Oeuvres complètes de M. de Bonald*, vol. 2, Paris, 1864, 703.

32. *La Minerve française*, 1818; see, for example, the first three volumes. The expression 'système libéral et constitutionnel' is in vol. 3, 32.

33. *Doctrines des libéraux ou extraits raisonnés*, Paris, 1819, 2.

34. *Minerve française*, vol. 1, 1818.

35. *Les Idées libérales*, in *Le Nouvelliste Francais ou Recueil Chosi de Mémoires*, no. 12, Pesth, 1815, 277, as quoted by J.L. at 154.

36. *Le Libéral, Journal philosophique, politique et littéraire*, 12 November 1816, 1.

37. 'Du Libéralisme', *La Quotidienne* 291 (19 October 1818), 3–4.

38. F. Jaunin, 'Les divisions libérales au moment des élections de 1818 : une explication partielle à l'échec de la candidature de Benjamin Constant à Paris', *Annales Benjamin Constant* 35 (2010), 57–75; and R. Alexander, *Re-writing the French Revolutionary Tradition*, Cambridge, 2003.

39. *Le Franc libéral ou le Censeur du Midi*, Avignon, 1818, 12.

40. *Avis aux libéraux par un libéral*, Paris, 1818, 4–5.

41. N. Boisson, 'Les Figures de Joseph Rey 1779–1885: conspirateur libéral, "philosophe" et socialist utopique', Mémoire de troisième année, Université de Grenoble, 2; A.B. Spitzer, *Old Hatreds and Young Hopes: The French Carbonari against the Bourbon Restoration*, Cambridge MA, 1971. Lafayette himself joined the conspirators; Benjamin Constant did not.

42. *National Gazette and Literary Register* 1(8) (29 April 1820), 2.

43. Jaunin, 'Les divisions libérales'.

44. See Constant's letter to his cousin, Rosalie, quoted in Rosenblatt, *Liberal Values*, 240.

45. R. Whatmore, 'Adam Smith's Role in the French Revolution', *Past and Present* 175(1) (2002), 65–89.

46. F. Ferrier, *Du gouvernement consideré dans ses rapports avec le commerce*, Paris, 1805, 14–15 and 37.

47. D. Todd, *L'Identité économique de la France : Libre-échange et protectionnisme, 1814–1851*, Paris, 2008, 43.

48. Ibid., 40–41.

49. On the propagandizing and educative efforts of the French liberal political economists, see P. Steiner, 'Competition and Knowledge: French Political Economy as a Science of Government', in *French Liberalism*, 192–207.

50. J.-B. Say, *Lettres à M. Malthus*, Paris, 1820, 19.

51. J.-B. Say, *A Treatise on Political Economy, or the Production, Distribution and Consumption of Wealth*, vol. 1, C.R. Prinsep (trans.), Boston, 1821, 173, 178, 179, 180 and 207–9.

52. D. Hart, 'Class Analysis, Slavery and the Industrial Theory of History in French Liberal Thought, 1814–1830: The Radical Liberalism of Charles Comte and Charles Dunoyer', retrieved 15 April 2019 from http://davidmhart.com/lib erty/Papers/ComteDunoyer/CCCD-PhD/CCCD-Book-2010.pdf.

53. *Nouveaux principes d'économie politique, ou de la richesse dans ses rapports avec la population*, vol. 1, Paris, 1819, 56 and 52.

54. In 1835, Jean Charles Léonard Simonde de Sismondi wrote to a friend: 'Je suis libéral et, mieux encore, républicain, mais jamais démocrate.' J.C.L.S. de Sismondi, *Fragments de son journal et correspondance*, Geneva, 1857, 182.

55. Quoted in G. de Bertier de Sauvigny, *La Restauration*, Paris, 1963, 168.

56. Speech delivered on 4 May 1821, *Archives parlementaires*, 2nd series, vol. 31, 222.

57. See Rosenblatt, *Liberal Values*, 164–68.

58. *Commentaire sur l'ouvrage de Filangieri*, Paris, 1822, 4, 17, 44–45 and 301.

59. *Plan des libéraux pour recommencer la Révolution*, Paris, 1821, 18.

60. *Avis à tous les bons francais: Catéchisme antilibéral. Projets impies, immoraux et anarchiques du libéralisme*, Marseille: iii.

61. P. Rosanvallon, *Le Moment Guizot*, Paris, 1985, 336.

62. *Mémoires posthumes de Odilon Barrot*, vol. 1, Paris, 1875–76, 337.

63. Speech delivered in the Chamber of Deputies on 28 May 1844, in *Histoire Parlementaire: recueil complet des discours prononcés dans les chambres de 1819 à 1848 par M. Guizot*, vol. 4, Paris, 1864, 381.

64. *Mémoires posthumes de Odilon Barrot*, 393.

65. R. Romani, 'Political Economy and Other Idioms: French Views on English Development, 1815–1848', *European Journal of the History of Economic Thought* 9(3) (2002), 359–83.

66. See, for example, F. Bastiat, *Sophismes économiques*, Paris, 1846, 139.

67. M. Lutfall, 'Aux Origines du Libéralisme Economique en France: *Le Journal des Economistes*. Analyse du contenu de la premiere série 1841–1853', *Revue d'histoire economique et sociale* (1972), 495–516; see also D. Sherman, 'The Meaning of Economic Liberalism in Mid-nineteenth Century France', *History of Political Economy* 6(2) (1974), 171–99.

68. *Journal des économistes* VIII (April–July 1844), 60; IV (December 1842–March 1843), 260.

69. As quoted in G. Minart, *Frédéric Bastiat (1801–1850): Le croisé du libre-échange*, Paris, 2004, 45.

70. F. Bastiat, 'À Messieurs les électeurs de l'arrondissement de Saint-Séver', in *Oeuvres complètes de Frédéric Bastiat*, vol. 1, Paris, 1862–64, 464.

71. See, for example, L. Blanc, *The History of Ten Years; or France under Louis Philippe*, Walter Kelly (trans.), Philadelphia, 1848, 83 and 19.

72. Ibid., 362 and 547.

73. C. Dupont-White, *Essai sur les relations du travail*, Paris, 1846, 369, C. Dupont-White, *L'Individu et l'état*, Paris, 1858, 293. Dupont-White translated *On Liberty* in 1859 and *On Representative Government* in 1861. For a recent defence of Dupont-White's 'liberalism', see J.-F. Spitz, 'The "Illiberalism" of French Liberalism: The Individual and the State in the Thought of Blanc, Dupont-White and Durkheim', in *French Liberalism*, 252 68.
74. G. Verucci (ed.), *L'Avenir. 1830–1831*, Rome, 1967, 170, 106–7, 213, 5 and 10.
75. In 1840, 170 deputies out of 450 were civil servants. L. Girard, *Les libéraux francais: 1814–1875*, Paris, 1985, 133.
76. A. de Tocqueville, *Selected Letters on Politics and Society*, Roger Boesche (ed.), Berkeley, 1985, 156.
77. *Dictionnaire politique : Encyclopédie du langage et de a science politiques*, Paris, 1842, as quoted in A. Jardin, *Histoire du libéralisme politique: De la crise de l'absolutisme à la Constitution de 1875*, Paris, 1985, 347.
78. A. de Tocqueville, *Recollections: The French Revolution of 1848*, J.P. Mayer and A.P. Kerr (eds), New Brunswick, 1987, 14.
79. For only a few examples, see Catherine Audard, *Qu'est-ce que le libéralisme ? : Ethique, politique, société*, Paris, 2009; Monique Canto-Sperber, *Le libéralisme et la gauche*, Paris, 2008; Michel Guénaire, *Les deux libéralismes*, Paris, 2011; Pierre Manent, *Histoire intellectuelle du libéralisme*, Paris, 2012.
80. I further develop the themes of this article in my *The Lost History of Liberalism*, Princeton, 2018.

Bibliography

Alexander, R. *Re-writing the French Revolutionary Tradition*. Cambridge, 2003.

Audard, C. *Qu'est-ce que le libéralisme? Ethique, politique, société*, Paris, 2009.

Avis a tous les bons francais. Catéchisme antilibéral : Projets impies, immoraux et anarchiques du libéralisme. Marseille, 1830.

Avis aux libéraux par un libéral. Paris, 1818.

Barrot, O. *Mémoires posthumes de Odilon Barrot*. Paris, 1875.

Bastiat, F. *Sophismes économiques*. Paris, 1846.

Bell, D. *The Cult of the Nation in France*. Cambridge, 2011.

Blanc, L. *The History of Ten Years; or France under Louis Philippe*, trans. W. Kelly. Philadelphia, 1848.

Boisson, N. 'Les Figures de Joseph Rey 1779–1885: conspirateur libéral, 'philosophe' et socialist utopique', Mémoire de troisième année, University of Grenoble, 2001.

Bonaparte, N. *Correspondances de Napoléon 1er*, vol. 6. Paris, 1862.

Bossuet, J. *Oraisons funèbres de Bossuet*. Paris, 1886.

Canto-Sperber, Monique. *Le libéralisme et la gauche*. Paris, 2008.

Clément, J.-P. *Aux Sources du libéralisme français: Boissy d'Anglas, Daunou, Lanjuinais*. Paris, 2000.

Comte, C., and C. Dunoyer (eds). *Le Censeur européen, ou examen de diverses questions de droit public*, vol I. Paris, 1817.

Constant, B. *Commentaire sur l'ouvrage de Filangieri*. Paris, 1822.
———. *Cours de politique constitutionnelle*. Paris, 1819.
———. *Doctrines des libéraux ou extraits raisonnés*. Paris, 1819.
Craiutu, A. *Liberalism under Siege: The Political Thought of the French Doctrinaires*. Lanham, MD, 2003.
———. *A Virtue for Courageous Minds: Moderation in French Political Thought, 1748–1830*. Princeton, 2012.
Le Dictionnaire de l'Académie françoise, vol. 1. Paris, 1694.
Diez del Corral, L. *El liberalismo doctrinario*. Madrid, 1956.
De Bertier de Sauvigny, G. 'Liberalism, Nationalism, Socialism: The Birth of Three Words'. *Review of Politics* 32 (1970), 151–52.
———. 'Libéralisme: aux origines d'un mot'. *Commentaire* 7 (1979), 420–24.
———. *La Restauration*. Paris, 1963.
De Bonald, L. *Oeuvres de M. de Bonald*. Paris, 1864.
De Dijn, A. *French Political Thought from Montesquieu to Tocqueville: Liberty in a Levelled Society?* Cambridge, 2008.
De la Rocque, G. A. *Traité de la noblesse : de ses différentes espèces*. Paris, 1678.
De Lyon, J.A.P. *De la Monarchie avec les philosophes, les révolutionnaires et les Jacobins*. Lyon, 1817.
De Sismondi, J.C.L.S. *Fragments de son journal et correspondance*. Geneva, 1857.
———. *Nouveaux principes d'économie politique, ou de la richesse dans ses rapports avec la population*, vol. 1. Paris, 1819.
De Tocqueville, A. *Selected Letters on Politics and Society*, Roger Boesche (ed.). Berkeley, 1985.
Dupont-White, C. *Essai sur les relations du travail*. Paris, 1846.
Faulche, S., and Compagnie. *Encyclopédie, ou dictionnaire raisonné des sciences, des arts et des métiers*, vol 9. Neuchatel, 1765.
Fernández-Sebastián, J. 'The Crisis of the Hispanic World: Tolerance and the Limits of Freedom of Expression in a Catholic Society', in Elizabeth Powers (ed.), *Freedom of Speech: The History of an Idea* (Lanham, MD, 2011), 103–32.
Ferrier, F. *Du gouvernement consideré dans ses rapports avec le commerce*. Paris, 1805.
Fiévée, J. *Histoire de la session de 1815*. Paris, 1816.
Geneens, R., and H. Rosenblatt (eds). *French Liberalism from Montesquieu to the Present Day*. Cambridge, 2010.
Girard, L. *Les libéraux francais: 1814–1875*. Paris, 1985.
Guénaire, M. *Les deux libéralismes*. Paris, 2011.
Guizot, M. *Histoire Parlementaire: recueil complet des discours prononcés dans les chambres de 1819 à 1848*. Paris, 1864.
Gunn, J.A.W. *When the French Tried to Be British: Party, Opposition, and the Quest for Civil Disagreement 1814–1848*. Montreal, 2009.
Hart, D. 'Class Analysis, Slavery and the Industrial Theory of History in French Liberal Thought, 1814–1830: The Radical Liberalism of Charles Comte and

Charles Dunoyer'. PhD dissertation. King's College, University of Cambridge, 1994.

Jainchill, A. *Reimagining Politics after the Terror: The Republican Origins of French Liberalism*. Ithaca, NY, 2008.

Jardin, A. *Histoire du libéralisme politique : de la crise de l'absolutisme à la Constitution de 1875*. Paris, 1985.

Jaunin, F. 'Les divisions libérales au moment des élections de 1818 : une explication partielle à l'échec de la candidature de Benjamin Constant à Paris'. *Annales Benjamin Constant* (35) (2010), 57–75.

Jaume, L. *L'Individu éffacé ou le paradoxe du libéralisme français*. Paris, 1997.

Jennings, J. *Revolution and the Republic: A History of Political Thought in France since the Eighteenth Century*. Oxford, 2011.

Kahan, A. *Alexis de Tocqueville*. New York, 2013.

Leonhard, J. 'From European Liberalism to the Languages of Liberalisms: The Semantics of *Liberalism* in European Comparison'. *Redescriptions. Yearbook of Political Thought and Conceptual History* 8 (2004), 17–51.

———. *Liberalismus: Zur historischen Semantik eines europäischen Deutungsmusters*. Munich, 2001.

Loyseau, C. 'Traité des ordres et dignitez', in K.M. Baker (ed.), *University of Chicago Readings in Western Civilization*, vol. 7, *The Old Regime and the French Revolution* (Chicago, 1987), 13–31.

Lutfall, M. 'Aux Origines du Libéralisme Economique en France : *Le Journal des Economistes*. Analyse du contenu de la premiere série 1841–1853'. *Revue d'histoire economique et sociale* (1972), 495–516.

Manent, P. *Histoire intellectuelle du libéralisme*. Paris, 2012.

Marichal, J. 'Espana y las raices semanticas del liberalismo'. *Cuadernos. Congresso per la libertad de la cultura* (March/April 1955), 53–60.

Massillon, J. *Oeuvres de Massillon*, vol 2. Paris, 1833.

M.H.B. *De l'abus des mots, de leur fausse interprétation et de leur influence sur la destinée des peuples*. Paris, 1815.

Minart, G. *Frédéric Bastiat (1801–1850) : Le croisé du libre-échange*. Paris, 2004.

Mélonio, F. *Tocqueville et les Français*. Paris, 1993.

Nemo, P., and J. Petitot (eds). *Histoire du libéralisme en Europe*, Part II. Paris, 2006.

Nussbaum, M. *Cultivating Humanity: A Classical Defense of Reform in Liberal Education*. Cambridge, MA, 1998.

Plan des libéraux pour recommencer la Révolution. Paris, 1821.

Raynaud, P. (ed.). *Des réactions politiques* in *De la force du gouvernement actuel de la France et de la nécessité de s'y rallier*. Paris, 1988.

Romani, R. 'Political Economy and Other Idioms: French Views on English Development, 1815–1848'. *European Journal of the History of Economic Thought* 9(3) (2002), 359–83.

Rosanvallon, P. *The Demands of Liberty: Civil Society in France since the Revolution*, A. Goldhammer (trans.). Cambridge, MA, 2007.

———. *La monarchie impossible : Les Chartes de 1814 et de 1830*. Paris, 1994.

————. *Le Moment Guizot*. Paris, 1985.

Rosenfeld, S. *A Revolution in Language: The Problem of Signs in Late Eighteenth-Century France*. Stanford, 2004.

Rosenblatt, H. *Liberal Values: Benjamin Constant and the Politics of Religion*. Cambridge, 2008.

————. *The Lost History of Liberalism: From Ancient Rome to the Twenty-First Century*. Princeton, 2018.

Say, J.-B. *Lettres à M. Malthus*. Paris, 1820.

————. *A Treatise on Political Economy, or the Production, Distribution and Consumption of Wealth*, C.R. Pinsep (trans.). Boston, 1821.

Sherman, D. 'The Meaning of Economic Liberalism in Mid-nineteenth Century France'. *History of Political Economy* 6(2) (1974), 171–99.

Spitzer, A.B. *Old Hatreds and Young Hopes: The French Carbonari against the Bourbon Restoration*. Cambridge, MA, 1971.

Swart, K. "Individualism' in the Mid-nineteenth Century (1826–1860)'. *Journal of the History of Ideas* 23(1) (1962), 77–90.

Todd, D. *L'Identité économique de la France: Libre-échange et protectionnisme, 1814–1851*. Paris, 2008.

Verucci, G. (ed.). *L'Avenir. 1830–1831*. Rome, 1967.

Vierhaus, R. 'Liberalismus', in O. Brunner, W. Conze and R. Koselleck (eds), *Geschichtliche Grundbegriffe: Historisches Lexikon zur politisch-sozialen Sprache in Deutschland*, vol. 3 (Stuttgart, 1982), 741–85.

Vincent, K.S. *Benjamin Constant and the Birth of French Liberalism*. New York, 2011.

————. 'Benjamin Constant, the French Revolution, and the Origins of French Romantic Liberalism', *French Historical Studies* 23(4) (2000), 607–37.

Von Leyden Blennerhassett, J. *Madame de Staël, Her Friends, and Her Influence in Politics and Literature*, trans. J.E. Gordon Cumming. Cambridge, 2013 [1889]), vol. 3.

Welch, C. *De Tocqueville*. New York, 2001.

Whatmore, R. 'Adam Smith's Role in the French Revolution'. *Past and Present* 175(1) (2002), 65–89.

————. *Republicanism and the French Revolution: An Intellectual History of Jean-Baptiste Say's Political Economy*. Oxford, 2000.

Chapter 6

Nordic Liberalisms

Sweden and Denmark in Comparison

Jussi Kurunmäki and Jeppe Nevers

The Nordic countries are today viewed as inherently belonging to the Western liberal political cultures, marked by liberal freedoms and liberal political institutions. However, liberalism has not been a dominant concept for describing the political cultures in the Nordic countries, and in the international literature on liberalism, the Nordic countries rarely make an entry. Instead, the Nordic countries are known as the site of a long history of peasant freedom as well as the welfare state, or the Nordic model. The alleged legacy of freedom and the prospect of welfare policies were articulated in the 1930s as a particular Nordic brand of democracy.[1]

In this chapter, we shed light on the ways in which liberals and liberal ideas have played important, yet quite different, roles in shaping political cultures in two Nordic countries: Sweden and Denmark. We argue that it would be impossible to describe and understand Nordic agrarian traditions, political democratization or the emergence and contestation of welfare policies in the Nordic countries without paying attention to the shifting roles of different types of liberals. We also point out that the concept of liberalism came to be linked with quite different positions in the respective countries by the early twentieth century, with Swedish liberalism taking a centre-left progressive position, not too unlike that of the 'new liberalism' in Britain, while Danish liberalism came to oppose the welfare state and social democracy.[2]

Sweden: From the Shadow of the French Revolution to Social Liberalism

The concept of liberalism entered into Swedish political language in the early 1820s in a debate that at a principled level dealt with the foundations of political order and at a more practical level with the powers of the monarch and the legitimacy of the government in Sweden. The debate was in many ways typical of the post-Napoleonic Age, in which many new 'ism' concepts were introduced to organize present political positions, visions of the future and interpretations of the past.[3] It was initiated in 1821 when Johan Johansson, the editor of the newly founded newspaper *Argus*, distinguished between 'liberalism' and 'ultraism'. The division referred to the antagonistic situation in the French Chamber of Deputies, but its roots were located deeper in the division between the theorists of social contract and those advocating a historical and organic constitution, which even in Sweden was discussed in terms of an 'historical school'. As the main representatives of the respective positions, Johansson identified such famous names as Rousseau, Fichte, Sieyes and Paine, on the one hand, and Müller, Savigny, Arndt and Burke, on the other. Johansson maintained that an unconstrained liberalism would lead to 'republicanism' and unconstrained 'ultraism' to 'theocracy'. He claimed a middle position, advocating a 'constitutional monarchy'. Johansson had, of course, the Swedish monarchy in mind. He defended its constitutional nature and claimed that, in fact, Sweden had the oldest constitutional tradition in Europe.[4]

The debate took off when *Stockholms Courier*, another new newspaper, openly defended 'liberalism' and held that *Argus* was taking a stand in favour of the 'ultras'. According to the editor, Johan Peter Theorell, there was little danger that liberalism would undermine monarchy and introduce a republic. His point was to claim that the government would be under popular control and that political representation would not be based on the estates.[5] The conservative *Svensk Litteratur-tidning* joined in and claimed that the liberals were advocating an artificial theory that was based on a system of control, i.e. checks and balances, as well as on a contract between those who govern and those who are governed. For the editor of the newspaper, Vilhelm Fredrik Palmblad, the king and the people did indeed possess joint power, but he also held that the king was 'the living voice of God on earth'.[6]

As the debate went on, the most important arguments with respect to the conceptual history of liberalism were, on the one hand, that the liberal paper associated liberalism with constitutionalism, publicist activity, control of civil servants, and the abolition of the estates and the guilds,[7] and on the other hand that liberalism was attacked by making a distinction between 'false' and 'true' liberalism in a lengthy essay by the philosophy professor Nils Fredrik Biberg, published in 1823.[8] This distinction, which has been an important aspect of how 'isms' have been established through contestation,[9] remained a common rhetorical element in conservative argumentation in nineteenth-century Sweden.[10] Biberg did not add much to the repertoire of conservative arguments when he depicted 'false liberalism' as based on the idea of artificial and ahistorical contract, but his attempt to argue against liberalism in the name of 'true liberalism' is a clear indication that 'liberalism' had in a short time become a label that was difficult to ignore.

'Liberalism' was established as a key concept in Sweden early on and with a surprisingly elaborate argumentation for and against. The debate in the early 1820s shows that 'liberalism' was intimately part of the debate over the French Revolution and its legacy in the Europe of the Holy Alliance. Although Sweden had not experienced any violent revolution, the Age of Revolution and the Napoleonic Wars had major consequences in the country. In 1809, Sweden lost the eastern part of its kingdom, Finland, to the Russian Empire; the king was deposed in a coup arranged by some leading officers and members of the political elite; and a new constitution was enacted within a couple of months. The loss of Finland sparked a wave of neoromantic (often conservative) literature as well as (often radical) political pamphlets, which claimed further reforms in the name of 'public opinion'. It is therefore no wonder that questions of constitutional tradition, the powers of the monarch and the popular basis of government were felt to be crucial and discussed with the help of the new concept that was spreading in Europe.

Further, when trying to explain why liberalism was so thoroughly debated so early, we may note that 'liberal' as a concept of political faction was in early use in Sweden as well. A group of men behind the 1809 Constitution employed the word 'liberal' in a manner that combined older connotations of being generous and the willingness to give away privileges in an enlightened spirit.[11] One of the leading founding fathers of the 1809 Constitution described it as being 'liberal and just' rather than 'aristocratic'.[12] Although the Constitution did not abolish the four-estate system of representation, the rhetoric of 'more liberal principles' was directed against the political privileges based on the estates. After the enactment of the Constitution, these men formed a club that defined itself as 'the liberal side', 'the liberals' and 'the liberal party'.[13] Political standpoints also began to be described in relation to the concept of 'liberal'. In 1818, the historian Erik Gustaf Geijer, the intellectual leader of the so-called historical school before his famous declared turn to liberalism in 1838, presented a critical characterization of both the advocates of 'liberal ideas' and the 'serviles'. To him, both ideological positions were counterproductive, the former causing anarchy and the latter despotism.[14]

During the following decades, several newspapers and political clubs that adhered to liberal ideas were founded. The period from the 1830s to the 1860s has been described as the era of association liberalism in Sweden, during which 'public opinion', 'the principle of persons', 'middle class', 'progress' and 'reform of representation' became political catchwords.[15] The newspaper *Aftonbladet*, founded in 1830, became the flagship of liberalism in the country. It argued against political and economic corporations, and held that the social question was best answered by voluntary associations and by enhancing workers' self-help. Alongside theories, for example, of Bentham and Constant as well as contemporary theories of market liberalism, it brought ideas of Saint-Simon and other utopian socialists into Swedish public discussion. It was also a forum of mid nineteenth-century European republican ideas.[16]

'Liberalism' became a concept of movement in the Koselleckian sense. Not only was it used to describe visions of the future, but it was also identified as the synonym to movement.[17] However, such identification did not mean that it was clear what liberalism meant or stood for. Several newspaper articles bear witness to the need to define what liberalism meant in practice by explaining how the general principle should be applied to concrete circumstances.[18] Moreover, 'liberalism' was constantly defined through associating or contrasting it with other 'isms', through pairing it with adjectives and through hyphenations. 'Liberalism' was presented as the opposite of 'absolutism',[19] it could be identified with 'republicanism'[20] or it was positioned amongst other ideological concepts by distancing it from (in this order) radicalism, socialism and communism.[21] Moreover, 'moderate liberalism' was often distanced from 'radicalism'.[22]

The most important conceptual distinction by the mid nineteenth century was nevertheless that between 'liberalism' and 'conservatism'. During the first half of the century, it was more common to claim that one was 'a true liberal' rather than 'a conservative',[23] but the increased self-conscious use of 'liberalism' invited a counterconcept that could reasonably be used as a contrast. *Aftonbladet* issued such an invitation in 1836 when it asked in the headline of an article dealing with liberalism: 'What is the Consequence of Monarchical Conservatism?'[24] Continuous attempts to make a conservative case by using 'true liberalism' in argumentation provoked the liberal paper to announce that 'true liberalism' and 'true conservatism' were one and the same thing.[25] One conservative paper moved away from the attempt to speak in the name of 'true liberalism' and held, instead, that 'conservatism' and 'liberalism' could mean the same thing when moderate – they were 'elastic concepts'.[26]

The language of liberalism in Swedish newspapers was predominantly about a 'political' rather than an 'economic' liberalism, if we accept the somewhat misleading distinction between the two. Nevertheless, the opponents of liberalism always described the liberals as adherents of atomistic individualism and economic egoism. In the 1820s, they were accused of being advocates of Adam Smith (which they often were)[27] and much of the liberals' argumentation dealt with the abolition of guilds and other economic hindrances. It has been rather common to view the mid nineteenth-century Swedish liberals as advocating a laissez-faire doctrine in economic matters, but it has also been argued that ideas of economic liberalism and freedom of trade were blended with a positive view of active economic measures taken by the state.[28]

The prominent liberals of mid nineteenth-century Sweden saw themselves most often as 'national liberals', the concept of nation being a blend of voluntary and primordial ideas. The Polish struggle for national liberation in the early 1860s and the campaign for national unification in Italy were not only supported but also taken as 'national liberal' arguments in favour of pan-Scandinavian unification, as well as ushering in a reform of political representation that would be based on 'the nation' instead of the estates. In mid nineteenth-century European politics, the most important liberals were not the advocates of Utilitarianism or the laissez-faire economy, but 'national liberals' who struggled for political reforms in the name of the nation. In the Swedish liberal reformists' language, de Tocqueville and J.S. Mill were often associated with Mazzini and Garibaldi. Unlike in Germany, where 'national liberals' came to be increasingly associated with 'conservative liberals', Swedish 'national liberals' were idealists, whose national enthusiasm was often expressed in terms of the principles of popular sovereignty and the freedom of oppressed peoples. However, after the pan-Scandinavian momentum was halted due to the Danish defeat in the war against Germany in 1864 and after the parliamentary reform of 1866 led to a 'national' representation, the language of 'national liberalism' became less significant.[29]

What followed was a distinction between 'old liberals' (*gammalliberala*) and 'new liberals' (*nyliberala*), the point of departure of the pamphlet penned by the leading late nineteenth-century liberal Adolf Hedin. In his distinction, the decisive question was whether a liberal should be satisfied with the 1866 parliamentary reform, which had abolished the political estates and created a bicameral Diet based on restricted voting rights, and with a liberalized economic life, or whether one should demand further reforms of suffrage and the 'social question'. The pamphlet was also a programmatic declaration for the first liberal party in Sweden. The New-Liberal Society (*Nyliberala sällskapet*) was founded in 1867, Hedin being one of the founders. However, it never gained any of the characteristics of a political party and after four years, its leaders joined the Farmers' Party, the dominant party in the lower chamber. In that pamphlet, Hedin presented himself as a 'democrat' and his party as 'the party of progress'. He advocated, for instance, universal (male) suffrage and parliamentarism.[30] It is noteworthy that Hedin did not say anything about 'liberalism' in the liberals' programmatic text. Even more striking is the absence of any discussion on 'liberalism' in his collected writings and speeches, which cover four decades, contain more than 1,200 pages and in which issues such as universal suffrage, parliamentary government, international law, nineteenth-century constitutions and the history of the French Revolution were discussed.[31] It seems that a leading advocate of people's rights and social and political reforms did not need 'liberalism' to make his point.

The first liberal central organization in the country did not have the word 'liberal' in its name, but was called Reform Association (*Reformförening*) (1879–85). The first workers' associations took shape within this and other smaller reform associations. One illuminating example of the merged intellectual reformism and political radicalism of the 1880s was the student association *Verdandi*, an initial platform for the future leaders of the Liberals and the Social Democrats, Karl Staaff and Hjalmar Branting, respectively. Terms such as 'reform', 'suffrage', 'labour' and 'the people' were more important than 'liberalism' for the reform-minded persons who we commonly identified as liberals. When they founded a party in 1895, it was called the People's Party (Folkpartiet). Even that attempt turned out to be short-lived. 'Liberal' appeared in the party name in 1900 when the Liberal Coalition Party (Liberala samlingspartiet) was founded (as a party in parliament). It was followed two years later by a nationwide party, the Free-Minded Land Union (Frisinnade landsföreninen). It has been suggested that 'free-minded' was thought more suitable than 'liberal' because by the end of the nineteenth century, the latter had begun to mark a political position that was sometimes characterized as 'grey'.[32] Nevertheless, it is difficult to pin down any general positioning of political radicalism between 'liberal' and 'free-minded'. Early party programmes and electoral manifestos did not identify any difference between those words.[33] However, 'free-minded' was more rurally bounded and came to be closely linked with the temperance movement that exerted a great influence on Swedish political life in the late nineteenth century and the early twentieth century. In 1923, the question of prohibition broke the unity of the party.[34]

The first edition of a major Swedish lexicon in 1885 did not include an entry for 'liberalism', but like 'conservative', 'liberal' was described as 'a highly stretchable concept'. The lexicon pointed out that the most common counterconcepts for 'liberal' were 'the Right', 'conservative', 'radical', 'reactionary' and 'the Left'.[35] However, although the distinction between 'liberal' and 'the Left' may have been drawn in some cases, it is not possible to view them as in opposition to each other. It was far more common in the late nineteenth and early twentieth-century political language to view 'the Left' as a coalition of the Liberals and the Social Democrats. Despite their divergent preferences regarding the role of parliamentary politics and the future political and economic organization of the society, the Liberals and the Social Democrats had common cause in their struggle for parliamentary democratization. Those parties had grown from a shared landscape of reform associations.

The terminological picture painted above, as well as the strategic cooperation between the Liberals and the Social Democrats, does not mean that there was no rhetorical battle over 'liberalism'. On the contrary, it is possible to maintain that the political mobilization of the socialist labour movement re-actualized liberalism from the late 1880s onwards, as it was attacked by theoretically conscious socialist debaters. Moreover, a protectionist wave among the Farmers' Party and many conservative intellectuals in the 1880s made the difference between liberalism and conservatism sharper than it had been after the 1866 Parliamentary Reform, when the 'old liberalism' and the 'old right wing' were sometimes associated.[36] While the relationship between liberalism and conservatism had been discussed and thus acknowledged them as the main rival ideologies,[37] the increased prominence of 'socialism' rendered 'liberalism' challenged from two directions, and often quite fiercely. On the one hand, the socialists attacked liberalism – depicted as their main contender – as a well-meaning ideology, but inherently and fatally flawed.[38] In their view, the future was about the struggle between socialism and liberalism.[39] On the other hand, the conservatives saw liberalism as belonging to the same camp as socialism. It was held that liberalism had nurtured socialism,[40] was under the influence of the latter,[41] and was based on radicalism and agitation.[42]

However, the Social Democrats and the Liberals needed each other in the struggle for parliamentary democratization. Due to the restricted suffrage, social democratic candidates rarely had any chance to get elected without being listed among the liberal candidates before universal male suffrage came in effect in 1909. The principle of universal male suffrage regarding elections to the lower chamber was accepted in principle even among the conservatives (i.e. the Right) in the early years of the new century, but they maintained that any significant reform of the upper chamber would jeopardize the constitutional government in the country, undermining the power of the monarch, as the government rested on a conservative majority in the upper chamber. Although universal suffrage that would include women was the first-order demand in electoral manifestos, the Left opted for universal male suffrage in the elections for the lower chamber through majoritarian elections, which would then enable – or so the argument went – the parliamentarization of the government.[43] The principle of parliamentarism was finally accepted in 1917 when the king promised not to intervene in the workings of the cabinet formed by the Liberals and the Social Democrats. A reform of suffrage that also included women and democratized even the upper chamber was passed in 1918.

Given the strategic collaboration between the Liberals and the Social Democrats, it is understandable that ideological differences were downplayed. However, it is still quite remarkable that the Liberals' electoral manifestos did not contain any direct attack on the socialists or socialism before 1920. Their main political opponents were 'the Right', 'conservatives' and 'reaction'.[44] Besides 'liberal' and 'free-minded', their own position was identified with the terms 'progressive' and 'democratic'.[45] The Social Democrats struck a balance between the explicit mention of the common cause with the Liberals and explanations that pointed out the instrumental nature of that cooperation. To that end, liberalism was criticized, although it was also held that liberalism was not as bad as the Right. According to the Social Democrats' electoral manifesto in 1911, liberalism (presented as an active subject) liked to see itself as representing political goals that were neutral and above class interests. The manifesto explained that the liberals did not have any clear economic programme.[46] The Liberals, in turn, pointed out the virtues of individualism and private ownership, and questioned the Social Democrats' nature as a class party. The antiparliamentarian and syndicalist factions within the party in particular provoked the Liberals' criticism.[47] Nevertheless, the rift between the Liberals and the Social Democrats, when seen from the Liberals' angle, became clearly visible first in the 1920 electoral manifesto, when it was held that 'according to the free-minded, class politics and class interests must not get power in society'. The party also launched its own preferable version of democracy, 'enlightened democracy', which was based on 'citizenry skills and the sense of responsibility'.[48] This was clearly a response to the Social Democrats' increased demands for 'industrial democracy' and 'socialization'.[49]

The Liberals forfeited their position as the leading party to the Social Democrats in the 1920s, but they were still able to exert considerable influence as a party that could forge minority governmental coalitions, despite the fact that the party split in 1923.[50] It took eleven years before the two liberal parties, the Free-Minded People's Party (Frisinnade folkpartiet) and the Liberal Party of Sweden (Sveriges liberala parti), were united again under the name the People's Party (Folkpartiet). The concept of the people had been one of the key concepts of Swedish liberals since the early nineteenth century, but it was not a particularly liberal concept, being the foremost positively laden political concept in Swedish politics in general. It is therefore possible to ask whether 'the people' was a label that could give the liberal party a profile of its own, especially when the Social Democrats were quite successful in their attempt to transform their class-based rhetoric to one increasingly built on the concept of the people.[51]

The liberals of the interwar years took two separate directions: the so-called city liberals, who were leaning to the right, and a younger generation of intellectuals, who drew on the heritage from the struggle for democratization, advocated social reforms, but were against the Social Democrats' demands for socialization.[52] Even those liberal intellectuals, who supported expansive social welfare policies and balancing economic measures of the state, made it clear that social democracy would lead to socialism. According to Bertil Ohlin, the professor of economics who collaborated with the leading social democratic experts on issues concerning the economy, socialism was mistakenly based on 'a theory of catastrophe', which ruled out any other solutions than state-socialism.[53] Drawing on Keynes, he described the older doctrine of liberalism as having been based on a laissez-faire noninterventionist theory, against which a new socially conscious mixed economy and progressive system of taxation should be created.[54] The British 'new liberalism' with its emphasis on 'social liberalism' had gained ground among the Swedish liberals in the 1910s, which partly explains the ideological ground on which Ohlin built. For example, Hobhouse's *Liberalism* was translated into Swedish in 1913, and the liberal newspapers had reported on the policies that were pursued by Lloyd George and others in Britain.[55]

On many social political and economic questions, Ohlin was close to the leading social democratic economist Ernst Wigforss, who in the 1920s on several occasions sought to build a bridge between socialism and liberalism. It was an attempt to link Swedish social democracy to the British new liberalism and elaborate on guild socialism or cooperative socialism. He held, for example, that Hobhouse had more followers in socialist parties than in the liberal ones. This was, obviously, also a critical remark directed against the Swedish Liberals, who, according to Wigforss, were still too partial to 'Manchester liberalism'.[56]

Together with Karl Staaff, Ohlin was the most influential twentieth-century liberal in Sweden. He became the leader of the People's Party after the Second World War and stayed in office until 1968, exerting an influence on the liberal agenda during half a century. As a young academic, he was in many ways closer to the Social Democrats than to his own party, admitting several times that many of the social policy measures taken by the cabinets led by the Social Democrats after 1932 were more or less correct. However, he disagreed over the ideological foundations of these policies, pointing out that the Social Democrats were advocating a 'state socialism' that would lead to economic inefficiency, labour-market corporatism and, eventually, to a deficit of freedom and democracy. In particular after the Second World War, he became openly critical of the Social Democrats' ideas of planned economy, being influenced by Hayek, as many other liberals were at the time. Ohlin had described his view of liberalism as 'social liberalism' in the 1930s, but it has been noted that the specific characterization did not surface in the party programme, where the term 'liberalism' was used instead. Although there were some attempts to form a bourgeois bloc against the Social Democrats in the 1950s, it is noteworthy that Ohlin did not want to identify his party's position as belonging to the 'Right' and that he was reluctant to see his position as 'bourgeois'. In that matter, he remained faithful to the late nineteenth-century and early twentieth-century image of the nonsocialist left.[57]

'Liberalism' continued to be the organizing ideological concept for the party after the Second World War. The 1962 programme was built on 'liberalism' to the extent that the concept functioned as an acting subject rather than the party itself. The party claimed to strive for individual freedom and justice in contrast to a commando discipline, which had, as it was held, two faces in the form of socialism and conservatism, as these ideologies either concentrated the power in the hands of the state or the capital.[58] The next programme in 1972 displayed a general left-wing orientation in Swedish (and Western European) politics, and 'liberalism' was mentioned only once when a difference was noted between the state and society,[59] but the 1982 programme drew again on 'liberalism' at the same time as it was distinguished from 'socialism', 'conservatism' and 'egoistic capitalism'. It is also noteworthy that the programme presented a historical account of the victorious liberal ideas and reforms in Sweden, harking back to the press freedom in the eighteenth century.[60]

A victorious tone was further emphasized in 1990 when the programme presented 'The Foundations of Liberalism', an account of a general history of liberalism beginning in seventeenth-century England, and an account that argued for an open society, individual rights and the rule of law. Not quite dissimilar to Fukuyama's idea of 'the end of history', the programme held that socialism and conservatism were no longer the main contender ideologies to liberalism. However, a new ideological threat was identified in 'populism' and 'neo-Nazism'.[61] The following party programmes from 1997 and 1999 had the same character of a winners' history. No opponent 'isms' were pointed out.[62]

To have a liberal party claiming a victory of liberalism at the end of the Cold War does not in itself say much about the political situation in Sweden. The People's Party, which changed its name to *Liberalerna* in 2015, had during the second half of the twentieth century become a minor party in Swedish politics. Parliamentary elections show a decline from almost a quarter of the total vote in the 1950s to a level of around 10 per cent during the last couple of decades. One way of assessing the political status of liberalism is to see how the other parties have regarded liberalism in their programmes.

It turns out that no other party claimed the ownership of 'liberalism'. More tellingly, there is no critical mention of 'liberalism' in the other parties' programmes. Although the Social Democrats, who have dominated Swedish politics since the 1930s, have recognized the Liberals as their collaborators in the struggle for parliamentary democracy,[63] there has not been any discussion on 'liberalism' in their programmes. The ideological self-identification has been 'democratic socialism' in the subsequent programmes from 1960 to 2001. Neither did the communist party throw out 'liberalism', but targeted 'democratic socialism',[64] 'capitalism' and 'imperialism' alongside the Social Democrats.[65] The conservative party, in turn, referred to 'conservative ideology combined with liberal ideas' in the 1978/1984 programme, thus modifying the party's previous adherence to a 'conservative tradition of ideas'. However, this move did not contain any discussion on liberalism.[66] The Centre Party (the former agrarian party), which today has a vocal liberal faction in the party organization, had 'equality' as the key concept in the 1970 programme,[67] and in 1990 the programme employed 'ecological humanism' as the concept around which the party was to be gathered. The latter programme held that 'the traditional ideologies – conservatism, liberalism, and socialism – are merely economic orientations' and that they belonged to the age of industrialization.[68]

While the lack of 'liberalism' in other than the Liberals' party programmes does not prove by itself the irrelevance of that concept in Swedish postwar political discourses, inasmuch as party programmes do not reflect the daily common use of any concept, it nevertheless gives an indication of how the major collective actors in parliamentary democracy have viewed their ideological position. In that picture, liberalism appears by the turn of the twentieth century as a rather noncontroversial 'ism', cherished by the somewhat weak liberal party.[69]

Denmark: From Bourgeois to Agrarian Liberalism

From 1660 to 1849, Denmark was an absolute monarchy. In spite of the many reforms in the late eighteenth century, most notably the reforms of the agricultural system and the rural education programmes that were central to empowering the Danish peasantry in the nineteenth century, the monarchy came under increasing pressure in the age of revolutions. This was, to put it briefly, the context for the emergence of 'liberals' and 'liberalism' in the Danish language of politics in the 1820s and 1830s. Before that period, 'liberal' was only used as an adjective and being 'liberal' meant, as in so many other European cultures, being open-minded and generous. The connotations could vary from one context to another, but being 'liberal' was always a moral quality, something that had to do with the character of an educated and (therefore) open-minded person.

However, in the 1820s and the 1830s, this field of moral semantics was supplemented by distinctly political references. In a dictionary of foreign words from 1827, one finds not only the adjective and the older moral semantics; now, 'liberal' was also a noun – it was nothing less than a 'friend of a free form of government'.[70] And in a dictionary from 1837, 'liberalism' was defined as 'free-mindedness, love of free constitutions'.[71] That same year, another dictionary of foreign words defined liberalism as a 'striving for a free form of government, for free development of mankind's spiritual abilities and for free exercise of inborn rights; free-mindedness (opposite of *Servilismus*)'.[72] Seven years later, a second edition of the same dictionary now also defined a 'liberalist', 'a new word by which someone has wanted to define believers in a misconceived and too radical liberalism'.[73] As indicated in these random examples, the politicization of the term 'liberal' did not extinguish the older field of moral semantics. Indeed, for many liberals, there was a connection between the self-understanding as an educated and free-minded citizen and support for the liberal case, most notably the struggle for a so-called 'free constitution'. But in public discourse, the political connotation was now dominant. In another dictionary of foreign words from 1849, the 'liberals' were simply defined as 'the political party that wants a free constitution' and liberalism as a 'striving for civic and political freedom'.[74]

The liberals of the 1830s and the 1840s, mostly educated men of the Copenhagen bourgeoisie, often self-identified as 'liberals', but in Danish historiography they are not primarily known as liberals. Their struggle for a free constitution that culminated in a nonviolent transition to a constitutional monarchy in 1848–49 has been studied by generations of Danish historians, but as a rule of thumb, liberals since that time have been labelled 'national liberals',[75] although they did not use that self-identification until the 1860s.

Although the 'national liberals' of the mid nineteenth century were central to the demolition of the absolute monarchy, it is a striking trait in modern Danish history that this nineteenth-century liberalism disintegrated before it became an actual tradition. Across the whole of Europe, of course, liberals and liberalism came under fire in the second half of the nineteenth century, but in Denmark the crisis was so profound that by 1900, only a few claimed to be liberals, and the term 'liberalism', if used at all, was a term of the past. But why was that so? We will point to three main reasons that all contributed to the fall of this more or less classical bourgeois liberalism and thus paved the way for the rise of a peculiar thing in a European context: an agrarian-based liberalism.

First, we must recall that throughout Europe, liberals and liberalism were attacked for having no response to what was called 'the social question'. Early socialists saw liberalism as closely connected to capitalist society, the theoretical foundation for bourgeois capitalism, but Christian conservatives too launched harsh criticisms. In Denmark, H.L. Martensen, the Bishop of Copenhagen, published his critique in 1878.[76] For Martensen, liberalism was simply the root of all evil in modern society. At its heart, liberalism was an ideology of individualism that completely neglected the importance of society and of the common good. In his view, liberalism was the philosophical foundation for a society of 'free competition', 'laissez-faire' and the struggle of all against all. Thus, he had more understanding for socialism as a response to the calamities of liberalism, although he was sceptical towards its advocacy of the abolition of private property, which he called 'revolutionary socialism'. His own position was that of a Christian socialist. D.G. Monrad, another bishop and one of the founding fathers from 1849 and a leading liberal voice of that time, who responded to Martensen, defending liberalism: 'It is true that it has destroyed many shackles and limitations that hindered the free movement of individuals, but it has not forgotten society.'[77] Instead, he listed a number of areas in which liberals had worked for society and for the common good, for instance, education, postal services, railroads, the implementation of telegraph technology, etc. He also mentioned that if Martensen could find good solutions to the social problems of the time, then he would 'find warm and loyal support in the camp of liberalism'.[78] When Martensen criticized the liberals for not seeking the common good, he simply did not understand what liberalism was all about. According to Monrad, it was precisely the essence of liberalism that the state should provide for the common good, and only for the common good, and thus never take sides: 'This is the reason why the state so often holds back and lets the forces in civil society fight for themselves. The fear is that interference will do more harm than good.'[79]

This type of answer to the social question led to a remarkable victory for the critics' definition of liberalism as free competition and the survival of the fittest. Before the 1860s and the 1870s, liberalism was only occasionally identified with 'laissez-faire' and noninterference in the economy. Undoubtedly, many liberals in the 1840s and 1850s subscribed to the demolition of the old guild system as their primary motivation (and they succeeded in 1857), but they never defined the free market as the essence of liberalism, and only rarely was the 'ism' used in the heated debate on free competition. However, after liberalism came under increasing fire in the 1870s, a liberal such as Monrad chose to defend what he called 'the great, economic law' that is 'by God built into human society'.[80] This negative 'economization' of the term 'liberalism' was an important factor in its demise in the early industrial society.

A second reason for the fall of bourgeois liberalism can be seen in the fact that many Danish liberals moved to the right in the political struggles over the question of democracy in the late nineteenth century. In Danish historiography, the last decades of the nineteenth century are known as the age of the constitutional battle, a parliamentary battle over the relationship between the government and the democratic forces in the parliament. On the one side of the parliament, 'the Right' (in Danish *Højre*), argued that the government, according to the Constitution, should be appointed solely by the king, while the growing section on 'the Left' (in Danish *Venstre*) argued that the government should not be able to appoint a government and govern against a majority in the lower chamber. In 1901, after three decades of struggle and various attempts to remain in power, the Right finally gave in.

The democratic alliance, which self-identified as 'the democracy', consisted of two major groups (and a number of subgroups): members of parliament elected as social democrats and members of parliament elected as members of the Venstre party. This party, the oldest still-existing party in Danish politics, was established in 1870 and consisted from the outset first and foremost of farmers and other representatives of the rural population. Since the agricultural reforms of the late eighteenth century, farmers and their representatives had risen to become an important political faction that was already active on the democratic left in the late 1840s, but throughout the nineteenth century, this political group did not proclaim liberalism to be its ideology. In nineteenth-century Denmark, 'the liberals' were the urban academics of Monrad's type. Even Niels Neergaard, a leading voice in Venstre, and an academic who had published books on British liberal politicians such as William Gladstone and Richard Cobden, did not self-identify as a liberal. In 1865, Frede Bojsen, another Venstre politician, talked in a private letter of the 'illiberality' of the liberal party, but he did not want to bear the name himself.[81]

The important point is that many older liberals wound up on the losing side in the constitutional battle. Monrad himself continuously pursued a Hegelian balance-oriented strategy and, towards the end of his life, moved towards Venstre, but many of the older liberals chose to side with the conservatives against the democrats. This surely also contributed to the discrediting both of liberalism as an ideology and of 'liberal' as a label. Although the British-style dichotomy of liberals vs. conservatives was sometimes used in the constitutional struggle, the term 'liberalism' was never connected to the strong mobilization of the rural population in the second half of the nineteenth century. On the contrary, leaders of Venstre, often inspired by the romantic writer N.F.S. Grundtvig, identified themselves against the urban environments, including the liberal academic elite of the mid nineteenth century.

Third, the 'national liberals' were also the driving force behind the foreign policy that led to the catastrophic defeat by Prussia in 1864. Here we must recall that the Danish monarchy was a conglomerate state, stretching from the Arctic Circle in the north to Hamburg in the south. Norway was ceded over to Swedish Crown after the Napoleonic Wars and, as regards the southern border, the national liberals such as Monrad wanted and tried to build a nation-state that included the duchy of Schleswig, with many German-speaking inhabitants, and that led to war and subsequently defeat by Prussia in 1864. That defeat was a national tragedy and contributed significantly to the unpopularity of the liberals. For a few years, Monrad even emigrated to New Zealand. He later returned to Denmark and resumed his political activities, for instance, defending liberalism against Bishop Martensen in 1878, but after the loss to Prussia in 1864, celebrating the liberals or liberalism was no easy feat. Instead, there are many examples demonstrating that the label 'national liberals', still the term most frequently used in scholarly literature with regard to the bourgeois liberals of the nineteenth century, came to possess negative connotations.[82]

Thus, around the turn of the twentieth century, the term 'liberalism' was not seriously claimed by anyone. As in other European countries, there was an urban environment of liberal academics who, towards the end of the nineteenth century, sought to develop an ideology of social reform on the basis of central elements of the liberal state, but, as in France, this ideology of social reform was not developed as a 'new liberalism' (as it was in England or Sweden).[83] Politically, this group of academics supported Venstre and inside that party they were known as 'the European Venstre' (because of their international orientation) and 'the radical left'. Politically, they gathered in the 'Copenhagen Liberal Voters Union' (Københavns Liberale Vælgerforening) with ties to the older generation of liberals, but it is noteworthy that this generation of academics never associated themselves with liberalism (though occasionally with 'liberal' as a moral quality and, as already mentioned, as a very general political label in opposition to the conservatives). Hence, in 1905, when this group broke with Venstre and formed 'The Radical Left' (Det radikale Venstre), the guiding concepts were not 'liberalism' or even 'liberals', but 'radicals' and 'radicalism'. In Denmark, the proponents of the new liberalism were simply 'the Radicals'. Only much later, in the mid twentieth century, did this party claim 'social liberalism' as its ideology.[84] Thus, in Danish political discourse, the term 'radical' has since served as a label for a member of the social liberal party and in the big picture a slightly left-of-centre party, parallel to the liberal People's Party in Sweden.

After the radicals left Venstre and formed their own party, Venstre became ever more closely tied to the farmers and their political and economic interests. In seeking to understand the semantics of liberalism in twentieth-century Denmark, this connection cannot be overemphasized, since it was the remaining faction of Venstre that eventually appropriated the concept of liberalism. Many historians have argued that Venstre was a liberal party from the outset: its members were democrats and also strong proponents of free trade. Thus, it is not difficult to reconstruct a liberal ideology in the early programmes of Venstre. Nonetheless, Venstre did not claim the term 'liberalism' in the late nineteenth century. This happened only after the First World War, and if we want to understand this peculiar link between peasantry and liberalism, it is important to realize that from the early days of Venstre, Danish farmers were strong proponents of free trade because they exported a large quantity of agricultural goods.

Economic interests were also central to Venstre's ideological arsenal during and after the First World War and the party's subsequent embrace of the term 'liberalism'. At the outbreak of the war, the Danish government was led by the Radicals (supported by the fast-growing social democratic group), facing the difficult task of remaining neutral while trading with both sides in the European conflict. This called for a significant regulation of all Danish production and trade, especially of the large agricultural production and its export to the British Isles. In other words, the unregulated market of the late nineteenth century was put on hold, and those who lost income were first and foremost the farmers. In this very tense situation, certain leaders in Venstre, especially Thomas Madsen-Mygdal, later a prime minister and for many historians the iconic Danish liberal of the twentieth century, launched a harsh rhetoric against the politics of regulation put forth by the government. During the war, this clash of interests was also given an ideological element: the radical minister of the interior, who was in charge of the regulated economy, expressed fascination with the possibilities that such regulation provided, and this brought his party, Det radikale Venstre, closer to the social democratic vision of the state. This situation became an important factor in the construction of a political coalition of huge importance for Danish politics in the twentieth century: the coalition of the Det radikale Venstre and the Social Democratic Party.

For Venstre, this was a coalition of 'radicalism' and 'socialism', and they argued that it would usher in a new age of tyranny. In the highly polarized climate of the years following the First World War, Venstre developed an antisocialist agenda, and from the early 1920s onwards some began to speak of liberalism as an ideology in opposition to the politics of regulation, and hence to the socialism of the Radical-Social Democratic government.[85] The youth organization of Venstre was the first to take action. As early as 1917, an article on 'Dansk Liberalism' in the journal of Venstre's Ungdom (Youth of Venstre) identified 'state absolutism' as the new enemy of liberalism.[86] In Venstre, this rhetorical move seems to have happened a little later, but in 1925 it was stated in official party literature that 'the dividing line in politics runs between Liberalism (Venstre) and Socialism (Social Democracy)'.[87] One of the first important figures to use liberalism as a key concept in Venstre was J.V. Christensen, a newspaper editor and from 1924 a member of the Landstinget (the upper house). In 1930, he published a book on Danish liberalism, *Liberalismen i Danmark*, making Venstre the inheritor of a liberal tradition stretching back to the Enlightenment and the Constitution of 1849.[88] Christensen was one of many Venstre leaders to stress that the coalition of Radicals and Social Democrats was the heir to the absolute monarchy and the old guild system, in opposition to political and economic freedom. He made references to the contributions of disparate theoreticians such as Ludwig von Mises and L.T. Hobhouse. A similar line of argument, alongside Venstre's increasing orientation toward liberalism, also found expression in another book entitled *Liberalismen i Danmark* from 1935. This book was published by Erik Eriksen (former chairman of the youth organization and later Prime Minister after the Second World War) and Harald Nielsen, and it contained a preface written by Madsen-Mygdal. Here liberalism was defined as an ideology that sought the limits of individual freedom to be as wide as possible and that viewed the state as an organization created to defend that individual liberty.[89] In other words, the rebirth of liberalism was agrarian because it was born out of agrarian interests and connected to the agrarian party as its ideology, but in theory it was a rather 'classical' form of liberalism, about individual freedom and clear limits to the powers of the state and, at its centre, the limits to economic regulation.

This period was also in broader terms one of ideological reorientation and the construction of new political alliances, resulting in two parties on the right that opposed state regulation, Venstre, and the new Conservative People's Party founded on the ruins of the old party on the right, as well as two left-leaning parties who favoured increased state regulation, Det radikale Venstre and the Social Democratic Party. These four parties still exist, and in public debate they are often referred to as the four old parties. Moreover, they still form the backbones of the two blocs in Danish politics, the 'blue bloc' (liberals and conservatives) and the 'red bloc' (radicals and social democrats). Thus, throughout the twentieth century, the semantics of liberalism were often (though of course not in all cases) developed in opposition to the welfare state and social democracy[90] – in short, in opposition to state regulation. And Venstre, literally 'left' in Danish, wound up as a right-of-centre party.

What is perhaps most fascinating is that this was never a winning strategy. From the 1930s to 2005, not a single prime minister of Venstre was re-elected and thus from time to time forces in Venstre tried to move away from too narrow a definition of liberalism as antiregulation. Such attempts at redefinition had already occurred in the 1930s when liberalism was seen by many as the cause of the Great Depression. Consequently, the party's programme of 1938 stated that: 'Modern economic liberalism is not, as it is falsely accused, a perception of society that puts the single individual in opposition to society and its common interests; on the contrary it is a profoundly social perception of society.'[91] Such ideas re-emerged at various points (not least in the 1960s) and are an important part of Venstre's ideological history. But this does not change the fact that the concept of liberalism from the 1920s and the 1930s onwards was, above all, connected to Venstre and was often seen as an ideology of antiregulation, politically influenced by the farmers' opposition to the politics of regulation in the 1910s.

This disintegration of the urban liberalism of the nineteenth century and the rise of an agrarian liberalism defined explicitly in opposition to state regulation in the early twentieth century is an important development for at least two reasons. First, it gave liberalism a firm position in Danish political language as a counterconcept to far-reaching regulation. Second, it paved the way for a rather strong liberal tradition in modern Denmark. On the one hand, liberalism was not a winning concept in the age of the social democratic welfare state between the 1930s and the 1970s; it was unrelated to the construction of the Danish variant of the Nordic model. On the other hand, liberalism was the ideology of the main opposition party and – through the base of this party – liberalism and 'being liberal' were transmitted as a political identity to groups and classes in the rural population, in some cases providing the semantics of liberalism with a layer of anti-elitism. In 1963, when Venstre was officially renamed 'Venstre: Denmark's Liberal Party', some even preferred it to be called 'Denmark's Liberal People's Party'.[92]

Throughout the last half-century, Venstre has increasingly intensified this orientation as the liberal party in Danish politics. Many supporters of Det radikale venstre still identify as 'social liberals', but that party has never really tried to claim liberalism as its ideology, a concept that step by step has been appropriated by Venstre.

Since the 1980s, this pattern has definitely re-emerged. The 1970s saw only little activity around the concepts of 'liberal' or 'liberalism', but in the early 1980s, younger voices in Venstre introduced neoliberal theory, most notably the thought of Friedrich Hayek and Milton Friedman, and combined this market-oriented liberalism with the history of Venstre. A key publication was *Ny-liberalismen – og dens rødder* (*New-Liberalism – and its Roots*), written by Bertel Haarder, Erik Nilsson and Hanne Severinsen.[93] Although the authors expressed some discontent with the 'ism' (liberalism), they accepted it and used it to bring together the intellectual and political legacy of Venstre with new theories of market regulation. Thus, an important feature of the more recent history of Danish liberal thought and politics is the sparseness of voices in Venstre that have been critical of neoliberalism. Instead, the history of Venstre and the agrarian tradition stretching back to the early nineteenth century, and not least the writings of Grundtvig, were intertwined with a more general European or international history of liberal thought, containing a political as well as an economic free-market dimension.

Another significant change in the more recent history of Danish liberalism has been Venstre's ability to modify its voting base. Already in the 1980s, Venstre was definitely an agrarian-based party – it was the Conservative Party that grew in size. But since the early 1990s, the Conservative Party has been in continuous decline. Venstre on the other hand has grown to be not only the leading 'bourgeois' (*borgerlig*) party (*borgerlig* continues to be the primary label for a Danish nonsocialist or the centre-right), but between 2001 and 2015, it was the largest party in the Danish Parliament. It is definitely an important back-drop for this development that, since the late 1990s, Venstre has increasingly embraced the welfare state, formerly a concept almost owned by the social democrats. Just one example will suffice: in 1993, the Vice-Chairman of Venstre, Anders Fogh Rasmussen, published a book entitled *From the Social State to the Minimal State: A Liberal Strategy*.[94] Only a few years later, Rasmussen, now as Chairman of Venstre, became Prime Minister on the basis of a much more welfare-friendly rhetoric, now emphasizing 'free choice' in the public sector.

Against this background, Venstre gained significant political ground, and in 2001 it became the biggest party in the Danish Parliament. The early twenty-first century also saw the coming of a new liberal party, the Liberal Alliance, a party that was framed as more 'liberal' than Venstre. So, if 'liberalism' was a word of the past in the early twentieth century, it was for many a concept of the future in the early twenty-first century. The agrarian influence had weakened, antiregulation had turned into free choice in the public sector and a strong critique of the state had made way for liberal visions of the welfare state, but the shift from a more or less classical bourgeois liberalism in the nineteenth century to an agrarian-based liberalism in the twentieth century still resonated in Danish politics.

Comparative Remarks

Despite many similarities between the Swedish and Danish histories of the language of liberalism, our analysis does not support any singular pan-Nordic or pan-Scandinavian liberalism. On the contrary, it seems to suggest the necessity of recognizing a high degree of particularity in national varieties of European political discourse, even in countries that are geographically close and, in many ways, have followed similar historical paths. In this final section of the chapter, we will point out some obvious commonalities and will discuss the most important differences between the two cases.

As elsewhere in Europe in general, most Swedish and Danish liberals in the early nineteenth century can be characterized as constitutionalists. Being a liberal constitutionalist could, of course, mean quite different things and carry various degrees of radicalism with it, but it was common for them to be against absolutism or absolutist tendencies as well as estate-based political and economic privileges. In Sweden, the early breakthrough of liberal language around 1810 was linked with the attempts to demarcate monarchical power, and the language of liberalism was associated with demands for rudimentary parliamentary control of the government from the 1820s onwards. The Danish liberals may not have preceded the Swedish ones, but their case for a 'free constitution' was certainly more urgent, as Denmark was an absolute monarchy until 1848. In both countries, the mid nineteenth-century liberals were mostly 'national liberals'. They had many personal contacts, not least due to their pan-Scandinavian ambitions, but while for the Swedish national liberals the termination of the pan-Scandinavian project, due to the Danish loss against Prussia in 1864, was a matter of lost prestige that could be compensated through the reform of parliament in 1866, the Danish failure was a blow against the liberals as such.

In both countries, liberal ideas on political and social reforms were promoted under a number of labels other than liberalism. In both countries some liberals organized themselves under the label 'the Left'. However, there was a crucial difference. The Swedish liberals were leftish in their willingness to cooperate with the Social Democrats and their ability to combine urban progressive ideas with some degree of agrarian reformism. In Denmark, where there was a similar call for political and social reforms as in Sweden, liberalism seemed to be a concept of the nineteenth century and the urban intellectuals around 1900 preferred a French-inspired language of radicalism, whereas neither agrarians nor social democrats took the liberal language on board. Later, in the 1920s and 1930s, there was a renaissance of liberalism in Denmark, as agrarians in the Venstre party embraced the concept and constructed an ideology of antiregulation in opposition to social democracy and the politics of regulation. This placed liberalism at the margins in the age of the social democratic welfare state. However, since the crisis of the welfare state in the 1970s and 1980s, the connection between the main opposition party and the concept 'liberalism' has been crucial for its reintroduction into the Danish language of politics.

In Sweden, on the other hand, the history of liberalism co-joined with the formation of the welfare state, even if the 1920s saw the liberals distancing themselves from social democracy and profiling themselves with the concept of liberalism. In fact, it has been held that the liberals should be acknowledged, as in the United Kingdom, as the forerunners of the welfare state due to their leading role in late nineteenth-century and early twentieth-century parliamentary democratization and social policy reformism.[95] However, in the longer run, it seems to be the case that the Swedish liberals were more or less marginalized, being as they were so close to the welfare state project that became identified with social democracy. Being a middle-ground party with no clear socially bounded interest anchorage, despite their resonance with the lower middle classes and civil servants, and being a party identified with 'the Left' has been too narrow a position for the Liberals in a country where the Social Democrats have been exceptionally successful.

In Denmark, a comparable tradition of progressive liberalism developed out of the radical tradition and, especially from the mid twentieth century, was identified as 'social liberalism'. Thus, in Denmark, the identification as 'liberal' today points to a right-of-centre position, not least to the Venstre party, whereas 'social liberal' points to a centre-left position comparable to Swedish liberalism. An explanation of these different trajectories since the mid nineteenth century would have to include many factors, not least the different developments of agrarianism and social democracy, and their underlying social structures in the two countries. In Denmark, the breakdown of bourgeois liberalism in the 1860s led to a political landscape in which agrarian mobilization in the late nineteenth century came to form a social force of its own, in opposition to bourgeois culture and later to social democracy, whereas in Sweden, agrarian mobilization merged to a higher degree with the social democratic movement. In this respect, it is a crucial and telling difference that Swedish social democrats enjoyed early and strong support in rural areas. This never happened in Denmark, where the agrarian movement, and its Venstre party, became the opposition to the social democrats, and the term 'liberalism' became the ideological label for this opposition.

The Social Democrats have not picked up 'liberalism' in either Sweden or Denmark as a guiding ideological label, although they have continuously claimed the concept of freedom and occasionally made references to aspects of the liberal heritage. In this vein, they have typically seen themselves as being able to combine liberal and socialist ideas, as Gunnar Myrdal put it in the early 1930s.[96] Whether or not this has been the case would demand an extensive study of its own, but it is at least possible to maintain that, in Sweden, the language of liberalism that the People's Party has cultivated, together with a strong liberal media in the country, has kept the Social Democrats aware of a progressive nonsocialist alternative that has been articulated in the terms of liberalism.

Jussi Kurunmäki is Associate Professor at the Centre for Nordic Studies, University of Helsinki, and at the Institute of Contemporary History, Södertörn University. He works in the fields of conceptual history and the history of political thought. He is one of the editors of the Finnish anthology of conceptual history *Käsitteet liikkeessä (Concepts in Motion)* (2003), *Rhetorics of Nordic Democracy* (2010), *Democracy in Modern Europe: A Conceptual History* (Berghahn Books, 2018) and the special issue on the political rhetoric of 'isms' in the *Journal of Political Ideologies* (2018). He is also the chairperson of the Concepta – International Research Seminars in Conceptual History and Political Thought network.

Jeppe Nevers is Professor of History at the University of Southern Denmark in Odense. He has written on a variety of topics in modern Danish and European history, including democracy, liberalism and capitalism. His books include *Fra skældsord til slagord: Demokratibegrebet i dansk politisk historie* (2011) and *Det produktive samfund: Seks kapitler af industrialiseringens idéhistorie* (2013), and he has also contributed to several comparative and international research projects.

Notes

1. J. Kurunmäki and J. Strang (eds), *Rhetorics of Nordic Democracy*, Helsinki, 2018.
2. The second section of the article draws on J. Nevers, 'Frihed over by og land: De liberale og liberalismen i Danmark, 1830–1940', in J. Nevers, N. Olsen and C. Sylvest (eds), *Liberalisme: Danske og internationale perspektiver*, Odense, 2013, 101–25; J. Nevers, 'The Rise of Danish Agrarian Liberalism', *Contributions to the History of Concepts* 8(2) (2013), 96–105; and J. Nevers and N. Olsen, 'Liberalism and the Welfare State: The Danish Case in a European Perspective', in A. Doering-Manteuffel and J. Leonhard (eds), *Liberalismus im 20. Jahrhundert*, Stuttgart, 2015, 239–367.
3. For 'isms' as future-oriented concepts, see R. Koselleck, *Vergangene Zukunft: Zur Semantik geschichtlicher Zeiten*, Frankfurt am Main, 1979.
4. *Argus*, 14 July 1821; 8 August 1821; 18 August 1821; 22 August 1821.
5. See N. Runeby, 'Konservatismens motståndare i det tidiga 1820-talets Sverige', *Statsvetenskaplig Tidskrift* 4 (1966), 292–315, at 309–10.
6. *Svensk Litteratur-tidning*, 17 December 1821.

7. *Courieren från Stockholm*, 7 February 1822.
8. N.F. Biberg, 'Om falsk och sann liberalism', *Svea* (1823), 13.
9. See also J. Leonhard, 'From European Liberalism to the Languages of Liberalisms: The Semantics of *Liberalism* in European Comparison', *Redescriptions: Yearbook of Political Thought and Conceptual History* 8 (2004), 17–51, 35f.
10. See e.g. *Post- och Inrikes Tidningar* 18 July 1851.
11. A. Thomson, '"Liberal": Några anteckningar till ordets historia', in *Festskrift tillägnad Theodor Hjelmqvist på sextiårsdagen den 11 April 1926,* Lund, 1926, 147–91, at 172. The word 'liberal' in itself was not new in the Swedish language. Early uses of the word 'liberal' had been associated with learning and generosity. According to the *Dictionary of Swedish Academy*, 'liberal' was used in the meaning of a learned people as well as denoting a scholarly concept in 1687, and its first use together with *frikostig* (generous) has been documented as early as 1675. See *Svenska Akademien: Ordbok över svenska språket*, Lund, 1942, vol. 16, 620.
12. Thomson, '"Liberal"', 178. The new Constitution put an end to the semi-absolutist era that had begun in 1772. The Constitution was based on the idea of the separation of powers, granting the monarch the executive powers that included the appointment of the members of the Council of the State.
13. Thomson, '"Liberal"', 174, 180–82.
14. E.G. Geijer, *Samlade skrifter: Andra bandet,* Stockholm, 1874, 275.
15. See T. Jansson, *Adertonhundratalets associationer*, Uppsala, 1985.
16. See e.g. L. Kihlberg, *Lars Hierta i helfigur*, Stockholm, 1968, 39–138.
17. See e.g. *Dagligt Allehanda*, 20 November 1833.
18. *Aftonbladet*, 1 April 1841.
19. *Dagligt Allehanda*, 20 November 1833.
20. *Aftonbladet*, 1 August 1835.
21. *Göteborgs Handels- och Sjöfartstidning*, 22 January 1851.
22. *Aftonbladet*, 16 November 1846.
23. G. Heckscher, *Svensk konservatism före representationsreformen I*, Uppsala, 1939, 88f.
24. *Aftonbladet*, 22 October 1836.
25. *Aftonbladet*, 2 February 1848.
26. *Post- och Inrikes Tidning*, 19 October 1860; see also *Post-och Inrikes Tidning*, 16 December 1844.
27. See e.g. *Odalmannen* 1823.
28. L. Magnusson, *Äran, korruptionen och den borgerliga ordningen: Essäer från svensk ekonomihistoria*, Stockholm 2001, 134–41.
29. J. Kurunmäki, *Representation, Nation and Time: The Political Rhetoric of the 1866 Parliamentary Reform in Sweden*, Jyväskylä, 2000, 179–94.
30. A. Hedin, 'Hvad folket väntar af den nya representationen: Femton bref från en demokrat till svenska riksdagens medlemmar', in V. Spångberg (ed.), *Adolf Hedin: Tal och skrifter*, Stockholm, 1904, 1–57.
31. Spångberg, *Adolf Hedin*; V. Spångberg (ed.), *Adolf Hedin: Tal och skrifter II*, Stockholm, 1915.

32. T. Vallinder, 'Folkpartiets ideologiska och organisatoriska bakgrund 1866–1943', in *Liberal ideologi och politik 1934–1984*, Stockholm, 1984, 38; G. von Bonsdorff, *Studier rörande den moderna liberalismen i de nordiska länderna*, Ekenäs, 1954, 44.

33. The party programmes and electoral manifestos have been available at the Swedish National Data Service: retrieved 25 February 2019 from http://snd.gu.se/sv/vivill/party/fp.

34. G. Johansson, *Liberal splittring: skilsmässa – och återförening, 1917–1934*, Gothenburg, 1980, 402–9.

35. *Nordisk familjebok: Konversationslexikon och realencyklopedi innehållende upplysningar och förklaringar om märkvärdiga namn, föremål och begrepp*, Stockholm, 1876–99, 1202.

36. E.g. *Upsala*, 14 July 1874; *Dagens Nyheter*, 25 January 1879.

37. E.g. *Dagens Nyheter*, 28 May 1881; *Härnösandsposten*, 22 October 1884.

38. E.g. *Arbetet* 5, April 1888; 1 December 1888; 9 May 1889, 3 July 1890; 30 March 1892.

39. E.g. *Arbetet*, 4 January 1890; *Dalpilen*, 9 May 1890.

40. *Svenska Dagbladet*, 29 October 1886.

41. *Svenska Dagbladet*, 16 September 1890.

42. *Svenska Dagbladet*, 22 April 1887; 18 September 1890.

43. See J. Kurunmäki, 'Different Styles of Parliamentary Democratisation in Finland and Sweden: An Analysis of Two Debates over Parliamentary Reform in 1906', in S. Soininen and T. Turkka (eds), *Parliamentary Style of Politics*, Helsinki 2008, 106–28.

44. Retrieved 25 February 2019 from http://snd.gu.se/sv/vivill/party/fp/manifesto/1908.

45. Retrieved 25 February 2019 from http://snd.gu.se/sv/vivill/party/fp/manifesto/1905; http://snd.gu.se/sv/vivill/party/fp/manifesto/1911.

46. Retrieved 25 February 2019 from http://snd.gu.se/sv/vivill/party/s/manifesto/1911.

47. See e.g. K. Staaff, *Politiska tal II*, Stockholm, 1918, 147–68.

48. Retrieved 25 February 2019 from http://snd.gu.se/sv/vivill/party/fp/manifesto/1920.

49. Retrieved 25 February 2019 from http://snd.gu.se/sv/vivill/party/s/manifesto/1920.

50. Johansson, *Liberal splittring*, 403.

51. J. Kurunmäki, '"Nordic Democracy" in 1935: On the Finnish and Swedish Rhetoric of Democracy', in Kurunmäki and Strang (eds), *Rhetorics of Nordic Democracy*.

52. See e.g. http://snd.gu.se/sv/vivill/party/lp/manifesto/1924 (retrieved 25 February 2019).

53. Quoted in O. Wennås, 'Bertil Ohlin om socialismen, liberalismen och folkpartiet', in *Liberal ideologi och politik 1934–1984*, Stockholm, 1984, 83.

54. Ibid., 82–87.

55. Vallinder, 'Folkpartiets ideologiska', 49.
56. E. Wigforss, 'Liberalism och socialism', *Tiden* 6 (1923), 321–35; *Tiden* 7–8 (1923), 385–405.
57. Wennås, 'Bertil Ohlin', 97–99, 116, 129–31.
58. https://snd.gu.se/vivill/fp/program/1962 (retrieved on 25 February 2019).
59. https://snd.gu.se/vivill/fp/program/1972 (retrieved 25 February 2019).
60. https://snd.gu.se/sv/vivill/party/fp/p/1982 (retrieved 25 February 2019).
61. https://snd.gu.se/vivill/fp/program/1990 (retrieved 25 February 2019).
62. https://snd.gu.se/vivill/fp/program/19907; https://snd.gu.se/vivill/fp/program/1999 (retrieved 25 February 2019).
63. http://snd.gu.se/sv/vivill/party/s/program/1975 (retrieved 25 February 2019).
64. http://snd.gu.se/sv/vivill/party/v/program/1953 (retrieved 25 February 2019).
65. http://snd.gu.se/sv/vivill/party/v/program/1967 (retrieved 25 February 2019).
66. http://snd.gu.se/sv/vivill/party/m/program/1984 (retrieved 25 February 2019).
67. http://snd.gu.se/sv/vivill/party/c/program/1970 (retrieved 25 February 2019).
68. http://snd.gu.se/sv/vivill/party/c/program/1990 (retrieved 25 February 2019).
69. This notion gains some support from an overview of the digitalized archive of Swedish newspapers at the Swedish National Library, which shows a relatively low-level use of 'liberalism' in Sweden after the Second World War. Scores for 'liberalism' are usually between 100 and 200 hits per year, which is basically at the same level as the hits on 'conservatism' and half as many as hits on 'socialism'. See http://tidningar.kb.se (retrieved 25 February 2019).
70. C.F. Primon, *Lexicon over alle de fremmede Ord og Udtryk, der jevnligen forekomme i det Danske Sprog i enhver Green af Videnskaberne og Kunsterne*, Copenhagen, 1827.
71. J.N. Høst, *Fuldstændig Fremmedordbog eller Lexicon over alle i vort Sprog brugelige fremmede Ord, med Angivelse af deres retskrivning, Udtale og Kjøn, samt Fordanskning, Omskrivning eller forklaring, i alphabetisk Orden*, Copenhagen, 1837.
72. L. Meyer, *Kortfattet Lexicon over fremmede, i det danske Skrift- og Omgangs-Sprog forekommende Ord, Konstudtryk og Talemaader; tilligemed de i danske Skrifter mest brugelige fremmede Ordforkortelser*, Copenhagen, 1837.
73. L. Meyer, *Kortfattet Lexicon over fremmede, i det danske Skrift- og Omgangs-Sprog forekommende Ord, Konstudtryk og Talemaader; tilligemed de i danske Skrifter mest brugelige fremmede Ordforkortelser*, 2nd ed., Copenhagen, 1844.
74. J.N. Høst, *Fuldstændig og udførlig Fremmed-Dansk ordbog for Hvermand*, 2 vols, Copenhagen, 1849.

75. For a recent example with many historiographical references, see C. Friisberg, *Ideen om et frit Danmark: Den nationalliberale bevægelses ideologi og politik – især i enevældens sidste år.*, Varde, 2003, 14–40.
76. H.L. Martensen, *Den christelige Ethik: Den specielle Deel*, 2 vols, Copenhagen, 1878.
77. D.G. Monrad, *Politiske Breve, nr. 14–18*, Nykøbing Falster, 1878, 71.
78. Ibid., 74.
79. Ibid., 126f.
80. Ibid., 129f.
81. S. Høgsbro, *Brevveksling og dagbøger*, 2 vols, Copenhagen, 1923, vol. 1, 170.
82. See e.g. V. Hørup, *V. Hørup i Skrift og Tale: Udvalgte Artikler og Taler*, 3 vols, Copenhagen, 1902–4, vol. 2, 8.
83. Cf. L. Andersen, 'Velfærdsmoral og solidaritet: Dansk socialliberalisme i europæisk kontekst, 1880–1910', in Nevers, Olsen and Sylvest (eds), *Liberalisme*, 149–72.
84. Cf. N. Olsen, 'Liberalismens revitalisering og afkulturalisering i Danmark 1945–70', in Nevers, Olsen and Sylvest (eds), *Liberalisme*, 221–46.
85. Cf. J. Nevers, 'Frihed over by og land: De liberale og liberalismen i Danmark, ca. 1830–1940', in Nevers, Olsen and Sylvest (eds), *Liberalisme*, 101–26.
86. H. Nygaard, 'Dansk Liberalisme', *Dansk Folkestyre* 13 (1917).
87. *Venstres Valgbog, 1925–26* (in Venstre's archives).
88. J.V. Christensen, *Liberalismen i Danmark*, Copenhagen, 1930.
89. E. Eriksen and H. Nielsen, *Liberalismen i Danmark*, Odense, 1935, 13f.
90. For some significant exceptions, such as Social Democrats talking about social liberalism in the postwar period, see Olsen, 'Liberalismens revitalisering'.
91. Venstre's programme of 1938.
92. Olsen, 'Liberalismens revitalisering'.
93. B. Haarder, E. Nilsson and H. Severinsen, *Ny-liberalismen – og dens rødder*, Holte, 1982.
94. A.F. Rasmussen, *Fra socialstat til minimalstat: En liberal strategi*, Copenhagen, 1993.
95. See e.g. Bonsdorff, *Studier rörande*, 10f; Vallinder, 'Folkpartiets ideologiska', 49f; S. Nycander, *Liberalismens idéhistoria: Frihet och modernitet*, Stockholm, 2009, 384–99.
96. G. Myrdal, 'Socialpolitikens dilemma I', *Spectrum* 3 (1932), 1–13.

Bibliography

Biberg, N.F. 'Om falsk och sann liberalism', *Svea*, 1823.
Christensen, J.V. *Liberalismen i Danmark*. Copenhagen, 1930.
Eriksen, E., and H. Nielsen. *Liberalismen i Danmark*. Odense, 1935.
Friisberg, C. *Ideen om et frit Danmark: Den nationalliberale bevægelses ideologi og politik – især i enevældens sidste år*. Varde, 2003.
Geijer, E.G. *Samlade skrifter: Andra bandet*. Stockholm, 1874.

Haarder, B., E. Nilsson and H. Severinsen. *Ny-liberalismen – og dens rødder*. Holte, 1982.

Heckscher, G. *Svensk konservatism före representationsreformen I*. Uppsala, 1939.

Hedin, A. 'Hvad folket väntar af den nya representationen: Femton bref från en demokrat till svenska riksdagens medlemmar', in V. Spångberg (ed.), *Adolf Hedin: Tal och skrifter* (Stockholm, 1904), 1–57.

Høgsbro, S. *Brevveksling og dagbøger*, 2 vols. Copenhagen, 1923.

Hørup, V. *V. Hørup i Skrift og Tale: Udvalgte Artikler og Taler*, 3 vols. Copenhagen, 1902–4.

Høst, J.N. *Fuldstændig Fremmedordbog eller Lexicon over alle i vort Sprog brugelige fremmede Ord, med Angivelse af deres retskrivning, Udtale og Kjøn, samt Fordanskning, Omskrivning eller forklaring, i alphabetisk Orden*. Copenhagen, 1837.

———. *Fuldstændig og udførlig Fremmed-Dansk ordbog for Hvermand*, 2 vols. Copenhagen, 1849.

Jansson, T. *Adertonhundratalets associationer*. Uppsala, 1985.

Johansson, G. *Liberal splittring: skilsmässa – och återförening, 1917–1934*. Gothenburg, 1980.

Koselleck, R. *Vergangene Zukunft: Zur Semantik geschichtlicher Zeiten*. Frankfurt am Main, 1979.

Kurunmäki, J. 'Different Styles of Parliamentary Democratisation in Finland and Sweden: An Analysis of Two Debates over Parliamentary Reform in 1906', in S. Soininen and T. Turkka (eds), *Parliamentary Style of Politics* (Helsinki, 2008), 106–28.

———. *Representation, Nation and Time: The Political Rhetoric of the 1866 Parliamentary Reform in Sweden*. Jyväskylä, 2000.

Kurunmäki, J., and J. Strang (eds). *Rhetorics of Nordic Democracy*. Helsinki, 2018.

Kihlberg, L. *Lars Hierta i helfigur*. Stockholm, 1968.

Leonhard, J. 'From European Liberalism to the Languages of Liberalisms: The Semantics of *Liberalism* in European Comparison'. *Redescriptions: Yearbook of Political Thought and Conceptual History* 8 (2004), 17–51.

Magnusson, L. *Äran, korruptionen och den borgerliga ordningen: Essäer från svensk ekonomihistoria*. Stockholm, 2001.

Martensen, H.L. *Den christelige Ethik: Den specielle Deel*, 2 vols. Copenhagen, 1878.

Meyer, L. *Kortfattet Lexicon over fremmede, i det danske Skrift- og Omgangs-Sprog forekommende Ord, Konstudtryk og Talemaader; tilligemed de i danske Skrifter mest brugelige fremmede Ordforkortelser*. Copenhagen, 1837 (1st edn) and 1844 (2nd edn).

Monrad, D.G. *Politiske Breve, nr. 14–18*. Nykøbing Falster, 1878.

Myrdal, G. 'Socialpolitikens dilemma I'. *Spectrum* 3 (1932), 1–13.

Nevers, J. 'Frihed over by og land: De liberale og liberalismen i Danmark, 1830–1940', in J. Nevers, N. Olsen and C. Sylvest (eds), *Liberalisme: Danske og internationale perspektiver* (Odense, 2013), 101–25.

———. 'The Rise of Danish Agrarian Liberalism', *Contributions to the History of Concepts* 8/2 (2013), 96–105.

Nevers, J., and N. Olsen. 'Liberalism and the Welfare State: The Danish Case in a European Perspective', in A. Doering-Manteuffel and J. Leonhard (eds), *Liberalismus im 20. Jahrhundert* (Stuttgart, 2015), 239–367.

Nordisk familjebok: Konversationslexikon och realencyklopedi innehållende upplysningar och förklaringar om märkvärdiga namn, föremål och begrepp. Stockholm, 1876–99.

Nycander, S. *Liberalismens idéhistoria. Frihet och modernitet.* Stockholm, 2009.

Nygaard, H. 'Dansk Liberalisme'. *Dansk Folkestyre* 13 (1917).

Primon, C.F. *Lexicon over alle de fremmede Ord og Udtryk, der jevnligen forekomme i det Danske Sprog i enhver Green af Videnskaberne og Kunsterne.* Copenhagen, 1827.

Rasmussen, A.F. *Fra socialstat til minimalstat: En liberal strategi.* Copenhagen, 1993.

Runeby, N. 'Konservatismens motståndare i det tidiga 1820-talets Sverige', *Statsvetenskaplig Tidskrift* 4 (1966), 292–315.

Spångberg, V. (ed.). *Adolf Hedin: Tal och skrifter II.* Stockholm, 1915.

Svenska Akademien: Ordbok över svenska språket. Lund, 1942.

Thomson, A. '"Liberal": Några anteckningar till ordets historia', in *Festskrift tillägnad Theodor Hjelmqvist på sextiårsdagen den 11 April 1926* (Lund, 1926), 147–91.

Vallinder, T. 'Folkpartiets ideologiska och organisatoriska bakgrund 1866–1943', in *Liberal ideologi och politik 1934–1984* (Stockholm, 1984), 12–79.

Von Bonsdorff, G. *Studier rörande den moderna liberalismen i de nordiska länderna.* Ekenäs, 1954.

Wennås, O. 'Bertil Ohlin om socialismen, liberalismen och folkpartiet', in *Liberal ideologi och politik 1934–1984* (Stockholm, 1984), 80–142.

Wigforss, E. 'Liberalism och socialism'. *Tiden* 6 (1923), 7–405.

Chapter 7

'Liberalism' and 'Liberality'

The Liberal Tradition in the Netherlands

Henk te Velde

⬦

It could be argued that the Netherlands has always been a 'liberal' country. At any rate, the word 'liberal' has always been there. As in France or Britain, the word 'liberal' was already used in the sixteenth and seventeenth centuries, but in the meaning of generous.[1] The word was not used for political purposes, and the accompanying noun was not 'liberalisme', but 'liberaliteit', liberality. Both words were derived from the French language, but 'liberaliteit' can be traced back to Cicero and the Latin words 'liberalitas' and 'liberalisme' arrived much later, in the nineteenth century. In that sense, the concept 'liberal' has two roots, which have remained visible almost to this day: on the one hand, the obvious meaning of holding principled liberal political views and, on the other, 'generous' – at first mainly in the sense of generous with money, but later also broad-minded, tolerant of diverging opinions and advocating pluralism.[2] In this chapter I will trace the vicissitudes of the two concepts, in particular the tension between them from the beginning of the nineteenth century until the Second World War.

The regime of the federal Dutch Republic from the sixteenth until the eighteenth centuries could be characterized as liberal in the sense of moderate, respecting certain rights, and tacitly (but often not openly) tolerating divergent views on political and religious matters. Meanwhile, the word 'liberal' was not employed in a political sense, not even at the end of the eighteenth century, when the Batavian Republic was founded in 1795 as a satellite of the French revolutionary republic in the wake of the French Revolution. Its revolutionary beginnings were celebrated by planting trees of liberty and, inspired by French revolutionary thought, its freedom was to be guaranteed by popular sovereignty. There have been some theoretical discussions among historians as to whether the political thought of the Batavian Republic was still republican or already proto- or early liberal,[3] but the word 'liberalism' did not exist, and no recognizable liberal current emerged. After much turmoil, the Netherlands became part of the French Empire in 1810; when the country regained its independence in 1813, the memory of the revolutionary episode was one of temporary madness or silliness, imported from France.

'Liberality' and the Emergence of 'Liberalism'

When the word 'liberalism' first appeared in the Dutch language in the 1820s, it was criticized as 'the new name' that was given to 'Jacobinismus'.[4] The term was used to underline the difference between Dutch moderate traditions and French theoretical and ultraradical projects. One member of the Dutch lower house said in 1832: 'We do not want to have anything to do with foreign ideas, we do not want absolutism nor liberalism; liberalism is the unlimited liberty to interfere with another person's affairs, absolutism is the prohibition to mind one's own business; we want neither.'[5] A year later, a colleague of his added: 'Our fatherland has nothing in common with the propaganda for either liberalism or légitimisme. Here, we do not hold on to one theory or another, but to experience.'[6] A newspaper that would later become one of the mainstays of liberalism still believed that 'liberalismus' equalled lawlessness, moral decay and unbridled licentiousness ('teugelloosheid') and 'an eternal revolt against everything that exists, against all law, order and government'.[7] Even though the journal said so in response to someone who argued that there was also a 'good' liberalism that defended (moderate) 'true freedom', the word 'liberalism' was in greater use by its opponents than by its adherents. The opponents based themselves on the widespread rejection of abstract reasoning and radicalism of every kind in Dutch intellectual and political circles. To be Dutch meant to be modest and practical.

Today, as in the examples I have just given, the Dutch word for liberalism is *liberalisme*, which is clearly derived from the French *libéralisme*. The famous Dutch historian Johan Huizinga was obviously wrong when he wrote that the Dutch and European history of the political meaning of the concept 'liberal' was determined by British developments.[8] During the heyday of Dutch liberalism in the second half of the nineteenth century, Britain was the great example, but the concept of liberalism was imported from France and Germany. As well as *liberalisme*, the word *liberalismus* was also used. It seems to be a Latin loanword, but it was probably borrowed from the German *Liberalismus*. *Liberalisme* and *Liberalismus* could be employed almost interchangeably to refer to the spirit of the dangerous French Revolution or to describe political movements or a spirit of enlightened rationalism. Gradually, the word *liberalismus* would disappear, though it was still in use until the Second World War, but then mainly as a term used by liberalism's opponents. When *liberalismus* became uncommon, it could be utilized to suggest the distance between the author and the untouchable thing he or she was describing.

The first mention of the word 'liberalismus' in a Dutch newspaper was a reference in 1815 to Spain, where some people were 'accused' of 'liberalismus'.[9] And one of the first defences of a political 'liberal' spirit in the Dutch language was also partly based on the Spanish case, which was made use of to argue that a freedom-loving liberal spirit had emerged in the struggle against Napoleonic despotism.[10] The first book in the Dutch language about liberalism was a translation of the German history of liberalism by Wilhelm Traugott Krug in 1823.[11] This book did not have a great impact on the history of Dutch liberalism, but its attempt at positioning liberalism as a middle force between revolution and reaction, or between despotism and anarchy, foreshadowed strategies that would later be used by Dutch liberals. Only a year later, another newspaper that would later vigorously advocate quite a radical liberalism defended 'liberaliteit' as a constructive form of politics that was not necessarily confined to opposition, let alone aiming to 'overthrow' the government.[12] A review of Krug even tried to argue that although 'liberalismus' was indeed a new word, it was, in fact, just another word for 'liberaliteit', that is to say, that it meant being broad-minded, generous and tolerant.[13] Early attempts at defending liberalism as a sensible response of financially and intellectually independent men to the necessary pluralism of (modern) politics – who refrained from inciting the common people – also used the word 'liberaliteit'.[14] In that way, they attempted to use the positive connotations of the old word, and their use of it demonstrated that the meaning of liberalism was still undefined, although many liberals would continue to claim that their way of thinking was characterized by all those marvellous qualities.

Whatever the case may be, in the 1830s the word 'liberalism' still alarmed people, as the author of a small Dutch book entitled *Liberalismus* explained. The author was a pupil of the Leiden professor of constitutional law Johan Rudolf Thorbecke, who would only a few years later, in 1848, definitely become the leader of the liberal party. At that time, however, he still rejected this radical defence of liberalism.[15] In around 1848, other members of parliament still argued that liberality (*liberaliteit*) was fine, but that it ran the risk of turning into an extreme 'liberalismus' or 'jacobinismus'. Liberal meant being generous and broad-minded, but forcing people to become liberal was despotism.[16]

The adjective *liberaal* retained at least part of its original meaning, although the party-political meaning of the word increasingly prevailed during the second half of the nineteenth century. But even then, the adjective remained less definite and more flexible than the noun. Interestingly, *liberalisme* and *liberalismus* were not used that much by liberals themselves, not even when they later became the dominant party in politics. When Johan Rudolf Thorbecke – Prime Minister and the most important nineteenth-century political and intellectual liberal leader – wrote his political testament in 1870, he set out to define the core of his political views. He called his Cabinet a 'liberal' Cabinet, in inverted commas. He explained that liberal did not signify the name of a political party; rather, it was the mark of a politics that stimulated the development of creative force in society, and a politics that concerned the law and only the law. He did not mention liberalism or a liberal party, which did not exist in a formal sense at that time.[17] There was liberal politics and there were liberals, but the 'ism' 'liberalism' sounded perhaps too much like an ideological system to become instantly popular in the Netherlands. Thorbecke and other liberals used the word 'liberalism', but not abundantly, and probably only after a while. At the end of his life, Thorbecke was still using 'liberaal' in a very broad sense too, when he described a contemporary as 'a liberal man', 'in the true, lofty sense of the word', which meant that he was politically and religiously tolerant.[18]

Liberal Breakthrough and Dominance

Between the 1830s and the 1870s, liberalism became the dominant force in Dutch politics. It took off with the revision of the Constitution in 1848. This was the moment Thorbecke really entered the political scene. The former professor of constitutional law now became a politician for the remainder of his life (after an earlier abortive attempt at changing the Constitution in 1844). He led the process of constitutional revision in 1848 and became the leader of a new Cabinet shortly after that, in 1849. The revision of 1848 defined the nature of Dutch liberalism unquestionably as in essence constitutionalism. This was not exactly a new idea, as it had already been called 'constitutionalism' previously, but until then liberalism could also be defined as almost anything ranging from conservative humanism to revolutionary Jacobinism: 'for sure no word exists, that at present is understood in more diverse ways, and that leads to more diverse feelings and judgments, than Liberalism' (1828).[19] According to a publication from the 1830s, 'the words liberal and liberal institutions are used and understood in so many different ways, that it would be impossible to give a fair description of liberalism'.[20] The words could be used in a pejorative sense or even as terms of abuse, and also to describe not only political but also diverse, and sometimes unrelated, forms of economic, religious and cultural liberalism. The political events of 1848 would decide the debate about the concept for a long time. As with their

German counterparts, the Dutch liberals were also called the 'constitutional party'.[21] They appeared to be the true advocates of ministerial responsibility in particular. That was the issue for which the constitutional revision of 1848 has remained famous in the Netherlands. 'The King is inviolable; the ministers are responsible' is the formula that was introduced into the Constitution. Moreover, direct elections for the lower house of parliament and elements of the rule of law such as freedom of assembly and association were introduced, and further steps were taken in separating church and state.

The liberals were very successful in picturing themselves as champions of the Constitution and their more conservative opponents as reactionaries. Curiously, though, there was hardly any debate about ministerial responsibility as such. Almost all parliamentarians agreed that ministerial responsibility should be introduced; they only differed in their views about what this meant in practice.[22] This shows that no real conservative party existed in the Netherlands; in addition, the most conservative elements left parliament when the new Constitution was introduced. Parliament now consisted of almost only liberal members of one shade or another. Often only the adherents of Thorbecke were called liberals, while most other members rejected the descriptor 'conservatives', and a number of them contested the monopolization of the liberal label by Thorbecke. To a large extent, the discussion about liberalism became one between liberals of different stripes. This was partly the heritage of the Dutch past. There existed a kind of patronizing, complacent and rather conservative 'liberaliteit', which in other countries would probably have shaded into a form of aristocratic conservatism.[23] In the Netherlands, no clear aristocratic identity existed, and a variant of moderate economic and constitutional liberalism was quite popular among the bourgeois, intellectual and commercial elites.

Meanwhile, the real debate of 1848 revolved around the other important change: the introduction of direct instead of indirect elections of the members of the Second Chamber, the Dutch House of Commons. The opponents of this change feared that it would bring demagogues into the parliament, although it turned out that Dutch politics remained rather quiet. Moreover, they argued that this democratization of the lower house would disturb the balance between the monarchical, aristocratic and democratic elements of the Constitution. They looked to England not as an example of 'liberalism', but as an example of the mixed constitution, which had preserved a pristine balance in politics and society. England was the cradle, the home, of 'well-ordered liberty'.[24] What makes this particularly interesting is that the idea of a balance was also a component of liberal discourse, though in another sense.

Thorbecke wrote that liberalism meant keeping within bounds (*maat*) and that its adversaries did not know how to do that.[25] One could even argue that

Thorbecke gave his own version of the mixed constitution. He was in favour of a strong, self-confident Cabinet and constitutional monarchy, as well as a strong parliament that should be directly elected by the constituency. He did not favour aristocracy in the ordinary meaning of the word, but he did famously talk about the 'aristocracy of the intellect'. Perhaps, after all, the constitutional liberalism of the middle of the nineteenth century was – in the Netherlands and elsewhere – a form of translating the older idea of the mixed constitution into written or positive law. Or, arguably, liberalism was the bridge from the early nineteenth-century mixed constitution to the separation of powers and to twentieth-century liberal democracy. In this volume, Michael Freeden quotes a letter from John Stuart Mill to Alexis de Tocqueville, which shows that Mill thought liberalism could be used as a way to find a balance between aristocracy and democracy.

However, constitutional liberalism was not an attempt to restore the old mixed constitution. The idea of the mixed constitution had been used in the Netherlands and elsewhere as a balance that would keep things as they were, as a negative check on the elements of the Constitution. Liberals wanted to use a balanced form of politics in a positive way to change society and to stimulate the development of a free society. They were appalled that so many Dutch intellectuals thought that the average should be praised as 'the golden mean' in society, rather than being rejected as a dull mediocrity. They wanted to open windows, take risks, change politics and cultural habits. This was indeed radical, and Thorbecke claimed that being 'moderately liberal' was just as undesirable as being moderately honest or moderately just.[26]

Moreover, in particular in the Dutch case, this new balanced politics was defined in constitutional, that is to say legal, terms. Thorbecke's liberalism resembled European doctrinaire liberalism, in particular its French and German variants.[27] He was partly educated in Germany and was intrigued by German liberalism, and later also by what happened in France. Commentators from other countries recognized the international family resemblance of the doctrinaires: the famous historian Leopold von Ranke called Thorbecke 'strenger Doktrinär' and others saw in him 'le Royer-Collard de la Hollande' (Royer-Collard being the leader of the French doctrinaires during the Restoration).[28] Just like his foreign counterparts, Thorbecke was opposed to democracy, revolution and popular sovereignty, and defended a systematic, constitutional and rather detached politics. The doctrinaire brand of liberalism was first and foremost preoccupied with changing the state; if the rule of law and the Constitution functioned as they should, society would develop and grow in a natural way – Thorbecke and other romantic liberals resorted to many organic metaphors. This continental form of liberalism devoted most of its energy to the legal organization of the state. Its goal was a free society, but liberals believed that a free society could only prosper when supported and guaranteed by the appropriate rules. In fact, Thorbecke wrote, the state was, or ought to be, nothing more than a juridical community.[29] Yet, for his Calvinist or less doctrinaire opponents, his brand of liberalism destroyed freedom because it was overly centralist, overly homogenizing and overly directive, and 'un Dutch'.[30]

François Guizot and his brand of doctrinarism were toppled by the revolution of 1848, and German liberalism was also severely damaged by the outcome of that revolutionary year. In contrast to developments in France and Germany, 1848 saw the beginning of the victory of Dutch doctrinaire liberalism. It was less conservative than the French doctrinarism that was used to contain the revolution, whereas its opponent was a Dutch conservatism that dared not speak its name. Thorbecke had set out with rather conservative views, but his constitutional approach served as a means to break into the closed shop of the Dutch elite, and his opponents thought that he was a radical or, even worse, a republican. His rigid and seemingly legalistic form of liberal politics proved to be a weapon of emancipation for middle-class newcomers on the sociocultural and political scene in the Netherlands. In order to be acceptable as a party of government, liberals had to demonstrate that they were not radicals, let alone revolutionaries. This conformed to their natural tendency to keep aloof from popular politics and stick to the parliament.

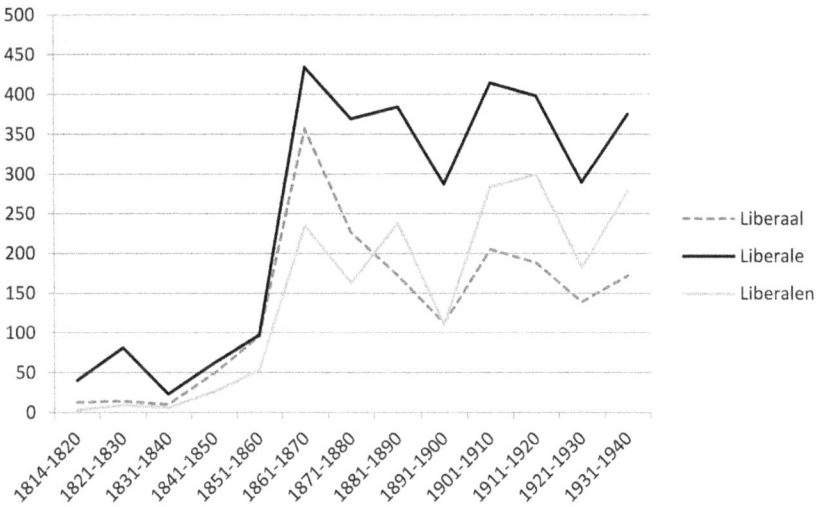

Figure 7.1 Use of the terms 'Liberaal', 'Liberale' and 'Liberalen' in the Dutch lower house. Source: Staten – Generaal Digitaal, http://www.statengeneraaldigitaal.nl.

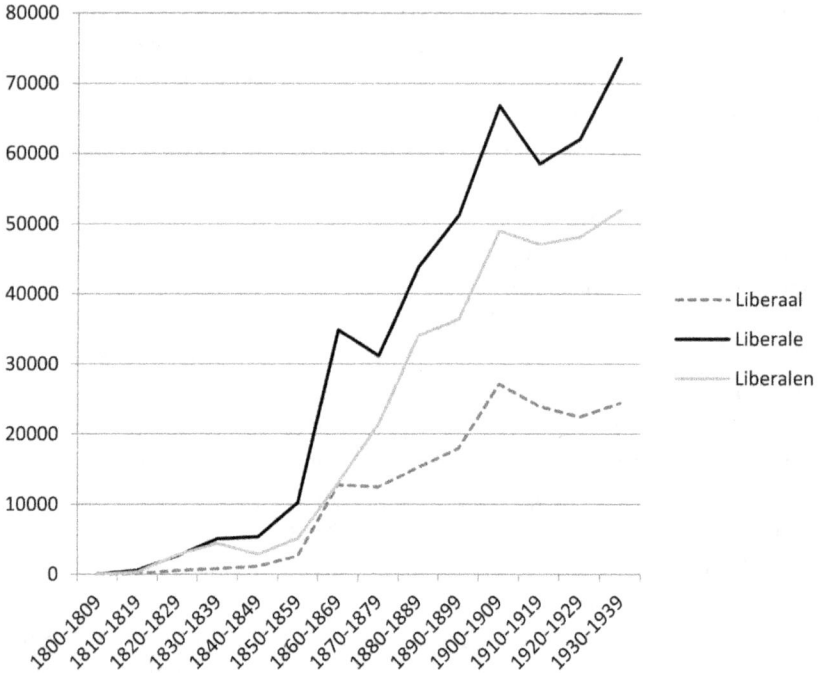

Figure 7.2 Use of the terms 'Liberaal', 'Liberale' and 'Liberalen' in Dutch newspapers, 1800–1939. Source: Delpher, https://www.delpher.nl/.

Perhaps the 1860s were the real pinnacle of liberal power and influence in the Netherlands. It was certainly the decade that the word 'liberalism' was the most used in the Dutch Parliament, relatively speaking (i.e. in proportion to the number of pages of the Dutch Hansard). This was partly caused by extensive debates about the meaning of the concept. Were only adherents of Thorbecke authorized to use the label or had the term become so vague that it now included almost everyone? And was liberalism a rising force or was it already on the decline? For Thorbeckean liberals, Britain was yet again the great example, but now due to its liberalism: the liberalism of Cobden, Bright and later Gladstone. John Stuart Mill was the most admired intellectual hero, in particular because of his *On Liberty*, which seemed to be their guidebook or 'vademecum'.[31] It is difficult to tell whether a real cultural transfer was taking place. Dutch intellectuals read British, French and German texts, and in their constitutional debates in parliament, MPs constantly quoted foreign experts, but it is not easy to distinguish between real transfer and the use of foreign examples as a way of boosting the fortune of one's own movement in the Netherlands. For instance, both Dutch liberals and orthodox Protestants claimed Gladstone as their example, because he was such a successful and well-known political leader. It is clear, though, that liberalism was to a large extent an international movement.

'Vrijzinnigheid' and Liberalism in the Late Nineteenth Century

Liberalism was now such a strong brand that even principled opponents tried to appropriate it. The emerging orthodox Protestant party operated under the banner of 'Christian liberalism' for a short while, before it started to use the expression Christian democracy.[32] The party used this label in order to argue that politics should free religion from all constitutional impediments and to promote the strength of the neo-Calvinists in civil society. The orthodox attempt to capture the word 'liberal' did not last very long, partly because the label was now quickly losing its attraction for newcomers, but probably also because Christian liberalism had already existed with a different meaning.

The Dutch language contains a synonym of 'liberal' that is close to the German word 'freisinnig', *vrijzinnig*. This word could denote 'liberal' in its political or social senses, but during the nineteenth century, its predominant meaning became liberal in a religious sense, as opposed to orthodox. Most liberals were Protestants, but liberal Protestants. This could sometimes mean that they were dissenters: Thorbecke was a Lutheran, whereas the main Protestant church was Calvinist. But usually they belonged to the national church, which, while not formally a state church, was the dominant church, thus enjoying some privileges. Their form of liberal Protestantism was rather dry, intellectual and elitist, and not at all evangelical. Just like political liberalism, liberal Protestantism attained dominance in the third quarter of the nineteenth century and then lost this position again to the emerging orthodox Protestant group, which attracted more lower-class Protestants. But the religious and cultural connotation of the word *vrijzinnig* remained, and because it had seldom been used for political purposes, it was still available at the end of the century for liberals who wished to find new paths in politics without really abandoning liberal premises.

By the end of the nineteenth century, all new parties – orthodox Protestants, Catholics and socialists – claimed to fight for freedom in one way or another, but liberalism was declining as a political force. In the 1860s, liberalism as a political movement had first begun to show signs of discord. The agenda of constitutional liberalism was almost completed and the question arose as to what to do next. The Thorbeckean liberals had now become the political and social establishment, and they showed some signs of the same conservative complacency that Thorbecke had fought when he started out as a politician.[33] On the other hand, a new generation of 'young liberals' were no longer satisfied with mere constitutional liberalism. They wanted to use liberal power to bring about a liberal society, and their main strategy was reforming the school system in order to spread liberal values through the national system of primary schools. After the death of Thorbecke, the young liberal Jan Kappeyne van de Coppello became their new leader, but only for a short period of time. In 1879, he introduced a new education bill that served as a rallying point for liberals of different persuasion, but also for their religious opponents, both Catholics and orthodox Protestants, who exploited the bill to mobilize religious opposition against liberalism. The nature of primary education was the main issue of political polarization in that period. For some years, Dutch liberalism seemed predominantly to become a party of anticlericalism, as was happening in some countries with a dominant Catholic party. However, this proved to be merely a passing episode. Its main political effect was that it helped their religious opponents to form a coalition of Catholics and orthodox Protestants.

In the 1890s, however, liberalism regained some of its energy, first by concentrating on broadening the suffrage and then on social legislation. Whereas the young liberals had concentrated on education, the new social liberals thought these relatively new issues were the most pressing political questions. At first, this new brand of liberals remained within the old, rather loose, liberal party, which only established its first formal national organization, the Liberal Union, in 1885. By the 1890s, the party had broken up over the issue of general suffrage. This resulted in a couple of separate parties, whose names also illustrate some of the linguistic problems liberalism had to face.

The conservative liberals were now using the rather pleonastic name of Free Liberals, as if liberalism itself had lost much of its original meaning, which was not altogether untrue. The progressive liberals thought the word 'liberalism' had been contaminated by laissez-faire economics and conservatism.[34] In the days of Thorbecke, laissez-faire had been a less important ingredient of liberalism than constitutionalism. Nonetheless, it had been important as a progressive weapon against the paternalist and interfering economic politics of the king and in around 1850, Thorbecke's first Cabinet had been the occasion for a considerable amount of discussion about a free economy.[35] Meanwhile, however, laissez-faire had become another term for an unfeeling kind of conservative liberalism. This was one of the reasons why progressives no longer favoured the term 'liberal' and instead chose the combination *vrijzinnig-democratisch*. In 1901, a *vrijzinnig-democratische* party was founded. There is a debate among historians as to whether they should still be counted as members of the liberal family. At the time, conservative liberals argued that they had forsaken their membership of the liberal family and had joined the family of social democrats instead.[36] The historian of the

Free Liberals also wants to exclude them from the liberal universe, partly because they themselves had freely chosen a different name.[37] Moreover, the historian of the *vrijzinnig-democraten* argues that they formed part of a separate, internationally recognizable group of democratic parties.[38] That is probably true, as the Dutch *vrijzinnig-democraten* were certainly looking abroad for inspiration to German *Kathedersozialisten* or British new liberals.

However, the *vrijzinnig-democraten* were so close to liberalism, and in particular to its culture and social circles, that it would be an unwarranted reduction of liberalism to exclude them, not least because they exhibited a clear family resemblance to British new liberalism. The change from classic liberalism to *vrijzinnig-democratisch* in the Netherlands clearly resembled the change from classic to new liberalism in Britain.[39] The fact that Dutch new liberals were not so keen on claiming the name 'liberal' as were their British counterparts[40] is also due to the nature of Dutch classical liberalism. This doctrinaire, professorial type of liberalism had consciously kept the common people at bay or, more precisely, they did not like rhetorical display, mass meetings or most of the popular aspects of politics. Thorbecke had looked down on politicians such as Gladstone or Palmerston, who according to him came close to opportunistically pandering to the common people instead of maintaining a strict legal, constitutional line.[41]

Even though they were also rather intellectual and sometimes even elitist, the democratic Dutch new liberals wanted to underline the distance that separated them from such attitudes, so they chose another name. In general, however, twentieth-century liberalism tried to steer a middle course between conservatism on the one hand and social democracy on the other, and there was always the risk of drifting off in one of those directions. At first, the new liberalism occasionally seemed to want to join forces with social democracy, but its proponents always underlined the differences. In addition, it was often rather hard to perceive the Free Liberals still as a liberal, instead of a purely conservative party. They may have claimed the name 'liberal', but that was also because no one in the Netherlands dared to claim the label 'conservative'. In contrast to the British use of the word, the Dutch term 'liberal' was already beginning to sound rather conservative by around 1900 and it was very diffi-cult to imagine an alliance between social -democrats and 'liberals' – such an alliance would only happen at the very end of the twentieth century. If one wanted to keep the door open to social democrats, one had to offer another word. In the interwar years, the *vrijzinnig-democraten* were the most dedi-cated champions of the rule of law, a classic liberal theme, and their record in this respect was certainly better than that of the liberal party, which was in that period more of a party of law and order. Many of their adherents also belonged to *vrijzinnig* (liberal) Protestantism.

The Dutch new liberals advocated general male and female suffrage, some social legislation, and comprehensive education of the people. They were more moralistic than previous generations of liberals and believed that the state should, to a certain extent, act as the keeper or guardian of every citizen. As in Britain, the main difference between classic and new liberalism lay in their conception of citizenship and freedom. Thorbecke's adherents had assumed that only independent men could become citizens bearing full political rights. Citizenship presupposed (material and intellectual) freedom and independence. The new liberals reversed the sequence: because everybody had the right to become a citizen, it was crucial to support and educate the people in order to realize their freedom. Initially they had hoped that voluntary societies would take care of the necessary support and education, but they quickly recognized that only the state had the wherewithal for the required effort. They now even quoted Rousseau: 'il n'y a que la force de l'état qui fasse la liberté de ses membres' ('the strength of the state can alone secure the liberty of its members').[42]

Decline

The new party was officially founded in 1901 and it would cooperate during the national elections with the other liberal forces under the name of *vrijzinnige concentratie*. All liberals considered themselves to be *vrijzinnig*, but not all *vrijzinnigen* wanted to be called liberals. Eventually, three *vrijzinnige* parties existed: the old Liberal Union, which tried to keep all liberal forces united, the conservative Free Liberals and the Vrijzinnig-Democraten (or Lib Dems). This was a sign not of liberal strength, but of dwindling forces. At the beginning of the twentieth century, it had become difficult to explain what liberalism was, and the liberal parties also began to lose elections. Already by around 1900, bourgeois liberalism appeared a spent force to many people. A conservative liberal was writing in his diary that 'liberalism was taken to its grave' and that 'for the moment, liberalism has lost everything in the Netherlands'.[43] 'The liberals are crushed between the extremes', one of his political friends observed.[44]

This was voiced after the liberal parties had lost the national elections of 1901. During the First World War, a liberal government and a last liberal prime minister were still in power, but in fact he led a minority government. When this ended in 1918, the liberals suffered a crushing defeat at the elections – the first elections with male general suffrage; full general suffrage would be introduced one year later. A liberal newspaper predicted the 'end of the liberal era' for the foreseeable future.[45] This was no sudden strange death of Dutch liberalism, but rather a crucial episode in the course of a prolonged agony. Ultimately, liberalism would rise again from the grave, but this revival was to take a very long time. The prediction proved to be quite accurate: throughout the entire twentieth century, the Netherlands would not have a liberal prime minister again.

An increasing amount of people, including many liberals, even wanted to avoid the term 'liberal'. When a number of small parties, which were more or less liberal in their orientation, merged in 1921, some partners were 'repelled' by the word 'liberal', which conjured up images of neglect of social questions. They agreed to use the noncommittal name 'Freedom League' (Vrijheidsbond) instead.[46] Some politicians and voters still wanted to hold on to the old label, and the Freedom League was also called 'Liberal State Party' (Liberale Staatspartij), but for most people, the label had lost its attraction and the liberal current in the strict sense of the word would be almost dead by the end of the interwar years. In the meantime, it had become very difficult to make out what the term 'liberal' meant in political terms. At the end of the 1930s, the Liberal State Party/Freedom League had dwindled to a mere four seats – alongside six *vrijzinnig-democratische* seats—in a parliament consisting of a hundred members, and all its original issues had disappeared. Constitutionalism was no longer a forte of the liberals as opposed to the *vrijzinnig-democraten*. They had even abandoned laissez-faire and free trade in the face of the economic crisis of the 1930s, and they were no longer the principal opponents of the confessional or denominational parties. One of their leaders argued that liberalism needed a thoroughly religious basis and he curiously believed that Voltaire supported him in this respect.[47]

The word 'liberal' now sounded like an echo of a nineteenth century that had been too materialistic, too rationalist and too individualist, or so the public opinion of the 1930s assumed. From the religious parties to the social democrats, almost everyone agreed that society needed a more socially oriented and moral form of politics. It was in this intellectual and politi-cal climate that Johan Huizinga tried to rehabilitate the word 'liberal', and reverse the history of the decline and fall of liberal values. This was part of an attempt to restore confidence in Western culture in the face of the crisis of fascism and the threat of Nazi Germany. Huizinga wanted to save the con-cepts of democracy and humanism as well, but for the present purposes, his comments on the word 'liberal' are particularly relevant. Already by around 1900, he maintained, the words 'liberal' and 'liberalism' were so seriously contaminated by their association with the bourgeoisie that many people were no longer prepared to use them. Paradoxically, this seemed to offer the opportunity to liberate the word from its narrow party-political meaning and restore its old meaning of befitting a free-born person, mild, generous and civilized, which Huizinga excavated from the Latin and from early modern texts in an essay he wrote during the German occupation in the Second World War.[48] The old and rather conservative historian disliked politics, and when he wrote about the Dutch national character, he referred to the social concept of 'burger', a Dutch word that could mean the burgher of an early modern town, the citizen of a modern state, or bourgeois and petty-bourgeois in the sense of belonging to the middle classes.[49] But when he described the values connected with 'burgerlijke' culture, he employed words that could have been used in connection with liberal in its nonpolitical sense: moderate, nonmilitaristic, commercial. Wasn't he arguing that the Netherlands had always been and should remain a 'liberal' country? He was echoing that other European intellectual, Thomas Mann, who had written in his very political tract *Betrachtungen eines Unpolitischen* that if he were liberal, it could only be in the sense of national and 'unpolitical' *Liberalität.*[50]

Huizinga's pupil, the Marxist historian Jan Romein seemed to draw a comparable conclusion during the first year of the German occupation. According to him, the Dutch tradition of freedom and tolerance had not only inspired Dutch liberals, but had further instilled a liberal spirit into all great Dutch politicians, be they socialist, Calvinist or Catholic.[51] He used the word 'liberalism', but in effect he was referring to what was still called 'liberaliteit' in the early nineteenth century. Then, as in the 1940s, *liberaliteit* was considered to be a feature of Dutch national identity. History seemed to have come full circle. Before liberalism there was already *liberaliteit*, and now liberalism was endowed with that meaning. Dutch political liberalism was at the lowest point in its history, yet a Marxist historian was suggesting that all major Dutch politicians had been imbued by a sense of liberalism!

Epilogue

Romein wrote under the spell of the German occupation and he used the concept of liberalism as a way to unite all Dutch currents as well as a weapon against Nazi ideology. He would not have been able to do so had liberalism still been a powerful political label. But if the Netherlands was a liberal country, this remained rather well hidden in politics. During a large part of the twentieth century, Dutch politics were dominated by religious parties and social democrats. A narrow definition of liberal and liberalism prevailed in politics. For instance, no one has ever called liberal democracy 'liberal' in the Netherlands. The Dutch expression was 'parliamentary democracy'; liberal would have sounded too much like a narrow party label. In the early postwar years, the former *vrijzinnig-democraten* first joined the new formed Dutch Labour Party (which also united social democrats and progressive Protestants), but their leader and a substantial following later decided to quit the party and found a new liberal party, together with the rump of the liberals. The new party was called 'People's Party for Freedom and Democracy' (VVD, 1948), but it remained rather small. In the 1960s, a new left-liberal party was founded and chose the name Democrats '66. D66 has sometimes employed the social-liberal label, and in certain respects it resembles the *vrijzinnig-democraten*.

Over the past few decades, the liberal parties have been the most constant factor in the Dutch coalition governments and, since 2010, the VVD has been the strongest party. At the time of writing, the Netherlands has a liberal prime minister again, the first since the First World War: Mark Rutte, a member of the rather neoliberal VVD, but possessing a democratic attitude akin to the Democrats. However, initially, Rutte ruled with the support of the Party for Freedom, which, notwithstanding its name, is the party of the right-wing populist Geert Wilders. Wilders launched his political party as a member of parliament for the VVD, but his party has developed into the very opposite of liberalism as well as liberality.

However, Wilders' party is to a certain extent reminiscent of the 'Jacobinism' that nineteenth-century commentators were so afraid of: aggressively favouring unity over diversity, fiercely anticlerical and antireligious (against Islam), and expecting the state to enforce 'national' morals. This is only a minority movement, but it is clear that the times when all important political currents were instilled by a liberal spirit are over. This is a strange conclusion at a time when more Dutch political parties then ever claim a part of the liberal heritage and the Netherlands has a liberal Prime Minister. Perhaps Dutch citizens are so convinced that freedom is a precious gift that even its opponents now have to dress up as its defenders.

Henk te Velde is Professor of Dutch History at Leiden University, the oldest history chair in the Netherlands. He studied history at the University of Groningen, where he subsequently worked as Professor of the History of Political Culture until he moved to Leiden in 2005. His Ph.D. on Dutch liberalism and nationalism in around 1900 was published as a book in 1992. He has also written a number of books on Dutch and comparative history. His latest English-language publications are *Organizing Democracy: Reflections on the Rise of Political Organizations in the Nineteenth Century* (co-edited with Maartje Janse, 2017) and *Democracy in Modern Europe. A Conceptual History* (co-edited with Jussi Kurunmäki and Jeppe Nevers, 2018).

Notes

1. According to the examples provided by the *Woordenboek der Nederlandsche Taal,* the Dutch counterpart of the *Oxford English Dictionary.*
2. J. Leonhard, *Liberalismus: Zur historischen Semantik eines europäischen Deutungsmusters,* Munich, 2001, 87 and passim for 'liberalitas' and its modern European equivalents.
3. See the contributions by Velema (classic republicanism) and Van Sas (early liberalism) in F. Grijzenhout, N. van Sas and W. Velema (eds), *Het Bataafse experiment: Politiek en cultuur rond 1800,* Nijmegen, 2013, 63 and 81.
4. Cf. the conservative and orthodox Protestant W. Bilderdijk, *De bezwaren tegen den geest der eeuw van mr I. da Costa toegelicht,* Leiden, 1823, 47.
5. D.F. van Alphen, *Handelingen Tweede Kamer,* 27 December 1832, 111. The Dutch parliamentary reports are available at http://wip.politicalmashup.nl and http://www.statengeneraaldigitaal.nl (retrieved 25 February 2019).
6. F. Fret, *Handelingen Tweede Kamer,* 12 June 1833, 261.
7. 'Vrijheidsdrift en vrijheidsgeest' and 'Aanmerkingen van de redactie', *Algemeen Handelsblad,* 7 June 1832.
8. J. Huizinga, 'The Spirit of the Netherlands' (1935), in *Dutch Civilisation in the Seventeenth Century,* London, 1968.
9. *Nederlandsche Staatscourant,* 2 November 1815 (I have used the digitized newspapers available at http://www.delpher.nl). Huizinga already mentioned the 'curious' Spanish connection in passing: J. Huizinga, *Geschonden wereld: Een beschouwing over de kansen van herstel van onze beschaving,* Haarlem, 1945, 238, but he did not really know the Spanish (and Latin American) background. See now the work of J. Fernández-Sebastián, for instance, Chapter 3 in this volume. The Netherlands were not directly influenced by Spanish 'liberalism', but newspapers contain scattered references to Spain.
10. *Arnhemsche Courant,* 30 March 1824.
11. W.T. Krug, *Geschiedkundig tafereel van het liberalismus van ouden en lateren tijd,* Amsterdam, 1823.
12. 'Liberaliteit', *Arnhemsche Courant,* 29 June 1824.
13. 'Liberaliteit en liberalismus', *De Weegschaal* (1823), 261–63, 268. Cf. P.J.E. Bieringa, 'Vrijheid in het Nederlandse politieke debat, 1814–1840', in E.O.G. Haitsma Mulier and W.R.E. Velema (eds), *Vrijheid: Een geschiedenis van de vijftiende tot de twintigste eeuw,* Amsterdam, 1999: 308.
14. Anonymus [= Antoni May van Vollenhoven], 'Patriotismus – Liberaliteit', *Vaderlandsche Letteroefeningen* 2 (1820), 518–23.
15. J.R. Thorbecke, *De briefwisseling,* G.J. Hooykaas III (ed.), The Hague, 1988, 110 and 116 (letters from 1837). Cf. T.M. Roest van Limburg, *Liberalismus,* Leiden, 1837. Roest was also a political journalist at the *Arnhemsche Courant.*
16. *Handelingen Tweede Kamer 1847–1848,* 23 August 1848, 783; *Handelingen Tweede Kamer 1849–1850,* 14 June 1850, 7–8.
17. J.R. Thorbecke, 'Narede', in *Politieke redevoeringen,* vol. VI, Deventer, 1870.

18. J.R. Thorbecke, *Historische Schetsen* [1860], The Hague, 1872, 36.
19. C. van Zuylen van Nyevelt, *Liberalismus*, Amsterdam, 1828, 1.
20. T.M. Roest van Limburg, *Liberalismus*, Leiden, 1837, 5.
21. Cf. H. te Velde, 'The Organization of Liberty: Dutch Liberalism as a Case of the History of European Constitutional Liberalism', *European Journal of Political Theory* 7 (2008), 65–79.
22. D. Slijkerman, *Het geheim van de ministeriële verantwoordelijkheid: De verhouding tussen koning, kabinet, Kamer en kiezer, 1848–1905*, Amsterdam, 2011.
23. Cf. J. van Zanten, *Schielijk, winzucht en bedaard: Politieke discussie en oppositievorming 1813–1840*, Amsterdam, 2004, 127–32.
24. Cf. the conservative G.W. Vreede, *De regtstreeksche verkiezingen tot de nationale vertegenwoordiging bestreden*, Amsterdam, 1848; cf. H. te Velde, 'Mixed Government and Democracy in 19th-Century Political Discourse: Great Britain, France and the Netherlands', in J. Kurunmäki, J. Nevers and H. te Velde (eds), *Democracy in Modern Europe: A Conceptual History* (New York, 2018), 42–64.
25. J.R. Thorbecke, *Briefwisseling*, vol. VI, The Hague, 1998, 552.
26. Ibid., 553.
27. Cf. A. Craiutu, *Liberalism under Siege: The Political Thought of the French Doctrinaires*, Lanham, 2003; L. Díez del Corral, *Doktrinärer Liberalismus: Guizot und sein Kreis*, Neuwied am Rhein, 1964; H. te Velde, 'Onderwijzers in politiek: Thorbecke, Guizot en het Europese doctrinaire liberalisme', *BMGN* 113 (1998), 322–43.
28. J. Drentje, *Thorbecke: Een filosoof in de politiek*, Amsterdam, 2004, 335, 423.
29. E.g. J.R. Thorbecke, *Briefwisseling*, vol. VII, The Hague, 2002, 474 (c. 1870); J.R. Thorbecke, 'Narede', in *Politieke redevoeringen*, vol. VI, Deventer, 1870.
30. See e.g. the Calvinist leader G. Groen van Prinsterer, *Handelingen Tweede Kamer*, 12 May 1851: 726–6; and the liberal conservative W. Wintgens, *Handelingen Tweede Kamer*, 27 March 1865: 744 ('extremely systemizing spirit').
31. R. Aerts, *De letterheren: Liberale cultuur in de negentiende eeuw: het tijdschrift De Gids*, Amsterdam, 1997, 363 and 465.
32. Letters and a memo by the future orthodox Protestant leader A. Kuyper to the old leader G. Groen van Prinsterer and his reply, in G. Groen van Prinsterer, *Briefwisseling*, vol. VI, The Hague, 1992, 507 and 736–37 (1874).
33. Cf. H. te Velde, 'Liberalism and Bourgeois Culture in the Netherlands, from the 1840s to the 1880s', in S. Groenveld and M. Wintle (eds), *Under the Sign of Liberalism: Varieties of Liberalism in Past and Present*, Zutphen, 1997.
34. G. Taal, *Liberalen en radicalen in Nederland, 1872–1901*, The Hague, 1980, 456.
35. Cf. http://kbkranten.politicalmashup.nl/#q/laissez faire.
36. S. van Houten, *Liberaal of vrijzinnig/sociaal-democraat*, The Hague, 1899.
37. P. van Schie, *Vrijheidsstreven in verdrukking: Liberale partijpolitiek in Nederland 1901–1940*, Amsterdam, 2005.
38. M.H. Klijnsma, *Om de democratie: De geschiedenis van de Vrijzinnig-Democratische Bond, 1901–1946*, Amterdam, 2008.

39. S. Stuurman, 'Samuel van Houten and Dutch Liberalism, 1860–1890', *Journal of the History of Ideas* 50 (1989), 135–52; S. Stuurman, 'John Bright and Samuel van Houten: Radical Liberalism and the Working Classes in Britain and the Netherlands 1860–1880', *History of European Ideas* 11 (1990), 593–604; S. Stuurman, 'Nineteenth-Century Liberalism and the Politics of Reform in Britain and the Netherlands', *Anuario del Departemento de Historia* 11 (1990), 153–70; and his comprehensive account in Dutch: S. Stuurman, *Wacht op onze daden: Het liberalisme en de vernieuwing van de Nederlandse staat*, Amsterdam, 1992.
40. See also S. Dudink, *Deugdzaam liberalisme: Sociaal-liberalisme in Nederland 1870–1901*, Amsterdam, 1997: 272.
41. Drentje, *Thorbecke*, 498.
42. Quoted by the prominent member of the Vrijzinnig-Democraten and future minister M.W.F Treub (1896), who is quoted in Stuurman, *Wacht op onze daden*, 314.
43. W.H. de Beaufort, *Dagboeken en aantekeningen 1874–1918*, H. de Valk and M. van Faassen (eds), 2 vols, The Hague, 1992, vol. 1, 134 (1901) and 213 (1903).
44. B. Reiger (1901), quoted by P. van Schie, *Vrijheidsstreven in verdrukking: Liberale partijpolitiek in Nederland 1901–1940*, Amsterdam, 2005, 55.
45. The liberal daily *Algemeen Handelsblad*, quoted in *Het Volk*, 11 July 1918.
46. P. Van Schie, *Vrijheidsstreven in verdrukking: Liberale partijpolitiek in Nederland 1901–1940*, Amsterdam, 2005, 244.
47. O.C.A. van Lidt de Jeude, *Londense dagboeken januari 1940–mei 1945*, 2 vols, The Hague, 2001, vol. 1, 364f.
48. J. Huizinga, *Geschonden wereld: Een beschouwing over de kansen van herstel van onze beschaving*, Haarlem, 1945, 237–39.
49. J. Huizinga, 'The Spirit of the Netherlands', in *Dutch Civilisation in the Seventeenth Century*, London, 1968.
50. Quoted in J. Leonhard, *Liberalismus: Zur historischen Semantik eines europäischen Deutungsmusters*, Munich, 2001, 552.
51. J. Romein, 'Oorsprong, voortgang en toekomst van de Nederlandse geest', in *In opdracht van de tijd: Tien voordrachten over historische thema's*, Amsterdam 1946, 163–67. Cf. H. te Velde, 'How High Did the Dutch Fly? Remarks on Stereotypes of Burger Mentality', in A. Galema, B. Henkes and H. te Velde (eds), *Images of the Nation: Different Meanings of Dutchness 1870–1940*, Amsterdam, 1993, 74f.

Bibliography

Aerts, R. *De letterheren. Liberale cultuur in de negentiende eeuw: het tijdschrift De Gids*. Amsterdam, 1997.
Bieringa, P.J.E. 'Vrijheid in het Nederlandse politieke debat, 1814–1840', in E.O.G. Haitsma Mulier and W.R.E. Velema (eds), *Vrijheid: Een geschiedenis van de vijftiende tot de twintigste eeuw* (Amsterdam, 1999), 305–24.
Bilderdijk, W. *De bezwaren tegen den geest der eeuw van mr I. da Costa toegelicht*. Leiden, 1823.

Craiutu, A. *Liberalism under Siege: The Political Thought of the French Doctrinaires.* Lanham, 2003.

De Beaufort, W.H. *Dagboeken en aantekeningen 1874–1918*, H. de Valk and M. van Faassen (eds), 2 vols. The Hague, 1992.

Díez del Corral, L. *Doktrinärer Liberalismus: Guizot und sein Kreis.* Neuwied am Rhein, 1964.

Drentje, J. *Thorbecke: Een filosoof in de politiek.* Amsterdam, 2004.

Dudink, S. *Deugdzaam liberalisme: Sociaal-liberalisme in Nederland 1870–1901.* Amsterdam, 1997.

Grijzenhout, F., N. van Sas and W. Velema (eds). *Het Bataafse experiment: Politiek en cultuur rond 1800.* Nijmegen, 2013.

Huizinga, J. *Geschonden wereld: Een beschouwing over de kansen van herstel van onze beschaving.* Haarlem, 1945.

———. 'The Spirit of the Netherlands', in *Dutch Civilisation in the Seventeenth Century.* London, 1968.

Klijnsma, M.H. *Om de democratie: De geschiedenis van de Vrijzinnig-Democratische Bond, 1901–1946.* Amterdam, 2008.

Krug, W.T. *Geschiedkundig tafereel van het liberalismus van ouden en lateren tijd.* Amsterdam, 1823.

Leonhard, J. *Liberalismus: Zur historischen Semantik eines europäischen Deutungsmusters.* Munich, 2001.

Roest van Limburg, T.M. *Liberalismus.* Leiden, 1837.

Romein, J. *In opdracht van de tijd: Tien voordrachten over historische thema's.* Amsterdam, 1946.

Slijkerman, D. *Het geheim van de ministeriële verantwoordelijkheid: De verhouding tussen koning, kabinet, Kamer en kiezer, 1848–1905.* Amsterdam, 2011.

Stuurman, S. 'John Bright and Samuel van Houten: Radical Liberalism and the Working Classes in Britain and the Netherlands 1860–1880'. *History of European Ideas* 11 (1990), 593–604.

———. 'Nineteenth-Century Liberalism and the Politics of Reform in Britain and the Netherlands'. *Anuario del Departemento de Historia* 11 (1990), 153–70.

———. 'Samuel van Houten and Dutch Liberalism, 1860–1890'. *Journal of the History of Ideas* 50 (1989), 135–52.

———. *Wacht op onze daden: Het liberalisme en de vernieuwing van de Nederlandse staat.* Amsterdam, 1992.

Taal, G. *De briefwisseling*, G.J. Hooykaas III (ed.). The Hague, 1988.

———. *De briefwisseling*, G.J. Hooykaas VI (ed.). The Hague, 1998.

———. *De briefwisseling*, G.J. Hooykaas VII (ed.). The Hague, 2002.

———. *Historische Schetsen.* [1860] The Hague, 1872.

———. *Liberalen en radicalen in Nederland, 1872–1901.* The Hague, 1980.

———. *Politieke redevoeringen*, vol. VI. Deventer, 1870.

te Velde, H. 'How High Did the Dutch Fly? Remarks on Stereotypes of Burger Mentality', in A. Galema, B. Henkes and H. te Velde (eds), *Images of the Nation: Different Meanings of Dutchness 1870–1940* (Amsterdam, 1993), 59–80.

———. 'Liberalism and Bourgeois Culture in the Netherlands, from the 1840s to the 1880s', in S. Groenveld and M. Wintle (eds), *Under the Sign of Liberalism: Varieties of Liberalism in Past and Present* (Zutphen, 1997), 62–77.

———. 'Mixed Government and Democracy in 19th-Century Political Discourse: Great Britain, France and the Netherlands', in J. Kurunmäki, J. Nevers and H. te Velde (eds), *Democracy in Modern Europe: A Conceptual History* (New York, 2018), 42–64.

———. 'Onderwijzers in politiek: Thorbecke, Guizot en het Europese doctrinaire liberalisme'. *BMGN* 113 (1998), 322–43.

———. 'The Organization of Liberty: Dutch Liberalism as a Case of the History of European Constitutional Liberalism'. *European Journal of Political Theory* 7 (2008), 65–79.

Van Houten, S. *Liberaal of vrijzinnig/sociaal-democraat*. The Hague, 1899.

Van Lidt de Jeude, O.C.A. *Londense dagboeken januari 1940–mei 1945*, 2 vols. The Hague, 2001.

Van Prinsterer, G. *Briefwisseling*, vol. VI. The Hague, 1992.

Van Schie, P. *Vrijheidsstreven in verdrukking: Liberale partijpolitiek in Nederland 1901–1940*. Amsterdam, 2005.

Van Vollenhoven, A.M. 'Patriotismus – Liberaliteit'. *Vaderlandsche Letteroefeningen* 2 (1820), part II, 518–523.

Van Zanten, J. *Schielijk, winzucht en bedaard: Politieke discussie en oppositievorming 1813–1840*. Amsterdam, 2004.

Van Zuylen van Nyevelt, C. *Liberalismus*. Amsterdam, 1828.

Vreede, G.W. *De regtstreeksche verkiezingen tot de nationale vertegenwoordiging bestreden*. Amsterdam, 1848.

Chapter 8

A Conceptual Scheme of Polish Liberalism

Six Pillars

Maciej Janowski

Is it possible to reconstruct a conceptual scheme of Polish liberalism through-out its history? Or to offer a short list of 'keywords', similar to those that are usually given at the beginning of any research article? In other words, can one treat the whole corpus of Polish liberal thought, from the late eighteenth to the early twenty-first centuries, as a single 'research article'? A conceptual scheme is of course something more than just a list of keywords; it should use them as a building block to construct a fabric, a three-dimensional model that would represent relations and tensions among all its elements.[1] The task is even more complicated by the fact that there exists no 'corpus' of liberal thinkers or liberal texts. The Polish nineteenth century witnessed so many political twists and turns that the institutional continuity of political groupings and intellectual threads was often broken. Deeper intellectual con-tinuity existed, to be sure, but the identification of various threads and their classification as 'liberal', 'conservative', etc. is a matter of interpretation – and the content of the 'corpus' changes accordingly. An even greater theoretical problem arises when we realize an obvious thing – liberalism at the European periphery is something different from liberalism in the European core. Again, the effect depends on what we are seeking: whether we look for ideas and people that possibly closely remind us of English 'core' liberalism or try to trace modifications in liberal ideas at the periphery.

I have tried elsewhere to outline the contours of Polish nineteenth-century liberalism and I do not wish to repeat the exercise. Rather, I prefer to show certain structural lines – pillars of construction if one prefers that metaphor – which, in my opinion, support the edifice of nineteenth and early twentieth-century (until 1939) Polish liberal thought. Needless to say, another historian could imagine a different edifice, with other pillars to support it; the source material is so rich that it allows for various, very different interpretations.

Let us start with some historical background. In 1795, the old Polish-Lithuanian Commonwealth ceased to exist, partitioned between Russia, Austria and Prussia. In Polish culture, it was a period of a still triumphant Enlightenment. In 1831, a great anti-Russian insurrection (the 'November uprising') failed and gave rise to more repressive politics by the partitioning powers. This moment is conveniently accepted as the start of the triumph of Polish romanticism. Romanticism, with its idea of Polish messianism, favoured radical solutions (democratic or conservative) and was hardly a place for liberal thought. The defeat of next great uprising (the 'January uprising' in 1863) triggered a new wave of repression and another cultural transformation, this time a decline of Romanticism and the victory of Positivism. It was precisely at the time of severest Russification, in the 1870s, that liberal thought in the Russian partition achieved its intellectually most interesting results. It was a truncated liberalism, with no possibility of expressing political opinions; even the term 'liberalism' was suspect and the term 'Positivism' was used instead. Nevertheless, in its social and economic ideas, Warsaw positivism was a genuine liberalism. The early twentieth century witnessed the growth of mass political parties in the Polish territories and with it, like elsewhere in Europe, a crisis of liberalism. Intellectually it was still interesting, but politically more and more marginalized.

The independent Polish state re-emerged in 1918. A short revival of liberal ideas (in the wake of the triumph of liberal Western powers over autocratic Germany) soon gave way, as everywhere, to more and more authoritarian ideas and politics. Cultural liberalism retained a certain position in intellectual circles, whereas mainstream Polish economists, whatever their political opinions, supported economic liberalism. The German assault in 1939 began the Second World War and created radically new conditions for everything – including the development of political thought.

With all this in mind, I propose a scheme of Polish liberal thought in the nineteenth and twentieth centuries in which the following ideas play a central role, organizing the hierarchy of all other issues. I will start, unsurprisingly, with the concept of liberty. Second comes 'normality', i.e. a normative image of Western Europe; third, the problem of economic backwardness and modernization; fourth, the modern state; fifth, nation-building; and, finally, a universalist ethics as an axiological fundament. I will attempt to show how the vocabulary and, with it, the imagery – which expresses itself by means of conceptualization – changed.

Liberty: Enlightenment and Romanticism

Let us begin with liberty. An excellent book by Anna Grześkowiak-Krwawicz has greatly augmented our understanding of the multiple uses of the concept of liberty in Polish political discourses up to the mid eighteenth century.[2] It demonstrated how the concept of liberty was a republican one, highlighting political participation rather than individual freedom as a core value. This 'old' republican trend in the second half of the eighteenth century could assume various versions and various ideological costumes. It could form the central concept of the 'old-noble' opposition to enlightenment reforms; it could become a basis for some new political ideas, as when the Confederates of Bar turned to Jean-Jacques Rousseau to outline for them a sketch of a Polish constitution. The Bar Confederation (1768–72) was a somehow Janus-faced movement, on the one hand opposing the Enlightenment reforms, especially religious tolerance, while on the other hand attempting to resist Russian intervention and the partition. Turning to Rousseau, the confederates initiated the creation of the *Considérations sur le gouvernement de Pologne*.

It may be seen as a feature of Polish liberal thought – and perhaps that of other countries in the European periphery as well – that liberty does not figure as a central category in liberal parlance. The Enlightenment reformers, mainly gathered around King Stanislaus Augustus (who ruled from 1764 to 1795) and opposing the old republicanism, could not succeed in winning over the concept of liberty for themselves – it was almost monopolized by the traditional defenders of noble privilege. Therefore, this concept was often employed by enlightened reformers in an ironic or an outwardly critical sense. 'Look for [the cause of] your misfortune in your own liberty' – thus Adam Naruszewicz, one of the leading Enlightenment intellectuals around King Stanislaus Augustus, addressed the 'misguided nation' in one of his poems, meaning obviously the political nation, i.e. the nobility. In a more sober mood, Wawrzyniec Surowiecki, an economist close to the German tradition of cameralism, complained in 1812 about the 'misunderstood liberty of disposing of one's private property', which he saw as one of the reasons for Poland's deforestation. The above sentence was uttered in a lecture he delivered to Warsaw law students, who were to become state officials in the Napoleonic Duchy of Warsaw. No wonder that he expressed the hope for enlightened governmental activity to repair the damage.[3]

Some other reflections appear closer to what we perhaps could classify as a liberal tradition. In 1790, Hugo Kołłątaj, a leader of radical reformers (who were to be called the Polish 'Jacobins' in 1794), attempted to distinguish between various meanings of liberty:

> The liberty of a nation should be treated in the same way as the liberty of an
> [individual] man. What is permitted to a [single] man, is permitted to men, to
> a nation, and the only difference between the liberty of a man and the liberty
> of a nation is the difference between the needs and relations of man with man,
> or the [needs and relations] of people with a government. From this follows a
> double liberty, or its double consequences: Civil liberty is related to the needs
> and security of [individual] man, political liberty – to persons and needs of
> society.[4]

This is a difficult and ambiguous fragment, even in Polish. It looks as if
Kołłątaj was struggling with the language to express the ideas that did not yet
have a proper conceptual apparatus in Polish. The general meaning seems to
be as follows: there exists something like individual liberty, and the liberty of
a nation is simply a 'multiplication' of a great number of individual liberties,
although with one important difference – in national liberty, there is an
added dimension of relations between individuals and government (whereas
individual liberty deals only with relations of individuals among themselves).
The sphere of relations among individuals is civil liberty, while the sphere of
relations between individuals and society (or state) is political liberty. The
sentence that follows after the above quotation is clear: 'Political liberty stems
from civil liberty; indeed, political liberty is bad and harmful if it does not
safeguard civil liberty.'

Kołłątaj's thoughts are interesting for numerous reasons, among others
because he attempted to take some of the traditional tenets of the political
culture of the gentry and transform the old estate liberty of the nobility
into the modern 'liberal' idea of liberty. That is the context of the analysed
fragment too.

In the same period, we witness a process analysed in depth by Reinhart
Koselleck with regard to Prussian political language – 'singularization',
as he called it, of political concepts. 'Liberties' were frequently employed
in the plural – as privileges, often in the phrase 'rights and liberties'.
Sometimes liberty in the singular also meant a privilege, an individual
exemption in a feudal system where privilege was a most typical instrument of socioeconomic policy. The final collapse of the state in 1795
brought about a certain diversification. Staunch 'enlighteners' kept a certain distance from the idea of liberty and extolled the merits of developed
state structures. At the same time, liberty began – more and more – to
mean political independence, and that would be a central meaning in Polish
political parlance until 1918.

The Polish Romanticism that developed especially in exile in France in the
1830s and 1840s contributed to the 'national' and 'universalist' (and certainly
not individualist) understanding of the concept of liberty. The great thinkers

and poets, especially Adam Mickiewicz, were disappointed with the mundane and prosaic reality of the French July Monarchy. They had their own idea of liberty that united the individual with the national, and the national with the universal, and that contemptuously rejected liberal constitutional institutions, because liberty had to be rooted in the souls of the people, not in dry legal formulae. Commenting on one of numerous failed attempts of the Polish émigrés at stirring a revolution in Europe, Mickiewicz wrote:

> The expedition of our brethren is exactly a fragment of this outspoken defence of liberty that was started by the [Polish] revolution [of 1830] and whose result will still have to be awaited for generations. Whatever its effect … it has demonstrated not through words but through a brave deed, how the Poles feel the brotherhood of peoples, how they are ready everywhere to spill their blood for liberty. They have put into practice one of the paragraphs of the future European law: *Mutual help in the fight for liberty.*[5]

Elsewhere, Mickiewicz wrote about the envisaged gathering of the Polish Diet in exile (which eventually did not happen). The Diet should:

> proclaim that, if any nation gains its liberty, the Polish Diet would invite its representatives for a common debate on the case of liberty … The idea that we are knights of universal liberty, would rouse everyone in his own eyes, and the great idea is indispensable for the awakening of the spirit of great sacrifice.[6]

A comment is required: Romanticism (Mickiewicz, obviously one of the most interesting thinkers of this stream in Poland, stays here as a *pars pro toto*) managed to reconcile the national and the universal, but the price for that was a lack of any practical, institutional recommendations. Therefore, the radical democratism of many leading personalities of the romantic generation, often tinged with mysticism, did not have much to offer to the liberal intellectual tradition. It was people's intuition, not constitutional theory, that was to build the political system of the future free Poland in free Europe. In this sense, we may say that Polish romanticism was essentially antiliberal. We do not need to introduce the conservative romantic thinkers (such as Zygmunt Krasiński) here because their antiliberalism is clear, but even democrats stressing the central importance of freedom were very far removed in their mentality from the liberal mind. It should also be added that the strong national element in Polish romantic thought could easily degenerate into chauvinism and xenophobia; there are various instances of such simplifying perceptions of the romantic philosophy of history.

At the same time, Polish romanticism also had a strong impact on Polish liberalism. Its influence on Polish positivism is visible in stressing the internationalism of national ideology. This universalist element ended partially only in the early twentieth century, about which more later.

In 1981, this interrelation between the 'national', patriotic and individualist understanding of liberty was analysed by the eminent historian Henryk Wereszycki (1898–1990). Himself an anticommunist Social Democrat rather than a liberal, Wereszycki belonged to those few Polish historians who kept a distrustful distance from the Communist authorities throughout the whole Communist period and therefore won great moral authority in the professional milieu. In his old age, Wereszycki reflected on the level of liberty in Galicia under Austrian rule. He recalled from his childhood a jubilee celebrating the seventy-fifth birthday of an eminent Polish Social Democrat, Bronisław Limanowski (1835–1935) in 1910 in Lviv. A Ukrainian Social Democrat taking part in the event said: 'We wish you, Comrade Limanowski, a free Warsaw.' And then – mused Wereszycki – twenty years later, in 1930, Limanowski could clearly see that in fact there was more liberty in Habsburg Lviv in 1910 than in Warsaw in 1930. There was more national freedom, but less individual liberty in 1930: Poland was independent, but Austria was more liberal. Wereszycki's reflections from that distant perspective[7] were not developed (by him or by anyone else) into a more systematic analysis. The interrelation between these two types of liberty was never a central topic of Polish thought.

Liberty: Economics

The relationship between liberty and the economic system was subject to periodic reassessment. The Romantic thinkers saw a reverse relationship between liberty and economic wellbeing: they demanded sacrifices to win liberty and they feared that the material conveniences of everyday life would seduce the Poles away from the pursuit of loftier ideals. The liberals tended, as a rule, to see a positive correlation between wellbeing and liberty. The Warsaw positivists in the second half of the nineteenth century noticed this connection, but the strong Russian state censorship made impossible a deeper discussion of this issue. It was only in the changed situation of an independent statehood that more subtle reflections could appear. One of the leading Polish interwar economic liberals, Adam Krzyżanowski, was pessimistic here: he supposed, contrary for example to Milton Friedman more than half a century later, that political despotism would soon trample economic liberty, not the other way round. A different accentuation characterized a book published in 1938 in Cracow entitled *The Decline or Renaissance of Liberalism* by the economist Ferdynand Zweig (a student of Krzyżanowski's). Without disregarding the power of antiliberal totalitarian regimes both to the east and to the west of Poland, Zweig permitted himself some cautious optimism. Just as classical liberalism, he wrote, was followed by the now-reigning 'neomercantilism', so would that 'neomercantilism' be followed by 'neoliberalism'.[8] The now so familiar term was not coined by Zweig. In 1927, one of the leading Romanian liberal theoreticians, Stefan Zeletin, published a small book entitled *Neoliberalism*. In his etatism, Zeletin was much more radical than Zweig. His book was never quoted by Zweig, who was probably unfamiliar with it (and who provides hardly any footnotes, as it happens). However, it is interesting that the thought of both these authors led in the same direction: new liberalism demands much more state activity than the old one; neoliberalism is social liberalism.

An interesting question is whether this 'new liberalism' (Zweig seems to have used 'new liberalism' and 'neoliberalism' interchangeably) can be seen as a conscious transposition of the 'new liberalism' of Leonard Hobhouse and other British social reformers. Without venturing a detailed study in transfer of ideas, I daresay that both Romanian and Polish intellectuals must have known about them; they observed the intellectual developments in Western Europe rather carefully. At the same time, it is clear that for the Polish culture French and German intellectual life was more important than the cultural developments in Britain. The influences of the German *Kathedersozialismus* or of the revisionist German Social Democracy were probably more important than the British ones. The transformation of liberalism in the direction of more socialization had been 'in the air' since the last decades of the nineteenth century and it took place in various ways in all European intellectual contexts. Sometimes, the patient did not survive the operation and was replaced by a movement that better understood (or better pretended to understand) the social problem – a rightist or leftist one, be it Christian Social, peasantist, Social Democratic or radical nationalist. Sometimes the liberals themselves were looking for a new term that would better express the shift of values: they called themselves radicals or democrats. It is possible that in this search for a new label, some of them coined the phrase 'new liberalism' independently from external influences (after all, the phrase is not that complicated).

Another question may be posed, but only as a digression, whether there is any connection between this neoliberalism of 1926 and 1936 and the 'new' neoliberalism of the 1980s and 1990s. On the one hand, they seem to differ: the 'old' one being 'social' liberalism, whereas the 'new' one heralded free-market orthodoxy. It was probably not a coincidence that Friedrich Hayek, considered one of the 'founding fathers' of the 'new' neoliberalism, called himself a 'paleoliberal' in order to distance himself from the 'new' social liberals. On the other hand, both neoliberalisms clearly took their inspiration from the

German ordoliberalism, while stressing different aspects of it. Zweig's book was republished in Poland (as one of the clandestine, noncensored publications) in the late 1980s, as one of the harbingers of the new 'liberal consensus' of the 1990s – another sign of the connection between the 'neoliberalisms' of the 1930s and 1980s. However, a serious answer to this question would demand research that is much more detailed.

Zweig included the concept of 'fairness' in his understanding of liberty as a justification of state action. It is fair play that demands of the state to protect the individual consumer against the monopolist, and the factory worker against the capitalist. It is interesting to note Zweig's reading of Adam Smith, whom he considers – contrary to the common stereotype – as a forerunner of social liberalism.

As regards the 'liberty and wealth' issue, Zweig believed that liberal economics and politics cause economic growth, but the reverse is also true:[9] economic growth makes liberal economic policy ever-more indispensable, for the more complicated the economy is, the less regulated it should be. A regime of regulation may be temporarily necessary to prevent catastrophe in a situation of extreme poverty, but once the population becomes even slightly richer, a free economy should be introduced so that individual enterprises can contribute to a still steadier growth. While repeating the classical liberal tenet of the close interconnection between liberty and property, Zweig stressed the necessity of democratizing property: 'Whoever fights in defence of liberty, has to fight for granting property to the masses, for providing them with a certain minimum of property that guarantees them freedom of movement … A programme of neoliberalism, i.e. of social liberalism is a programme of a broad democratisation of property.'[10]

Liberty: Social and Cultural Aspects

There were also thinkers in the interwar liberal tradition who stressed the social element more emphatically than Zweig did. Antoni Słonimski, an eminent poet and journalist and one of the leading collaborators of the Warsaw liberal weekly *Wiadomości Literackie* (*Literary News*), writing his feuilletons in the years of the Great Crisis and immediately after, could on different occasions identify himself both with socialism (stressing his fundamental distance from Soviet totalitarianism) and liberalism.[11]

Another axis of transformation of the concept of liberty is its relation to customs and morals. Zweig is rather traditional here. Political and economic liberty demands a modicum of social discipline: if society is not kept in check by external coercion, its cohesion can be only preserved by discipline internalized in social customs and by strong individual moral feeling. In a sense, Zweig strongly remains here in the tradition of Warsaw positivism: one of its important ideas was that people could make up for the absence of their own independent national institutions through individual and collective activities 'up from the bottom'. Individual consciences can fulfil the tasks ministries and other government agencies fulfil in other countries. However, already by the late nineteenth century, the idea according to which a strong internalization of moral norms is a condition of liberalism's success came under attack. Aleksander Świętochowski, the leader of the positivists, started campaigns for divorce and on many occasions attacked the 'hypocritical' traditional morality. Others followed suit. Yet, it was only in the interwar period that the concept of liberty acquired a very strong meaning of liberty from the oppressive and hypocritical traditional morals. Tadeusz Boy-Żeleński was the central actor here.

I am not sure whether Boy-Żeleński has ever called himself a liberal. A rationalist and Francophile, a prolific translator of French *belles-lettres* (his Francois Villon, Pascal, Montesquieu and Proust, to name but a few, still remain the standard Polish translations to this day), he considered himself an apostle of *raison* and *clarté* in a country of prejudice and bigotry. Boy (he was known mostly by this pen name, although his identity was obvious to everyone) did not analyse the concept of liberty in his writings. His books are collections of essays and feuilletons that were published previously in various journals; such a form did not, of course, favour systematic analysis. When he writes, for example, 'Doctors are, as a rule, less liberal than lawyers' (in a feuilleton dealing with attitudes towards the penalization of abortion),[12] it is obvious that he uses the term 'liberal' in an everyday 'commonsensical' way, not as an analytical category. Nevertheless, he once wrote:

> An interesting thing: eighteenth-century rationalism cared more for purifying life from the prejudices within the sphere of morals than for a political revolution. It happened contrariwise: the French Revolution has brought about a political turnover, but almost did not touch all these prejudices ... The skeptical and liberal bourgeoisie turned out to be in many cases – e.g. as regards virginity – more strict than old-fashioned aristocrats or peasants. And so, after having lost almost one and half centuries, we start the debate at the moment it was broken, listening, as to something new, about things that were proclaimed – often more audaciously – 150 years ago.[13]

This was already a programme: to provide the rationalist purge of prejudices, a purge that eighteenth-century rationalism promised, but failed to deliver. Thus, the importance of his feuilletons in broadening the scope of understanding of liberty in Polish liberal discourse is beyond any doubt. Boy advocated contraception and (in certain extreme cases) abortion, and the introduction of civil marriages (with the possibility of divorce). However, beyond these specific issues, he engaged in fighting what he considered a general atmosphere of hypocrisy and moral dual standards. He criticized above all the attitudes of the Roman Catholic clergy, whom he dubbed 'our occupants'. Together with the above-mentioned Antoni Słonimski, poet and journalist, he was one of the pillars of the Warsaw weekly *Wiadomości Literackie*, one of the most important cultural periodicals of the interwar period. Vigorously attacked by the nationalist right and the Church, he enjoyed a great amount of popularity in the milieus of the liberal intelligentsia.

We may wonder whether the Polish fortunes of the idea of liberty submit themselves to Isaiah Berlin's famous dichotomy of 'negative' and 'positive' liberty or – to use the nineteenth-century conceptualization of the same problem – of the 'ancient' liberty as participation versus the 'modern' liberty as lack of coercion. It is, as it seems, somewhere inbetween. It is essential to bear in mind that the strength of the idea of national, collective liberty somehow places the history of the concept of liberty in Polish culture beyond the alternative of 'positive' versus 'negative' or 'ancient' versus 'modern' models. One should perhaps look to German culture with its collectivist, Hegelian and state-centered understanding of freedom for a possible parallel, bearing in mind that the Polish version of this 'collectivist' liberty was much less dependent on Hegelian philosophy.

Normality, Development, Backwardness

Parallel with 'liberty' goes 'normality'. In the late eighteenth century, the generalized West, under different names, became the normative point of reference. However, it was Warsaw positivism that developed a more complicated picture (almost a theory) of 'normality'. It was connected with the positivist elaboration of the idea of organic work. A 'normal' society is an organic one, in which all social strata cooperate one with another, where no cell of the social organism is left aside, and social development benefits not just some cells but every one of them. This type of argumentation is very common, even if the term 'normal' itself does not appear. Some elements of this type of discourse resurfaced without any consciousness of the existence of their predecessors in the 1980s as the idealized 'West' became the 'norm' against which to measure Polish society. Needless to say, Polish society was found wanting in every respect.[14]

The opposition of the 'normal' West and the 'abnormal' Polish situation is not far removed from the notion of 'backward' and 'developed' countries or regions. Many authors since the late eighteenth century wrote about 'medieval' conditions, 'Gothic' barbarity, 'feudal' remnants, etc., thus implying linear development (which means that Poland followed, although with a certain time lag, the same path as the West). On the other hand, some voices depicted the specific features of Polish society not as if they were the earlier stage of the same developmental line, but treating them as a different, self-contained system that was ruled by its own internal logic. Thus, one often wrote about the 'caste' system of social divisions in Polish society, suggesting rather a comparison with India than with the earlier 'stages' of European history. These two attitudes were far from being mutually exclusive. One could – and this was probably the most common route – mix the two and present a view of development that to a certain degree mirrored the Western one, but nevertheless had some peculiar elements. These peculiar elements may have proceeded either from the different historical starting points or from the fact that the very development of the West somehow affected the development of the backward region. Wherever this last attitude is discernible, we confront something like the idea of dependent development *avant la lettre*. As an example, Wawrzyniec Surowiecki distinguished between the countries he called 'przemyślne' and those he called 'zaodłożone'. 'Zaodłożony' means 'fallow' (as an adjective), whereas the first meaning of 'przemyślny' is 'industrious', but for Surowiecki, it means 'industrial' too. The dichotomy between the 'fallow countries' and the 'industrial/industrious' ones does not convey the impression of chronological continuity that the dichotomy backward/modern clearly possesses. Surowiecki draws a short synthesis of Poland's economic history, starting with a highly mythologized picture of Poland's economic flourishing in pre-Christian times, which incidentally also illustrates the early reception of some Romantic ideas in Poland. What is important is Surowiecki's analysis of the decline of Polish towns in the early modern period and the resulting condition of Polish society at the turn of the eighteenth and nineteenth centuries. Lack of towns, of transportation and of trade (and, more broadly, any exchange of people or ideas) fashioned a society that was passive and unable to change. An important role was played by foreigners, who kept the meagre trade and industrial life going (incidentally, Surowiecki was among the few Polish economic writers who regarded the economic role of the Jews very positively).[15]

Half a century later, Józef Supiński represented a less optimistic picture; he feared Western economic and cultural supremacy more than Surowiecki did. When he wrote in the 1850s, the political prospects of Polish national development looked much bleaker than during the Napoleonic period or immediately after 1815. At the same time, he was an occidentalist and a liberal; there was no other option for Poland than to 'catch up' with the West, not only in the economic but also in the cultural sense. Supiński reproached all those who saw in the 'West' only moral decline. Between the danger of annihilation of Polish national culture by the unifying force of capitalist modernization and the need to adapt capitalist solutions to Poland, there was only one way to proceed: to develop a specific Polish road to modernity. The 'Polish school of national economy' that was announced in the title of his main work would have to differ not only from the laissez-faire model of classical political economy, but also from the German model as advocated by Friedrich List. List, as is well known, advocated the role of the state as the initiator of industrialization; Supiński could not follow suit as the Polish state did not exist and the industrialization of 'peripheral' Polish lands was hardly a priority for the partitioning powers. He therefore hoped for a gradual development that would use the potential of the Polish village as regards agricultural and artisan skills in order to raise, step by step, the capital necessary for industrialization.

The utopian character of this solution was soon very obvious, as the Austrian railway system had connected Galicia with the economic core of the monarchy, which resulted in the influx of cheaper industrial goods to Galician markets and in effect the collapse of the traditional rural industries. Nevertheless, the attempts of 'self-modernization' (as some historians call it), or modernization from below, abounded in the late nineteenth and early twentieth centuries in the Polish territories. The concept of 'organic work' provided it with ideological backing. In that sense, Supiński's work had some results; it was certainly influential.

Many more authors within the broadly understood liberal tradition were developing ideas about the specificity of backward societies. Thus, Stanisław Szczepanowski's well-known book *Poverty of Galicia* (1888) attempted to characterize the socioeconomic system of Galicia as a coherent whole, where every individual feature is conditioned by the whole system. In the early twentieth century, on a more sophisticated intellectual level, the economist Zofia Daszyńska-Golińska presented characteristics of 'passive' and 'active' capitalism. It seems that in the period to which we refer, liberal authors were more outspoken about the specificity of backwardness and dependent development than the Marxists. This was because the first generation of Polish Marxists were mostly orthodox and they hoped for a repetition of the classical scheme: first the growth of industrial capitalism and then a proletarian revolution. Even the discussions on the role of the peasantry in the class struggle did not challenge Marxist orthodoxy. It is only with Rosa Luxemburg (as far as she can be counted as part of the Polish intellectual tradition) that the role of the periphery in socioeconomic development was accorded profound treatment in Marxist theory. This happened a century after Surowiecki and half a century after Supiński.

State

All the concepts presented are closely interwoven, but no pair of them perhaps as strictly as the concepts of backwardness and of state. With most of the theoreticians of Polish socioeconomic backwardness, it was the state that was to supply the remedy. If some thinkers tried to do without it, as did Supiński or the Warsaw positivists, it is only because they did not see any possibility of using the state, which they perceived as alien and not as a tool of Polish economic politics. The idea of state socioeconomic activities, i.e. of modernization 'from above' developed in the eighteenth century in parallel with the Germanic idea of enlightened absolutism; it happened at the same time when the very idea of the state, in the modern sense of the term, was only developing.

The relation of the concepts of liberty and of state in the conceptual framework offered here is twofold. On the one hand, the state was considered to be an ally, not an enemy, of liberty. The estate privileges and other 'feudal' institutions constituted the real limits of individual liberty and they could be curbed only by a strong enlightened state structure. On the other hand, liberty was seen as the sphere outside the domain of state action. In an 1881 essay entitled 'Political Directions', Aleksander Świętochowski, one of the leaders of the Warsaw positivists, stressed that, individually, people do not need 'their own' states, generals or diplomats; what they needed were conditions for a free and unhampered life and development. Rather than a libertarian manifesto, this statement was an attempt to show the Poles the possibility of living as if 'without' a Russian state. Nevertheless, with its faith in the social consequences of individual actions, it is still an example of an attitude atypical of peripheral liberalisms, where the state is usually seen as a moving principle of modernizing changes. However, both above-mentioned views, one seeing the state as an ally of individual liberty and another stressing the importance of the private sphere, have a common 'Hobbesian' aspect. Both assume that liberty is positioned in the private sphere outside state activity and both see a certain role for the state in safeguarding it. In the case of Surowiecki (who was writing in the Duchy of Warsaw, which was a Polish state), the government should actively introduce certain legal conditions and conduct certain political actions in order to guarantee both economic growth and individual liberty. With Świętochowski, as in classical laissez-faire liberalism, the state merely had to guarantee internal and external safety and justice.

Nation

The next concept in this overview is that of the nation. It is clearly central to the Polish politics of the nineteenth (and in part the twentieth) century and there are relatively more works dealing with its role in Polish political thought than with any other concept presented in this chapter.[16] The problem with 'nation' is that it is such an overwhelming idea used by everyone and analysed from so many different angles of intellectual history, political history and sociology that it is very difficult to select those usages that can, with some credibility, be seen as connected with liberalism. 'Nation' was used in highly emotional, and therefore imprecise, ways. Without going into details on this, the central line of tension seems to exist between the nation understood politically and ethnically; the first of these in turn may be understood in a traditional or modern way. The traditional political nation is the estate nation or, more or less, the noble estate. The modern understanding of the political nation is the 'Jacobin' idea of a nation consisting of all the (male?) adult inhabitants of a polity, irrespective of their religion, language or ethnicity. The ethnic idea of nation can also have two very different meanings. It can be connected with the idea of the nation-state, in which case it implies the assimilation (by force if necessary) of all ethnic minorities (if the nation is understood inclusively) or the exclusion of some minorities (usually the Jews) from the national body. Alternatively, the ethnic nation can be understood as an ethnoculturally defined entity, possessing various political aspirations but not necessarily aiming at separate statehood (such was the Austromarxist idea of nationality put forward in the books of Karl Renner and Otto Bauer).

Now an interesting confusion occurred in liberal ideology. On the one hand, we have the 'Jacobin' idea of nation: democratic, inclusivist and ready to assimilate by force the 'reactionary' Bretons or Occitanians into the political French nation of citizens. On the other hand, we have the ethnic idea of a nation connected with the idea of the nation-state. It is interesting to see how both ideas intermingle. In various instances of liberal journalism, and at times also in liberal nationality politics, it is impossible to discern and to disentangle the threads: whether a given attempt at ethnocultural unity is motivated by Jacobin democratism or by nationalist intolerance. To give but a single example, Józef Supiński, later to became an eminent liberal economist, wrote in Lviv in 1848, in opposing the existence of a separate Ruthenian (Ukrainian) national movement: 'All this construction of bifurcation [i.e. creating a separate 'Ruthenian' nationality parallel to the Polish one] rests on ice' that would be melted by 'the spring of [Polish] national life'.[17] Did Supiński write it as a democrat/liberal who believed (as the French Jacobins did) in a close connection between centralism and freedom, or did he write it as a Polish nationalist? As usual, the answer is 'both'. In the 'original' case of French revolutionary Jacobinism, an ethnic element is also clearly discernible in spite of (or, rather, hand in hand with) a universalist revolutionary phraseology. It seems that in East Central Europe, this similarity of revolutionary Jacobin ideas with the nationalist idea of a monoethnic nation-state facilitated the reception of liberalism for a while and at the same time did much to 'nationalize' it.

Universal (Humanitarian) Ethics

Finally, we have the concept of universalism. It manifested itself in various phrases, bearing both practical and moral importance. Practically, it ensured that – to return to the concepts discussed above – 'normality' would at last triumph over 'backwardness', as the general laws of social development were the same in Warsaw as in London. As regards the moral side, universalism was as important. The novelist Bolesław Prus (the pen name of Aleksander Głowacki), who had week by week for some forty years been repeating his liberal, gradualist and rationalist credo in his 'Weekly Chronicles' in various Warsaw journals, constantly opposed the very idea of a social struggle, considered by what he called 'pseudo-Darwinists'[18] (the Positivist that he was, he would never recognize social Darwinism as true Darwinism) as the main factor of social development.

Against both national rivalry and class struggle, Prus endorsed an ideology of gradualist meliorism, preaching cooperation between nations and classes, compromise and practical work aiming at economic development:

> It is true that politics and the national chauvinisms aroused by it still divide nations; however, above distrust and enmity one can already discern certain common ideals, unclearly felt by all inhabitants of Western Europe but openly and hotly desired by people of higher intellectual and ethical culture. Brotherhood of peoples, liberty, justice, respect for human persons, for their feelings, convictions and property, exchange of services, fullest possible participation, active and passive, in the benefits of civilization – these are catchwords that are common to the inhabitants of Europe today ... These are three levels of social duties: towards individuals, towards nation and towards civilization. On each of these levels one cannot, one should not, be harmful, and one should, one has to, be useful.[19]

Prus wrote this in 1909. In 1937, the poet and essayist Antoni Słonimski (who called his feuilletons 'Weekly Chronicles' as a homage to Prus, whose admirer he was) quoted Mickiewicz's understanding of liberty as an international European and not just Polish phenomenon. He subscribed to this idea and expressed hope that this currently 'unfashionable liberty' had slowly started to regain its position in Europe.[20]

This idea of universal human values was grounded, I believe, to the same degree both in the universalism of the Enlightenment and in the universalist understanding of liberty adopted by Mickiewicz and some other Romantic thinkers.

However, this universalism was openly challenged by the new generation of radical nationalists after 1900. Of course, it is not to be claimed that texts stressing the priority of the national interest over humanitarian sentiments were rare in the nineteenth century – they are also easily to be found within the liberal tradition, as the distance between the 'progressivist' centralism of a Jacobin pedigree and national chauvinism was often close. Florian Ziemiałkowski, a rather moderate democrat from Galicia (Austrian partition), criticized in 1861 the idea of possible cooperation of the Habsburg nationalities in the Vienna Parliament: each nationality 'cares only for itself … remembers only its own land: demands only what is good for itself, with no regard for others. It cannot be otherwise, as there are no emotions in politics – interest above all!'[21]

Such phrases were often repeated, but they were not built up to a level of political theory; this happened only in the early twentieth century. This is perhaps the central distinction between the liberal tradition and the tradition of modern ideological nationalism, as represented in Poland by Roman Dmowski and Zygmunt Balicki. Their doctrine renounced any universalist legitimization for their nationalism, having defined the nation as the highest moral value from which all other were derived and that in turn needs no legitimization – it is at the top of the pyramid of values. Balicki, less important as a practical politician, but the more theoretically minded among the two, developed an idea of a national ethics, different from Christian ethics (valid only in relations between individuals). This ethics of 'national egoism' is in essence a military ethics that glorifies struggle in a blend of social Darwinism and neo-Romantic irrationalism that was typical for the culture of the early twentieth century.

The liberals, living in the increasingly antiliberal atmosphere of the early twentieth century, did sometimes accept, half unconsciously, some elements of this ideology; thus, anti-Semitic elements are discernible in the journalism of Bolesław Prus after 1905. Even so, liberal thought, however nationalist and intolerant it could be in practice, could not dispense with the Enlightenment-universalist framework on which its whole axiology was based. The polemics of the Polish liberals against the new nationalist doctrine of national egoism are among the most eloquent expressions of this universalism (the above-quoted fragments from Prus and Słonimski are a good instance of this).[22]

Conclusions

The question of the mutual relations of the above concepts can be tackled here only superficially. There are several general ideas that permeate all these concepts and thus provide them with a certain underlying unity. One of them is the idea of national identity (or nationalism, in various meanings of this extremely ambiguous term). It influenced not only the concept of nation but was also important in shaping the context for all the concepts discussed here. The consciousness of economic backwardness (not necessarily formulated in these terms) was another key factor.

Another element that was central to Polish (and not only Polish) culture as a whole was what could be called cultural dependency – or perhaps 'reactiveness' would be a better term. Polish culture reacted to European ideas and tried to rework them so that they fitted local conditions. Polish liberalism obviously shares this 'reactive' character with most of the continental European liberal ideologies.

These general features are evident in all the concepts that were presented above. Both the strength of national ideology and the consciousness of backwardness made this version of liberalism more centralist than the original. Both backwardness and hope for producing national unity called for state activity. In the Polish case, this centralism was more often ideological than real, as until 1918 there was no Polish state to conduct the centralist policy. It is clear that liberty in Polish liberal parlance has a strong centralist and *étatiste* component, and that the normative element based on the idealized vision of the Western European societies is one of the formative components of Polish liberal thought. This normative attitude facilitated the acceptance of the concept of backwardness. The idea of the nation, multifold and protean in its diverse meanings, was usually embraced by the liberals as a democratizing idea: the nation, whether understood politically or culturally, would overcome estate differences and unite the nobility with the peasantry into a single conception of Poles/citizens. Thus, the nation was in a certain way connected with the universalist idea: it was a social organism, developed along the same general laws as other nations and was also bound by the same moral principles. The ethical universalism of the liberal authors of course had its roots in the Enlightenment, as was the case everywhere, but it was also influenced by the romantic tradition of the struggle for universal freedom, particularly strongly represented by Adam Mickiewicz.

Contrary to what may perhaps have been expected, the Romantic tradition, with its strong democratic and revolutionary elements, acted here as a check against more chauvinist versions of nationalism. This seems to me a very important phenomenon. Equally interesting is what I have called the 'reactive' character of Polish liberal thought. By selecting and transforming various elements of Western ideas, Polish liberal thought provides the student with a perspective to observe the potentialities implicitly present in the ideas produced by the 'core' Western European countries. This is perhaps the central benefit one has from studying the provincial versions of European ideologies.

Maciej Janowski is Professor at the Institute of History, Polish Academy of Sciences (Warsaw), and Recurrent Visiting Associate Professor at the Department of History, Central European University (Budapest), Among his publications are *Birth of the Intelligentsia, 1750–1831* (2014); and *A History of Modern Political Thought in East Central Europe, Volume I: Negotiating Modernity in the 'Long Nineteenth Century'* (co-authored with Balázs Trencsényi, Mónika Baar, Maria Falina and Michal Kopeček, 2015).

Notes

1. The research for this chapter was financed by the National Science Centre, Poland (Research Project No 2015/19/B/HS3/03737).
2. A. Grześkowiak-Krwawicz, *Regina libertas: Wolność w polskiej myśli politycznej w XVIII wieku*, Gdańsk, 2006.
3. W. Surowiecki, 'Moje lekcje statystyki dawane w 1812/1813', in J. Grzywicka and A. Łukaszewicz (eds), *Wybór pism*, Warsaw, 1957, 273–492 and 297.
4. H. Kołłątaj, *Uwagi nad pismem, które wyszło w Warszawie z drukarni Dufourowskiej, pod tytułem: Seweryna Rzewuskiego, hetmana Wielkiego Koronnego, o sukcesji tronu w Polszcze rzecz krótka*, Warsaw, 1790, 18.
5. A. Mickiewicz, 'Bracia nasi w Szwajcarii' [1833] in L. Płoszowski (ed.), *Dzieła: Wydanie narodowe*, vol. 6, Warsaw, 1950, 113.
6. A. Mickiewicz, 'Myśli o sejmie polskim', [1832], L. Płoszowski (ed.), *Dzieła: Wydanie narodowe*, vol. 6, Warsaw, 1950, 158–59.
7. H. Wereszycki, 'Życzymy ci towarzyszu Limanowski wolnej Warszawy', in *Niewygasła przeszłość: refleksje i polemiki*, Cracow, 1987, 234-46.
8. F. Zweig, *Zmierzch czy odrodzenie liberalizmu*, Lwów, 1938, 15.
9. Ibid., 176–77.
10. Ibid., 41.
11. For his sympathy with 'rotten liberalism', cf. A. Słonimski, 'Kronika Tygodniowa', *Wiadomości Literackie*, 18 October 1936, reprinted in A. Słonimski, *Kroniki tygodniowe 1936–1939*, R. Habielski (ed.), Warsaw, 2002, 93. For his endorsement of a form of socialism that is different from the Soviet system, see his 'Kronika Tygodniowa', *Wiadomości Literackie*, 25 December 1932, reprinted

in Rafał Habielski and A. Słonimski (eds), *Kroniki tygodniowe 1932–1935*, Warsaw, 2001, 65.
12. T. Żeleński (Boy), 'Paragraf a lancet', in *Reflektorem w mrok: Wybór publicystyki*, A.Z. Makowiecki (ed.), Warsaw, 1985, 266.
13. 'Ekonomia miłosna', ibid., 386.
14 On the relation of Polish culture towards the real or imagined 'West', cf. an interpretative overview by J. Jedlicki, 'Europe's Eastern Borderland: An Essay on the History of Flows of Civilization Innovations', *East Central Europe* 41 (2014), 86–104 (with comments by L. Wolff and O. Sereda).
15. Cf. W. Surowiecki, 'O upadku przemysłu i miast w Polsce', in J. Grzywicka and A. Łukaszewicz (eds), *Wybór Pism*, Warsaw, 1957, 33–246 (on Jews, see 208–16).
16. The literature on the concept of nation is immense. I have profited most from the texts by A. Walicki, among others *The Enlightenment and the Birth of Modern Nationhood: Polish Political Thought from the Noble Republicanism to Tadeusz Kościuszko*, Notre Dame, IN, 1989, and his studies in Polish collected in his *Prace Wybrane*, A. Mencwel (ed.), 4 vols, Cracow, 2009–10, and from the pivotal book by T. Kizwalter, *O nowoczesności narodu: Przypadek polski*, Warsaw, 1999.
17. J. Supiński, in *Dziennik Narodowy*, 9 May 1848, quoted in O. Arkusza, 'Rusini galicyjscy drugiej połowy XIX – początku XX wieku między ukraińskim a wszechruskim wariantem tożsamości narodowej', *Zeszyty Naukowe Uniwersyetu Jagiellońskiego. Prace Historyczne* 144(2) (2017), 284.
18. B. Prus, 'Kronika tygodniowa', *Tygodnik ilustrowany*, 28 March 1908, reprinted in B. Prus, *Kroniki. Wybór*, S. Fita (ed.), 2 vols, Warsaw, 1987, vol. 2, 191.
19. B. Prus, 'Kronika Tygodniowa', *Tygodnik Ilustrowany*, 30 October 1909, reprinted in ibid., vol. 2, 218–19.
20. A. Słonimski, 'Kronika tygodniowa', *Wiadomości Literackie*, 26 September 1937, reprinted in Habielski and Słonimski (eds), *Kroniki tygodniowe 1936–1939*, 198–99.
21. F. Ziemiałkowski's speech in the Galician diet, 26 April 1861, in *Sprawozdania stenograficzne z posiedzeń Sejmu krajowego galicyjskiego we Lwowie, odbytych od dnia 15 do 26 kwietnia 1861 r*, Lviv, 1861, 508.
22. For another instance, see W. Spasowicz, 'Etyka Egoizmu', in *Liberalizm i narodowość: Wybór pism*, D. Szpoper (ed.), Cracow, 2010, 257–76.

Bibliography

Arkusza, O. 'Rusini galicyjscy drugiej połowy XIX – początku XX wieku między ukraińskim a wszechruskim wariantem tożsamości narodowej'. *Zeszyty Naukowe Uniwersyetu Jagiellońskiego. Prace Historyczne*, 144(2) (2017), 277–302.
Grześkowiak-Krwawicz, A. *Regina libertas: Wolność w polskiej myśli politycznej w XVIII wieku*. Gdańsk, 2006.
Jedlicki, J. 'Europe's Eastern Borderland: An Essay on the History of Flows of Civilization Innovations'. *East Central Europe* 41 (2014), 86–104.

Kizwalter, T. *O nowoczesności narodu: Przypadek polski.* Warsaw, 1999.

Kołłątaj, H. *Uwagi nad pismem, które wyszło w Warszawie z drukarni Dufourowskiej, pod tytułem: Seweryna Rzewuskiego, hetmana Wielkiego Koronnego, o sukcesji tronu w Polszcze rzecz krótka.* Warsaw, 1790.

Mickiewicz, A. *Dzieła: Wydanie narodowe*, L. Płoszowski (ed.). vol. 6. Warsaw, 1950.

Prus, B. 'Kronika tygodniowa', *Tygodnik ilustrowany*, 28 March 1908, reprinted in B. Prus, *Kroniki. Wybór*, vol. 2, S. Fita (ed). Warsaw, 1987.

Słonimski, A. *Kroniki tygodniowe 1932–1935*, R. Habielski (ed). Warsaw, 2001.

———. *Kroniki tygodniowe 1936–1939*, R. Habielski (ed). Warsaw, 2002.

Spasowicz, W. 'Etyka Egoizmu' (1904), in *Liberalizm i narodowość: Wybór pism*, D. Szpoper (ed). Cracow, 2010.

Sprawozdania stenograficzne z posiedzeń Sejmu krajowego galicyjskiego we Lwowie, odbytych od dnia 15 do 26 kwietnia 1861 r. Lviv, 1861.

Surowiecki, W. 'Moje lekcje statystyki dawane w 1812/1813', in J. Grzywicka and A. Łukaszewicz (eds), *Wybór pism* (Warsaw, 1957), 273–492.

Walicki, A. *The Enlightenment and the Birth of Modern Nationhood: Polish Political Thought from the Noble Republicanism to Tadeusz Kościuszko.* Notre Dame, IN, 1989.

———. *Prace Wybrane*, A. Mencwel (ed), 4 vols. Cracow, 2009–10.

Wereszycki, H. 'Życzymy ci towarzyszu Limanowski wolnej Warszawy', in *Niewygasła przeszłość. refleksje i polemiki* (Cracow, 1987), 234–46.

Żeleński (Boy), T. *Reflektorem w mrok: Wybór publicystyki*, A.Z. Makowiecki (ed). Warsaw, 1985.

Zweig, F. *Zmierzch czy odrodzenie liberalizmu.* Lwów, 1938.

Chapter 9

Liberal Politics without Liberal Thought?

The Strange Career of Italian Liberalism

Paolo Pombeni

It may seem strange to argue that Italy was never dominated by liberal theory despite the constant shaping of its political system on liberal principles – except during the fascist interlude.[1] The single name of Benedetto Croce ought to rebut any such claim, given Croce's eminence as a liberal philosopher and his unflagging defence of liberal Italy, even at times that were unfavourable to such a task – meaning both the fascist dictatorship and the period ushering in the democratic republic after 1946.

Obviously, I do not intend to deny that Croce was a major exponent of liberal thought, still less forget liberalism's contribution to the formation of a unified state between the 1840s and 1880s. I single out that phase since it was then that liberalism played a truly leading role in building a 'constitutional ideology', whereas later on it would no longer enjoy the lead and began to wane: first because the ideological framework of constitutionalism grew unduly legalistic and rigid, and then because liberal intellectualism inclined towards nationalism after some flirtation with socialism by the new generations.[2]

My focus is on another phenomenon that can be stated thus: although the Italian state came into being in the mid nineteenth century through the desire of the national elites to get into line with political developments afoot in Europe – namely liberal constitutionalism as propounded by the legendary 'English model' – let us not forget that it struck roots in somewhat unreceptive soil.[3]

A few decades ago, Raffaele Romanelli summed up the issue under the neat slogan 'an impossible command'.[4] Italian liberalism would have had to apply state authority or command in order to force through a system based on *liberty*: the citizens' ability to take their destiny in hand and actively shoulder their responsibilities. Hence, Italian constitutionalism rested on a pure contradiction in terms: 'I order you to be free'.

This idea may, perhaps, be reformulated along different lines. The way in which the Italian political system worked was shaped by liberal constitutional values (except for the fascist interval, and there too, some ambiguity applies), but it was not supported by liberal ideology as such. An ideology is something different from a line of philosophical thought: it aims not to supply the rational tools by which to analyse the facts, but to build mechanisms bestowing sense and meaning on the historical developments that engulf our lives.[5] The studies by Quentin Skinner and Reinhart Koselleck, and the historical approach they generated[6] teach us that ideas must be framed both in terms of Skinner's *meaning/intention* tandem[7] and within the logical-historical setting that conditions the way these 'liberal' ideas were employed from one period to the next.[8]

The entire history of Italy from 1848 to the present day has been geared towards producing a political system based on the principles of modern constitutionalism: political decision by representation, recognition of free expression by the individual as the linchpin of social behaviour, the exercise of power within a checks-and-balances framework, support by the public sphere for the development of individual potential, and social organizations through which to engage. Naturally these premises have been given a different reading throughout the various historical phases that have made up these 150 years of the unified Italian state. But, with the exception of the fascist interlude, I would claim they have basically gone unchallenged in their constitutional formulation (their mode of practice is another matter entirely).

There is no doubt that such values underlay the 'constitutional science' that was developed in Italy from the late nineteenth to the early twentieth centuries.[9] True, they were questioned towards the end of that period (and even earlier), but more in regret at the failure to implement them than in rejection of them *tout court* (for example, the reappraisals of parliamentarianism and representation). But if one asks how much currency those values enjoyed outside academic circles and the ruling elite, that is a different business altogether. One can hardly expect to find 'mass adoption' (in any country, come to that, but especially in Italy, where school attendance was low), but, to my knowledge at least, there was no serious attempt to 'popularize' such values, except for some instances of representation within 'democratic' party organization, especially on the Left.

As Quintino Sella, one of the leaders of Italian liberalism, said in an electoral speech on 18 November 1874: 'I openly state that I am revolted by the slightly different parties among men who swore an oath to the Constitution and substantially tend towards the same unity, liberty, and moral, intellectual, economic progress for their country, diverging only in the ways and times for gaining these supreme goals. Perhaps the greatest danger for the constitutional institutions is the break-up of politicians into many parties.'[10] Not until the Resistance, and subsequently the parties under the Republic, were the aforementioned liberal values upheld on any scale, and that was largely because they were values that fascism had dismissed as irrelevant.

It is hard to deny that these were 'liberal' values in the proper sense of the term. Yet while support for them was expressed in terms of 'political thought' – albeit in different ways and timeframes – this never transformed into an ideology, that is, a system reflecting what D.E. Apter called the dual function of ideology – 'binding the community together' and 'organizing the role personalities of the maturing individual' so that they 'generate a by-product, the legitimation of authority'.[11]

In Italian history, the task of performing these two functions was not entrusted to liberal ideology or, at any rate, not to liberal ideology as such.[12] It is well known that from the outset, Italian society divided up the undertaking of 'binding the community together' among a range of actors. It would be wrong to deny that a kind of 'liberal culture' figured among these, though it suffered from a lack of confidence in its own capacity to gain this goal within the fragmented Italian social context. Consequently, liberal culture was pushed to entrust state authority with the task of doing it. Thus, the school system, especially in the more senior classes, was shaped and dominated by liberal culture,[13] but it would be a long time before such general training worked its way into the social system, and just when that was on the verge of happening – roughly at the outbreak of the First World War – the war machine and the social transformations it brought about checked this social development, while fascism, when it came, knocked it on the head once and for all.[14]

In terms of ideology, the weak point of the Italian political system was the lack of any normal dialogue between progressive and conservative liberalism, a dialogue that characterized the development of that ideological system in the Anglo-Saxon world. And once again, Catholic ideology, with which it had to reckon, proved crippling. Of course, one ought to delve more deeply into the real picture of Italian liberalism as it dealt with the first wave of secularism that demoted religion to a practice for the culturally immature.[15] Liberalism also had to fight the oligarchic tendency of its own ruling class to close ranks and hold at bay popular-rooted forces that they were unable to control, such as the Catholic movements.

A specific instance of this situation is illustrated through the young Alcide De Gasperi[16] and his antiliberal stand. In Trento where he lived, the 'Rome issue' was only a distant murmur: as a Habsburg subject, he surveyed quite a different horizon, but there too the prevailing features of liberalism were a contempt for religion and a bid by the liberal oligarchy to keep the popular leaders away from power. In a public meeting in September 1905, De Gasperi claimed that 'he had to proclaim once more that at times in which liberals call themselves democrats and the socialists had proclaimed the realm of democracy in Trentino, one forgets the peasants' boots that are the majority in this country and that are obliged to sustain the heaviest burdens imposed by the State, the Provinces, and the municipalities'.[17]

This liberal-social Catholic polarity was curiously accentuated by what should have been its sworn enemy, socialist ideology. In Italy, socialism emerged not as a development of liberal premises, but as a break with them. The clash did not concern the movement's leaders, many of whom shared a large measure of liberal culture, but related to the ideology that was generated to bind the rank and file's consensus. In this case, we have a simple reversal of the community tradition found in Catholic culture, with which socialism maintained ties. (Many of its leaders exhibited an affinity by having gone through the ranks of Masonry, an organization that in many ways resembled a form of the secularized Church.) This is another case of the parallel existence between an antiliberal attitude and the promotion of political values that might be considered liberal. That, however, could not be admitted: to acknowledge such an affinity would have meant legitimizing the claim to leadership by a conservative ruling class that was not so much blinkered about the pressures of modernization as unwilling to accept that this would jeopardize the existing social and political pecking order.[18]

It is interesting to weigh up the reasons for this rift. Some reasons are indubitably bound up with historical contingency. Liberal thinking ('liberal ideology' would be a misnomer here) tied itself closely to a scheme for standardizing the nation willy-nilly, so that it looked askance on all 'cultural' movements that claimed recognition in the public arena. One may definitely admit that, for all the ideological complexity that dogs the dawn of the twentieth century, there was a Europe-wide bid[19] to defend the terrain gained by the traditional 'constitutional equilibrium' that had come to the fore in the course of the nineteenth century. However, in a number of countries, there was also awareness that a change of climate needed to be reckoned with. This was markedly the case in Great Britain, with the phenomenon that went by the name of the 'new liberalism'. [20] A different, though significant, development occurred in France with the great debate on the 'decadence' issue.[21]

Italy's political system arose from a national revolution unifying a broad range of community cultures and civil traditions, and bound up with differing historical developments that were often quite separate from one another. It was no easy matter, therefore, to take the theoretically acclaimed British model and extract from it that respect for traditional self-government that had so fascinated Italian observers, at least on paper. The result was that Italian liberal culture got driven towards two opposite extremes. The first, in which it resembles some episodes in German liberalism, was the entrenched idea that the state was the only possible form of community and, above all, the only unit that deserved public protection and promotion.[22] The second was the opposite-sounding championing of the individual as an abstract social monad, devoid of any legal ties to intermediate echelons of the community.

As already emphasized, the force of Italian liberalism was, at least on the cultural side, its monopoly on constitutional thought, especially in its juridical interpretation. British 'new liberalism' found no audience in Italy and the same could be said for American progressive liberalism. Referring to the will of the people was dangerous to an elite that had difficulty in penetrating the spaces occupied either by Catholic organizations or by the increasingly ascendant power of socialist ideology. Relying firmly on the field of traditional constitutional thought, forged in the mid nineteenth century, seemed safer.

The state as the sole fount of law is paramount in V.E. Orlando's theory of the person-state, and equally so in the view of the 'administrative state' during the Giolitti era, which saw the alleged 'scientific neutrality' of the executive arm of political power as a guarantor of civil liberty. This feature of liberalism's political/juridical ideology is well known and frequently studied.[23] To overlook this trait is to fail to understand the crisis that Italian liberalism first underwent between the 1890s and 1914. This would peak between 1918 and 1924, never to arise again.

The crisis in liberal thinking also infected the constitutional ideology. Spurred on by socialism's sense of a creed, the liberals lamented that their brand of democracy lacked the ethical and religious spirit that de Tocqueville had long before identified as the real engine of American democracy – now seen as the democracy of the future. This provided a nudge towards nationalism as the bourgeoisie's version of socialist zeal. By the same token, it detracted from party spirit at a time when the works of Ostrogorski and Michels rode the crest of the wave in Italy as elsewhere.[24] On the other hand, such crippled liberal thinking would be too weak to stand up to fascism when the latter explicitly challenged its claim to validity.

One might plausibly argue that there was a strange streak of weakness in Italian liberal ideology as it helped to build a unified state along the lines of European constitutionalism. Historians have attributed this to various causes:

the conflict between the new state and the Church – an entity that possessed strong powers of social cohesion and, above all, it should be noted, cultural penetration. Then there was the difficulty experienced by a central power, keen to bolster its new governance, in winning legitimation from populations habituated to a lower degree of expected participation (the classic novelty was compulsory military national service – a practice most of the country had never hitherto known). Again, there was a dearth of social elites accustomed to stable relations with natural communities that possessed other channels of leadership selection.

The liberals in Italy never really engaged with the thorny issue of nationally standardizing a piecemeal community network. The superiority of liberal culture was deemed to be self-evident.

If this was challenged, only one way was open, as Vilfredo Pareto wrote to G. Jonas on 14 October 1903:

> The choice by now is between reaction and revolution. Every middle way is barred. One who hopes to fight socialism following a middle way helps reaction and vice versa ... One who wants to defend society must in some way fortify conservatives, also called reactionaries; must principally work to unite various factions, in order to foster a government, be it of whatever kind, that will fight that enemy; must reveal the vanity and nonsense of democratic formulas ... and of new masters' heresy.[25]

Any soul-searching there might have been about liberalism's political doldrums was set aside with the consolatory observation that the British system too was buckling under the advance of mass society. As Giulia Guazzaloca has shown in a study, it appeared to Italians that the British Parliament Act of 1911 was emblematic of that crisis, as it had destroyed the legendary balance between electoral representation and representation by 'settled superiorities' grouped in the House of Lords.[26]

This phenomenon can be seen in the growing rift between the juridical thinking of scholars of constitutional law and broader political attitudes. The basic framework of Italian constitutional science remained closely linked to the construct that was liberal constitutionalism. Not only was there no backtracking on its load-bearing structures (representation as paramount in legitimizing power, government answerable to parliament, individual citizen rights, etc.), but they were constantly modified and revised to suit the changing conditions of history. To illustrate, one need only cite the name of Santi Romano and his institutional theory (somewhat along the lines of Maitland and Gierke).[27]

If we move away from this dimension and look at political theory proper, we will find liberal thinkers barricaded behind the old walls, refusing to consider a change in the relationship between former certitudes and the shifting times. To compress the analysis at the risk of oversimplification, constitutionalism had been devised for a limited citizen body that was now expanding to embrace a social spectrum that was not necessarily 'educated' to grasp the basic system: adjustment to the change called for a serious revision of key concepts. This is what occurred in various parts of Europe: suffice it to cite Britain's new liberalism or the complex shifts in Max Weber's thought.

Italian liberalism deluded itself that it might solve the problem by emphasizing the old tenet: the 'political community' equals the state, seen more or less in a Hegelian light. Plainly the question of the political education of the new ranks admitted to citizenship[28] was never mooted. It was simply delegated to the school system – state-run, needless to say – although based on a broad cultural background that had little to do with the civil values that were supposed to have inspired liberalism. This inevitably raised the issue of what Italy came to call 'civil religion' – the very ideology that was meant to bind the political community. The pronounced positivist slant to liberal culture in Italy, its links with the general enlightenment critique of religion, not to mention its roots in elitism, prevented the liberals from grasping the relationship between mass culture and political community-building that could lead to incorporation into the broader national community. On the contrary, they were provoked into setting up a shortcut between 'community identity' and 'state identity'; this transformed civil religion into a kind of ascetic idolatry of the public sphere that ran the state.

In fact, the banal way of solving the problem of the relationship between a juridical liberal theory that regarded the state as the true (and only existing) form of the political community, and the lack of social legitimacy among people at large for that approach pushed Italian liberalism to support the growth of nationalist ideology. 'Nation' signalled in a sense the social decline of state pre-eminence as the source of political integration. But nationalism was a divisive ideology because it was inclined to expel from the community those people indisposed to recognize the superiority of the so-called (and artificially constructed) 'national needs'.

Obviously, Italy's involvement in the First World War presented a golden opportunity to give that shortcut between community identity and state identity a war-mongering twist; it was hoped that the experience of the trenches might supply that 'school of citizenship' and finally make good the ideological deficit of Italian liberalism.[29] To some extent, this did actually happen, since the war clearly achieved a 'nationalizing of the masses' to a degree that had hitherto not been accomplished. At the same time, though, it propelled Italian liberalism into the arms of fascism, albeit via nationalism, a far from insignificant stepping-stone.[30]

Italian liberalism seems not to have detected that transitional phase in the liberal political system: the return of social and political bodies (to borrow Maitland's famous definition) as constitutional entities. The crucial issue was obviously to acknowledge what public weight such organizations might come to have and – by no means a secondary question – foresee which of them would make the grade. It seemed unacceptable simply to recognize as 'guilds' what were de facto social groups, on top of which was the tricky question of what to call the religious formations. To lump them all together as latter-day medieval guilds (as though this boiled down to economic enterprises) would have entailed ideological acrobatics. No doubt, this is what the trade unions indeed were, but one way or another, all such groups had to be given some legal sanction, which meant subjecting them to the constricting embrace of 'state' power.[31]

It is sometimes asked why the Italian political system was unable from 1919 to 1924 to develop antibodies against the seizure of power by Mussolini and his entourage. There are many reasons, of course, and many factors, bound up with chance conditions, but since we are analysing ideologies, it seems indisputable that on the political market fascism offered a 'good' that liberalism did not possess: it propounded the unification of the body politic within the framework of an elementary ideology that nonetheless managed to include all the loose ends of the Italian community system. In contradistinction, liberalism was clearly unable to accept the principle of combining different social forms as the basis for national rebirth.

It could be argued that fascism succeeded – with many limitations and a vast amount of manipulation – in posing as a 'national ideology' claiming to hold all the traditions together: Catholic and socialist, as well as national liberal. The single party achieved that coalition far more than did the corporative system, and as a state-party upheld the very *statalismo* towards which a sizeable swath of Italian liberalism had itself been inclined.[32]

The close analysis of crisis management undertaken by the Italian Parliament between 1919 and 1924 makes this point crystal clear. In the 1920–22 crisis, as Giovanni Orsina[33] has shown so well, not only did the Italian liberals – with the odd exception – remain puzzled as to how to organize parties in the modern shape required by the proportional electoral system, but they were implacably hostile to parliament negotiating a coalition government. This reached its climax when in 1922, V.E. Orlando made it a condition of agreeing to form a government that he should not have to bargain with the parties over how the team was formed. He made this clear in an article in an Argentinian newspaper: 'If in fact the Cabinet had to become the government of a plurality or of a college, no doubt it would be the worst of all government forms, because it would deny the first and most essential necessity, which requires unity of thought and action in directing the State.'[34]

Given such a background, it is obvious that fascism ultimately stood as the authoritarian but plausible solution to what had already been dubbed the crisis of the liberal or the 'modern' state. In addition, fascist ideology offered a certain element of Italian liberalism support for the insertion of society into the state-lead socio-institutional system. True, this goal was pursued by a distinct party, the Partito Nazionale Fascista, which seemed odd to liberal minds, but the primacy of the state, which Mussolini strongly reaffirmed, was sufficient to make the new panorama acceptable, also taking into account that the force of the Fascist Party was more proclaimed than had been realized.[35]

Crucially and paradoxically, the experience of fascism – in its highly peculiar way – fielded a series of principles typical of the new phase of liberalism (the experiment of national mass education, the party as the tool for social and political discipline, state consensus-building via welfare management and so on). Concurrently, it showed how impossible it was to have a modern state without a real liberal ideology. In a nutshell, the constitutional novelties of fascism proved void of content precisely because they lacked two vital ingredients of a proper liberal system: *representation* created as a link with a civil society that pre-dated, and was distinct from, the state, as well as *government by discussion*, the dialectical core of political consensus (where not only are opinions debated, but so are the powers of reciprocal control and limitation).

Restoration of those liberal principles, without denying that they were associated with the tools forged by the new liberalism, would come about in Italy with the republican Constitution of 1948.[36] Curiously, it was not the work of Italian liberalism at all, but – especially in its purely ideological content – largely the product of the two forces that opposed and condemned liberalism in theory: social Catholicism and communism. To these, one should add the juridical thinking that matured between the two wars, the outstanding exponent of which was Costantino Mortati. Mortati cannot merely be styled a 'liberal', although he voiced the new-style reappraisal of 'government by discussion'; in that he was proudly rejected by the old doyen of classical juridical liberalism, the eighty-year-old Vittorio Emanuele Orlando, who himself sat in the Constituent Assembly.[37]

As I have shown elsewhere,[38] the young representatives of social Catholicism who clustered around Giuseppe Dossetti were the prime supporters of that pluralist democracy that they thought alien to liberalism, but that in actual fact was far from being so.[39] From this perspective, it can be noted that the core of largely jurist, youthful university teachers grouped under Dossetti's lead, who had a fundamental input into the Italian Constitutional Charter, were fired by the idea of 'surpassing the principles of 1789' – as one of them,

Giorgio La Pira, explicitly said when quoting Taine in the Chamber in so many words. His message was that the 'individualistic' principles of Rousseau were to be supplanted; we had to return to an 'organic' universe.[40] La Pira drew on the personalistic philosophy of the French thinker Emmanuel Mounier and his *Déclarations des droits des personnes et des communautés*, written in 1941 and then published at the height of La Résistance in his review *Esprit* under the question: 'Must we rewrite the declaration of the rights of man?'[41] Apart from that source, the fledgling-professor group was fascinated by the entire French social/legal movement: authors such as Duguit, Hauriou and Gurvitch, as well as the 'institutional' thinking of the Italian constitutionalist Santi Romano, who had kept a careful watch on the social reality underpinning the regulatory framework of the jurists.

What was being argued was exactly what the traditional Catholic (antiliberal) social doctrine saw as different from modern constitutionalism: liberty was unacceptable as the freedom to do what everyone wanted and could only be accepted as the positive freedom to desire the good. This formulation sprang from a basic principle: that man was antecedent to the state. It was clearly opposed to Hegel's view of political philosophy – or, to be even more precise, the Hegel-derived German legal-constitutional philosophy that had also held sway in Italy prior to fascism. This argued that subjective rights did not exist per se, but came into existence when 'constituted' by state law.

In parallel with this controversial issue was another, regarding the communal nature of the human *person*. Again in La Pira's words, taken from a famous article in which he commented on the 1948 Charter: 'the human personality unfolds by the organic belonging to successive social communities in which it is included and through which it develops in proper order and attains perfection'.[42]

The arguments for the 'communal' approach were based both on ideology and on expediency: the Catholics wanted to defend not only their right to religious freedom, but also the Church's own right to be a juridical institution on par with the modern state. For that reason, the person–community link became so important. Denying it was therefore held to be typically liberal.

But this last claim, if truth be told, needs further dissecting. Recognition of communities as subjects deserving legal protection is technically a thorny issue. One should recall that the attack on them, initially conducted by the liberal system, was not so much aimed at the 'social' kind of community, which would be safeguarded by the new postwar constitutionalism, as against those corporative institutions that claimed (or could be expected to claim) normative power regardless of, and antecedent to, their own members. The problem, to put it simply but effectively, was to avoid 'dual citizenship' rather than to demand that individuals be defined as monads divorced from their community roots. Many instances can be cited for this. One might recall that the very model adopted by liberalism, the British system, was underpinned by a fabric upholding *comunitarismo* (community-mindedness) – whether of the sort connected with geographical identity, or professional associationism, or the offshoots of Protestant sects.

At the time of the great postwar debate, the subject of national communities was actually a bone of contention that served a twofold and diverging purpose: on the one hand, to restore the 'private' value of such experiences, protection of which had not been lacking in the liberal age or indeed under the great dictatorships that had turned them into 'public' functions and had subordinated them to the state; yet, on the other hand, to proclaim and uphold these was a ploy to regain leeway for religious freedom, especially for Catholics, removed from the sphere of summit agreements between Church and state. As Dossetti claimed of the modern state's duties, in a famous speech in 1951 (when he concluded 'we must assume this premise: not to fear the state'), it was necessary that 'the state asserts its duty not only to effect a static bridge-building among existing social forces, but to promote a dynamic synthesis and hence a *reformation* of the social body'.[43]

At the Constituent Assembly, as well as throughout the preparatory debates conducted in periodicals, the liberals stood out neither for their participation nor for their inventiveness. Apart from being much divided, they found it hard to assemble a rounded ideological proposal shaping the proposed course of the new political system. They split roughly into a large collection of economists more or less wedded to traditional 'free market' thinking, and a more political grouping who largely engaged in a formalistic criticism of the new democracy and considered all the clauses of the first part of the Constitution Charter to be an 'outmoded' text, 'both anachronistic and rash'.[44]

The considerable amount of liberal thinking contained in the Italian Constitution was thus curiously owed to antiliberals, such as Dossetti's group, who were explicitly anxious to replace the term 'individual' – a liberal expression they saw as reducing political subjects to monads devoid of social connection – by the new term 'person'. In Emanuel Mounier's thinking, this stood for the new political subject complete with his multiple community affiliations. However, if we ponder the concrete outcome of that battle with due detachment, it was a slim victory, at least in the pages of the 1948 Italian Constitution. The term 'person' is used in the sense intended by that battle only once, in Article 3, which states: 'it is the duty of the republic to remove economic and social obstacles that actually limit the liberty and equality of citizens and thus *impede the full development of the human person*'. One other phrasing in Article 2 may stem from the same line of argument: 'the Republic acknowledges and guarantees the inalienable rights of man, *both as a single being and in the social formations where his personality unfolds'*. For the rest, wherever 'person' recurs, it is used in a generic sense or is interchangeable with 'man' and 'citizen', with no appreciable difference in usage.[45]

Was all this an antiliberal attitude? Many a theoretician of Anglo-Saxon liberalism might blithely subscribe to such a blueprint.[46] Of course, there is some shift of perspective when dealing with 'continental' liberalism, not just as a form of political philosophy but also as a political ideology bound up with the problem of defending and proclaiming the state.[47] But then, one has only to look at American liberalism, or British liberalism for that matter, and one will detect their robust attachment to a view of the political sphere encapsulated in the old terms of the *communitas communitatum*.

A question that demanded considerable energy on the part of the representatives of the Liberal Party at the Constituent Assembly was the method of selecting deputies for the Chambers, especially for the new Senate, now to become elective. They, and especially Luigi Einaudi, argued for the electoral majority system against the Proportional Representation approach. Their idea was that basing selection on uninominal constituencies was the best way to promote the choice of 'eminent personalities' by the voters, instead of handing them over to the hated propaganda of political (manipulative) ideologies with their party machines. The battle was nearly won, and it was only at the last minute, due to a complicated parliamentary strategy, that the liberal proposal was defeated and the P.R. system was applied to the Senate.[48]

Another crucial feature of postwar Catholic antiliberalism is the controversy over economic rights. It also marks the divide from socialist antiliberalism, whose mainstay was the cult of the state, duly purged by proletarian revolution, needless to say. Economic rights found their way into all postwar constitutions, but one can hardly maintain that the results were all that appreciable.[49] Unlike the case with rights to freedom, so-called economic rights lacked the juridical leverage to command respect. Nearly everywhere they remained at the stage of 'good intentions' that were included without any chance of becoming real engines of political action. The obverse of what might have been expected actually appears to have happened. They were a convenient excuse to legitimise simple 'declarations of intent' (i.e. promising, but doing nothing about it) – so often a means by which politicians pretended to flesh out what they had promised. This is as clear as day in the Italian Constitution that never got anywhere on this particular wicket.[50] Ultimately, even the 'Keynesian' policies implemented long afterwards (from the end of the 1950s) failed to find the kind of firm constitutional basis that supported the development of civil rights. Significantly, the historic decision to nationalize the electricity grid in 1962–63 was solidly supported by the Catholic and socialist parties, staunchly opposed by the liberal party[51] and – a fraction more tepidly – by the Communist Party, though the last was mainly moved by considerations of tactical opposition to the Christian Democrats.

Another point that undeniably deserves attention is the emerging issue of economic planning, within which the welfare question is also included. This inclusion should come as no surprise, although some might see welfare as belonging more appropriately to economic, or even civil, rights. Though this is a grey area, the management of what the continent significantly calls the 'social state' pertains more appropriately to the range of activities governing the system of economic relations rather than to the sphere of rights.[52] Such operations relate to the redistribution of income rather than to equality *erga omnes*, as is the case with rights issues. That they were later incorrectly shifted into this last category brought about further, and still ongoing, crises.[53]

As concerns the management of the economy, we should note that these issues were only passed down to post–1945 liberalism as 'second generation' matters. The defence of free competition and keeping state intervention to a minimum was a dogma of nineteenth-century Anglo-Saxon liberalism, whereas continental attitudes and practices here have been much less univocal, even though there existed broad agreement about accepting the model in theory.

A debate over the relationship between liberalism and what 'free economy' could signify was held between Luigi Einaudi, the 'guru' of Italian economic liberalism, and the eminent philosopher Benedetto Croce. As is well known, it began in 1928 with Einaudi's article, in which he criticized Croce's distinction between 'liberalism' and what he termed *liberismo*, indicating a view of liberalism that prioritized an economic principle over 'ethical liberalism'.[54] The core of the question was state intervention in the economy. Croce viewed the state as a possible form of the Spirit regulating events above individual interests. He rejected any idea of the supremacy of economics in organizing social life, regarding the latter instead as the domain where the life of the Spirit – Ethics in a superior sense – would dominate. Einaudi did not dismiss the possibility of regulatory action by the state in the economic field and opposed the confusion of liberalism with laissez-faire, but vigorously emphasized that free competition should not have to meet any kind of obstacle.[55]

With the advent of the twentieth century, the problem of public intervention in the economy became the order of the day across Europe, while the use of the public sphere in a regulatory capacity was not always seen as a breach of the liberal tradition. From this standpoint, the input of Keynesian theory must be seen as decisive. Although there were those who failed to notice Keynes was a liberal (the prime example is the Dossetti group in Italy),[56] compatibility between public intervention and the liberal system became a fairly routine matter, especially after the New Deal. It was ultimately bolstered when the Americans decided to support the postwar European economies (the Marshall Plan was a typical post-Keynesian scheme hinging on a degree of top-down regulation of the economic market, which was one of the conditions attaching to operating and stabilizing it).[57]

It would be short-sighted to underestimate the decisive part played in this experience by the first steps of state regulation of the economy under the great dictators. Evidence has recently been found that even Ludwig Erhard's *Soziale Marktwirtschaft* theorizing had its roots in work carried out under the Weimar Republic and matured under Hitler's dictatorship.[58] Yet, what kept the planning experiments of the second postwar period within the bounds of liberalism, without for one moment jeopardizing the situation, was the target they set themselves: to enhance individual affluence by a continuously increased reliance on personal and family consumption. Here too, we must note that in Italy the most convinced upholders of solidarity and social intervention in the economy were the Catholic left-wing. Einaudi, on the contrary, had little sympathy with Keynes and his ideas. In a leading article in *Il Corriere della Sera* in 1948, he criticized planning as a third way between liberalism and communism.[59] The target of his polemic was Wilhelm Röpke—who was also a liberal thinker, founder of the so-called *Ordoliberalism* – and his *Die Gesellschaftkrise der Gegenwart* (1942). Croce himself took sides against Röpke in 1943,[60] having already stressed in 1941 that 'liberty as morality cannot have any other basis than itself, because it would cease to be moral if linked to economic data'.[61] Academic economists of the interwar generation were basically monetarists, obsessed by the hyperinflation of Weimar; the greatest authority among them, Bresciani-Turroni, had indeed witnessed it at first hand. To them, the state had to keep out of economics and only ensure that the currency was solid. Or so ran the theory; in practice, things worked out differently.

There is another interesting point for discussion here. In 1950–51, when that orthodox monetarist, the DC Treasury Minister Luigi Pella, decided to use Marshall funds largely to build up reserves and prop up the national currency, he drew the fire first of the Catholic left, who defended what La Pira famously called the 'poor people's expectations'[62] – namely, that development would bring in its wake bread and work . It should be noted that also that many American Marshall Plan experts, who were none other than Keynesian liberals, shared La Pira's approach.[63] At about the same time, an address by Croce to the Congress of the Liberal Party in Turin on 7–8 December 1951 met with little success when he appealed to his audience 'always to examine and discuss measures that are left- and right-oriented, progressive and conservative, and to adopt something from the one side and something from the other, if you so wish, but more frequently [measures] of progress than those of conservatism'.[64]

The truth is that in paving the way for an 'affluent democracy', new-style public intervention in the economy kept its historical links to liberalism with its 'pursuit of happiness'. One is tempted to quip that in the end, socialism became liberalized far more than liberalism turned socialist. This would emerge during the vexed 'opening to the left' when the Italian liberals, or rather such liberals as identified with the party that claimed to represent them officially, closed ranks in defence of a quite obsolete version of their ideology. They carried it off with verve and with some of the cultural snobbery that distinguished their leader, Giovanni Malagodi. Malagodi was a man of culture, but was unable to understand the world around him as the 1950s morphed into the early 1960s.[65]

The roots of the problem went back a long way. As early as 1955, one of the most influential liberal ideologists, Panfilo Gentile, who was also a respected leader-writer for the *Corriere della Sera*, had published a significant treatise[66] that displayed the true limits of the Italian approach to liberalism. It ranged from defence of the individual against the state, to the issue of containing the state within set limits. But that was academic orthodoxy of no particular novelty – what also transpired was a distrust of 'mass democracy': a lofty disdain for politics with its inevitable requirement to hobnob with the people. All this seemed like the road to perdition, a slide towards 'religious'-style manipulation, just – lest we forget – as Gaetano Mosca had claimed in his day.

A quotation from Panfilo Gentile will suffice to understand what is meant here: 'Therefore, once and for all, a democratic system based on universal suffrage simply is … a regime in which many elites agree to submit themselves to the judgment of crowds in order to be installed in power. This means that a democratic regime is an oligarchy installed by crowds.'[67]

Such an approach to politics would ultimately devalue the entire postwar Italian constitutional system. The age-old chant would be heard that this was a far cry from the legendary 'British' and now also 'American' model, which only existed in the imagination of the malcontents. One typical example is Giuseppe Maranini, a belated convert to liberalism, who invented the term *partitocrazia* (unchallenged party dominance); it was a scarcely subtler way of rejecting omnipresent forms of modern politics, even in the countries whose virtues he sang (especially Great Britain and the United States). The only difference was that in the latter, the liberals, or their secular heirs, profited from political developments after the Second World War, whereas in Italy, this gave the whip-hand to the Christian Democrat party – a formation that sprang from an historical antiliberalism that the Catholics could never forget.[68]

Italian liberalism would never make much progress down such a road. Significantly, the most original and innovative Italian liberal thinker, Nicola

Matteucci, would preface his aptly entitled *Liberalism in a Changing World* with these words:

> I hope it is clear to the reader that this book intends no defence of liberal democracy as it exists in Italy today. All of us – some more, some less – have done our bit in rendering it less and less credible to the young. It no longer arouses genuine feeling capable of defending it from external enemies and, above all, internal enemies. If anything, I would like to sketch a model of liberal society for a future that belongs to everyone.[69]

Paolo Pombeni is Emeritus Professor in the History of Political Systems at the University of Bologna. From 2010 to 2016, he was Director of the Italian-German Historical Institute in Trento. He is also a member of the editorial board of *Ricerche di Storia Politica* and *Journal of Political Ideologies*. His most recent books include *La ragione e la passione: Le forme della politica nell'Europa contemporanea* (2010); *Der Junge De Gasperi: Werdegang eines Politikers* (2012); *Giuseppe Dossetti, L'avventura politica di un riformatore cristiano* (2013); *La questione costituzionale in Italia* (2016); *Che cosa resta del 68* (2018); and *La buona politica* (2019). He is editor of *The Historiography of Transition: Critical Phases in the Development of Modernity 1494–1973* (2016).

Notes

1. I am aware that there still exists discomfort at styling the fascist period as an interval or parenthesis. My aim is far from playing down the impact of that phase, or disputing the undeniable 'continuity' of Italy's history. I only mean to point out that fascism was an 'interval' in terms of my attempt to trace the fortunes of liberal constitutionalism as the load-bearing structure of the Italian political system.
2. Cf. L. Lacché, *Il costituzionalismo liberale*, in *Il contributo italiano alla storia del pensiero*, Rome, 2012, 294–301. For a general view of this problem, see P. Grossi, *Scienza giuridica italiana, 1860–1950*, Milan, 2000.
3. On the wide-ranging debate in Italian political thought concerning the 'English model' and its significance, see P. Pombeni, *La ragione e la passione: Le forme della politica nell'Europa contemporanea*, Bologna, 2010, which reviews the topic extensively.
4. R. Romanelli, *Il comando impossibile: Stato e società nell'Italia liberale*, Bologna, 1988.
5. See D.E. Apter (ed.), *Ideology and Discontent*, New York, 1964. One should not confuse 'ideology' with 'culture': had the focus of this chapter been on 'culture', its scope would be quite different.

6. I am well aware of the differences between these two authors, but the fact that both of them broadly dealt with 'political theory' and its key terms has tended to bracket them together. Taking it for granted that these two authors' main output is already familiar, I would also mention H. Joas and P. Vogt (eds), *Begriffene Geschichte: Beiträge zum Werk Reinhart Kosellecks*, Frankfurt am Main, 2011; H. Jordheim, 'Conceptual History between *Chronos* and *Kairos*: The Case of Empire', *Redescriptions* 11 (2007), 113–45; H. Jordheim, 'Against Periodisation: Koselleck's Theory of Multiple Temporalities', *History and Theory* 51 (2012), 151–71.

7. Q. Skinner, *Dell'interpretazione*, Bologna, 2001. As we shall see later on, the same distinction holds when it comes to interpreting antiliberalism. There are cases where liberal ideology was disclaimed or even condemned when the subsequent intention would be to uphold liberal-style values and principles.

8. Here again, as we shall see later, much of the Italian problem with liberalism depends on what position might be taken at any one time by the 'party' styling itself 'liberal', though not actually being so – or at least insufficiently so to qualify as the sole faithful interpreter of that ideology.

9. F. Lanchetser, *Pensare lo Stato: I giuspubblicisti nell'Italia unitaria*, Rome, 2004; M. Fioravanti, *Dottrine dello Stato e della Costituzione tra Otto e Novecento*, Milan, 2001; A. Mazzacane (ed.), *I giuristi e la crisi dello stato liberale in Italia fra Otto e Novecento*, Naples, 1986; G. Cianferotti, *Il pensiero di V.E. Orlando e la giuspubblicistica italiana fra Ottocento e Novecento*, Milan, 1980.

10. Quoted in L. Lucchini, *La politica italiana dal 1848 al 1897: Programmi di governo*, Roma, 1899, vol. I, 510.

11. 'Introduction', in Apter, *Ideology and Discontent*, 18–21.

12. That said, at the turn of the nineteenth century in particular, certain jurists did review the problem of 'society', which could not be absorbed *sic et simpliciter* by the state (as one line of German doctrine, then in vogue, maintained). See L. Lacché, 'Lo stato giuridico e la costituzione sociale: Angelo Majorana e la giuspubblicistica di fine secolo', in *Il 'giureconsulto della politica': Angelo Majorana e l'indirizzo sociologico del diritto pubblico*, Macerata, 2011, 23–53.

13. See. V. Fiorelli, *La nazione fra i banchi: Il contributo della scuola alla formazione degli italiani fra Otto e Novecento*, Soveria Mannelli, 2012.

14. One gathers this, for example, from the way in which the concept of 'fatherland' (*patria*) developed (with the associated term 'Risorgimento'). A prime case of this was when many intellectuals who had previously subscribed to the membership of socialist movements rediscovered and appropriated the terms. R. Pertici has drawn attention to this point in his 'Il "ritorno alla patria" nel sovversivo del primo Novecento: Percorsi politico-culturali di una generazione di intellettuali italiani', *Ricerche di Storia Politica* 11 (2008), 153–75; R. Pertici, 'Il "ritorno alla patria" nel sovversivismo primo novecentesco e l'incontro con Mazzini', in A. Bocchi and D. Menozzi (eds), *Mazzini e il Novecento*, Pisa, 2009, 65–107.

15. In this one sees the clear influence of positivism and its associated scientism. There was also little connection between the intellectual elite and the lower

classes. On the first point, it is interesting to examine how Italian radicalism had formed: cf. G. Orsina, *Seenza Chiesa né classe: Il partito radicale nell'età giolittiana*, Rome, 1998.

16. P. Pombeni, *Il primo De Gasperi: La formazione di un leader politico*, Bologna, 2008; P. Pombeni, 'Uno strumento di conquista dello spazio politico: De Gasperi e i liberali 1900–1914', in F. Cammarano and S. Cavazza (eds), *Il nemico in politica: La delegittimazione dell'avversario nell'Europa contemporanea*, Bologna, 2010, 121–54.

17. A. De Gasperi, *Scritti e discorsi politici*, 4 vols, Bologna, 2006, vol. I, 365.

18. We are now beginning to see studies investigating this point of rupture. There is a very interesting study by G. Guazzaloca, *Fine secolo: Gli intellettuali italiani ed inglesi e la crisi tra Otto e Novecento*, Bologna, 2004. F. Cammarano also touches on the evolution of Italian liberalism in his *Storia dell'Italia Liberale*, Rome, 2011; F. Cammarano 'Das Zeitalter des klassischen Liberalismus: Politische und nationale Identität in Italien nach der Einigung', *Jahrbuch des italienisch-deutschen historischen Instituts in Trient* 38(2) (2012), 11–50. A first attempt to analyse the career of a leader of progressive liberalism is to be found in R. Chiarini (ed.), *Alle origini dell'età giolittianaL La 'svolta liberale' del governo Zanardelli-Giolitti 1901–1903*, Venice, 2003. Another useful text is M. Scavino, *La svolta liberale 1899–1904: Politica e società nell'età giolittina*, Milan, 2012.

19. J.W. Müller, *Contesting Democracy: Political Ideas in 20th Century Europe*, New Haven, 2011.

20. On this M. Freeden's *The New Liberalism: An Ideology of Social Reform*, Oxford, 1978 is still fundamental. The other classic on this topic is P. Clarke, *Liberals and Social Democrats*, Cambridge, 1978.

21. E. Weber, *La Francia fin de siècle*, Bologna, 1990; M. Battini, *L'ordine della gerarchia: I contributi reazionari e progressisti alle crisi della democrazia in Francia 1789–1914*, Turin, 1995.

22. On this issue, the jurists obviously played a key role, especially Vittorio Emanuele Orlando. I refer the reader to M. Fioravanti, *La scienza del diritto pubblico: Dottrine dello Stato e della Costituzione tra Otto e Novecento*, Milan, 2001. For a more general view of the state vis-à-vis constitutional theory, see M. Fioravanti, *Costituzionalismo: Percorsi della storia e tendenze attuali*, Rome, 2009; and P. Grossi, *Introduzione al Novecento Giuridico*, Rome, 2012.

23. Besides the works cited in notes 18 and 22, see also P. Costa, *Lo Stato immaginario: Metafore e paradigmi nella cultura giuridica italiana fra Ottocento e Novecento*, Milan, 1986.

24. See G. Quagliariello, *Gaetano Salvemini*, Bologna, 2007. For a perfect case in point from many angles, see R. Pertici, 'Antonio Anzilotti da Marx a Gioberti: parabola di uno storico "realistico"', *Archivio Storico Italiano* 170 (2012), 477–533; P. Pombeni, 'La teoria del partito politico nell'età di Michels', *Annali della Fondazione Luigi Einaudi* XVLI (2012), 85–119.

25. Quoted in M.L. Sergio, *Dall'antipartito al partito unico: La crisi della politica in Italia agli inizi del Novecento*, Rome, 2002, 146.

26. Guazzaloca, *Fine secolo*. That certain jurists and politicians influenced the Italians against the British transformation that straddled the *fin de siècle* is argued by Pombeni, *La ragione e la passion*, 377–94.

27. On this point, see the interesting article by M. Fotia, 'L'Istituzionalismo in Santi Romano tra Diritto e Politica', *Democrazia e Diritto* 1–2 (2011), 135–74. See also Grossi, *Introduzione*, 41–62.

28. The question of citizenship is obviously central to liberal ideology. See P. Costa, *Civitas: Storia della cittadinanza in Europa*, vol. III, *La civiltà liberale*, Rome, 2001; A. Fahrmeir, *Citizenship: The Rise and Fall of a Modern Concept*, New Haven, 2007.

29. On this topic, see the penetrating notes by R. Vivarelli, *Storia delle origini del fascismo. I: L'Italia dalla Grande Guerra alla marcia su Roma*, Bologna, 1991. Materials and notes on the subject are also to be found in E. Gentile, *La Grande Italia: Il mito della nazione nel XX secolo*, Rome, 2006; M. Mondini and G. Schwarz, *Dalla guerra alla pace: Retoriche e pratiche della smobilitazione nell'Italia del Novecento*, Verona, 2006; A.M. Banti, *Sublime madre nostra: la nazione italiana dal Risorgimento al fascismo*, Rome, 2011.

30. E. Papadia, *Nel nome della nazione: l'Associazione nazionalista italiana in età giolittiana*, Rome, 2006.

31. L. Ornaghi, *Stato e Corporazione*, Milan, 1984.

32. P. Pombeni, *Demagogia e tirannide: Uno studio sulla forma partito del fascismo*, Bologna, 1984.

33. G. Orsina, 'L'organizzazione politica nella Camera della proporzionale (1920–1924)', in F. Grassi Orsini and G. Quagliariello (eds), *Il partito politico dalla Grande Guerra al fascismo*, Bologna, 1996, 397–489.

34. Quoted in G. Orsina, 'L'organizzazione politica nella Camera della proporzionale', *La Nacion*, 10 May 1922, 440. On the elaborate question of the position of political parties within the framework of the Italian constitutions, see M. Gregorio, *Parte totale: Le dottrine costituzionali del partito politico in Italia fra Otto e Novecento*, Milan, 2013.

35. G. Melis, *La macchina imperfetta*, Bologna, 2018.

36. On the problem of the constitutional thinking in modern Italy from the Risorgimento until now, see P. Pombeni, *La questione costituzionale in Italia*, Bologna, 2016.

37. See P. Pombeni, 'L'ultimo Orlando: Il costituente', in [Senato della Repubblica, Convegni della Sala Zuccari], *Vittorio Emanuele Orlando: Lo scienziato, il politico, lo statista*, Soveria Mannelli, 2003, 33–35.

38. P. Pombeni, 'Il contributo dei cattolici alla Costituente', in S. Labriola (ed.), *Valori e principi del regime repubblicano*, vol. I, *Sovranità e Democrazia*, Rome, 2006, 37–80; P. Pombeni, 'Cultura politica e legittimazione della costituzione', in M. Fioravanti and S. Guerrieri (eds), *La Costituzione Italiana*, Rome, 1999, 139–89; P. Pombeni, 'Individuo/Persona nella costituzione italiana: Il contributo del dossettismo', *Parole Chiave* 10–11 (1996), 197–218.

39. For a close reconstruction of antiliberalism as proclaimed by Giuseppe Dossetti, see E. Galavotti, *Il professorino G. Dossetti tra crisi del fascismo*

e costruzione della democrazia 1940–48, Bologna, 2013. More generally, see
P. Pombeni, *Giuseppe Dossetti: L'avventura politica di un riformatore cristiano*,
Bologna, 2013.

40. La Pira's policy statement on the design for the Constitution was delivered on
11 March 1946. The address can now be read in N. Antonetti, U. de Siervo and
F. Malgieri (eds), *I cattolici democratici e la costituzione*, Bologna, 1998, vol. III,
1051–72.

41. Originally published in *Esprit*, December 1944, the text has been reissued in
E. Mounier, *Oeuvres*, Paris, 1963, vol. IV, 99–104.

42. *Cronache Sociali*, 15 January 1948. On the context of this thought within the
framework of the development of the Catholic political thought, see P. Pombeni,
'Christian Democracy', in M. Freeden, L.T. Sargent and M. Stears (eds), *The
Oxford Handbook of Political Ideologies*, Oxford, 2013, 312–28.

43. G. Dossetti, *'Non abbiate paura dello stato', Funzioni e ordinamento dello stato
moderno*, E. Balboni (ed.), Milan, 2014, 32.

44. The judgment by Mario Paggi, one of the liberals who best appreciated the
substantial novelty of the postwar situation, is quoted in L. Ornaghi, 'I progetti
di Stato (1945–1948)', in R. Ruffilli (ed.), *Cultura politica e partiti nell'età della
Costituente*, Bologna, 1979, vol. I, *L'area liberal democratica, il mondo cattolico e
la Democrazia Cristiana*, 96. (The whole chapter, at 39–102, is enlightening as to
the liberal approach to the constitutional issue.)

45. For a detailed analysis of this subject, see Pombeni, 'Individuo/persona'.

46. See M. Freeden, *Liberalism: A Very Short Introduction*, Oxford, 2015.

47. See M. Fioravanti, *Costituzione e popolo sovrano*, Bologna, 2004.

48. This is explained in detail in Pombeni, *La questione costituzionale in Italia*.

49. M. Cau, 'Culture costituzionali in transizione: Italia e Germania nel secondo
dopoguerra', in P. Pombeni and H.G. Haupt (eds), *La transizione come problema
storiografico*, Bologna, 2013, 363–87.

50. P. Pombeni, 'Fanfani Costituente: un approccio della cultura cattolica alla "questione economica" nel secondo dopoguerra', in P. Capuzzo, C. Giorgi, M. Martini
and C. Sorba (eds), *Pensare la contemporaneità: Studi di storia per Mariuccia
Salvati*, Rome, 2011, 465–84.

51. G. Orsina, *L'alternativa liberale: Malagodi e l'opposizione al centrosinistra*, Venice,
2010.

52. P. Pombeni, 'La democrazia del benessere e l'evoluzione della forma partito nel
quadro dei sistemi costituzionali europei 1943–1968', in E. Francia (ed.), *Luciano
Cafagna tra ricerca storica e impegno civile*, Venice, 2007, 85–104.

53. Paolo Pombeni, 'La Democrazia sociale: Una sfida per il XXI secolo?', in
P. Pombeni and G. Consorte (eds), *Democrazia Sociale: La sfida europea e
l'anomalia italiana*, Padua, 2010, 1–31.

54. L. Einaudi, 'Del concetto di liberismo economico e sulle origini materialistiche
della Guerra', *La riforma Sociale* (1928), 501–16; L. Einaudi, 'Dei diversi significati del concetto di liberismo economico e dei suoi rapporti con quello di
liberalismo', *La Riforma Sociale* (1931), 186–94.

55. L. Einaudi, 'Intorno al contenuto dei concetti di liberismo, comunismo, interventismo', *Argomenti* (1941), 18–34.
56. E. Biagini, 'Keynesian Ideas and the Recasting of Italian Democracy 1945–1953', in E.H.H. Green and D.M. Tanner (eds), *The Strange Survival of Liberal England*, Cambridge, 2007, 212–44.
57. M. Campus, *L'Italia, gli Stati Uniti e il piano Marshall*, Rome, 2008; F. Fauri, *Il piano Marshall e l'Italia*, Bologna, 2010.
58. A.J. Nicholls, *Freedom with Responsibility: The Social Market Economy in Germany 1918–1963*, Oxford, 2000.
59. *Corriere della Sera*, 15 April 1948.
60. B. Croce, 'La terza via', *La Critica* (1943), 109–12.
61. B. Croce, 'Liberalismo contro il duplice dommatismo liberistico e comunistico', *Rivista di Storia Economica* (1941), 6.
62. This is the title of a famous article by La Pira published in *Cronache Sociali*, 15 April 1950.
63. C. Spagnolo, *La stabilizzazione incompiuta: Il piano Marshall in Italia (1947–1952)*, Rome, 2001.
64. *Il Giornale* (a newspaper published in Naples), 8 December 1951.
65. An acute reconstruction of events showing the protagonist in a favourable light is to be found in Orsina, *L'alternativa liberale*.
66. P. Gentile, *L'idea liberale*, Soveria Mannelli, 2000 [1955].
67. Ibid., 51.
68. On the Maranini episode, see the acute work by E. Capozzi, *Il sogno di una costituzione. Giuseppe Maranini e l'Italia del Novecento*, Bologna, 2008. On the postwar deadlock of Italian liberalism, see R. Pertici's stimulating reconstruction, 'La crisi della cultura liberale in Italia nel primo ventennio repubblicano', *Ventunesimo Secolo* 8 (2005), 121–49.
69. N. Matteucci, *Il liberalismo in un mondo in trasformazione*, Bologna, 1972, 10. On this thinker, see T. Bonazzi and S. Testoni Binetti (eds), *Il liberalismo di Nicola Matteucci*, Bologna, 2007, especially the essay by G. Cotroneo (at 15–32), which highlights the progress made since Croce's legacy. Matteucci accepted that Italian liberalism had no future without coming to terms with that world of 'social sciences' that Croce had eyed with suspicion. It was natural for Matteucci to figure among the founders of that Bolognese adventure, the 'Il Mulino' group, where the various traditions of Italian 'democracy' managed to engage in dialogue and cross-fertilization without the neurotic fear that someone would always stake a prior claim.

Bibliography

Antonetti, N., U. de Siervo and F. Malgieri (eds). *I cattolici democratici e la costituzione*. Bologna, 1998.
Apter, D.E. *Ideology and Discontent*. New York, 1964.

Banti, A.M. *Sublime madre nostra: la nazione italiana dal Risorgimento al fascismo.* Rome, 2011.

Battini, M. *L'ordine della gerarchia: I contributi reazionari e progressisti alle crisi della democrazia in Francia 1789–1914.* Turin, 1995.

Biagini, E. 'Keynesian Ideas and the Recasting of Italian Democracy 1945–1953', in E.H.H. Green and D.M. Tanner (eds), *The Strange Survival of Liberal England* (Cambridge, 2007), 212–44.

Bonazzi, T., and S. Testoni Binetti (eds). *Il liberalismo di Nicola Matteucci.* Bologna, 2007.

Cammarano, F. 'Das Zeitalter des klassischen Liberalismus: Politische und nationale Identität in Italien nach der Einigung'. *Jahrbuch des italienisch-deutschen historischen Instituts in Trient* 38(2) (2012), 11–50.

———. *Storia dell'Italia Liberale.* Rome, 2011.

Campus, M. *L'Italia, gli Stati Uniti e il piano Marshall.* Rome, 2008.

Capozzi, E. *Il sogno di una costituzione: Giuseppe Maranini e l'Italia del Novecento.* Bologna, 2008.

Cau, M. 'Culture costituzionali in transizione: Italia e Germania nel secondo dopoguerra', in P. Pombeni and H.G. Haupt (eds), *La transizione come problema storiografico* (Bologna, 2013), 363–87.

Chiarini, R. *Alle origini dell'età giolittiana: La 'svolta liberale' del governo Zanardelli-Giolitti 1901–1903.* Venice, 2003.

Cianferotti, G. *Il pensiero di V.E. Orlando e la giuspubblicistica italiana fra Ottocento e Novecento.* Milan, 1980.

Clarke, P. *Liberals and Social Democrats.* Cambridge, 1978.

Costa, P. *Civitas. Storia della cittadinanza in Europa. Vol. 3: La civiltà liberale.* Rome, 2001.

———. *Lo Stato immaginario: Metafore e paradigmi nella cultura giuridica italiana fra Ottocento e Novecento.* Milan, 1986.

Croce, B. 'La terza via'. *La Critica* (1943), 109–12.

———. 'Liberalismo contro il duplice dommatismo liberistico e comunistico'. *Rivista di Storia Economica* (1941), 6.

De Gasperi, A. *Scritti e discorsi politici,* 4 vols. Bologna, 2006.

Dossetti, G. *'Non abbiate paura dello stato', Funzioni e ordinamento dello stato moderno,* E. Balboni (ed.). Milan, 2014.

Einaudi, L. 'Del concetto di liberismo economico e sulle origini materialistiche della Guerra'. *La riforma Sociale* (1928), 501–16.

———. 'Dei diversi significati del concetto di liberismo economico e dei suoi rapporti con quello di liberalismo'. *La Riforma Sociale* (1931), 186–94.

———. 'Intorno al contenuto dei concetti di liberismo, comunismo, interventismo'. *Argomenti* (1941), 18–34.

Fahrmeir, A. *Citizenship: The Rise and Fall of a Modern Concept.* New Haven, 2007.

Fauri, F. *Il piano Marshall e l'Italia.* Bologna, 2010.

Fioravanti, M. *Costituzionalismo: Percorsi della storia e tendenze attuali.* Rome, 2009.

———. *Costituzione e popolo sovrano.* Bologna, 2004.

————. *Dottrine dello Stato e della Costituzione tra Otto e Novecento*. Milan, 2001.

————. *La scienza del diritto pubblico: Dottrine dello Stato e della Costituzione tra Otto e Novecento*. Milan, 2001.

Fiorelli, V. *La nazione fra i banchi: Il contributo della scuola alla formazione degli italiani fra Otto e Novecento*. Soveria Mannelli, 2012.

Fotia, M. 'L'Istituzionalismo in Santi Romano tra Diritto e Politica'. *Democrazia e Diritto* 1–2 (2011), 135–74.

Freeden, M. *Liberalism: A Very Short Introduction*. Oxford, 2015.

————. *The New Liberalism: An Ideology of Social Reform*. Oxford, 1978.

Galavotti, E. *Il professorino G. Dossetti tra crisi del fascismo e costruzione della democrazia 1940–48*. Bologna, 2013.

Gentile, E. *La Grande Italia: Il mito della nazione nel XX secolo*. Rome, 2006.

Gentile, P. *L'idea liberale*. Soveria Mannelli, 2000.

Gregorio, M. *Parte totale: Le dottrine costituzionali del partito politico in Italia fra Otto e Novecento*. Milan, 2013.

Grossi, P. *Introduzione al Novecento Giuridico*. Rome, 2012.

————. *Scienza giuridica italiana, 1860–1950*. Milan, 2000.

Guazzaloca, G. *Fine secolo: Gli intellettuali italiani ed inglesi e la crisi tra Otto e Novecento*. Bologna, 2004.

Joas, H., and P. Vogt. *Begriffene Geschichte: Beiträge zum Werk Reinhart Kosellecks*. Frankfurt am Main, 2011.

Jordheim, H. 'Against Periodisation: Koselleck's Theory of Multiple Temporalities'. *History and Theory* 51 (2012), 151–71.

————. 'Conceptual History between *Chronos* and *Kairos*: The Case of Empire'. *Redescriptions* 11 (2007), 113–45.

Lacché, L. *Il costituzionalismo liberale*, in *Il contributo italiano alla storia del pensiero* (Rome, 2012), 294–301.

————. 'Lo stato giuridico e la costituzione sociale: Angelo Majorana e la giuspubblicistica di fine secolo', in *Il 'giureconsulto della politica': Angelo Majorana e l'indirizzo sociologico del diritto pubblico* (Macerata, 2011), 23–53.

Lanchetser, F. *Pensare lo Stato: I giuspubblicisti nell'Italia unitaria*. Rome, 2004.

Lucchini, L. *La politica italiana dal 1848 al 1897: Programmi di governo*. Roma, 1899.

Matteucci, N. *Il liberalismo in un mondo in trasformazione*. Bologna, 1972.

Mazzacane, A. (ed.). *I giuristi e la crisi dello stato liberale in Italia fra Otto e Novecento*. Naples, 1986.

Melis, G. *La macchina imperfetta*. Bologna, 2018.

Mondini, M., and G. Schwarz. *Dalla guerra alla pace: Retoriche e pratiche della smobilitazione nell'Italia del Novecento*. Verona, 2006.

Mounier, E. *Oeuvres*. Paris, 1963.

Müller, J.W. *Contesting Democracy: Political Ideas in 20th Century Europe*. New Haven, 2011.

Nicholls, A.J. *Freedom with Responsibility: The Social Market Economy in Germany 1918–1963*. Oxford, 2000.

Ornaghi, L. 'I progetti di Stato (1945–1948)', in R. Ruffilli (ed.), *Cultura politica e partiti nell'età della Costituente*, vol. 1 (Bologna, 1979), 39–102.

———. *Stato e Corporazione*. Milan, 1984.

Orsina, G. *L'alternativa liberale: Malagodi e l'opposizione al centrosinistra*. Venice, 2010.

———. 'L'organizzazione politica nella Camera della proporzionale (1920–1924)', in F. Grassi Orsini and G. Quagliariello (eds), *Il partito politico dalla Grande Guerra al fascismo* (Bologna, 1996), 397–489.

———. *Seenza Chiesa né classe: Il partito radicale nell'età giolittiana*. Rome, 1998.

Papadia, E. *Nel nome della nazione: l'Associazione nazionalista italiana in età giolittiana*. Rome, 2006.

Pertici, R. 'Antonio Anzilotti da Marx a Gioberti: parabola di uno storico "realistico"'. *Archivio Storico Italiano* 170 (2012), 477–533.

———. 'Il "ritorno alla patria" nel sovversivismo primo novecentesco e l'incontro con Mazzini', in A. Bocchi and D. Menozzi (eds), *Mazzini e il Novecento* (Pisa, 2009), 65–107.

———. 'Il "ritorno alla patria" nel sovversivo del primo Novecento: Percorsi politico-culturali di una generazione di intellettuali italiani'. *Ricerche di Storia Politica* 11 (2008), 153–75.

———. 'La crisi della cultura liberale in Italia nel primo ventennio repubblicano'. *Ventunesimo Secolo* 8 (2005), 121–49.

Pombeni, P. 'Christian Democracy', in M. Freeden, L.T. Sargent and M. Stears (eds), *The Oxford Handbook of Political Ideologies* (Oxford, 2013), 312–28.

———. 'Cultura politica e legittimazione della costituzione', in M. Fioravanti and S. Guerrieri (eds), *La Costituzione Italiana* (Rome, 1999), 139–89.

———. *Demagogia e tirannide: Uno studio sulla forma partito del fascismo*. Bologna, 1984.

———. *Giuseppe Dossetti: L'avventura politica di un riformatore Cristiano*. Bologna, 2013.

———. 'Il contributo dei cattolici alla Costituente', in S. Labriola (ed.), *Valori e principi del regime repubblicano*, vol. I, *Sovranità e Democrazia* (Rome, 2006), 37–80.

———. *Il primo De Gasperi: La formazione di un leader politico*. Bologna, 2008.

———. 'Individuo/Persona nella costituzione italiana: Il contributo del dossettismo'. *Parole Chiave* 10–11 (1996), 197–218.

———. 'La democrazia del benessere e l'evoluzione della forma partito nel quadro dei sistemi costituzionali europei 1943–1968', in E. Francia (ed.), *Luciano Cafagna tra ricerca storica e impegno civile* (Venice, 2007), 85–104.

———. 'La Democrazia sociale: Una sfida per il XXI secolo?', in P. Pombeni and G. Consorte (eds), *Democrazia Sociale: La sfida europea e l'anomalia italiana* (Padua, 2010), 1–31.

———. *La ragione e la passione: Le forme della politica nell'Europa contemporanea*. Bologna, 2010.

———. *La questione costituzionale in Italia*. Bologna, 2016.

———. 'La teoria del partito politico nell'età di Michels'. *Annali della Fondazione Luigi Einaudi* XVLI (2012), 85–119.

————. 'L'ultimo Orlando: Il costituente', in [Senato della Repubblica, Convegni della Sala Zuccari], *Vittorio Emanuele Orlando: Lo scienziato, il politico, lo statista* (Soveria Mannelli, 2003), 33–35.

————. 'Uno strumento di conquista dello spazio politico: De Gasperi e i liberali 1900–1914', in F. Cammarano and S. Cavazza (eds), *Il nemico in politica: La delegittimazione dell'avversario nell'Europa contemporanea* (Bologna, 2010), 121–54.

Quagliariello, G. *Gaetano Salvemini*. Bologna, 2007.

Romanelli, R. *Il comando impossibil:. Stato e società nell'Italia liberale*. Bologna, 1988.

Scavino, M. *La svolta liberale 1899–1904: Politica e società nell'età giolittina*. Milan, 2012.

Sergio, M.L. *Dall'antipartito al partito unico: La crisi della politica in Italia agli inizi del Novecento*. Rome, 2002.

Skinner, Q. *Dell'interpretazione*. Bologna, 2001.

Spagnolo, C. *La stabilizzazione incompiuta: Il piano Marshall in Italia (1947–1952)*. Rome, 2001.

Vivarelli, R. *Storia delle origini del fascismo. I: L'Italia dalla Grande Guerra alla marcia su Roma*. Bologna, 1991.

Weber, E. *La Francia fin de siècle*. Bologna, 1990.

Chapter 10

Encounters with Liberalism in Post-Soviet Russia

Olga Malinova

❧❖❧

Despite the fact that the concept 'liberalism' had a significant history in Russia in the nineteenth and early twentieth centuries,[1] its reappearance in political practice during perestroika and after the collapse of the Soviet Union should be considered as essentially a new stage in its semantic evolution. As we shall see later, some particular meanings associated with the term before 1917 finally became salient in the post-Soviet period as well. At the same time, there were significant differences that indicate a break in semantic continuity.

According to research conducted by Mikhail Kalashnikov, the French term *idées libérales* appeared in the lexicon of the Russian educated elite at the very beginning of the nineteenth century, and the concept 'liberalism' as a label for constitutionalist political practices took shape around 1816–19.[2] However, the meaning of the term remained vague, which allowed its application to rather different ideas and groups that vaguely resembled their counterparts in Western Europe; this was often the reason for denying the 'authenticity' of Russian liberalism. Because of this ambiguity, there is no common opinion regarding the starting point of Russian liberalism as a particular set of social and political ideas. Those who use this term in a broad sense move it back in time to the middle of the eighteenth[3] or the beginning of the nineteenth centuries.[4] Others take as a benchmark the preparation of reforms in the 1860s.[5] Many scholars identify the beginnings of the intellectual history of liberalism in Russia with conceptions developed in the 1840–50s by intellectuals affiliated with the Westernizers' (*zapadniki*) circle – Timofey Granovsky, Konstantin Kavelin and Boris Chicherin.[6] Liberal political parties appeared in Russia in 1905, during the first revolution, when they were legalized. There were two major liberal parties – the Constitutional

Democrats Party (formally the Party of People's Freedom, informally the Kadets) and the Union of the 17th of October (informally the Oktiabrists) – and several smaller ones. None of them used the word 'liberal' in the party name because due to its discrepant connotations, it could not be a trustworthy label.[7] It might be argued that up to the beginning of the twentieth century, the concept 'liberalism' had passed the stages of semantic transformation and translation described by Jörn Leonhard's chapter in this volume.

In the USSR, the pre-1917 liberal tradition became a shadowy part of the narrative of the 'liberation movement' (*osvoboditel'noe dvizhenie*) that culminated in the Bolshevik Revolution: it was portrayed as weak, half-hearted and irrelevant to the actual problems of Russian society. Opportunities for the academic study of this tradition were considerably limited. According to the testimony of Victor Prilenskiy, a scholar of early Russian liberalism, 'in the years of the absolute domination of Marxism-Leninism any mention of liberalism, in particular Russian, should be followed by a considerable measure of relentless criticism, and not just criticism, but disdain'.[8] Even in the mid 1980s, when I commenced my studies of liberalism, this term had to be coupled with the adjective 'bourgeois'. This meant that it could not refer to 'our' experience and pointed either to alien Western ideas or to the 'old' and fallacious national tradition. However, even then, liberalism was not considered to be as 'bad' as conservatism or nationalism.

According to my records, it was in 1987–88 that the words 'liberal' and 'liberalism' began to be employed in contemporary domestic discourse. Remarkably, it appeared to be used both by sympathizers and critics. For example, Nina Andreeva, the author of the notorious letter in the newspaper *Sovetskaia Rossija* criticizing Mikhail Gorbachev's perestroika policy, wrote about a 'left-liberal socialism' that contrasts the idea of the value of the individual with proletariat collectivism and tends towards cosmopolitism.[9] A few months earlier, in his equally famous article in the magazine *Novyi mir*, Igor Kliamkin articulated the 'left-liberal' programme of perestroika, arguing for a new synthesis of the liberal tradition of Westernizers and Slavophiles.[10] By that time, however, this tradition had essentially been 'forgotten'. Those who were eager to be counted under the liberal banner had to reinvent it almost from scratch.

The Political Trajectory of Post-Soviet Russian Liberalism

With the commencing of economic and political reforms in post-Soviet Russia, the perspectives of liberalism became a matter of active public discussion. Many people in the early 1990s shared the frame of mind reflected in Francis Fukuyama's conception of 'the end of history'. Liberal ideology, as the most obvious alternative to Soviet orthodoxy, seemed to be the most appropriate justification of the forthcoming transformations that would see totalitarian institutions substituted by a market economy and democracy. In Russia, as well as in the other Eastern European countries – at least at the first stage of reforms – liberal ideas were taken up with genuine enthusiasm.[11] But dissatisfaction with the initial results of the reforms made the slogans of politicians who called themselves liberals much less popular. The faith in a quick 'return to normality' was replaced with disillusionment with the 'Western recipes'. However, neither enthusiasm nor dissatisfaction was based on a clear understanding of the meaning of liberalism. The survey of value attitudes conducted in 1993 by the 'Public Opinion' Foundation revealed that even the most liberal-minded respondents adopted liberal values rather selectively; freedom, autonomy, tolerance, rule of law, etc. were often misunderstood and seemed to have no deep roots in the 'material' aspects of respondents' everyday lives.[12] Hence, in the mid 1990s, Russia was at an early stage of adopting liberal ideas, with no guarantee that this process would be successful.

In the 1990s, liberalism as a political programme became one of several currently competing alternatives – not the most popular one, but still influential. However, its relative success was brief: in the mid 2000s, following the transformation of the party system initiated by President Vladimir Putin, the liberal parties became marginalized. In effect, they never enjoyed firm electoral support. Neither one of the liberal parties or electoral blocs ever gained more than 15 per cent of the seats in the State Duma – the lower chamber of the Russian Parliament. From election to election the results became less and less satisfactory. Until 2003, the State Duma was formed through a mixed electoral system, with one half of the seats distributed by a majoritarian, and one half by a proportional, system with a 5 per cent barrier. Liberal parties had not surpassed the 5 per cent barrier since 1999; with several mandates in electoral districts, they could obtain 29 (Sojuz pravykh sil) and 20 (Yabloko) seats out of 450. In 2003, they only obtained three at that time (Soiuz pravykh sil) and four (Yabloko) mandates in electoral districts. And since 2007, after the introduction of a proportional system with a 7 per cent barrier, both parties have lost representation in the State Duma. In 2011, according to official results, Yabloko obtained 3.43 per cent and 'Pravoe delo' (the successor of Soiuz pravykh sil) 0.6 per cent of votes. There were accusations of fraud in the 2011 campaign that probably affected the actual results of liberal parties (though hardly to a large degree). Both parties failed to gain seats in the State Duma. In 2016, the elections took place after a new reform that brought back the mixed electoral system with a 5 per cent barrier. However, not one liberal party was able to return their representatives to parliament.

Some scholars consider the marginalization of liberal parties in the mid 2000s a result of political reforms aimed at the creation of a limited number of strong parties and the elimination of smaller ones, as well as of unfair competition – there is a suspicion that electoral results are distorted by the semi-legal interference of so-called 'administrative resources' as well as through fraud.[13] Other scholars attribute liberalism's electoral failings to the poor performance of liberal parties and politicians[14] or to organizational and strategic errors in party-building.[15]

Despite the weak representation of the liberal parties in the State Duma, many reputed liberals held positions in the government during 1991–93, when the cabinet of Yegor Gaidar launched market-oriented economic reforms, as well as later. It provides opponents with the opportunity to blame liberals for political mistakes that had unfortunate consequences for the country at large.

The political marginalization of liberalism in Russia in the 2000s was determined not only by the unfavourable circumstances caused by Putin's authoritarian reforms (though that factor should not be underestimated), but also by the particular form in which it was introduced into post-Soviet political discourse. Shaping the image of *liberalism*, politicians who were considered liberals reproduced certain visions of the concept, within the framework of which some elements of liberal tradition were considered urgent and others less relevant. Their choice was particularly important because the general public had little theoretical knowledge and no practical experience of non-communist ideologies. This also applied to those who were considered liberals, but who were not well acquainted with the liberal tradition in Russia and other countries. So, the emerging representations of liberalism were evidently determined by the education, former social experience and communicative practices[16] of their advocates, and also by the liberal ideas that were most salient in the West at that time. Of course, after 1991, liberalism became the subject of intensive academic scholarship. Many works were translated and republished, and much effort was invested in the 'revival' of the Russian liberal tradition.[17] Hence, up to the 2000s, there was a solid body of literature relating to Western and Russian liberalism. But the political fate of the latter was largely determined by the set of ideas with which it became associated at the beginning of the 1990s as well as with the performance of leaders and parties that were reputedly liberal.

In this chapter, I will analyse this set of ideas based on my previous research into the programmes and public rhetoric of the two major political organizations of this segment of the political spectrum in the mid 1990s – the Democratic Choice of Russia party and the public association (and, since 2001, political party) Yabloko.[18] I shall then attempt to discover connections between what liberal politicians and public intellectuals meant by liberalism in the 1990s and the meanings of the term circulating in current discourse that refers to its crisis. In so doing, I will focus not on the political performance of liberals, but on how their rhetoric and public activity shaped the image of liberalism in post-Soviet Russia.

Liberalism as a Quest for Modernization

The term 'liberalism' can be applied to different things: it may refer to certain traditions of political thought, to a set of liberal values, to the 'moderate progressive' part of the political spectrum[19] or to a set of social and political institutions and practices that include religious tolerance, freedom of discussion, the restriction of state intervention in private life, constitutionalism, the rule of law, representative government, division of powers and free elections, as well as an economy based on private property, the market and freedom of contract. At the end of the twentieth century, liberalism was developed in Russia mostly in the latter sense, as a quest for modernization, as a political ideology that asserted the possibility of creating Western-type political and economic institutions, and that outlined the ways of achieving this goal. More than ever before, liberalism became associated with straightforward 'Westernism'.

Liberalism as a quest for modernization was most successful in Russia in 1989–91, when it was represented as an ideology of anticommunism. The reasons for this success were much more connected with the general enthusiasm, caused by the collapse of the communist regime, than with well-thought-out programmes proposed by 'democrats' (the common label for all political currents that supported the transition towards a market economy and democracy). At that time, such programmes barely existed. During the break-up of communism, liberal terminology was used by politicians whose ideological positions differed greatly. Many of those who called themselves 'liberals' did not deserve that description in any sense (the best example is the populist Liberal-Democratic Party of Vladimir Zhirinovsky, created in 1990). In countries with established liberal traditions – even if liberal values are widespread – people feel that they need some special grounds to call themselves 'liberals'. As J. Szacki put it, 'even though there is no precise definition of liberalism anywhere ... where it has a longer history this lack is somewhat made up for by the existence of precedents and stereotypes, which prevent people from letting the concept of liberalism stand for anything they wish'.[20] In Russia, as well as in Eastern Europe, liberalism was perceived as the most obvious alternative to communism during the first years of the democratic reforms, so it became a common label for politicians who developed anticommunist ideas.[21] However, in the mid 1990s, the disillusionment with 'liberal' reforms rendered the boundaries in politics clearer, and liberalism became limited to a particular part of the political spectrum.

In the mid 1990s, several Russian parties and movements were considered 'liberal' (though none of them used that term as an exclusive label of choice; the terms 'Democrats' and 'Liberals' at that time were synonymous, and the former was employed more often than the latter): Democratic Choice of Russia (DCR, led by Yegor Gaidar), Yabloko (Grigory Yavlinsky), *Vperiod, Rossia* (Boris Fiodorov), Obschee delo (Irina Hakamada), the Party of Economic Freedom (Konstantin Borovoi), etc. The liberal section of the party spectrum in Russia was highly fragmented from the very beginning, a factor that contributed to its political weakness. There were different currents of liberal ideas, all of which were represented by more than one political party or movement. Scholars distinguished between radical, social and national liberalism. The first was associated with the programme and political practices of the DCR, the second with Yabloko and some smaller liberal movements, and the third with Sergei Shakhrai's Party of Russian Unity and Agreement (which abandoned the political arena after failing at the second elections to the State Duma in 1995).[22] The following analysis is based on the discourses of the two longest-lived liberal political organizations: the political party DCR and the public association (since 2001, a political party) Yabloko.[23]

In order to deal with such fuzzy and heterogeneous political programmes, scholars require a definition of liberalism that can provide some criteria for their analysis. Of course, to define any 'ism' is a problematic task, because any definition constructs a particular understanding of 'the essence' of a multiform ideology. I follow the approach proposed by the Polish scholar Jerzy Szacki in his work on liberalism in Eastern Europe. According to Szacki, we should study the ideas of the politicians and ideologists who call themselves (and whom others call) liberals, despite differences between them and liberals in Western countries, though he also insisted on a conceptual analysis of their programmes, 'in which some knowledge about different varieties of liberalism and a personal view on liberalism in general are required'.[24] A similar approach to the identification of liberalism was also employed by some scholars of Western liberalism. Thus, Michael Freeden wrote that 'a liberal would be one who defined himself as such, or who was considered as such by his contemporaries, but also one whose political and social thought revolved round issues that had always concerned liberals'.[25] Hence, an approach based on the 'reputation' of those who profess to be liberals should be complemented by conceptual analysis, grounded in certain ideas about the historical heritage of liberalism and about its core principles.

At the end of the twentieth century, as well as earlier, liberalism in the Russian context meant certain 'civilizational choices' associated with taking a specific side in the long debate between Westernism and Fundamental Nationalism (Slavophilism, Nativism (*pochvennichestvo*), etc.), a debate that recommenced with every modernizing effort, although some differences between the DCR and Yabloko remained in that respect.

The ideologists of the DCR were probably the most radical Westernizers in Russian history. They argued for a drastic change of the existing social order so as to become 'like the West'. In the words of Andrey Kozyrev, the Minister of Foreign Affairs from 1990 to 1996 and one of the party leaders, 'our "supertask" is literally to pull ourselves up by the bootstraps ... into the club of the most developed democratic countries. Only by moving along this path will Russia gain the national self-consciousness and self-respect that it needs so much, and tread on firm ground'.[26] Less emotionally, but more thoroughly, similar ideas were developed by the former Prime Minister Yegor Gaidar. According to his conception, Russia occupies a place somewhere between the East and the West: whilst under the cultural and ideological influence of the West since at least the seventeenth century, it preserved for a long time the Eastern type of economic and political structures. Russian history during the past three centuries was determined by the struggle of two strategies of 'accelerated modernization': the first assumed the assimilation of the ready-made products of Western civilization instead of adopting necessary economic structures and was aimed at growth at the cost of mining all resources to the full; the second strategy was connected with the development of Russian institutions in a manner similar to those of the West – it was predicated on the creation of stimuli for self-development, but demanded the restriction of the state's activity. Both strategies reacted to the challenge of the West. In the words of Gaidar, 'to replace virtue with need, the conflict between those two strategies was called "our peculiar way", though it was actually the struggle between the two ways in circumstances in which it was impossible to choose either of them'.[27] The alternative of 'civilized', 'liberal capitalism' proposed by the DCR was considered as a realization of the second, intensive strategy.

The latter strategy was represented as the realization of universal social and economic laws that would work in Russia in spite of its cultural and historical peculiarities. In Gaidar's words, 'our main task is to solve strategic problems of the state, i.e. to complete the market reforms and create a steady, dynamic, rich, Western type society in our country', though he specified that by this he 'does not mean a crazy unification of cultures'.[28] The leaders of the DCR argued that 'universal' liberal values and institutions are entirely appropriate for Russia, even if in adapted form. They consequently concentrated their efforts on the technological aspects of the problem, seeking ways to implement 'civilized' institutions.

Yabloko's ideology was less decisive in this respect: its leaders expressed far less confidence in the easy assimilation of liberal institutions in Russia and tended to stress the difficulties of post-Soviet transformation. According to Vladimir Lukin, Russia encounters the problem of essential 'civilisation differences' on its path towards liberal institutions: 'The experience of the 1990s demonstrated probably even more clearly than the former experience of confrontation, that Russia and the West live in different fields of civilisation, have different historical traditions ... There are obvious distinctions in civilisations, and all attempts to ignore them have not and will not secure positive results for Russia.'[29] These cultural distinctions should be taken into consideration. This is why Yabloko considered a purely technological approach to liberal reforms irrelevant. In the opinion of Sergei Mitrokhin (the formal leader of the party from 2008 to 2015), the mistake of 'those Russian liberals who were orientated towards the West' was in 'defending technologies of reforms that, being effective in the other countries, in Russia met with a strong resistance of the national mentality, because they contradicted the dominant forms of social conscience and behaviour of the Russians. In spite of their abstract virtues such political technologies cannot suit Russian national interests'.[30] The ideologists of Yabloko saw a transition to Western liberal institutions as desirable, but problematic.

In the 1990s, the main point of concern and the main source of disagreement of the liberals was the strategy of economic reforms. Both the DCR and Yabloko considered the effective transformation of post-Soviet economics as a guarantee of the democratization of political life, the successful reform of state government, the development of social welfare, the improvement of Russia's international positions, etc. But their programmes of economic reforms were different. The distinctions concerned not so much the list of the basic issues, but their priorities and the role of the state.

The DCR supported the strategy of reform initiated in 1992 by the government led (though not headed at that time) by Yegor Gaidar. The party programme held that the liberalization of economics and financial stabilization were not the only possible way of reviving the destroyed economy, but also the most appropriate path towards its transformation. In Gaidar's words, the Russian government in 1991 was forced 'to start up a market mechanism immediately, with no preparation', assuming that it would be possible to 'build in' necessary details in the process.[31] Gaidar and his colleagues repudiated the charges of taking the wrong route. They claimed that the further problems resulted from the inconsistency in following the line on liberalization and privatization. In the long run, even if the reforms of 1991–96 created the unpleasant reality of 'nomenclature capitalism', the DCR's general line of politics had to be the struggle for further liberal economic reforms that would finally lead to 'civilised capitalism'.[32]

The ideologists of the DCR argued that the time to make a final choice between the classical liberal or the welfare model had not yet come: even if one wanted to have a welfare state, the road towards it led through a strict limitation of state expenses, including social ones. As a result, in Stephen Fish's words, 'post-Soviet Russian liberalism has combined social laissez-aller with a large measure of economic laissez-faire'.[33]

Yabloko's economic programme proposed a more gradual variant of reforms and criticized the policies of Gaidar's government. According to the 1995 party programme, 'the liberalisation of prices and economic connections ... can and should be achieved gradually; those processes should be started at different times in various sectors of economics, depending on the results of institutional and structural changes ... The choice of an orthodox variant of stabilisation policies for the transformation of the Russian economy was a serious strategic mistake'.[34] In the opinion of Grigory Yavlinsky, Yabloko's leader, 'the Russian economy was not damaged or injured by command centralisation, it was created by it'; therefore, pure liberalization was insufficient to make it work according to the laws of the market. The task was to make institutional and structural changes and thus to create conditions for activating market laws. But it needed additional efforts by the state.[35]

Yabloko insisted on the necessity of structural and institutional reforms that would create conditions for a civilized market. It also confirmed that the final choice between models of market economy was a matter for the future, but argued for a more 'social' model with a well-developed welfare state. However, it was remarkable that Yabloko avoided labelling itself as a social-liberal party. In 1996, it proclaimed adherence both to 'liberal and social approaches' (evidently implying that those were different). The *liberal* part of its programme was associated with the defence of private property and free enterprise, competition and rational government, while its *social* part was connected with various aspects of social politics.[36]

Despite the fact that the DCR and Yabloko personified two clearly different versions of liberalism, they both represented liberalism first and foremost as the 'ideology of [civilized] capitalism'. They distinguished between economic liberalism, understood as a movement for free enterprise, competition, guarantees of private property and a small but effective state, and political liberalism, identified as the struggle for human rights, civil society and democracy. The first was seen as the prerequisite for the second. It was precisely this programme of economic liberalism that was interpreted by Yabloko as the liberal part of their ideology. 'Civilized capitalism', the market economy and private property were represented as the key liberal values.

There could be three reasons behind such a vision of liberalism in the post-Soviet context. *First*, the 'economy-centric' character of liberalism in postsocialist countries was a consequence of the fact that economic reforms were the central factor in the break-up of socialism. It was no mere coincidence that there were many professional economists among the leaders of liberal parties. *Second*, the Russian liberals adopted those Western economic theories that seemed to be the most successful in the late 1980s, that is to say, the neoliberal conceptions often referred to as 'the Washington Consensus'. However, according to Peter Rutland, even if the 'prevailing ideas of the Washington Consensus undoubtedly encouraged Russia's leaders to embrace radical reforms', the actual policies 'diverged considerably from the prevailing neoliberal orthodoxy and were heavily shaped by the self-interest of the elites who were making the policy decisions'.[37] *Third*, liberalism appeared in post-Soviet Russia as an anticommunist ideology that, in contrast to Marxism, sanctified capitalism instead of socialism, but employed the same pattern of justification:[38] a 'proper' form of property must be the basis of the 'good society'. It was suggested that all social, political, national etc. problems would automatically be solved through a successful economic transformation. Economic transformation was portrayed as the 'magic key' that would help to solve all problems. During the first years of post-Soviet transformation, this type of thinking facilitated a vision of liberalism as the most obvious alternative to a totalitarian order. But it also led to the neglect of the other important aspects of the liberal order. This tendency was most obvious in the ideology and practices of the DCR, which explicitly proclaimed the struggle for 'civilized capitalism' as its main task. The leaders of Yabloko were less in the thrall of vulgar economism. They considered the development of social welfare, science, education, the rule of law and international politics to be taken into account as no less important tasks. But they represented their desire to develop these spheres, without reliance on the opportunities of the market, as a departure from liberalism. They consequently shared an interpretation of liberalism first and foremost as 'an ideology of building capitalism'. The unwillingness to represent Yabloko as the liberal party stemmed from an identification of 'true' liberalism with neoclassical theories.

Locating the project of 'good capitalism' at the heart of liberalism was the main source of its weakness in post-Soviet Russia. All analyses of surveys demonstrate that 'economic liberalism' had minimal chances of being adopted in Russia: the audience that could support the values of free market economy was rather limited.[39] If liberals in the 1990s could extend their repertoire, foregrounding public discussions over the issues of the rule of law, public administration, the reform of education, the development of a civic nation, etc., they could strengthen their position by attracting a cross-section of educated professionals, many of whom had suffered as a result of economic reforms. Unfortunately, those issues were not actively discussed, even if they were presented in official programmes. Liberalism thus continued to be strongly associated with 'civilized capitalism'.

The next obstacle for liberalism in post-Soviet Russia was conceptualizing the role of the state. Both liberal parties shared the ideal of a 'minimal but effective' state that obviously contrasted with the huge and omnipresent Soviet state. Liberalism was associated with the reduction of state machinery as well as state regulation of social and economic life, and the leaders of the DCR and Yabloko never missed an opportunity to emphasize this vector of change in their public rhetoric. More radically, the DCR insisted on 'breaking the tradition of the Eastern type of state' that is 'programmed for total suppression' of the economy and society.[40] Yabloko was more moderate, but it also stood for 'the state for the people', which meant decisive changes in Soviet practices.[41]

At the same time, the realization of the post-Soviet reforms presupposed an active role for the state in creating the liberal order. The question was how to reconcile the liberal ideal of a minimal state with its constructivist activity. Liberalism does not exclude social engineering, but normally it is aimed at the development of already-existing institutions. In the post-communist countries, not only liberal institutions but also social structures that provide their basis –legitimate private property, the middle class, civic society, etc. – had to be created from scratch. The DCR and Yabloko entertained different conceptions of the role of the state at the transition stage. According to the DCR, its activity should be limited to the formation of necessary conditions for a free market. Its leaders stood for minimizing administrative regulation; they maintained that welfare functions should be coordinated with economic growth. Of course, in a society lacking a habitual feeling of social security, the idea of cutting state welfare functions could only be unpopular. In accordance with its social liberal orientation, Yabloko supported a more dirigist role for the state, arguing for direct regulation at the opening phase; its leaders saw welfare functions as a priority that the state could not sideline. However, they considered the active role of the state as temporary, determined by the transitory conditions of the economy.

As a result, irrespective of the actual content of party programmes (much more welfare-permissive in the case of Yabloko), liberalism became associated with the idea of a minimal state. And it was an unfortunate choice, given that the collapse of the Soviet state machinery brought with it a significant dissolution of the social order, 'an unrestricted liberty' (*bespredel* in Russian, a term that became popular at the beginning of the 1990s) that caused insecurity and violation of individual rights. This aspect of the problem was essentially neglected by the liberals. In the words of Stephen Fish, even if 'Russia's social chaos cannot be blamed entirely on the country's liberal leaders', they could not be ignorant about it, but 'have shown gross negligence on issues of crime and corruption'.[42] However, to a great extent, it resulted from a perception of the liberal agenda that was widely shared in other European countries (the British case, as explored by Michael Freeden, was an evident exception). As Stephen Holmes observed, one of the lessons the liberals should learn from the Russian experience was that 'the largest and most reliable human rights organisation is the liberal state. Beyond the effective reach of such a state, rights will not be consistently protected or enforced'.[43] Russian liberals could hardly have known about it, but if they had, they would have been more successful.

The political programme of both liberal parties included the standard set of individual freedoms, the rule of law, the division of power and representative democracy; however, their approaches to political reforms differed slightly. The watershed was the attitude to the constitutional crisis of October 1993, when the conflict between President Boris Yeltsin and the Supreme Soviet led to armed clashes in the streets of Moscow. It resulted in the adoption of the new Constitution in a referendum in December 1993, which vested wide powers in the president. 'The Democrats' found themselves facing an uneasy choice: either to support this result despite the doubtful legitimacy of the victorious side, or to criticize it as a forcible cessation of the power of the legitimate representative body and an infringement of democracy. There were different personal decisions on that matter, but in its official documents, the DCR actually supported the division of power introduced by the new Constitution because a strong president was considered to be a guarantee for the continuation of reforms that lacked firm electoral support. The programme of the party backed the idea of governmental subordination to the president, but insisted on the differentiation of the functions of the government as the official executive body, and the president's Administration and Security Council as subordinate technical bodies.[44] It gave the opponents of the DCR a reason to argue that they 'treat democracy as the dictatorship of democrats'.[45] Yabloko assessed the new political system more critically, arguing for a constitutional amendment that would make Russia a parliamentary republic, but suggested it for the future, as it was also concerned that the domination of the Communists in parliament would set back reform.[46] Despite their differences, the positions of both liberal parties was determined by the understanding that, insofar as the desired reforms lacked mass support, strong presidential power was the only hope for the minority that strove for market and democratization. Ultimately this turned out to be a mistake, as in the 2000s, the construction of power adopted in 1993 facilitated the

antiliberal reforms of President Putin that, in addition to its other consequences, significantly affected the liberal parties.

Probably even more decisive was those parties' attitudes to the issues of
nation-building, the imperial legacy and Russia's place in the world. Even if
these issues are not considered as the core of a liberal agenda, they were quite
often a matter of concern for liberals. As has become retrospectively clear,
they were critically important for a country with new borders, a new ethnic
composition and a new role in the international arena. Two major liberal
parties were, for the most part, preoccupied with these issues. Their position
might be characterized as a moderate civic nationalism of the type expressed
in different contexts by J.S. Mill, T. Masaryk and W. Wilson, and in Russia
by B. Chicherin, P. Miljukov and P. Struve. It assigns primary importance to
the interests of individuals over the interests of the nation and of society over
the state. It considers citizenship as a criterion of belonging to the nation and
insists on ethnic nondiscrimination. In the particular context of the 1990s, it
also meant the endorsement of the break-up of the Soviet Union, a principled
refusal to restore the empire and a reconsideration of national priorities. In
Gaidar's words, there was a clear alternative: either 'restoration of a military
superpower' or 'renouncing imperial ambitions, and emancipating society
for free economic, cultural and social development'; these things 'could not
coexist, both as a matter of principle and due to a lack of resources'.[47] In the
same vein, the programme of Yabloko declared: 'Our aim is the wellbeing
of Russia. But we are against building the greatness of the country on the
blood and bones of its citizens.'[48] Both the DCR and Yabloko had to confront
the Chechen war. They blamed both sides of the military conflict, which
meant that they actively criticized the actions of the federal centre. They
also opposed the idea of interference in the sovereign affairs of the former
Soviet republics under the pretence of defending the rights of Russia's ethnic
population. Their opponents perceived this as a refusal to defend 'national
interests'. This stance, coupled with the above-mentioned advocacy of the
minimal state, saddled the liberals with the reputation of an 'antinational'
political force. Interestingly, before 1917, right-wing opponents also associated liberalism with cosmopolitianism and the lack of 'national orientation',
so the previous meaning was 'restored' in a new context.[49]

No less problematic was the issue of foreign policy strategy. Both the
DCR and Yabloko held that foreign policy should be subjected to domestic
policy. They argued that Russia should abstain from superpower ambitions
and collaborate with other countries for the development of an international
climate that would facilitate its transition to markets and democracy. Liberals
believed that after the end of the Cold War, former enemies had become
partners, and Russia should seek allies among Western democratic countries.

At the beginning of the 1990s, Russian diplomacy, headed by Andrey Kozyrev – one of the DCR leaders – moved in that direction. However, the decision to enlarge the North Atlantic Treaty Organization (NATO) to the East, and especially NATO's military operation against the Federal Republic of Yugoslavia during the Kosovo War in 1999, proved the failure of this strategy. These events created deep disillusionment with the West and significantly contributed to the loss of popularity of the DCR, and of liberalism in general, as far as it was associated with Westernism.

Finally, there was a problem of political tactics, given the circumstances of the lack of sufficient social support. Liberals could not therefore expect to obtain much political influence through elections. The choice was between collaboration with an illiberal government that would distort liberal proposals even while accepting them, and an oppositional status that offered few chances of attaining power in the near future. Both alternatives had negative consequences. Collaboration with illiberal power entailed moral responsibility for unpopular 'reforms from above' that harmed the image of liberals, but did not guarantee the fulfilment of their plans. However, the refusal to collaborate was also unfortunate, as it led to what the patriarch of the Russian liberal tradition Boris Chicherin described as 'oppositional liberalism', i.e. 'a liberal current that ... does not seek any positive goals, but just enjoys the splendour of the status of opposition'.[50]

The DCR and Yabloko solved this dilemma in different ways. Having been created to support the acting government following defeat in the parliamentary elections in 1995, the DCR had consciously adopted the role of the 'party of experts' that would formally or informally collaborate with the government (the fact that the government in Russia does not depend on support of the Duma facilitates this tactic). Collaboration with an illiberal government was considered to be 'the real way' towards 'the strategic promotion of our ideas', but it was not conducive to the party's popularity. However, it became the main reason for blaming liberalism for the negative results of state policy, while disregarding the extent to which their ideas were fulfilled. And Yabloko preferred the role of 'democratic opposition' without any real prospect of the opportunity to gain power, thus fully confronting the same problem described by Chicherin. The inability to realize its stated ideas gave it the appearance of a 'party of moralists'. Eventually both strategies turned out to be unsuccessful, taking into account the fact that Yabloko and the parties that succeeded the DCR had finally lost their support, and liberals came to be blamed for the policy mistakes of the 1990s.

In sum, in the 1990s, liberalism became strongly associated with the unpopular ideas of 'civilized capitalism' and a minimal state, as well as with the principles of civic nationalism and the rejection of imperial ambitions that in the long run became less favoured. Besides, it had clear connotations with Westernism that made it vulnerable to changing attitudes towards the West. It was also significant that liberals, despite their unquestionable adherence to the rule of law, democracy and human rights, could not – because of their political weakness and, frequently, for tactical reasons – defend these values effectively and consistently.

Post-Soviet liberalism was not a direct continuation of the pre-1917 political tradition. They shared some basic principles like Westernism, 'antinationalism' and a critical attitude to the state, yet distinctions were nonetheless significant. The 'revolutionary', 'radical liberalism' of the 1990s was an obvious deviation from the prerevolutionary tradition that emphasized the value of law[51] and guarantees of individual rights, and insisted on moderate, gradual means for implementing liberal aims.'[52]

The Crisis of Russian Liberalism in the Eyes of Opponents and Analysts

The peculiar features of post-Soviet Russian liberalism contributed to its negative image in public discourse that has become increasingly salient since the mid 2000s. This evolution resulted from the general political development towards authoritarianism, particularly after the 'coloured revolutions' of 2004–5, that is to say, mass protest movements supposedly supported from abroad that led to coup d'états in the neighbouring countries. Since the beginning of the 2000s, access of liberal politicians to the central TV channels – the most popular means of public communication – has been limited by unofficial censorship, while their critics have enjoyed more opportunities for expression. Moreover, the evolution of the official discourse was not favourable to the liberals. Even if Putin and Dmitry Medvedev – Putin's successor to the presidential office from 2007 to 2011 – never explicitly discarded the liberal aims of the 1990s and from time to time spoke in liberal voices, the idea of the 'revival of Great Russia' that became central to their policy was clearly inconsistent with the programme of post-Soviet liberalism with its critical attitude towards the idea of a strong state.[53] The failure at the parliamentary elections of 2003 became a clear indicator of the crisis of liberalism in Russia. The discourse of the liberals, and of their opponents and analysts, concerning the reasons for this unhappy condition reveals a further development of the meaning of 'liberalism' that partly follows from the peculiarities of its representations in the 1990s and partly reflects the particular ideological oppositions of the 2000s. Several features of post-Soviet liberalism are considered to be crucial factors in its evident decline in the mid 2000s.

Liberals are often portrayed as a Westernized elite seeking to engineer reforms from above without taking into consideration either the opinions of the conservative majority or national traditions. Mikhail Khodorkovsky noted that 'the Russian liberalism has failed because it ignored, first, some important national and historical traditions and, second, vitally important interests of the great majority of the Russian people'.[54] Of course, any reform encounters the problem of mass support. However, the manner in which market reforms were communicated in Russia actually gave some cause for such criticism: Yegor Gaidar and his team represented their case for change in a purely academic manner, appealing to the experience of other countries as if it represented 'objective' economic laws. They did not significantly modify their arguments even when the painful effects of the reforms became apparent. As S. Fish commented, 'liberal politicians who have served in Yeltsin's government, such as Gaidar, as well as those who have not, such as Yavlinsky, have consistently shown far more interest in educating and edifying voters than in listening to them, convincing them, and mobilizing public support for reform'.[55] This contributed to the image of liberalism as a doctrine addressing the needs of a prosperous minority.

Combined with the obvious economocentrism and unwillingness to support state paternalism, this image gave opponents a reason to represent liberalism 'as an economic and social doctrine preaching the necessity to sacrifice the health of a society to the health of the economy'.[56] Liberalism is strongly associated with the de-statization (*razgosudarstvlenie*) of the economy, denationalization and the reduction of the state's social responsibility. The fact that in the 2000s some reputed liberals held important governmental positions offers grounds for arguing that in spite of the prominent role of the state, the economic policy of Putin and Medvedev has remained 'neoliberal'. According to Peter Rutland, this inaccurate term is used for tactical reasons. It 'appealed to the laws of Western economic science to camouflage an asset grab by their friends and allies', while their opponents 'pointed to neoliberalism to "prove" that the reformers were merely serving the interests of the West'.[57] Either way, *liberalism* has been firmly linked to a certain type of economic policy that, according to its opponents, was practised by the government, even if the *liberals* are not formally in power. A good example of such arguments is the lecture 'The Limits of Liberalism for Russia' given by former Prime Minister Yevgeny Primakov at Moscow State University in 2012. Primakov argued that 'in spite of Putin's restraints, the neoliberals champion an essential decrease of the economic role of the state as owner'; however, in the Russian case, there are clear 'red lines' that should not be crossed as 'it is impossible to reach the level of competition that is necessary for scientific and technical progress ... without state interference'.[58] As a result of such interpretations, liberalism in Russian public discourse is often identified with a weakening of the state, which is deemed to be a contributory factor to social insecurity.

The wary attitude of the liberals towards the state, as well as their willing acceptance of the collapse of the Soviet Union and their critical assessment of Russia's imperial past, gave their critics grounds for blaming them for antipatriotism and antinationalism. According to one of those critics, 'today we deal with anti-national, anti-Russian liberalism that regards the traditional Russian statehood and its pretence for great power status ... as its main enemies'.[59] Seeking to modernize their country, the post-Soviet liberals shared the typical attitude of the Russian intelligentsia that Peter Struve in 1909 called 'apostasy from the state' (*otschepenstvo ot gosudarstva*): in their public rhetoric, they overstated their critical approach towards state activity, which led to negative assessments of any performance of that institution. It would be unfair to assert that the liberals do not appreciate the need to overcome that attitude.[60] However, in the 2000s, when deprived of access to the mass channels of public communication, liberals exploited the rare occasions of appearing on TV talk-shows to criticize illiberal state policies, thus confirming their reputation as 'nonpatriots'.

Finally, an important source of weakness of post-Soviet Russian liberalism is its strong identification with Westernism that not only supports claims for its irrelevance to the national context, but also makes it dependent on the fluctuations in public attitudes towards the 'West'. The Westernism of early post-Soviet liberalism followed from the need to have a convincing practical ideal that could justify the aims of the liberal reforms. While in the beginning this was actually helpful, it later made liberalism dependent on the sustainability of this ideal. Hence, the more complicated the image of the 'West' in Russia is and the more salient its unfavourable aspects are, the more problematic the tight connection between Russian liberalism and Westernism becomes. As soon as the expansion of NATO to the East made the disagreements between Russia and its Western partners on security issues obvious, the early romantic Westernism that was based on a desire 'to live like in the West' gave way to more critical attitudes. Some of those who perceive the West as a source of threat tend to represent liberalism as 'a weapon' of 'Americanism and globalism' aiming at destroying Russia.[61] This kind of criticism first appeared in the conspirologist fantasies of the extreme Right and Left, but since 2012, it has increasingly become an element of mainstream discourse.

Matters became particularly troublesome after Vladimir Putin's re-election as President in March 2012. His campaign took place in the context of the rise of protest activity in Moscow and some large cities. The liberals played a remarkable (though not a leading) role in the protest movement that started with rallies against fraud in the elections to the State Duma in December 2011 and developed into broader criticism of the regime. In this context, anti-Westernism was actively used as a means to marginalize the opposition. The idea of the opposition of 'ordinary people' against the 'pro-Western intelligentsia' played a significant role in Putin's electoral campaign. After his inauguration, the struggle against the 'pro-Western' opposition had brought about a series of political decisions, probably the most remarkable of which was the Foreign Agents Bill adopted by the State Duma in July 2012. The Bill obliged nongovernmental organizations (NGOs) that 'participate in politics' and are beneficiaries of sponsorship from abroad to register as foreign agents and refer to this status in their publications. The anti-Westernist turn in Russian domestic politics became even more apparent with the annexation of Crimea (based on the results of a referendum held on 16 March 2014), unleashing the war on the east of Ukraine, and the subsequent international sanctions against Russia. The strategy of counterposing the 'patriotic' pro-Putin majority and 'antinational' anti-Putin minority became particularly uncomfortable for the liberals who had been sullied with the reputation of 'Westernists'. In the midst of the anti-Westernist propaganda, they became stigmatized as the West's 'fifth column'. Phrases such as 'condemning to liberalism', 'the impasse of the liberal consciousness' or 'a good liberalism is a dead liberalism', which were previously not restricted to the extreme Right and Left press, could now be found in respectable national newspapers.

Even those who consider themselves liberals admit that the policy of the Western countries does not always correspond to proclaimed liberal ideals. As Andrey Tsygankov put it, 'today not only in Russia, but in most of the world, the West is more often associated with geopolitical games than with ideals of tolerance, justice and freedom'.[62] In the twenty-first century, especially following the 2008 economic crisis, 'the West' had lost the image of a group of flourishing societies with advanced economies and a considerable measure of social justice. Besides, due to a different historical experience, the Russian public is not receptive to postmodernist values like multiculturalism or tolerance to certain kinds of cultural diversity. As soon as liberalism is associated with such 'Western' practices, it loses its appeal in the eyes of most Russians.

The current crisis of Russian liberalism is to a great extent a result of the general path of evolution of the political regime. However, the way in which it became represented on the political scene in the 1990s was significant for its subsequent failure. Liberalism in Russia is associated with Westernism, an obsession with market economic reforms, a paternalist approach to the illiberal majority, criticism of the authoritarian regime and renunciation of imperial ambitions. In the context of political and ideological shifts of the 2000s and 2010s, this combination of ideas has facilitated the development of liberalism's negative image and of its political marginalization.

Olga Malinova is Professor of the School of Political Science at the National Research University Higher School of Economics, Moscow, and chief research fellow of the Institute of Scientific Information for Social Sciences, Russian Academy of Sciences. She is the author of books and articles on political ideologies and political discourse, symbolic politics, politics of memory and Russian identity construction. Her recent publications include 'The Embarrassing Centenary: Reinterpretation of the 1917 Revolution in the Official Historical Narrative of Post-Soviet Russia (1991–2017)', *Nationalities Papers* 46(2) (2018), 272–89; and 'Russian Identity and the "Pivot to the East"', *Problems of Post-Communism* (2019, forthcoming).

Notes

Some of the research in this chapter was first presented in O. Malinova, 'Konstruirovanie "liberalisma" v post-sovetskoi Rossii: nasledie 1990-kh v ideologicheskikh bitvah 2000-kh' ('Constructing "Liberalism" in Post-Soviet Russia: The Legacy of the 1990s in the Ideological Battles of the 2000s'), *Politeia* no. 84 (1) (2017), 6–28.

1. There is a large corpus of literature describing different stages of the intellectual and political development of liberalism in Russia, but few comprehensive works. The first attempt was a book by the Russian émigré Victor Leontovich published in Germany and later in a Russian translation in Paris: V. Leontovich, *Geschichte des Liberalismus in Russland*, Frankfurt am Main, 1957; V. Leontovich, *Istorija liberalizma v Rossiii 1762–1914*, Paris, 1980. There is a fundamental book by Andrzej Walicki focusing on the most important aspects of pre-1917 Russian liberalism that strikingly distinguished it from other currents of social thought – its commitment to the rule of law: A. Walicki, *Legal Philosophies of Russian Liberalism*, Notre Dame, IN, 1992. There are also several edited volumes, the fruits of recent scholarship aimed at reconstructing the legacy of Russian liberalism: V. Pustarnakov and I. Hudushina (eds), *Liberalizm v Rossii*, Moscow, 1996; B.S. Itenberg and V.V. Shelophaev (eds), *Rossijskije liberaly*, Moscow, 2001; A. Kara-Murza (ed.), *Rossijskij liberalism: idei i ljudi*, Moscow, 2007; V. Shelokhaev et al. (eds), *Rossijskij liberalism serediny XVIII – nachala XX veka*, Moscow, 2010. For a useful semantic analysis of the evolution of the concept of 'liberalism' in the nineteenth century, see: M. Kalashnikov, 'Poniatie *liberalisma* v russkom obschestvennom soznanii XIX veka', in A. Miller et al. (eds), *Poniatija*

o Rossii: K istoricheskoi semantike imperskogo perioda, Moscow, 2012, vol. 1, 464–513; L. Bibikova, 'Politicheskaia politcija, conservatory i sotcialisty: igra *liberalizmami* v publichnom i nepublichnom politicheskom prostranstve Rossijskoi imperii v konce XIX – nachale XX veka', in A. Miller et al. (eds), *Poniatija o Rossii: K istoricheskoi semantike imperskogo perioda*, Moscow, 2012, vol. 1, 514–58.

2. Kalashnikov, 'Poniatie *liberalisma*', 472 and 478.

3. Leontovich, *Istorija liberalizma*; Shelokhaev et al. (eds), *Rossijskij liberalism*; Kara-Murza (ed.), *Rossijskij liberalism*.

4. The outline of reforms prepared for Alexander I by the 'Secret Committee' (*Neglasnyi komitet*) headed by Mikhail Speransky is usually labelled as 'liberal', i.e. inspired by European *idées liberales*.

5. V. Pustarnakov, *Liberalizm v Rossii*, Kazan, 2002, 7.

6. V. Prilensky, *Opyt issledovanija mirovozzrenija rannikh russkikh liberalov*, Moscow, 1995; A. Walicki, *Legal Philosophies*; Itenberg and Shelophaev (eds), *Rossijskije liberaly*.

7. Kalashnikov, 'Poniatie *liberalisma*', 510.

8. Prilenskiy, *Opyt issledovanija*, 3.

9. *Sovetskaia Rossija*, 13 March 1988.

10. I. Kliamkin, 'Kakaia ulitsa vedet k khramu?', *Novyi mir* 11 (1987), 150–88.

11. See J. Szacki, *Liberalism after Communism*, Budapest, 1995, 2.

12. B. Kapustin and I. Kliamkin, 'Liberal'nye tsennosti v soznanii rossijan', *Polis* 1 (1994), 68–93; 2 (1994), 39–75.

13. D. White, 'Victims of a Managed Democracy? Explaining the Electoral Decline of the *Yabloko* Party', *Demokratizatsiya* 15 (2007), 209–29.

14. S.M. Fish, 'The Predicament of Russian Liberalism: Evidence from the December 1995 Parliamentary Elections', *Europe-Asia Studies* 49 (1997), 191–220.

15. H.E. Hale, '*Yabloko* and the Challenge of Building a Liberal Party in Russia', *Europe-Asia Studies* 56 (2004), 993–1020.

16. For a useful analysis of political culture of Russian liberals in 1985–91, see A. Lukin, *Political Culture of the Russian 'Democrats'*, Oxford, 2000.

17. For example, the activity of 'The Russian Liberal Inheritance' Foundation (see http://www.rusliberal.ru) resulted not only in the publication of Kara-Murza (ed.), *Rossijskij liberalism*, but also established a number of memorials to prominent liberals in several Russian cities.

18. O. Malinova, *Liberalizm v politicheskom spektre Rossii (na primere partii 'Demokraticheskij vybor Rossi i obschestvennogo ob'edinenia "Yabloko"')*, Moscow, 1998.

19. In prerevolutionary Russia, the word 'liberal' was often used in this sense, referring to adherents of stable and legal constitutional reforms. Radicals sometimes conferred on it epithets such as 'rotten', 'feeble', etc. By contrast, in the 1990s, liberalism became associated with radical reforms. It was therefore not a coincidence that in the 2000s, the opposite approach that supported stability and continuity with the national past was called the 'conservative' one.

20. Szacki, *Liberalism*, 8.
21. Ibid.
22. V. Sogrin, 'Liberalizm v Rossii: peripetii i perspektivy', *Obschestvennye nauki i sovremennost'* 1 (1997), 13–23. Sogrin also applied the term 'social liberalism' to the pro-Kremlin party 'Our Home is Russia', as well as to the electoral programme of President Boris Yeltsin in 1996, but such an interpretation obscures important distinctions between various approaches to post-Soviet reforms.
23. Both these organizations emerged as electoral blocs in 1993, on the eve of the first parliamentary elections. The DCR originated from the 'Choice of Russia' ('Vybor Rossii') bloc created to support economic reforms that the government under Yegor Gaidar initiated in 1992, and was reorganized as a political party in 1994. In 2001, the DCR dissolved itself to become a cofounder of the new right-liberal party 'Union of the Right Forces' ('Soiuz Pravykh Sil'), which in turn made way in 2008 for 'The Right Case' ('Pravoe delo'). *Yabloko* was also formed in 1993 as an electoral bloc (its name is an abbreviation of family names of its three leaders – Yavlinsky, Boldyrev and Lukin) as a coalition of liberal and social-democratic forces. In 2001, it was reorganised as a political party that has functioned since then.
24. Szacki, *Liberalism*: 24.
25. M. Freeden, *The New Liberalism: An Ideology of Social Reform*, Oxford, 1978: 5.
26. A. Kozyrev, *Preobrazhenie*, Moscow, 1995: 22.
27. Y. Gaidar, *Gosudarstvo i evolutsia*, Moscow, 1995: 57.
28. Ibid., 202.
29. V. Lukin and A. Utkin, *Rossia i Zapad: Obschnost' ili otchuzhdenie?*, Moscow, 1995, 142–43.
30. S. Mitrokhin, 'Natsional'nyi interest kak teoreticheskaia problema', *Polis* 1 (1997), 34.
31. Y. Gaidar, *Dni porazhenij i pobed*, Moscow, 1997, 255.
32. Gaidar, *Gosudarstvo i evolutsia*, 162–64.
33. Fish, 'Predicament', 209.
34. *Reformy dlia bol'shinstva: Ob'edinenie "Yabloko"*, Moscow, 1995, 103 and 105.
35. G. Yavlinsky, *Ekonomika Rossii: nasledstvo i vozmozhnosti*, Moscow, 1995, 33.
36. *Reformy dlia bol'shinstva*, 176–81.
37. P. Rutland, 'Neoliberalism and the Russian Transition', *Review of International Political Economy* 20(2) (2013), 332.
38. This feature of liberalism in postcommunist countries was mentioned by several scholars. See B. Ackerman, *The Future of the Liberal Revolution*, New Haven, 1992, 34–35; Szacki, *Liberalism*, 5–9; D. Furman, '"Pereviornutyi istmat?" Ot ideologii perestroika k ideologii "stroitel'stva kapitalizma" v Rossii', *Svobodnaia mysl'* 3 (1995), 15–21.
39. Kapustin and Kliamkin, Liberal'nye tsennosti; cf. A. Riabov, 'Liberalizm mozhet sostoiatsa v nashei strane tol'ko kak sotsial'nyi', *Politicheskij klass* 2 (2006), 23–27; N. Tikhonova, 'Sotsial'nyi liberalism: est' li al'ternativy?', *Obschestvennye nauki i sovremennost'* 2 (2013), 32–44.

40. Gaidar, *Gosudarstvo i evolutsia*, 41.
41. *Reformy dlia bol'shinstva*, 9–10.
42. Fish, 'Predicament', 208.
43. S. Holmes, *What Russia Teaches Us Now: How Weak States Threaten Freedom*, Washington DC, 1997, 4. Retrieved 27 February 2019 from http://www.ucis.pitt.edu/nccccr/1997-810-31-Holmes.pdf.
44. 'Programma partii "Demokraticheskij vybor Rossii"', *Politicheskij kurier partii 'Demokraticheskij vybor Rossii'* 2 (1995), 14.
45. S. Mitrokhin, 'Reabilitatsija demokratii', *Yabloko* 9 (17–24 April 1995).
46. *Materialy k V c'ezdu 'Yabloka'*, Moscow, 1995, part 1, 28–31.
47. Gaidar, *Gosudarstvo i evolutsia*, 185.
48. *Reformy dlia bol'shinstva*, 9–10.
49. L. Bibikova, 'Politicheskaia politsia', 543.
50. B. Chicherin, 'Razlichnye vidy liberalizma', in M. Abramov (ed.), *Opyt russkogo liberalizma*, Moscow, 1997, 44.
51. See Walicki, *Legal Philosophies*.
52. According to Kalashnikov, liberalism was contrasted with revolutionism in Russian public discourse since the 1850s, which later gave it a connotation of spinelessness: Kalashnikov, 'Poniatie *liberalism*', 490 and 510.
53. In 2003, reacting to this new attitude, Anatoly Chubais, one of the leaders of the DCR's successor party, even put forward the idea of Russia as a 'liberal empire'; however, that was too overstated to be supported by his party. See A. Chubais, 'Rossiia kak liberal'naia imperiia', retrieved 27 February 2019 from http://www.prpc.ru/library/civ_09/01.shtml; see also O. Malinova, 'Defining and Redefining Russianness: The Concept of "Empire" in Public Discourses in Post-Soviet Russia', in A. Guelke (ed.), *The Challenges of Ethno-Nationalism*, New York, 2010, 68–69.
54. *Vedomosti*, 29 March 2004. Khodorkovsky is an 'oligarch' and philanthropist, who subsidized the electoral campaigns of the liberal parties. In October 2003, shortly before the parliamentary elections, he was arrested and charged with fraud. The cited letter was written in prison; on publication in a national newspaper, it provoked widespread debate.
55. Fish, 'Predicament', 210.
56. E. Kholmogorov, 'Liberalizm – smert' Rossii', *Molodaia gvardija* 7 (2010), 105.
57. Rutland, 'Neoliberalism', 358.
58. Y. Primakov, 'Predely liberalizma dlia Rossii', *Vestnik Moskovskogo universiteta* 12(6) (2012), 7–8.
59. A.S. Tsipko, 'Razmyshlenija o prirode i prichinakh krakha postsovetskogo liberalizma', *Vestnik analitiki* 17(3) (2004), 20.
60. In particular, that was one of the points in Khodorkovsky's aforementioned letter.
61. A. Dugin, 'Patriotism ili liberalism?', *Politicheskij klass* 1 (2005), 57.
62. A. Tsygankov, 'Sumerki liberalizma: chto sulit porazhenie global'noi reformatsii', *Politicheskij klass* 9 (2005), 53. In order to understand how disillusionment with the Western Other contributed to a reconsideration of liberalism in

the Russian context, see Andrey Tsygankov's very instructive article about the intellectual evolution of the political philosopher Alexander Panarin, who started out as a confirmed Westernizer and ended his life as a nationalist conservative. A. Tsygankov, 'Aleksandr Panarin kak zerkalo russkoi revoliutsii', *Ideologija i politika* 3(1) (2013), 4–36.

Bibliography

Ackerman, B. *The Future of the Liberal Revolution*. New Haven, 1992.

Bibikova, L. 'Politicheskaia politcija, conservatory i sotcialisty: igra *liberalizmami* v publichnom i nepublichnom politicheskom prostranstve Rossijskoi imperii v konce XIX – nachale XX veka', in A. Miller et al. (eds), *Poniatija o Rossii: K istoricheskoi semantike imperskogo perioda* (Moscow, 2012), 514–58.

Chicherin, B. 'Razlichnye vidy liberalizma', in M. Abramov (ed.), *Opyt russkogo liberalizma* (Moscow, 1997), 38–51.

Dugin, A. 'Patriotism ili liberalism?'. *Politicheskij klass* 1 (2005), 57–63.

Fish, S.M. 'The Predicament of Russian Liberalism: Evidence from the December 1995 Parliamentary Elections'. *Europe-Asia Studies* 49 (1997), 191–220.

Freeden, M. *The New Liberalism: An Ideology of Social Reform*. Oxford, 1978.

Furman, D. '"Pereviornutyi istmat?" Ot ideologii perestroika k ideologii "stroitel'stva kapitalizma" v Rossii'. *Svobodnaia mysl'* 3 (1995), 15–21.

Gaidar, Y. *Dni porazhenij i pobed*. Moscow, 1997.

———. *Gosudarstvo i evolutsia*. Moscow, 1995.

Hale, H.E. '*Yabloko* and the Challenge of Building a Liberal Party in Russia'. *Europe-Asia Studies* 56 (2004), 993–1020.

Holmes, S. *What Russia Teaches Us Now: How Weak States Threaten Freedom*. Washington DC, 1997.

Itenberg, B.S., and V.V. Shelophaev (eds). *Rossijskije liberaly*. Moscow, 2001.

Kalashnikov, M. 'Poniatie *liberalism* v russkom obschestvennom soznanii XIX veka', in A. Miller et al. (eds), *Poniatija o Rossii: K istoricheskoi semantike imperskogo perioda*, vol. 1 (Moscow, 2012), 464–513.

Kapustin, B., and I. Kliamkin. 'Liberal'nye tsennosti v soznanii rossijan'. *Polis* 1 (1994), 68–93.

Kara-Murza, A. (ed.). *Rossijskij liberalism: idei i ljudi*. Moscow, 2007.

Kholmogorov, E. 'Liberalizm – smert' Rossii'. *Molodaia gvardija* 7 (2010).

Kliamkin, I. 'Kakaia ulitsa vedet k khramu?'. *Novyi mir* 11 (1987), 150–88.

Kozyrev, A. *Preobrazhenie*. Moscow, 1995.

Leontovich, V. *Geschichte des Liberalismus in Russland*. Frankfurt am Main, 1957.

———. *Istorija liberalizms v Rossii 1762–1914*. Paris, 1980.

Lukin, A. *Political Culture of the Russian 'Democrats'*. Oxford, 2000.

Lukin, V., and A. Utkin. *Rossia i Zapad: Obschnost' ili otchuzhdenie?* Moscow, 1995.

Malinova, O. 'Defining and Redefining Russianness: The Concept of "Empire" in Public Discourses in Post-Soviet Russia', in A. Guelke (ed.), *The Challenges of Ethno-nationalism* (New York, 2010), 60–77.

————. 'Konstruirovanie "liberalism" v post-sovetskoi Rossii: nasledie 1990-kh v ideologicheskikh bitvah 2000-kh' ('Constructing "Liberalism" in Post-Soviet Russia: The Legacy of the 1990s in the Ideological Battles of the 2000s'). *Politeia* 84 (1) (2017), 6–28.

————. *Liberalizm v politicheskom spektre Rossii (na primere partii 'Demokraticheskij vybor Rossi ii obschestvennogo ob'edinenia "Yabloko '")*. Moscow, 1998.

Materialy k V c'ezdu 'Yabloka'. Moscow, 1995.

Mitrokhin, S. 'Natsional'nyi interest kak teoreticheskaia problema'. *Polis* 1 (1997), 32–37.

————. 'Reabilitatsija democratii'. *Yabloko* 9 (17–24 April 1995).

Prilensky, V. *Opyt issledovanija mirovozzrenija rannikh russkikh liberalov.* Moscow, 1995.

'Programma partii "Demokraticheskij vybor Rossii"', *Politicheskij kurier partii 'Demokraticheskij vybor Rossii'* 2 (1995).

Primakov, Y. 'Predely liberalizma dlia Rossii'. *Vestnik Moskovskogo universiteta* 12(6) (2012), 3–15.

Pustarnakov, V. and I. Hudushina (eds). *Liberalizm v Rossii.* Moscow, 1996.

Reformy dlia bol'shinstva. Ob'edinenie 'Yabloko'. Moscow, 1995.

Riabov, A. 'Liberalizm mozhet sostoiatsa v nashei strane tol'ko kak sotsial'nyi'. *Politicheskij klass* 2 (2006), 23–27.

Tikhonova, N. 'Sotsial'nyi liberalism: est' li al'ternativy?'. *Obschestvennye nauki i sovremennost'* 2 (2013), 32–44.

Tsipko, A.S. 'Razmyshlenija o prirode i prichinakh krakha postsovetskogo liberalizma'. *Vestnik analitiki* 17(3) (2004), 4–24.

Rutland, P. 'Neoliberalism and the Russian Transition'. *Review of International Political Economy* 20(2) (2013), 332–62.

Sogrin, V. 'Liberalizm v Rossii: peripetii i perspektivy'. *Obschestvennye nauki i sovremennost'* 1 (1997), 13–23.

Shelokhaev, V. et al. (eds). *Rossijskij liberalism serediny XVIII – nachala XX veka.* Moscow, 2010.

Szacki, J. *Liberalism after Communism.* Budapest, 1995.

Tsygankov, A. 'Aleksandr Panarin kak zerkalo russkoi revoliutsii'. *Ideologija i politika* 3(1) (2013), 4–36.

————. 'Sumerki liberalizma: chto sulit porazhenie global'noi reformatsii'. *Politicheskij klass* 9 (2005), 45–54.

Walicki, A. *Legal Philosophies of Russian Liberalism.* Notre Dame, IN, 1992.

White, D. 'Victims of a Managed Democracy? Explaining the Electoral Decline of the *Yabloko* Party'. *Demokratizatsiya* 15 (2007), 209–29.

Yavlinsky, G. *Economica Rossii: nasledstvo i vozmozhnosti.* Moscow, 1995.

Chapter 11

Temporal Evolution and Morphological Complexity

The Multiple Layers of British Liberalism

Michael Freeden

As is often the case across Europe, liberalism in Britain emerged from multiple sources that have never entirely coalesced. It is also the case that the political and social senses of the term 'liberalism' were developed in Britain at a later stage than, say, in Spain or France. However, it could be argued that many of the conceptual features of liberalism either originated in Britain or attained an advanced stage of development there, even if in recent decades the United Kingdom has no longer occupied its former respected role as a net exporter of liberal ideas to the rest of Europe and beyond. Generally speaking, the origins of British liberalism and the pathways of its complex conceptual history are located variously in a particular tradition of political philosophy, in the evolution of the Liberal Party from the nineteenth century onwards, and in the consolidation of a broad ideology that emerged in parallel to the institutional manifestations of party politics, while becoming considerably distinct from them. If we merely remain concerned with the emergence of the terms 'liberalism' or 'liberals' (rather than 'liberal'), this account would have to begin in the first third of the nineteenth century. But lexicographical history may shed insufficient light on conceptual history for a number of reasons. Among those are the following: the indisputable evidence that a rich reservoir of liberal ideas can be traced back to seventeenth-century England; the obscuring of part of the political and conceptual history of liberalism under the labels 'Whig' or, conversely, 'radical'; and the presence of ideational features that flowed into liberal thinking from philosophical movements such as utilitarianism and Idealism, notwithstanding elements of either movement that could easily be interpreted as illiberal. As a consequence, it is not only the origins of liberalism that are pluralist; rather, British liberalism presents itself at any moment in time as a multilayered and flexible ideology.

That is not the only problem with a lexicographical approach to liberalism. For if liberalism is a concept, it is also a 'super-concept'. By that is meant not a qualitatively superior concept, but one that embraces a complex cluster of other concepts, each of which displays an intricate morphology and history of its own, and each of which may independently be necessary, yet insufficient, to pass muster as an indicator of liberalism. Hence, the justification of including 'proto-liberals', or the principal collocations of English liberalism such as 'liberty' and 'individuality', in the following analysis lies in the distinction between word and concept. Whereas a word can be singular, a concept is not, and the internal morphology of the concept 'liberalism' needs to be appreciated when delivering an account of its conceptual history.[1]

Nonetheless, if we attempt to answer the synchronic question 'what does the concept 'liberalism' look like in Britain?' rather than the diachronic question 'what are the ideational origins of the concept of liberalism in Britain?', the older reservoir is of limited use. For while there are many 'proto-liberalisms' – John Locke's *Second Treatise* is one archetypal example – these ideas did not consolidate for a long while into a recognizable ideological family bearing the name of liberalism. It is only in the nineteenth century that British liberalism began to exhibit a distinct identity and conceptual fingerprint, as older conceptions of liberty coalesced with the dual sets of commercial and trading freedoms on the one hand and newer notions of progress, evolution and civilization on the other. The salience of the individual in liberal thought was revealed as an amalgam of respect for personal separateness and conscience on the one hand, and the cultivation of human individuality, initiative and growth on the other. Even this convergence was left incomplete until theories of social interdependence were grafted onto the emerging conceptual combination at the turn of the twentieth century.

Liberalism Politicized and Liberalism Prefigured: The Arrival of a Concept

The timing of the introduction of the word 'liberal' into English as a political term is somewhat controversial, and it hinges significantly on whether we adopt a broad or narrow interpretation of the 'political'. Thus, whereas Adam Smith almost always used the term 'liberal', in the sense of 'generous', he also referred to 'the freedom of the exportation and importation trade' as a 'liberal system' – clearly a social practice with economic consequences.[2] Even more tellingly, the term 'oppressive' is conjoined with 'illiberal' as a denunciation of European national policy towards its colonies, and Smith comments on a policy of nonintervention as permitting the pursuit of individual interest 'upon the liberal plan of equality, liberty and justice' – a conceptual configuration that was to become a mainstay of nineteenth-century social and political liberal discourse.[3] Edmund Burke too, though well-established in the conservative pantheon, employed in 1790 a political sense of 'liberal' when referring to 'a liberal order of commons to emulate and to recruit' the spirited virtue of the nobility, and he invoked 'the pleasing illusions, which made power gentle, and obedience liberal' and that 'incorporated into politics the sentiments that beatify and soften private society'. Of the French revolutionaries, on the contrary, Burke pronounced: 'Their liberty is not liberal.'[4]

However, the linking of 'liberal' with a viewpoint attributed to cultural and political groupings commenced in Britain in the 1820s, some ten years after its advent in Spain, although as early as 1816, the poet Robert Southey disparagingly dubbed Napoleon as 'This perfect Emperor of the British Liberales',[5] confirming Napoleon's own attempts to depict himself as a liberal in the French context.[6] Initially the connotations of 'liberal' were largely negative, partly because it was employed in the 1820s by conservatives and traditionalists to denigrate the attempts of radical political reformers to introduce moderate change, and partly because it was seen as a foreign, imported term. In parliamentary debates, an early appearance of 'Liberal' in a political sense was in the context of a proposed Alien Bill, which contained, unsurprisingly, the cursory and derogatory reference 'as if the provisional committee at Glasgow were Spanish Liberals'.[7] More significantly, in the course of a parliamentary debate on foreign affairs in 1823, discontent with the then British Foreign Secretary, George Canning, from amongst circles close to Continental monarchs was reported (and ironically welcomed) by John Cam Hobhouse: '"Oh," said they, "matters will go poorly with us now in England: the patron of legitimacy is no more; and in his place we find a liberal; nay, more, a very radical," – to which he (Mr. H.) only replied, "I am afraid not quite" [A laugh!].'[8] Among its detractors, the linking of 'liberal' and 'radical' was a step too far.

The title of the literary periodical *The Liberal*, launched briefly in 1822 by the poets Lord Byron and Percy Bysshe Shelley (who drowned before the first issue was published) and the essayist Leigh Hunt,[9] was the first public manifestation of liberalism's political dimensions, not so much in its actual political contents as in the biased eyes of its opponents. They associated some of its contributors, including Byron and Hunt, with a moral depravity that was socially pernicious and subversive of religious ethics. The concept of liberty at the centre of liberal thinking could, as some critics asserted, degenerate into unbridled freedom. However, for the contributors to the periodical, in addition to the conventional meaning of liberal as generous, it was now also politically domesticated, while linked to an internationally directed humanitarianism.[10] As the Preface to *The Liberal* expressed it: 'We wish the title of our work to be taken in its largest acceptation, old as well as new ... All that we mean is that there are advocates of every species of liberal knowledge and that by a natural consequence in these times, we go the full length in matters of opinion with large bodies of men who are called Liberals.' Vague as the political allusions were, they pertained to 'the noblest and boldest sympathies in behalf of the human race' and to seeing 'the mind of man exhibiting powers of its own, and at the same time helping to carry on the best interests of human natures'. There, concluded the editors, 'we recognise the demi-gods of liberal worship'.[11]

For most of the nineteenth century, despite those initially unhappy with the semantic connection, the term 'radical' did much of the reformist work later connected to liberalism. One such connection was generated via the philosophic radicals, whose intellectual parentage was rooted in the Enlightenment, particularly in the positivist search for a rational reorganization of society on scientific principles.[12] Centred around figures such as Jeremy Bentham and James Mill, they advanced a psychological theory that focused entirely on individuals and their motivation. A desire to maximize their pleasure or utility and minimize their pain could be harnessed to a plethora of reforming policies that would produce the 'greatest happiness of the greatest number'. Rational policies could be pointedly engaged in to expedite the pursuit of happiness through radically reshaping constitutions, legal codes and even prisons. Nonetheless, it would be wrong to assimilate that movement into the broad liberal tradition in its entirety, for its logic commanded that the few could often be sacrificed on the altar of majoritarian happiness. But its default position was to minimize state interference and to rely on individual self-interest as the basis of a well-coordinated and harmonious society. The ideas and cultural attitudes it put at the disposal of liberals included an emphasis on socially generated change and reform, the identification of the individual as the unit of agency and action, the primacy of happiness as the end of social life – rather than prioritizing stability, power or wealth – and the call for social and philosophical thinking to rely on empirical evidence instead of custom or ideal theory. All these nuances were to be assimilated into typical nineteenth-century understandings of liberalism. Although it was more common to collocate the words 'radicalism' and 'reform', we find that even Mill, a sparing user of the term 'liberal', occasionally ran 'liberal' and 'reform' together. Thus, when Mill referred to the reform of the civil service through introducing a competitive examination, he saw this competence-building measure as offering liberals 'the realization of the principal object which any honest reformer desires to effect by political changes'.[13] And in 1835, Mill commended Tocqueville for utilizing the liberalism of his age to find a balance between aristocracy and democracy.[14] Even Mill's seminal *On Liberty* refers to liberalism only once, tellingly in the context of the popular limits to power sought by the previous generation espousing 'European liberalism', especially its 'Continental section'.[15] In another sphere, liberalism in its economic sense was considered as a desirable exportable practice. A book published by a British official at the British Embassy in Istanbul declared: 'Liberalism, appropriate for natural laws and reason, is the best economic policy from which both Turkey and England will benefit.'[16]

However, the emergence of liberalism in England began far earlier than that.[17] Many ideas now contained in the concept of liberalism were in public circulation long before the coining of the word. At the end of this chapter, we shall observe that liberalism is a constantly fluctuating morphological amalgam of the differing meanings that each of its core concepts carries. But to begin with, we need to note that the so-called liberal tradition is a mixture of at least five different historical trends, loosely layered on each other, but often in ill-fitting and patchy continuities. Those five subtraditions cannot be added up into a unified whole, because they too often pull in irreconcilable directions. Hence, no layer on its own can capture the intricacy of liberalism, yet liberalism cannot be understood without acknowledging their interplay. Nor would it be correct to claim that they are neatly historically sequential, as Reinhart Koselleck's 'geological' understanding of historical layers implies.[18] Rather, more than one of them has coexisted with others synchronically to this very day, while each excludes those segments of the other layers it finds incompatible with its own preferred emphases. An idealized optimal liberalism would include the features of all five layers, yet that is as logically and substantively impossible as it is historically false. All known liberalisms are therefore at most only second-best approximations of the overarching conceptual riches that liberal ideology can host.

The Layer of Boundaries

The first, and most durable, layer is a proto-liberal one. The seeds of liberalism sprouted as an uncoordinated movement to release people from the social and political shackles that constrained, and frequently exploited, them. Tyrannical monarchs, feudal hierarchies and privileges, and heavy-handed religious practices required a restraining doctrine separating rulers from the ruled and curbing their capacity for arbitrary conduct. These proto-liberalisms of resistance and relocation of governance, an early instance of which is the endorsement in Marsilius' 'valentior pars' of a limited form of popular participation, were powerfully reinforced by the burgeoning individualism that contract theory brought with it. Philosophers such as John Locke introduced early traces of the individualism that was now coupled to liberalism's emancipatory drive, inasmuch as human beings were seen to possess attributes whose removal would profoundly dehumanize them, in particular the capacity for life, liberty and the creation and ownership of property.

Hobbes had already offered a famous attempt at a scientific and precise definition of liberty as 'the absence of externall Impediments'.[19] Locke, however, significantly distinguished liberty from licence, liberty being not one for 'every Man to do what he lists', but to 'dispose, and order, as lists, his Person, Actions, Possessions, and his whole Property, within the allowance of those laws under which he is; and therein not to be subject to the arbitrary Will of another, but freely follow his own'.[20] Although Hobbes' conception has endured to this very day, it has flitted in and out of mainstream liberalism. On the contrary, Locke's conception is at the heart of the reasonable, constrained and constitutional conduct that future liberals have expected members of a society to display and governments to respect. The point here is not to extend the historical range of this chapter, but to recognize the installing and persistence of certain ideas in the progressive psyche. Thus, the philosopher, sociologist and journalist L.T. Hobhouse quoted Locke in his seminal 1911 book *Liberalism*, observing that 'the first condition of universal freedom ... is a measure of universal constraint', there being 'no essential antithesis between liberty and law'.[21]

As part of this first layer, two theoretical discursive devices became integral to a new anthropocentrism that profoundly impacted on future liberal thinking: natural rights and contract theory. Although rejected by advanced liberals, as we shall observe below, natural rights performed a number of critical services for embryonic liberalism. They identified individuals as the locus of certain irremovable qualities, around which social arrangements had to be organized. By naturalizing them, they were ostensibly placed *hors de combat*, due to their being the prepolitical and inalienable features that were the most vital and essential aspects of being human, and that consequently demanded preferential protection. Natural rights thus began to enshrine the idea of 'no-go' areas where rulers, governments and states were refused unauthorised entry, thus moving towards establishing boundaries and spaces as central to the languages of liberalism. Contract theory endeavoured to formalize a specific relationship, that between governed and governors, placing in the hands of the people the ultimate right to remove arbitrary and oppressive rulers from office and introducing the notion of permanent conditionality into macropolitical relationships. Beginning with invented and artificial time – the state of nature – contract theory proceeded to invented and artificial timelessness – the rule of reason. However, in the absence both of mass participation and of the power of the people to instruct governments to deliver certain policies, it did not signal a democratization of the body politic. The reconciliation of liberalism with democracy had to wait until the mid nineteenth century.

The main impact of the first liberal layer was therefore in the field of political rights and constitutionalism through the idea of separate spatial arrangements, manifested especially in the distinction between public and private. Mill had of course written eloquently about the distinction between self-affecting and other-affecting action, and had reminded his readers that 'in England ... there is considerable jealousy of direct interference, by the legislative or the executive power, with private conduct', warning that 'there are, in our own day, gross usurpations upon the liberty of private life actually practised'.[22] Herbert Spencer noted in 1884 the Whig 'desire to resist and decrease the coercive power of the ruler over the subject', observing that 'liberalism habitually stood for individual freedom versus State-coercion', and added: 'The function of Liberalism in the past was that of putting a limit to the powers of kings. The function of true Liberalism in the future will be that of putting a limit to the powers of Parliaments.'[23]

The Layer of Exchange

The second layer of liberalism involved its emergence as a vehicle for the expression of individual preferences under conditions of noninterference by others, in which markets epitomized a sense of open boundaries. Hobbes' 'technical' or 'philosophical' definition of liberty was transferred from a theory of individual motion to that of the unbounded economic and commercial activity of entrepreneurial initiative-takers and leaders of industry and finance, directing the toil and labour of the newly industrialized working class. The freeing of markets from arbitrary control, or from bureaucratic fetters, was added to the fundamental rights that individuals could claim, but was mainly perceived as a necessity for social and national flourishing, particularly in the nineteenth century. Increased production and consumption would stimulate wealth and endorse the virtues of a self-helping population. Individualism, honest work and inventiveness would combine, in John Bright's words, 'to promote the comfort, happiness, and contentment of a nation'.[24] Whether or not all the above can describe the actual practices of trade and commerce is beside the point, for the mythology of unadulterated economic exchange and expansion was firmly embedded in liberal discourse, and also pervaded what became known as liberal imperialism.[25]

Freedom of economic intercourse and movement could hardly be formulated as a natural right, for commerce could obviously not be presocial.

Rather, those freedoms grew to become rights the state was expected to deliver. Instead of just assuming its traditional role of maintaining internal order and external defence, and raising taxes for those purposes, the state was reinvented as the guarantor of a further set of property and trading rights. This differed from the Lockean right to property that protected the personal association between a man and his labour and product. The new economic role of the state was seen as the oversight of a set of socially beneficial practices – an extension of Adam Smith's 'invisible hand'. Phrases such as 'holding the ring', 'honest broker' or ensuring a 'level playing field' enhanced state responsibility. They also came to reinforce the more recent misconceptions about liberal neutrality, misconceptions that had additional roots in constitutional theory, particularly in the United States, where the illusion of the Supreme Court embodying a superpolitical impartiality was cultivated, despite its being an impossibility viewed through the lens of ideological analysis.

For many campaigners, free trade had an ethical as well as an economic rationale. Liberal aspirations were vented by Richard Cobden, who saw in the free trade principle 'that which shall act on the moral world as the principle of gravitation in the universe – drawing men together, thrusting aside the antagonism of race, and creed, and language, and uniting us in the bonds of eternal peace'.[26] Indeed, as the new liberal theorist, writer and economist J.A. Hobson observed, free trade was for liberals such as Cobden an instrument of internationalism.[27] Liberal universalism, contra most liberal philosophers, was not the timeless and rational realization of the creed of humanity, but was conceptualized as a gradual and hard-won process of expanding the reach of open human interaction through the solid, urban and respectable activities of the middle classes. More than its continental counterpart of *bürgerliche Gesellschaft*, it was occasionally kitted out in the garb of humanist idealism.

The Layer of Development

The third layer involved a conceptual and ideological breakthrough in the semantics of liberalism. The notion of individual development, of which John Stuart Mill was yet again the most able advocate, combined with continental ideas of *Bildung* to unlock human potential. Temporal movement and flow were superimposed on the constitutional stasis of the first layer, without of course dispensing with the spatial structure of liberalism, which Mill had retained. But more importantly and innovatively, British conceptions of the nature of liberalism were indebted through Mill to some German political philosophers and Wilhelm von Humboldt in particular. Liberalism now took on board the cultural creation of a maturing and progressing individual whose will was not to be identified at a point *in* time, but was exercised through continua of points *across* time. If the present self was only part of the future self, liberals had to engage in new strategies for the protection and promoting of individuals in the longer run.

That is the real significance of Mill's crucial phrase 'the free development of individuality':[28] the creation of a social and political, as well as cultural, environment in which liberty would be assigned new significance. Individualism asserted the fixed uniqueness of persons as separate units, casually joined in social relationships; individuality identified a dynamic process at the centre of human existence. It was a direct reaction to the utilitarianism on which the young Mill was nourished. While Bentham exhibited the same reformist and radical drive that the third layer of liberalism was now displaying, his utilitarianism was detached from any notion of time or development. No less significantly, it was also detached from the incipient teleology that nineteenth-century liberalism was beginning to cultivate, despite liberal pretensions to advocate open-ended futures – a teleology of process rather than of foreseeable outcomes. Contrary to Bentham's focus on utilitarian interest as always being that of the moment,[29] Mill referred to 'the permanent interests of man as a progressive being' and invoked von Humboldt in defining those permanent interests as 'The end of man, or that which is prescribed by the eternal or immutable dictates of reason, and not suggested by vague and transient desires, is the highest and most harmonious development of his powers to a complete and consistent whole'.[30]

The rise of a time-oriented liberalism, be it ever so open-ended, that regarded human growth as complementary to human autonomy and independence, signalled a new stage in its history. Von Humboldt's *The Limits of State Action*, from which Mill quoted selectively but enthusiastically, had in fact argued for a more libertarian version of liberalism than the one Mill was content to espouse,[31] but a typical characteristic of conceptual adaptation is to reassemble the ingredients of a concept by picking and choosing, retaining only those that serve the intentions of the reformulator and jettisoning the others. As will be noted below, this is a crucial feature of the conceptual morphology at the heart of the ideational interrelationships that constitute a political theory or an ideology.

The Layer of Interrelationships

In the fourth layer of the mutation processes undergone by liberalism, social space was no longer thought of as separating individuals by constructing protective barriers around them – as in early liberalism or even in Mill's developmental version, parts of which elaborated on the concerns of the first layer of liberalism – but as interweaving them, personally, politically, economically and, not least, culturally. Although liberalism had always displayed a modicum of sociability – its forerunner Locke regarded the state of nature as eschewing a war of all against all – it was patently and openly discovering its affinity with groups as well. National self-determination was one of the first manifestations of that affinity, but the flame of sociability now began to blaze powerfully not as liberal nationalism, but as liberal communitarianism. This involved a number of ideological and conceptual novelties. First, the new liberalism at the turn of the twentieth century emphasized the close interdependence among members of a society, suggesting that they could not survive on their own without assistance from and the support of others, and insisting on that backing as essential to individuality and human liberty themselves. Second, the conventional net of protection cast over individual space was extended. It now included the blocking of newly discovered menaces to individual flourishing – poverty, ignorance, disease, squalor and unemployment – that did not just involve inappropriate physical or legal intervention. Third, the democratically monitored state was enlisted to assist in this mammoth task because some important activities were held to be beyond the capacity of private initiative and because society was reimagined as a harmonizable, unitary entity with shared rational ends.[32] British new liberalism pushed out the boundaries of liberalism in its integration of the individual and the social more than any other European liberalism, thus making an indispensable contribution to the twentieth-century welfare state. It nonetheless remained on the liberal side of a porous boundary, though it overlapped heavily with positions occupied by the term 'social democracy', in Scandinavia, France, Germany and the Low Countries.

The late nineteenth and early twentieth centuries were undoubtedly the liveliest and most intense period in British history as far as the struggle over the concept of liberalism and the attempts either to reformulate or to consolidate its meanings are concerned. They therefore merit especial scrutiny in this chapter. As usual in such cases, there is a gap between the party-political rise of Liberalism and its theoretical and ideological manifestations. The use of the label 'Liberal Party' itself began only at the end of the 1850s, at a time when the theorists and philosophers we now regard as central to the liberal tradition were ideologically far ahead of the party system – not an unusual relationship between political parties and ideological innovators. As noted above, Mill rarely used the term 'liberal' to describe his views. When he did, he instead opted to call himself an advanced liberal.[33] In so doing, liberals such as Mill could keep one foot in the radical tradition while fighting to bring official Liberalism into step with their ideas. The political reforms associated with radicalism entailed the extension of the franchise, corrections to the

underrepresentation of large sectors of the population, and the strengthening
of Parliament in relation to the monarchy concurrently with the weakening,
or even abolition, of the House of Lords. Radicalism and liberalism continued
to be partly interchangeable As the MP Henry Labouchere asserted: 'I have
used throughout the word "Liberal" as the name of our party. I have done so
because the vast majority of Liberals are now Radicals.'[34] That linguistic association was also evident in Joseph Chamberlain's 1885 'Radical Programme',
which emphasized reformed local government, free schools, religious equality through disestablishing the Church of England, manhood suffrage in
equal-sized constituencies, payment of MPs and a graduated income tax.
Shortly after that, and unfortunately for advanced liberalism, Chamberlain
aligned himself with the Liberal Unionists and later the Conservatives, thus
contributing to watering down the political effect of the word 'radical'.

Contrast this with the semantic revolution incurred as the fourth layer of
liberalism penetrated further into left-wing politics forty years later, when
Charles Trevelyan wrote, upon joining the Labour Party: 'I have not been
required to shed anything of my Liberalism, except the party name, in joining
the Labour Party.' He then went on to list the late nineteenth-century tenets
of British liberalism, while ignoring its twentieth-century metamorphosis
into a social liberal ideology in which, ironically, he had himself played a part:
'Faith in Democracy, belief in Free Trade, love of personal freedom, respect
for national liberties, are all part of the Labour creed. The Labour Party is,
indeed, the safest custodian of these cherished Liberal principles.'[35]

Representatives of the Liberal Party came together in 1886 to issue a
book entitled *The New Liberal Programme* – not to be confused with the then
barely existing new liberalism. For some, it was a matter of preserving 'the
grand old watchword of Liberalism' – peace, retrenchment, and reform.[36]
For others, the aims of liberalism were different. The future cabinet minister
R.B. Haldane argued that 'because freedom to develop implies liberty, not
merely from material but from moral fetters, the policy of the Liberal Party
must be largely an educational one'.[37] On the whole, the term 'liberalism'
did not evoke grand principles for those at the coalface of representative
politics, but dissolved into a set of very concrete and time-specific measures.
Things were very different when it came to commentators, theorists and conscious ideological pacesetters, though conceptual disputes continued to rage.
Thus, just before the end of the nineteenth century, a group of six Oxford
graduates, some of whom were to achieve renown in later life, published a
collection of essays in which they attempted to move against the rising tide
and – in the words of the leading nineteenth-century Liberal politician W. E.
Gladstone – to make a particular effort 'on behalf of individual freedom and
independence as opposed to what is termed Collectivism'.[38] Hilaire Belloc,

in a blast redolent of past liberal discourses, enumerated the ideals of the liberals of Europe as including 'the sanctity of contract, the love of freedom, the virtue of self-control, and the inviolable right to property acquired by labour or by self-denial'.[39] Francis Hirst was hardly alone in distancing liberalism from socialism and in insisting that 'individual freedom and national prosperity would be as incompatible with Collectivism as they once proved to be with Protectionism and class monopoly'. Nonetheless, a minimalist and somewhat paternalist agenda of social reform was attached to the above: 'the advance of the just claims of the labouring classes, the improvement of their material condition, their elevation socially, morally, and intellectually … are embedded in Liberal principles'.[40] The older liberalism of the first layer – 'great abstract conceptions', 'rights which should belong to every man', 'human equality' and 'freedom' – was accorded prominence, while sharply disengaged from what those writers, biologically young, but ideologically ageing and themselves well-off, described as a collectivism of 'materialist programmes and promises of increased comfort'.[41]

Liberal Organicism

The concept of liberalism, however, was gravitating towards another sphere. Its fourth layer departed significantly from the second layer of entrepreneurial free trade, of 'Manchester liberalism'. Hobson accused the Manchester School of creating 'for its own special purposes an economic man, an embodiment of the selfish motives only'. Moreover, 'it completely failed to recognise the part which Society plays in the production of wealth and consequently could not recognise Society's claim as a consumer'.[42] The future Liberal Party leader Herbert Samuel insisted that the root idea of the new liberalism 'must be the unity of society – complex in its economic, cooperative, ethical and emotional bonds', together with 'a determination to abolish every evil condition from life'.[43]

In a book published in 1909, *The Crisis of Liberalism*, Hobson called for a 'restatement of the Liberal creed'. In a crucial passage that comes close to the core of the transformation of the concept of liberalism, he wrote:

> Liberalism is now formally committed to a task which certainly involves a new conception of the State in its relation to the individual life and to private enterprise … From the standpoint which best presents its continuity with earlier Liberalism, it appears as a fuller appreciation and realisation of individual liberty contained in the provision of equal opportunities for self-development. But to this individual standpoint must be joined a just apprehension of the social, viz., the insistence that these claims or rights of self-development be adjusted to the sovereignty of social welfare.[44]

Hobson now matched the idea of liberalism with that of organicism – two concepts that were hitherto understood to pull in opposite directions, one opening up individual liberty and the other ostensibly sacrificing it in the name of overriding collective interests.

This variant of social liberalism appealed to evolutionary and biological theory in order to revitalize the conceptual content it carried. The Enlightenment idea of progress embraced by the third layer of liberalism was now reanchored in a reading of evolution that did away with its overcompetitive 'survival of the fittest' interpretation. Instead, it promoted what Hobson's colleague Hobhouse called orthogenic evolution. Its hallmark was a growth of sociable rationality measured by an increasing ethicality, involving a conscious awareness of human interdependence. Competition was being replaced with intelligent cooperation, and central to this view was a perception of society as an organic interconnected entity. Evolution entailed the emergence of a guiding social intelligence, coordinated by a benevolent, enabling and democratically controlled state, which would assist in redistributing life chances in the name of the common good.

Lest the individual disappear in that quasi-teleological conception, Hobson inverted the organic analogy. Belloc had contended that 'the organic unity of the State is one of those pretentious metaphors ... which suggest one kind of unity by a totally different kind'. For Belloc, 'evolution is a long and somewhat stupid substitute for progress' and it depended on individual free will, not on 'the organized monotony and mechanical unity of a Socialist State'.[45] But Hobson, in another passage highly evocative of the new liberalism, asserted that 'the full organic formula' implied that 'it is doubtless to the real interest of the organism as a whole to distribute blood in accordance with the needs of the individual members and their cells ... Accept the view of Society as an organism, corresponding rights remain to its individual members, and a political machinery for enforcing them must exist'.[46] Although there were potentially illiberal and paternalistic undertones to Hobson's extolling of expertise and a version of 'democratic centralism',[47] he insisted that without attention to each of the parts, the body-politic would atrophy – thus injecting into organicist thinking a liberal content that was sensitive to the individual. This was later elaborated upon when Hobson wrote of the unity of socioindustrial life as a federal unity in which:

> the federal government ... conserves ... individual rights, not, as the individu-
> alist maintains, because it exists for no other purpose than to do so. It conserves
> them because it also recognises that an area of individual liberty is conducive to
> the health of the collective life. Its federal nature rests on a recognition alike of
> individual and social ends, or, speaking more accurately, of social ends that are
> directly attained by social action and of those that are realised in individuals.[48]

Hobhouse, author of the most important twentieth-century book on British liberalism, made a similar point. 'Mutual aid is not less important than mutual forbearance', he wrote, 'the theory of collective action no less fundamental than the theory of personal freedom.' The fissiparous spatiality still retained by liberalism's third layer was replaced by a new interlocked spatiality: 'So far as Mill rested his case on the distinction between self-regarding actions and actions that affect others, he was still dominated by the older individualism ... there is no side of a man's life which is unimportant to society.' Yet Hobhouse also echoed Mill's emphasis on temporal development, on the idea of growth as the 'foundation of liberty'. 'Liberalism', he affirmed, 'is the belief that society can safely be founded on this self-directing power of personality, that it is only on this foundation that a true community can be built ... Liberty then becomes not so much a right of the individual as a necessity of society.'[49] The inverted conceptualizations here are telling. Liberalism had travelled from extolling natural, presocial rights that constituted claims against governments and states to conceiving individual rights – as did Hobson – as essential to the interests and flourishing of a society, organically interwoven. A rational society would therefore demand that its members have rights as an existential fact of membership, not as a natural set of personal properties.

From Negative Restraint to Positive Assertiveness

A more expansive notion of liberty was vital to expressing the greater sensitivity of liberals to the hindrances to liberty. Liberals followed the lead of the Oxford philosopher Thomas Hill Green, who rejected the spurious and effectively inegalitarian freedom of contract in the industrial sphere and famously contended that freedom was 'a positive power or capacity of doing or enjoying something worth doing or enjoying ... in common with others'.[50] The association of liberty with movement, activity and community took Mill's temporal development one step further towards infusing liberalism with the dynamism it had begun to parade. Hobson reasserted that rejection of laissez-faire when he claimed that 'the negative conception of liberalism, as a definite mission for the removal of certain political and economic shackles upon personal liberty, is not merely philosophically defective, but historically false'.[51] When advanced social liberals expounded their vision, they conjured up a pioneering programme that set the agenda for the future welfare state and inspired the legislation at the heart of the 1906–14 Liberal governments. Hobson's argument shifted the balance of liberalism from 'absence of restraint' to 'presence of opportunity' and he optimistically foresaw a state that would guarantee 'free land, free travel, free power [electric or other], free credit, security, justice and education', for 'no man is "free" for the full purposes of civilised life to-day unless he has all these liberties'.[52]

Liberals, moreover, had made their peace with the state; indeed, they actively courted the state in its new guise of a disinterested, democratically accountable and benign agent, undertaking all the vital social activities that individuals were unable or unwilling to assume on their own. There were still many conventional voices reflecting the second layer of liberalism, such as Herbert Spencer's, for whom the state was solely a guarantor of security and property, but otherwise charged with nonintervention due to the self-balancing and voluntaristic view of society to which those liberals subscribed. Indeed, Spencer bemoaned the fact that 'popular good has come to be sought by Liberals, not as an end to be indirectly gained by relaxations of restraints, but as the end to be directly gained'.[53] However, Hobhouse, in singling out the state as an agent of compulsion acting in the name of social justice with moral and spiritual value, endorsed a contrasting view: 'Liberty and compulsion have complementary functions, and the self-governing State is at once the product and the condition of the self-governing individual.' Indeed, society's close-knit structure 'has accordingly allowed the development of certain nodes, or perhaps certain connecting fibres, to cut which is to destroy life while to ligature them is to induce temporary paralysis. This being so, society itself, through its own direct organs of government, is being compelled, apart from any Collectivist theory, to exercise a closer and more effective control over all that passes at these vital spots'.[54] Unlike the case with so many liberals, power was recognized rather than ignored. Hobhouse subtly observed that 'it is a question not of increasing or diminishing, but of reorganizing, restraints'.[55] And Hobson commented: 'Society, whether through the State or otherwise, can never do too much for individuals; for whatever it does well in its own interests as a society must furnish a richer soil for individual growth.'[56] This is not to say that the state could do no wrong, which is why constitutional constraints of the first layer were not overlooked in the new liberal mindset. But the three additional functions of the state, as Hobson saw it, were: to undertake routine industries, freeing individuals for more artistic and creative activity; to supply goods and services that all required – 'the necessities of physical, intellectual, or moral life'; and to protect the public as producers or consumers against 'dangers arising from the technical or the economic conditions of private trades'.[57]

The fourth layer of liberalism deemed as absurd the prospect of individual life detached from the community that sustained it. It effected a conceptual revolution in the semantic content of liberalism, while being careful not to cross the line to monistic forms of socialism or collectivism. It was a liberalism that, while recognizing the uniqueness of persons, also held to a national unity and recognized the emotional content of liberalism, affirming ties that incorporated 'feelings and ideas, sentiments of patriotism, of kinship, a common pride, and a thousand more subtle sentiments that bind together men who speak a common language, have behind them a common history, and understand one another as they can understand no one else'.[58] The social anchoring of society thus also entailed a restatement of the link between liberalism and nationalism, though not primarily as the principle of self-determination to be found elsewhere in nineteenth-century Europe, but as an acknowledgement of the local and concrete embodiment of liberalism in a geopolitical and cultural setting. And yet the international drive promoted by free trade liberalism had not evaporated. Hobhouse thought that 'nothing has been more encouraging to the Liberalism of Western Europe in recent years than the signs of political awakening in the East'.[59] Internationalism had sprung from the earlier universalism of liberalism, which remained a motif of significance. For example, the Liberal MP politician and writer J.M. Robertson maintained that 'the function of Liberalism is to recognize the element of "right" which is established by the universal moral law of reciprocity'.[60]

Twentieth-Century Hesitations

The similarities between the new liberalism and some varieties of continental social democracy, as well as French *solidarisme*, are striking, yet equally remarkable is the insistence of British left-liberals on placing themselves within a rejuvenated liberal tradition, bolstered by the legislative successes of a buoyant Liberal Party before the First World War. But the excessive state intervention brought about during the war was not received kindly even by the once new liberals, in contradistinction to their previous readiness to accept such intervention in the domain of compulsory social insurance. After that, many patently liberal discourses lost their public visibility as they were overshadowed by the rise of a growing Labour Party, which assimilated much of the left-liberal agenda, mainly without acknowledgement. The rump of liberal intellectuals and activists who remained true to their historical traditions retreated into a more modest version of progressive liberalism, shorn of the organic vision of its fourth layer and returning to a mixture of political reformism and a modified free market with a limited social agenda.[61] The term 'liberal' forewent its sheen and radical edge, and many of those speaking in its name reverted to a more centrist position. Centrist liberals retained a commitment to basic liberties and provision for the disadvantaged, but they preferred to resort to the virtues of individual enterprise and initiative as centrepieces of their ideology, and to restrict the functions of the state to specific areas. In the interwar years, security, economic efficiency and property assumed equal status to social justice within liberal discourse, and the pursuit of grand social visions was relaxed in favour of piecemeal reform until the advent of the 1942 Beveridge Report.[62] The massive problems of reconstruction following the First World War occasioned a new stress on economic and industrial productivity as a condition for domestic recovery and reform. Most interestingly, the attention of progressive liberals turned to the sphere of industry as the arena from which the necessary remedies could emerge. When the celebrated liberal weekly *The Nation* was taken over by a group headed by J.M. Keynes in 1923, having previously been a key mouthpiece of the new liberals, it immediately announced that 'Liberalism entails, in our view, a recognition that the economic structure of society requires radical and far-reaching change' towards 'the virtue of variety in industrial structure and experiment'.[63] Although *The Nation*'s editors insisted that 'our own sympathies are for a Liberal Party which has its centre well to the Left, a Party definitely of Change and Progress',[64] they nonetheless concluded, in a sharp about-turn from the concerns of the new liberalism, that 'it is clear that the technique of Capitalist production requires a degree of specialization and a strictness of discipline which are bound to be distasteful, and which involve some sacrifice of the quality of human life'.[65]

The President of the National Liberal Federation, the commentator and activist Ramsay Muir – a typical if hardly inspiring voice of British interwar liberalism – introduced a survey of Liberal policy with the following pedestrian observation: 'Liberalism – the belief in freedom of thought, freedom of enterprise, freedom of intercourse, and freedom in government – has been the chief guide of modern civilisation in all its progress during the last four centuries.'[66] Gone were the mutualism and distributive justice of advanced social reform, gone was the organic conception of society. Instead, a watered-down and cautious version was proposed, which was more in tune with liberalism's second layer: 'Social Reform aims at improving and strengthening the existing social order by removing its defects without destroying its mainspring, which is free enterprise.' The objective had radically changed yet again: 'By improving the health, fitness, and mental capacity of the people, Social Reform also improves their ability to produce wealth.'[67] It was left to Keynes and to Beveridge to reflect on their personal relationship to a liberalism of their own understanding. In his 1926 essay entitled 'Am I a Liberal?', Keynes – no radical himself when it came to political thinking – wrote in strikingly conventional terms: 'the *Class* war will find me on the side of the educated *bourgeois*'. For him, the existing achievements of the Liberal Party were either successful or obsolete and 'as dead as last week's mutton': self-government, reform of the House of Lords and social insurance. He too associated liberalism with free trade, not as an individualist, but as an economist, but he also envisaged that future progressive issues would concern disarmament, political devolution, birth control and 'directing economic forces in the interests of social justice and social stability'.[68] Beveridge, who had been a Conservative in his youth, moved gradually towards a liberal position and, following his famous 1942 report, published a short book in 1945, anticipating the General Election, entitled *Why I am a Liberal*. One of the points he focused on was that 'the outstanding merit of the Liberal creed – that it stands for the general interest alone – means that the Liberal Party, unlike both its rivals [Conservatives and Labour], cannot count on automatic support from any sectional interest'. That was combined with a distillation of the Beveridge Report: freedom from want by social security and full employment in a free society.[69]

The Layer of Group Particularism

For the sake of completeness, mention should be made of a fifth layer of liberalism, although it is not the focus of this chapter. In recent decades, diversity and uniqueness have been reintroduced into the liberal lexicon, partly displacing its past universalism. But whereas with J.S. Mill the diversity was one of eccentric individuals whose cultivation may enrich social life, since the last third of the twentieth century it has been one in which the distinctiveness of groups – ethnic, gender or religious, whose claims are often referred to as 'identity politics' – has been added to the core list of what many British liberals profess to hold dear.[70] On the continent, in contrast, nineteenth-century autonomous religious, ethnic and cultural entities, such as those under the aegis of the Habsburg Empire, had already attracted liberal narratives of tolerance and partial self-rule. Notably, this new layer illustrates the typical, disruptive and messy features of contemporary liberalism, exemplified in debates surrounding female Muslim head coverings, the caricaturing of religious holy men, the unequal status and power of women in many social spheres, or the disproportionate number of 'nonwhites' subject to police scrutiny. The emphasis on such liberal particularisms would have seemed retrograde to those pre-1914 new liberals who professed faith in harmonious and organic unity. A related issue at stake concerns whether liberals wedded to the idea of inclusive, universalizable practices can tolerate group preferences in their midst solely in the name of diversity and group self-determination if those preferences harbour practices that are deemed illiberal, discriminatory or even oppressive. This indeterminacy and inconclusiveness cuts liberalism down to size as its analysts recognize that, like any ideology, its conceptual arrangements permanently lack solutions to major social and political issues in which conflict seems intractable.

The Conceptual Morphology of Liberalism

If liberalism requires disaggregation in terms of the different contextual and temporal inputs with which it has been associated over the years, it also needs to be disaggregated as a concept that itself serves as a container for an internal range of constitutive concepts. The word 'liberalism' includes conceptual components that deliver persistently variable semantic content. Hence, the question of the conceptual arrangements that characterize the family of liberalisms needs to be addressed as a key element in conceptual history. All ideologies have recognizable conceptual morphologies in which a specific cluster of core concepts holds the ideology together, surrounded by adjacent and peripheral concepts that flesh it out. The study of the history of a single concept does not offer sufficient information on how that concept intersects with others, thereby potentially accruing additional meaning, or how particular conceptual combinations colour and alter the semantic content of each member of the assemblage. In the concrete worlds of social and political thought, concepts are invariably encountered within larger conceptual combinations, but never on their own. Hence, we cannot approach a concept as a single mass, or point, of meaning, nor can we trace the mutation of a concept on its own isolated timeline. Concepts are always located in fields of other intertwined or intercutting concepts.[71] These concrete conceptual clusters may display a fleeting and ephemeral presence, or longer durabilities, in which case such durability is achieved through conceptual decontestation. Like any ideology, liberalism engages in decontesting the essentially contested meanings of each of its concepts, choosing one or more conceptions out of the multiplicity of conceptions that each concept can embrace. This is necessitated not least by the mutually exclusive relationships that can obtain among such conceptions.[72]

Whereas conceptual historians normally focus on the process through which concepts change over time, the speed at which such change occurs and the disruptions incurred in that process, it is equally important to understand liberalism both synchronically and diachronically in two further ways: as a configuration of mutating spatial arrangements among concepts that affects their relative longevity as well as their concrete specificity; and as a combination of conceptual components whose relative weight is in constant flux, thus affecting their proportionate significance in any particular instance. In the case of liberalism, the spatial arrangements in which a radial structure stretches from centre to periphery contain seven empirically identifiable core concepts. This applies to all its versions, not only to the British example. Liberty, rationality, progress, individuality, the general interest, limited and accountable power, and sociability provide the fundamental features that all known liberals can be demonstrated to share.[73] But within this overriding pattern, the essential contestability of concepts produces a contest among the many conceptions that each of the above concepts possesses. This essential contestability is not only the consequence of the contingent and contextual filters through which meaning is attributed to each of these fundamental liberal core concepts, but is a property of the indeterminacy and frequent semantic overload of language itself. No version of liberalism can contain all the potential meanings it can carry. We have just observed this historically, but the phenomenon can be reinforced morphologically.

To illustrate this, if we take the manner in which liberty has been interpreted in the British liberal tradition, there is a considerable difference between the conceptualization of liberty that understands it as the absence of physical inter-vention in other people's actions – linked to the static implications of the first layer of liberalism; and the conceptualization of liberty that sees it as the absence of hindrances to human development and well-being – linked to the dynamic view of human nature that the third and the fourth liberal layers propounded. A revealing asymmetry emerges: the first conception of liberty often rules out the second, but the second conception acknowledges a modified and restricted version of the first. Particularly in the thought-practices associated with the fourth layer, the space surrounding human activity is simply reconceptualized as having additional undesirable economic, social or gender barriers that also need to be overcome. The shrinking of the concept of liberty merely to denote the ruling out of uninvited physical or legal constraints then renders it obliv-ious to the further activities that such shrinking would still permit and that would – deliberately or unintentionally – intrude on human activity in other ways. For that reason, the second liberal layer of free trade – lauding nonin-tervention in the commercial and financial lives of entrepreneurs – omitted to take into account the heavy costs of such liberty to other members of society. Within the liberal family, only the fourth liberal layer revealed what the first and second layers had concealed by dint of the narrow conceptual apparatus available to their proponents, because only that fourth layer was equipped with the intellectual tools to identify the consequences of interdependent human interaction, as well as the far greater complexity accorded to wellbeing and welfare, far beyond the material worlds of private pursuers of self-interest. Conceptual history is therefore composed of the continuous fragmentation and recombination of the components of the concept under inspection.

The switch from individualism to individuality – symptomatic of the third liberal layer – is illustrative of another decontestation of a central liberal concept, each conception being partly antagonistic to the other. The association of individualism with an atomistic self-sufficiency was incompatible with the re-emphasis on the centrality of human growth and flourishing to the liberal ethos, as distinct from human security and independence. And the means-end rationality as a calculating personal utilitarianism was supplemented and partly replaced by the ethical rationality of cooperation towards a common good preferred by the likes of Green and Hobhouse. As for progress, it was continuously torn between its material and moral paths, with either prosperity or educational and cultural improvement claiming alternative control over the concept. The main contribution of the first liberal layer was in establishing constraints on governmental and state power, and launching the adjacent concept of accountability – a theme running through all liberal variants, though itself under constant modification as the demands of democratic control grew ever more intricate.[74]

Political power as a permanent feature of human societies is already evident in Locke's writing, and the onus on rulers to wield it properly and ethically preceded the democratization of societies. But the requirements of representation necessitated ever-more inclusive and sophisticated conversations between government and governed. From the extension of the franchise in late nineteenth-century liberal programmes, the new liberals moved on to a more elaborate insistence on votes for women, devolution, proportional representation and reform of the House of Lords. Here too, the association of liberals with the general interest comes into play.[75] The implicit egalitarianism that was a product of allotting rationality to each individual, in terms of their life plans and political participation, prevented liberals – at least on the surface – from hitching their wagon to specific political, social or cultural groups, in contrast – as they argued – to the practice of conservatives or socialists. However, the second layer of liberalism did indirectly favour those adept at entrepreneurial skills, and the models of education that even Mill espoused were derived from narrow conceptions of a cultivated elite. As for sociability, it experienced rises and falls in intensity, from the Lockean indication that property, and hence social relationships, are endemic to human beings even in their natural state, through theories of invisible harmony by means of the pursuit of self-interest, or pleasure, to the strongly communitarian ideas of the left-liberals. These were accompanied by frequent decrescendos of the sociability component of liberalism, as the individualism and property features of liberalism kept reasserting themselves.

Liberalism, of course, has many additional adjacent and peripheral conceptual environments in which the conceptual core is situated. Thus, if liberty is surrounded by property and security, it acquires a very different significance within liberal morphology than if it is surrounded by democracy and welfare.

The British welfare state – above all a product of liberal thinking – accorded concrete interpretations to individuality and progress, associating them with a fuller equality of opportunity in the form of health and unemployment insurance, old-age pensions and free education, ministered in part through the direct activities of the state, but chiefly through voluntary arrangements underpinncd by it. In particular, the British welfare state normalized frailty and risk, inasmuch as they were beyond human control and therefore had to be minimized through the endeavours of a humane society. What was once restricted to passive toleration now become the active concern for others, and being liberal increasingly meant replacing individual egoism with social altruism – an updating of Mill's mission to civilize society.[76]

No chapter on the concept of liberalism can overlook its continuous negative connotations, from which the British term initially surfaced. Within the arena of ideological contestation, both conservatives and socialists picked at the term in varying degrees of denigration. The leading socialist theorist H.J. Laski, while respectful of liberalism's achievements in promoting individual originality, constitutionalism and human rights, was highly critical of liberalism's stated universalism, which was, in his view, 'more narrow in its benefit than the society it sought to guide'. 'As a doctrine', he asserted, liberalism 'was, effectively, a by-product of the effort of the middle class to win its place in the sun'. Though in an aside, Laski conceded that fourth-layer liberals such as Green and Hobhouse displayed 'more generous minds', it is symptomatic of the ideological conflicts in twentieth-century Britain that the evolution of liberal thinking was denied, obscured or misrecognized by those on the left of the political spectrum.[77] On the other hand, Conservatives preferred to restrict their understanding of liberalism to the ideals of negative liberty. Tellingly, Quintin Hogg – a leading mid twentieth-century Conservative – when reflecting on the party's view of liberalism, saw its nineteenth-century conceptualization as 'the great attack upon constituted authority', aiming at 'reducing the authority of the state to a minimum', freeing trade and abolishing privilege, to the dismay of Conservatives.[78] For these Conservatives, liberalism under laissez-faire was a creed of avarice, reduced to its second layer without the latter's moral undertones.

Such criticisms notwithstanding, if in much of Europe liberalism is considered to be a centrist ideology embracing economic freedoms and entrepreneurship – despite some salient continental liberal theorists to the contrary – the British variant has for the past 150 years established itself firmly on the centre-left and even on the social democratic segment of the spectrum. Of course, it has championed toleration, the rule of law and a deep respect for individual rights and protected private spaces, drawing from what is now inaccurately termed 'classic' liberalism. It has also increasingly emphasized an active participatory citizenry, alongside devolution, as part of widening the net of political decision-making – again an inclusivist emphasis not always present in other European liberalisms. But its most prominent hallmark since the 1890s has been an increasing highlighting of the triple relationship between individuality, sociability and welfare.

Michael Freeden is Emeritus Professor of Politics, University of Oxford. His books include *The New Liberalism: An Ideology of Social Reform* (1978); *Liberalism Divided: A Study in British Political Thought 1914–1939* (1986); *Ideologies and Political Theory: A Conceptual Approach* (1996); *Ideology: A Very Short Introduction* (2003); *Liberal Languages: Ideological Imaginations and 20th Century Progressive Thought* (2005); *The Political Theory of Political Thinking* (2013); *Liberalism: A Very Short Introduction* (2015); and *Conceptual History in the European Space* (coedited with W. Steinmetz and J. Fernández-Sebastián, Berghahn Books, 2017). He is the founder-editor of the *Journal of Political Ideologies* and a Fellow of the Academy of Social Sciences.

Notes

1. See W. Steinmetz and M. Freeden, 'Introduction: Conceptual History: Challenges, Conundrums, Complexities', in W. Steinmetz, M. Freeden and J. Fernández-Sebastián (eds), *Conceptual History in the European Space*, New York, 2017, 26.
2. A. Smith, *An Inquiry into the Nature and Causes of the Wealth of Nations*, vol. 1, Oxford, 1976, 538.
3. Ibid., 590 and 664.
4. E. Burke, *Reflections on the Revolution in France*, C.C. O'Brien (ed.), Harmondsworth, 1969, 124, 171 and 174.
5. R. Southey, *Quarterly Review* (October 1816), quoted in E. Dodds, 'Liberty and Welfare', in G. Watson (ed.), *The Unservile State*, London, 1957, 13.
6. See H. Rosenblatt, Chapter 5 in this volume.
7. J.W. Ward, 'Alien Bill', *Hansard*, 7 July 1820, 297.
8. John Cam Hobhouse, 'Negotiations Relative to Spain', *Hansard*, 28 April 1823, 1345.
9. See W.H. Marshall, *Byron, Shelley, Hunt and* The Liberal, Philadelphia, 1960.
10. See D.M. Craig, 'The Origins of "Liberalism" in Britain: The Case of *The Liberal*', *Historical Research* 85 (2012), 469–87.
11. L.P. Pickering, *Lord Byron, Leigh Hunt and the 'Liberal'*, New York, 1966, 31, 34 and 36.
12. See the still-excellent study by E. Halevy, *The Growth of Philosophic Radicalism*, London, 1972 [1928].

13. J.S. Mill, 'Reform of the Civil Service', in *Essays on Politics and Society: The Collected Works of John Stuart Mill*, vol. 18, Toronto, 1977, 207.
14. J.S. Mill, 'De Tocqueville on Democracy in America', in ibid., 56.
15. J.S. Mill, 'On Liberty', in J.M. Robson (ed.), *The Collected Works of John Stuart Mill*, vol. 18, Toronto, 1977, 218.
16. D. Urguarth, *Turkey and its Resources: Its Municipal Organization and Free Trade*, London, 1833, 168 (cited in B. Turnaoğlu, *The Formation of Turkish Republicanism*, Princeton, 2017, 48).
17. For a meticulous and extensive study of the mutating conceptualizations of liberalism in England (as well as in France, Germany and Italy), see J. Leonhard, *Liberalismus*, Munich, 2001.
18. R. Koselleck, 'Introduction' to *Zeitschichten*, Frankfurt am Main, 2000, 9.
19. T. Hobbes, *Leviathan*, Harmondsworth, 1968, 189.
20. J. Locke, *Two Treatises of Government, Second Treatise*, Cambridge, 1963, 348.
21. L.T. Hobhouse, *Liberalism and Other Writings*, J. Meadowcroft (ed.), Cambridge, 1994, 11.
22. Mill, 'On Liberty', 223, 225 and 287.
23. H. Spencer, *The Man versus the State*, Harmondsworth, 1969, 65, 67 and 18.
24. Quoted in R. Eccleshall, *British Liberalism: Liberal Thought from the 1640s to 1980s*, London, 1986, 131.
25. H.C.G. Matthew, *Liberal Imperialism*, Oxford, 1973.
26. A. Bullock and M. Shock (eds), *The Liberal Tradition*, Oxford, 1956, 53.
27. J.A. Hobson, *Richard Cobden: The International Man*, London, 1919, 22.
28. Mill, 'On Liberty', 261.
29. J. Bentham, *An Introduction to the Principles of Morals and Legislation*, Kitchener (Ontario), 2000, 15 and 205.
30. Mill, 'On Liberty', 224 and 261.
31. Ibid., 261–62.
32. For an analysis of the fourth layer, see M. Freeden, *The New Liberalism: An Ideology of Social Reform*, Oxford, 1978.
33. See S.O. Hansson, 'John Stuart Mill's Political Self-Identifications', *Journal of Political Ideologies* 18 (2013), 348–57.
34. A. Reid (ed.), *The New Liberal Programme*, London, 1886, 14.
35. H. Langshaw, *Socialism: And the Historic Function of Liberalism*, London, 1925, viii.
36. Reid, *The New Liberal Programme*, 80.
37. Ibid., 119.
38. Six Oxford Men, *Essays in Liberalism*, London, 1897, x.
39. Ibid., 30.
40. Ibid., 95–96.
41. Ibid.: 270 and 272.
42. M. Freeden (ed.), *Minutes of the Rainbow Circle 1894–1924*, London, 1989, 18–19.
43. Ibid., 28.

44. J.A. Hobson, *The Crisis of Liberalism*, London, 1909, xii and xiv.
45. Six Oxford Men, *Essays in Liberalism*, 60.
46. Hobson, *The Crisis of Liberalism*, 81–82.
47. See M. Freeden, 'Democracy and Paternalism: The Struggle over Shaping British Liberal Welfare Thinking', in A. Kessler-Harris and M. Vaudagna (eds), *Democracy and Social Rights in the 'Two Wests'*, New York, 2009, 107–22.
48. J.A. Hobson, *Work and Wealth: A Human Valuation*, New York, 1916, 304.
49. Hobhouse, *Liberalism*, 58–60.
50. T.H. Green. *Liberal Legislation and Freedom of Contract*, Oxford, 1881, 9.
51. Hobson, *The Crisis of Liberalism*, 92.
52. Ibid., 113.
53. Spencer, *The Man versus the State*, 67, 70, 177 and 205.
54. L.T. Hobhouse, 'The Conditions of Permanent Peace', *Manchester Guardian*, 21 August 1911.
55. Hobhouse, *Liberalism*, 74.
56. J.A. Hobson, *The Social Problem*, London, 1901, 225.
57. Ibid., 173.
58. Hobhouse, *Liberalism*, 61.
59. Ibid., 114.
60. J.M. Robertson, *The Meaning of Liberalism*, London, 1912, 47.
61. For a detailed discussion, see M. Freeden, *Liberalism Divided: A Study in British Political Thought 1914–1939*, Oxford, 1986.
62. W.H. Beveridge, *Social Insurance and Allied Services*, Cmd. 6404, London, 1942.
63. 'Liberalism and Labour', *The Nation*, 12 May 1923.
64. 'Editorial Foreword', *The Nation*, 5 May 1923.
65. 'Hints for Socialists', *The Nation*, 21 July 1923.
66. R. Muir (ed.), *The Liberal Way*, London, 1934, 7.
67. Ibid., 182–83.
68. J.M. Keynes, *Essays in Persuasion*, London, 1931, 324, 325 and 335.
69. W. Beveridge, *Why I am a Liberal*, London, 1945, 15–16.
70. See e.g. N. Dholakia, 'Towards Cultural Pluralism', in J. Margo (ed.), *Beyond Liberty: Is the Future of Liberalism Progressive?*, London, 2007, 198-208.
71. See Steinmetz and Freeden, 'Introduction', 27.
72. For a recent statement, see M. Freeden, 'The Morphological Analysis of Ideology', in M. Freeden, L.T. Sargent and M. Stears (eds), *The Oxford Handbook of Political Ideologies*, Oxford, 2013, 115–37.
73. For an elaboration, see M. Freeden, *Ideologies and Political Theory: A Conceptual Approach*, Oxford, 1996, 137–225.
74. See e.g. P. Starr, *Freedom's Power: The True Force of Liberalism*, New York, 2007, 32–41.
75. Hobson, *The Crisis of Liberalism*, 3–49.
76. See M. Freeden. 'The Coming of the Welfare State', in R. Bellamy and T. Ball (eds), *The Cambridge History of Twentieth-Century Political Thought*, Cambridge, 2003, 7–44.

77. H.J. Laski, *The Rise of European Liberalism*, London, 1962, 14, 167 and 168.
78. Q. Hogg, *The Case for Conservatism*, West Drayton, 1947, 48–53.

Bibliography

Bentham, J. *An Introduction to the Principles of Morals and Legislation.* Kitchener (Ontario), 2000.
Beveridge, W.H. *Social Insurance and Allied Services.* London, 1942.
———. *Why I am a Liberal.* London, 1945.
Bullock, A., and M. Shock (eds). *The Liberal Tradition.* Oxford, 1956.
Burke, E. *Reflections on the Revolution in France*, C.C. O'Brien (ed.). Harmondsworth, 1969.
Craig, D.M. 'The Origins of "Liberalism" in Britain: The Case of *The Liberal*'. *Historical Research* 85 (2012), 469–87.
Dholakia, N. 'Towards Cultural Pluralism', in J. Margo (ed.), *Beyond Liberty: Is the Future of Liberalism Progressive?* (London, 2007), 198–208.
Dodds, E. 'Liberty and Welfare', in G. Watson (ed.), *The Unservile State* (London, 1957), 13–26.
Eccleshall, R. *British Liberalism: Liberal Thought from the 1640s to 1980s.* London, 1986.
Freeden, M. 'The Coming of the Welfare State', in R. Bellamy and T. Ball (eds), *The Cambridge History of Twentieth-Century Political Thought* (Cambridge, 2003), 7–44.
———. 'Democracy and Paternalism: The Struggle over Shaping British Liberal Welfare Thinking', in A. Kessler-Harris and M. Vaudagna (eds), *Democracy and Social Rights in the 'Two Wests'* (New York, 2009), 107–22.
———. *Ideologies and Political Theory: A Conceptual Approach.* Oxford, 1996.
———. *Liberalism Divided: A Study in British Political Thought 1914–1939.* Oxford, 1986.
———. 'The Morphological Analysis of Ideology', in M. Freeden, L.T. Sargent and M. Stears (eds), *The Oxford Handbook of Political Ideologies* (Oxford, 2013), 115–37.
——— (ed.). *Minutes of the Rainbow Circle 1894–1924.* London, 1989.
———. *The New Liberalism: An Ideology of Social Reform.* Oxford, 1978.
Green, T.H. *Liberal Legislation and Freedom of Contract.* Oxford, 1881.
Halevy, E. *The Growth of Philosophic Radicalism.* London, 1972.
Hansson, S.O. 'John Stuart Mill's Political Self-Identifications'. *Journal of Political Ideologies* 18 (2013), 348–57.
Hobbes, T. *Leviathan.* Harmondsworth, 1968.
Hobhouse, L.T. *Liberalism and Other Writings*, J. Meadowcroft (ed.). Cambridge, 1994.
Hobson, J.A. *The Crisis of Liberalism.* London, 1909.
———. *Richard Cobden: The International Man.* London, 1919.
———. *The Social Problem.* London, 1901.

————. *Work and Wealth: A Human Valuation*. New York, 1916.

Hogg, Q. *The Case for Conservatism*. West Drayton, 1947.

Keynes, J.M. *Essays in Persuasion*. London, 1931.

Koselleck, R. 'Introduction' to *Zeitschichten*. Frankfurt am Main, 2000.

Langshaw, H. *Socialism: And the Historic Function of Liberalism*. London, 1925.

Laski, H.J. *The Rise of European Liberalism*. London, 1962.

Leonhard, J. *Liberalismus*. Munich, 2001.

Locke, J. *Two Treatises of Government, Second Treatise*. Cambridge, 1963.

Marshall, W.H. *Byron, Shelley, Hunt and* The Liberal. Philadelphia, 1960.

Matthew, H.C.G. *Liberal Imperialism*. Oxford, 1973.

Mill, J.S. *Essays on Politics and Society: The Collected Works of John Stuart Mill*, J.M. Robson (ed.), vol. 18. Toronto, 1977.

Muir, R. (ed.). *The Liberal Way*. London, 1934.

Pickering, L.P. *Lord Byron, Leigh Hunt and the 'Liberal'*. New York, 1966.

Reid, A. *The New Liberal Programme*. London, 1886.

Robertson, J.M. *The Meaning of Liberalism*. London, 1912.

Six Oxford Men. *Essays in Liberalism*. London, 1897.

Smith, A. *An Inquiry into the Nature and Causes of the Wealth of Nations*, vol. 1. Oxford, 1976.

Spencer, H. *The Man versus the State*. Harmondsworth, 1969.

Starr, P. *Freedom's Power: The True Force of Liberalism*. New York, 2007.

Steinmetz, W., and M. Freeden. 'Introduction: Conceptual History: Challenges, Conundrums, Complexities', in W. Steinmetz, M. Freeden and J. Fernández-Sebastián (eds), *Conceptual History in the European Space* (New York, 2017), 1–46.

Turnaoğlu, B. *The Formation of Turkish Republicanism*. Princeton, 2017.

Urguarth, D. *Turkey and its Resources: Its Municipal Organization and Free Trade*. London, 1833.

Conclusion

Michael Freeden

The conceptual history of European liberalism enjoys a uniquely important standing in the ideational and political life of the continent. To be sure, all ideologies and movements leave a marked imprint on their times, on the reimagining of a society's past, on its future expectations or indeed fears. But liberalism is endowed with a different order of visibility that applies to the trails it bequeaths and to those it blasts ahead, and that is ascribed even to the detritus of its failures. The malleable ease with which it has transformed the public languages and significations employed by the cultures it inhabits – in contrast to the political hurdles with which it is often confronted – and the profound impacts on the nations and groups it interweaves are unparalleled in the modern era. Liberalism is also the first comprehensive ideology imbued with secular values. Moreover, many of its ideational and local variants, however much they diverge from one another, can each in their own special way lay claim to have been dynamic and irreversible contributions to the identities of the peoples they affect. Liberalism's conceptual history encompasses a complex aggregate of principles, reasons, arguments and decontestations, but also of rhetorics, emotions, traditions and styles that enrich and colour the discourses in which its concepts operate. In that ideational tapestry, retrospectively invented continuities coexist with partial, interrupted and fractured narratives and practices, and are in turn interwoven with social movements and concrete historical experiences.

The historical trajectories examined in the volume are remarkable for drawing in certain notions and interpretations at different moments in their national journeys. Russian, French or Polish liberalisms, for example, each undergo the maturing, shifting or decline of their conceptual clusters and arrangements at disparate temporal points and with very varied accentuations. Notions of revolution and disruption filter, constrain and release the plethora of available liberal guises in those and similar instances, alongside aspirations for modernity, economic prosperity, individual liberty and competing senses of community. The outcome is that the meaning of the overarching term 'liberalism' embraces a range of flexible, always mutating, occasionally fragile, connotations and associations that serve multiple purposes, and either become entrenched or marginalized in a welter of fluctuating fortunes of the societies in question. No less intriguing is liberalism's ability to shift gear, and cross tracks, to secure – or at least enhance – its viability and staying power as it travels across dimensions that are both parallel and intersecting: the political, the ideological, the philosophical and the cultural. As its strength may wane in one such domain, it will wax in another. There are as many European liberalisms as there are regions, nations and localities. Moreover, some countries are powerful drafters of liberal languages; other tend to be borrowers or amenders. However, these roles are not fixed and permanent; they have frequently changed over time. This applies, for instance, to the prominent influence of Spanish constitutional liberalism in the first decades of the nineteenth century, which extended beyond the European continent although, in the main, Spanish liberals were inspired by other European political theorists. Emphatically, though, no contribution to the forging of liberalism's conceptual history can be ignored. Despite their nuances and subdivisions, several of those liberal strains have exercised a hold on other European liberalisms and have reached out to form pools of shared or overlapping international understandings, including on the global stage.

Perhaps the most striking feature of the term 'liberalism' is that it has led a triple life. As a political concept, it has been subject to the same measures of support and antagonism that other ideologies face. Its strategic positioning in party and constitutional languages has been very central to a society such as the United Kingdom, which cannot be comprehended unless its political liberalism is factored into any analysis. Other European countries have experienced the notion of liberalism in various degrees of political centrality or marginalization, and they have drawn on different sources. In Portugal, France and to some extent in Italy, it was associated with constitutionalism and the state, rather than party; in Spain, both facets – liberal constitution and liberal party – were closely intertwined from 1812; and in Germany, liberalism was tied more specifically to a constitutional nation-state, the *Rechtsstaat*. In the Netherlands, liberalism adopted a more conservative tinge in the political arena, but was deemed lacking a social orientation. Denmark and Sweden have placed liberalism, respectively, to the right or the left of the political spectrum. In Poland, liberalism became collocated with modernization and nationalism, and it has more recently also been coupled with modernization in Russia.

The ideal of liberal universalism thus became not merely a much-acclaimed philosophical, supratemporal and supraspatial attribute, but reflected the aspiration to draw less-developed societies into a transnational liberal orbit. Early signs of an institutionalized pluralism, as in the Habsburg lands, hint at another liberal theme – the toleration of diversity. In the United Kingdom, being a liberal also meant adopting the political project of taming and reformulating governance in pursuit of an inclusive and mutually respectful democracy. This bifurcated more generally either into displacing entrenched hierarchies or as a driving force in establishing new emancipated national identities – notably in the Iberian world, but also in Italy with iconic figures such as Mazzini harnessed both to liberal and republican ends. This latter version of liberalism, whether sustaining national independence or, more commonly, directed at autocratic governments from which release was eagerly sought was central to the concerns of numerous mainland liberal movements.

As a philosophical and cultural concept, liberalism has attached itself to powerful reforming tendencies, incorporating self-determining objectives that transcend the narrowly political. Notably, the etymological link between liberty and liberalism has sustained manifold European conceptions of what liberalism can achieve both in the private and public domains. But European cultures possess their own peculiar liberal flavours. A sense of broad-mindedness pervaded the Dutch cultural overtones of liberalism, even as its political manifestations shrank. Polish liberalism was suffused with an ardent romanticism. Above all, through a host of discourses at different levels of articulation and sophistication, liberalism has identified society as the location in which a free individual secures both personal and social progress, thus projecting a horizon of expectations that enhances a civilized and humane way of life.

Not infrequently, liberalism has also been pared down to, and extolled as, a set of economic arrangements that optimize material benefits, respect the private interests of a society's members, encourage cross-national commerce and exchange, and even on occasion act as a force for international peace. In France, commerce and political economy were co-opted in the liberal cause. The re-emergence on a large scale of liberalism in Russia is of that variety, focusing as it did on economic transformation as the path to stability and prosperity, and reclaiming liberalism as an effective, private property-based strategy and policy rather than a humanist vision of social relations. Historic hostility towards the state propelled the language of such liberalisms on a rather different path than the welfare responsibilities with which salient conceptualizations of liberalism were entrusted in the United Kingdom and Sweden.

As has been emphasized throughout this volume, we can only supply asymmetrical and sporadic snapshots of European liberalisms, which can at best capture segments of the complex features of their national manifestations, while recognizing that others may slip away. All such scholarship is tentative and provisional, but the outlines and glimpses it offers aim in each case at shedding light on representative, critical or illuminating properties of the conceptual histories under investigation, revealing their distinct patterns. Liberalism has, of course, been misrecognized, misnamed, renamed and usurped, and this constitutes a permanent challenge to the scholarly sensitivity of conceptual historians. Although those too form part of the peripheral historical environment of liberalism, they can lead down blind alleys or can unexpectedly be resurrected and legitimated as part of the long-term liberal narrative. Not least, specific liberalisms can often be acknowledged by paying heed to the voices of their most outspoken enemies, who latch on to one or another of liberalism's real or imagined features. Ultimately, as this volume has illustrated, the durability and adaptability of liberalism have secured its indispensable and distinguished role in shaping Europe's history.

Michael Freeden is Emeritus Professor of Politics, University of Oxford. His books include *The New Liberalism: An Ideology of Social Reform* (1978); *Liberalism Divided: A Study in British Political Thought 1914–1939* (1986); *Ideologies and Political Theory: A Conceptual Approach* (1996); *Ideology: A Very Short Introduction* (2003); *Liberal Languages: Ideological Imaginations and 20th Century Progressive Thought* (2005); *The Political Theory of Political Thinking* (2013); *Liberalism: A Very Short Introduction* (2015); and *Conceptual History in the European Space* (coedited with W. Steinmetz and J. Fernández-Sebastián, Berghahn Books, 2017). He is the founder-editor of the *Journal of Political Ideologies* and a Fellow of the Academy of Social Sciences.

Index

absolutism; absolutists, 8, 22, 30n9, 42–43, 46, 49, 61n52, 79, 85, 109, 113, 124n17, 135–136, 143–145, 147, 152, 154, 164, 172, 188, 195–196, 201, 204, 207n12, 214, 245. *See also* monarchy

agriculture, 139, 141, 171, 195, 198, 200, 244

Alcalá Galiano, Antonio, 114

Alembert, Jean-Baptiste le Rond d', 162, 165

Alfonso X of Castile, 112

Alien Bill, 304

Almagro San Martín, Melchor, 15

Almeida Garret, João Baptista da Silva Leitão de, 143, 147, 151

America; Americanism, 9, 11, 16, 104–105, 108–122, 161, 167, 176, 257, 264, 266–267, 294. *See also* United States, Latin America

ancien régime, 28, 39, 77, 145, 151, 155, 163, 174

Andreeva, Nina, 279

anticlericalism, 28, 38, 42, 52, 81, 106, 149, 222, 227. *See also* culture wars

anticommunism; anticommunist, 238, 282, 287

antiliberalism; illiberalism, 8, 11, 13, 17, 19, 22, 44, 78–79, 81, 102, 106, 138, 150, 163, 198, 237–238, 248, 256, 262–264, 267, 269n7, 271n39, 290–291, 294, 296, 302–313, 314, 319

antinationalism; antinational, 290, 292, 294–295

antipatriotism. *See* patriotism

antiquity, 25, 75, 78, 120, 162

Apter, David E., 255

Aretin, Johann Christoph von, 76

Aragão Morato, Francisco Manuel Trigozo, 142

Aranda, Pedro Pablo Abarca de Bolea, Count of, 115

Armitage, David, 119

aristocracy; aristocrats, 18, 39, 74, 80, 90, 113, 135, 138, 145, 162–164, 168, 187, 217–218, 235–236, 241, 249, 304, 306

Arndt, Ernst Moritz, 186

Arnold, Matthew, 73

Assunção Brandão, Mateus d', 144

Aquinas, Thomas, 112

atheism, 107, 114, 168. *See also* deism

Austria-Hungary; Habsburg Empire; Austria, 14, 27, 28, 37–71, 84, 234, 238, 248, 256, 319, 331

authoritarianism; authoritarian, 8, 16, 120, 135, 176, 234, 261, 281, 292, 296

backwardness, 25, 81, 103, 234, 242–245

Balicki, Zygmunt, 248

Bamberger, Ludwig, 88

Barrot, Odilon, 172, 173

Barth, Theodor, 88

Bastiat, Frédéric, 173, 174

Bayly, Christopher A., 104

Bauer, Otto, 246

Baumgarten, Hermann, 85

Belloc, Hilaire, 312, 314

Bentham, Jeremy, 9, 40, 110–111, 115, 153, 188, 305, 310

Condorcet, Marie Jean Antoine Nicolas
 Caritat de, 17
Colbert, Jean-Baptiste, 169
Collingwood, Robin G., 16
collectivism, 8, 279, 312–313, 316
colony; colonialism; empire; imperial, 1,
 24, 27–29, 88, 90, 103, 106, 108, 111,
 141, 290–291, 294, 296, 303
commerce; commercialization, 114,
 137–138, 141, 169–170, 173, 217,
 226, 303, 308, 321, 331
common good, 10, 12, 197, 314, 322
communism; communists; Communist
 party, 6–8, 30n11, 86, 188, 195, 238,
 261, 265–266, 281–282, 288–289
communitarianism, 8, 28, 118, 121, 311
comparison; comparative research, 4, 6,
 38, 73–74, 89–91, 118, 128n68, 173,
 203–206, 243
Comte, Charles, 170
Conrad, Joseph, 103
Constant, Benjamin, 9, 17, 20, 76, 110,
 115, 144, 163–168, 170–171, 188
Couthino, Rodrigo de Sousa, 137–139
Croce, Benedetto, 16, 253, 265–266,
 273n69
Croker, John Wilson, 78
concepts of movement;
 Bewegungsbegriffe, 6, 40, 188. *See
 also* -isms
conceptual history; history of concepts,
 2–5, 18, 20, 39, 121, 122, 186,
 233–234, 245, 302–304, 320,
 329–330, 332
Congress of Panama, 119
Congress of Vienna, 119
conservatism; conservatives, 1, 6, 8–9,
 12–13, 18–19, 21, 26–27, 41, 43,
 50–51, 73, 75, 79, 82–83, 90, 110,
 136–137, 142, 146–147, 149, 154,
 164, 172–173, 186–192, 194–195,
 197–199, 201, 203, 216–217, 219,
 221–224, 226, 233–234, 237,
 255–256, 258, 266, 279, 293, 297n19,
 300 n62, 304, 312, 319, 322–323, 330
constitution; constitutionalism, 7, 9, 11,
 13, 19, 21, 25, 41, 49–50, 76, 80–85,
 104–105, 107–108, 112, 117–119,

135–136, 138, 140–150, 153–155,
 163–164, 166–168, 171, 173, 175,
 186–187, 190–191, 196–198, 201, 204,
 207n12, 215–219, 221–223, 225, 235,
 237, 253–264, 268n1, 272n40, 278,
 282, 289, 308, 323, 330
contractualism. *See* social contract
cosmopolitism; cosmopolitanism, 105,
 116, 279, 290
counterconcepts, 42, 75, 109, 120, 188,
 190, 202
Counter–Enlightenment, 50. *See also*
 Enlightenment
Counterrevolution. *See* revolution
Crimea, 295
Culture. *See* civilization
culture wars; *Kulturkampf*, 46, 72, 81, 86.
 See also anticlericalism

Darwinism, Darwinists, 247, 314
 social-Darwinism, 247–248
Daszyńska-Golińska, Zofia, 244,
Daunou, Pierre Claude François, 110
decentralization, 148. *See also*
 centralization
deism, 7, 38, 46, 49–51, 168. *See also*
 atheism
democracy; democratism;
 democratization, 8, 21–22, 25–27, 79,
 80, 82–89, 104, 109–110, 119–121,
 129n83, 146–148, 150–153, 165, 172,
 185, 189, 191–193, 195, 198, 200,
 205, 217–218, 221, 223, 225–227,
 234, 237, 239–240, 246, 248–249,
 253–254, 256–258, 261, 263, 267–268,
 273n79, 279–286, 289–292, 306, 308,
 311–312, 314, 316, 322–323, 331
 Christian democrats, 221, 265, 267,
 272n49
Denmark, 12, 15, 22, 26–27, 185–212, 330
despotism; dictatorship; tyranny, 39,
 76–77, 107–108, 112–115, 139,
 142–143, 147, 150, 166, 187, 200,
 215, 253, 263, 266, 289
dictatorship. *See* despotism
Diderot, Denis, 162, 165
diversity, 227, 295, 319, 331
division of powers, 282, 289

Mably, Gabriel Bonnot de, 115
Macdonald, John A., 105
Madison, James, 115
Madsen-Mygdal, Thomas, 200–201
Maistre, Joseph de, 164
Maitland, Frederic William, 258, 260
Malagodi, Giovanni, 267
Mann, Thomas, 72–73, 226
Maranini, Guiseppe, 267
Maria II of Portugal, 153
Maria Theresa of Austria-Hungary, 41
Mariana, Juan de, 112
market. *See* economy
Marsilius of Padua, 306
Martensen, Hans Lassen, 197, 199
Martínez Marina, Francisco, 112
Marx, Karl, 86
Mascov, Johann Jacob, 45
Masaryk, Thomas, 17, 290
Marxism(–Leninism); Marxists, 17, 27,
    226, 244, 246, 279, 287
Massillon, Jean–Baptiste, 162
Matteucci, Nicola, 268, 273n69
Mayans, Gregorio, 107
Mazzini, Guiseppe, 28, 189, 331
Medvedev, Dmitry, 292–293
Metternich, Klemens von, 7, 41, 80
mercantilism, 48–49, 51, 168–169, 239.
    See also economy, political economy
Michels, Robert, 257
Mickiewicz, Adam, 237, 247–249
Mier, Servando Teresa de, 111
Miguel I of Portugal, 136, 144, 146–147,
    152
Middle Ages; medieval, 14, 112, 143, 147,
    162, 242, 260
middle class; bourgeoisie, 14–15, 22,
    26, 39, 72–73, 80, 84–87, 174–175,
    187, 194–199, 203, 205, 217, 219,
    224–226, 241, 257, 279, 288, 309,
    318, 323
Miljukov, Pawel, 290
Mina, Javier, 110, 113
Mises, Ludwig von, 9, 201
Mill, James, 305
Mill, John Stuart, 9, 17, 20, 23–25, 27,
    90, 174, 189, 218, 220, 290, 305–306,
    308–311, 315, 319, 322–323

Mitrokhin, Sergei, 285
moderation; moderate; juste milieu, 10,
    12–13, 18, 40, 46, 53n1, 84–85, 110,
    115–116, 136, 142–146, 148, 163,
    167, 188, 213–214, 217–218, 229,
    248, 282, 288, 290, 292, 304, 317, 323
modern; modernity; modernization,
    1–3, 6–8, 25, 50, 103, 87–88, 112,
    114–115, 119, 122, 136, 144–145,
    147–148, 151, 155, 165, 173,
    196–197, 202, 215, 225–226, 234,
    236, 244–245, 254, 256, 260–263,
    267, 282, 284, 294, 318, 330
monarchy; monarchism, 11, 21–23, 52,
    76, 79–83, 85, 103, 106, 108, 109,
    112–114, 117, 135–140, 142–143,
    145–149, 153–155, 164–165, 167,
    186–188, 191, 195–199, 201, 204,
    207, 217–218, 244, 304, 306, 312. *See
    also* absolutism, royalism
Monrad, Ditlev Gothard, 197–199
Monroe, James, 119
Monteagudo, Bernardo de, 110
Monteiro, Francisco Xavier, 141
Montesquieu, Charles de Secondat de, 40,
    45, 107, 115, 241
Mora, José Joaquin de, 113
Morais Silva, Antonio de, 139–140, 144,
    148
morality; ethics, 4, 23, 82, 117, 150, 153,
    162, 196, 199, 214, 224–225, 227,
    234, 240–243, 247–249, 255, 257,
    265–266, 304, 309, 313–314, 322. *See
    also* virtue
Mortati, Constantino, 261
Mosca, Gaetano, 267
Mounier, Emmanuel, 262–263
Mouzinho da Silveira, José Xavier,
    144–145, 151–153
Muir, Ramsay, 318
Müller, Adam, 186
Mussolini, Benito, 260–261
Myrdal, Gunnar, 205

Napoleon Bonaparte, 10, 19, 28, 39,
    75–77, 79–80, 83, 90, 103, 105, 107,
    112, 138, 145, 164, 169, 174, 304
Napoleon III, 80, 150, 176

9 781800 736351